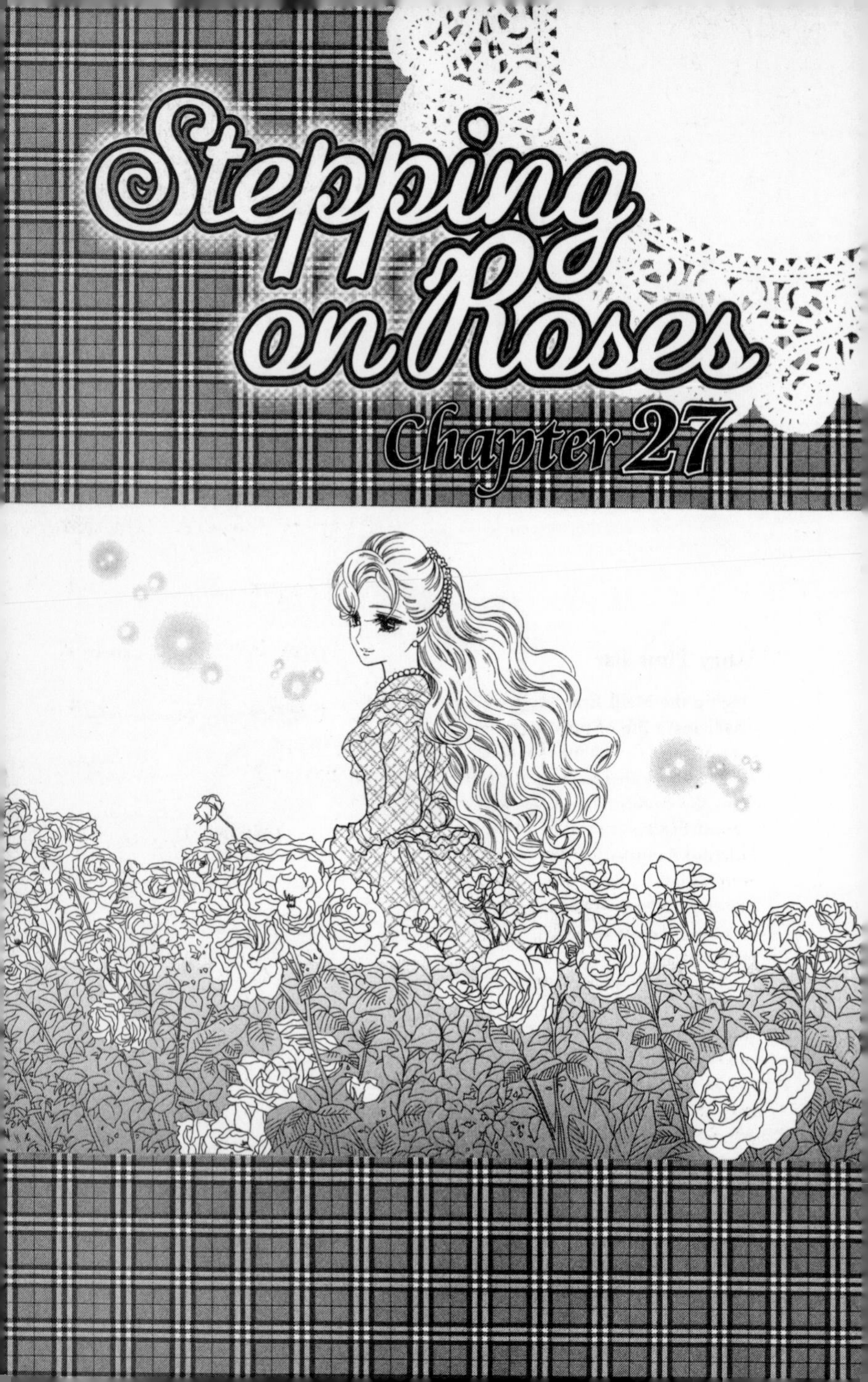
Stepping on Roses
Chapter 27

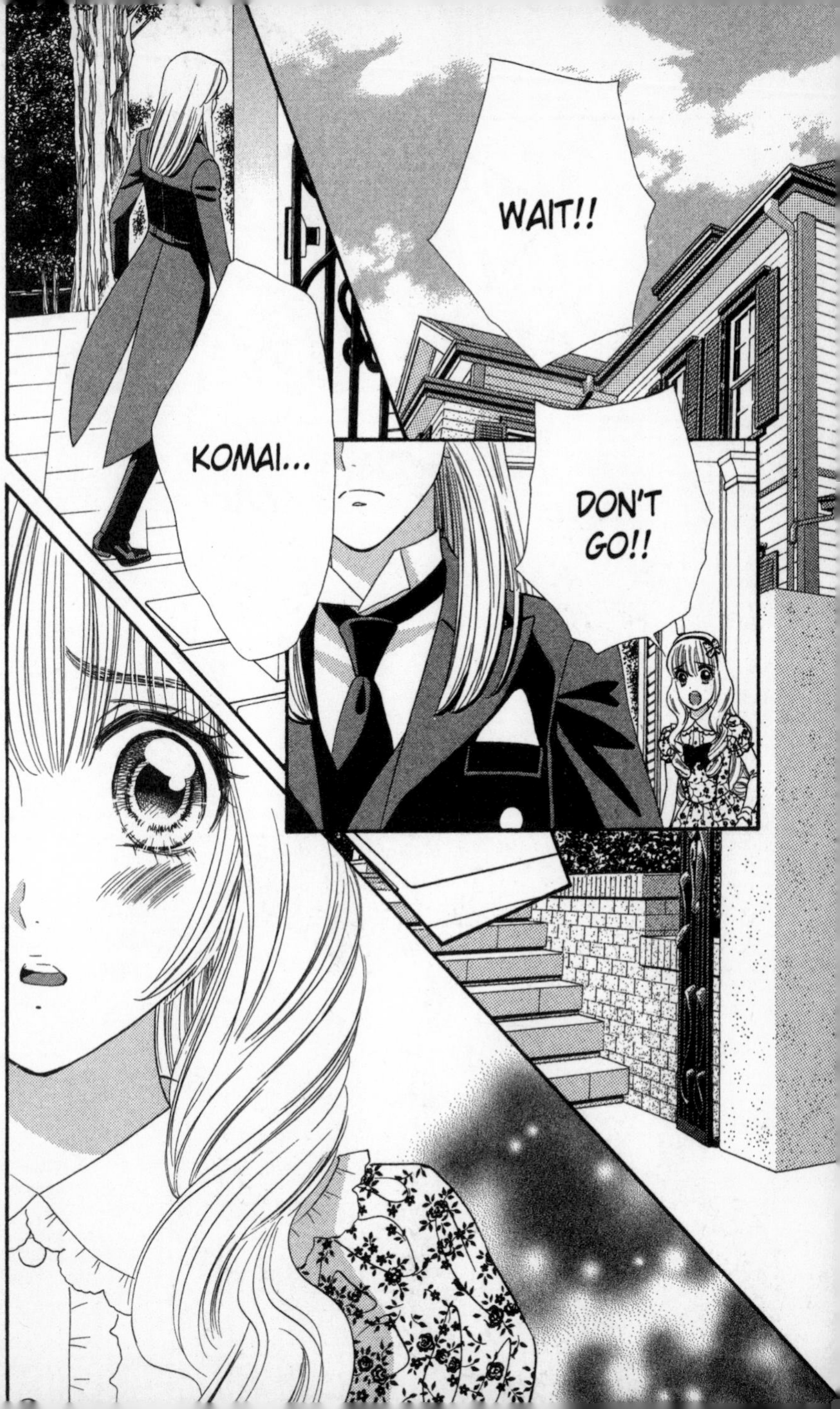
WAIT!!
KOMAI...
DON'T GO!!

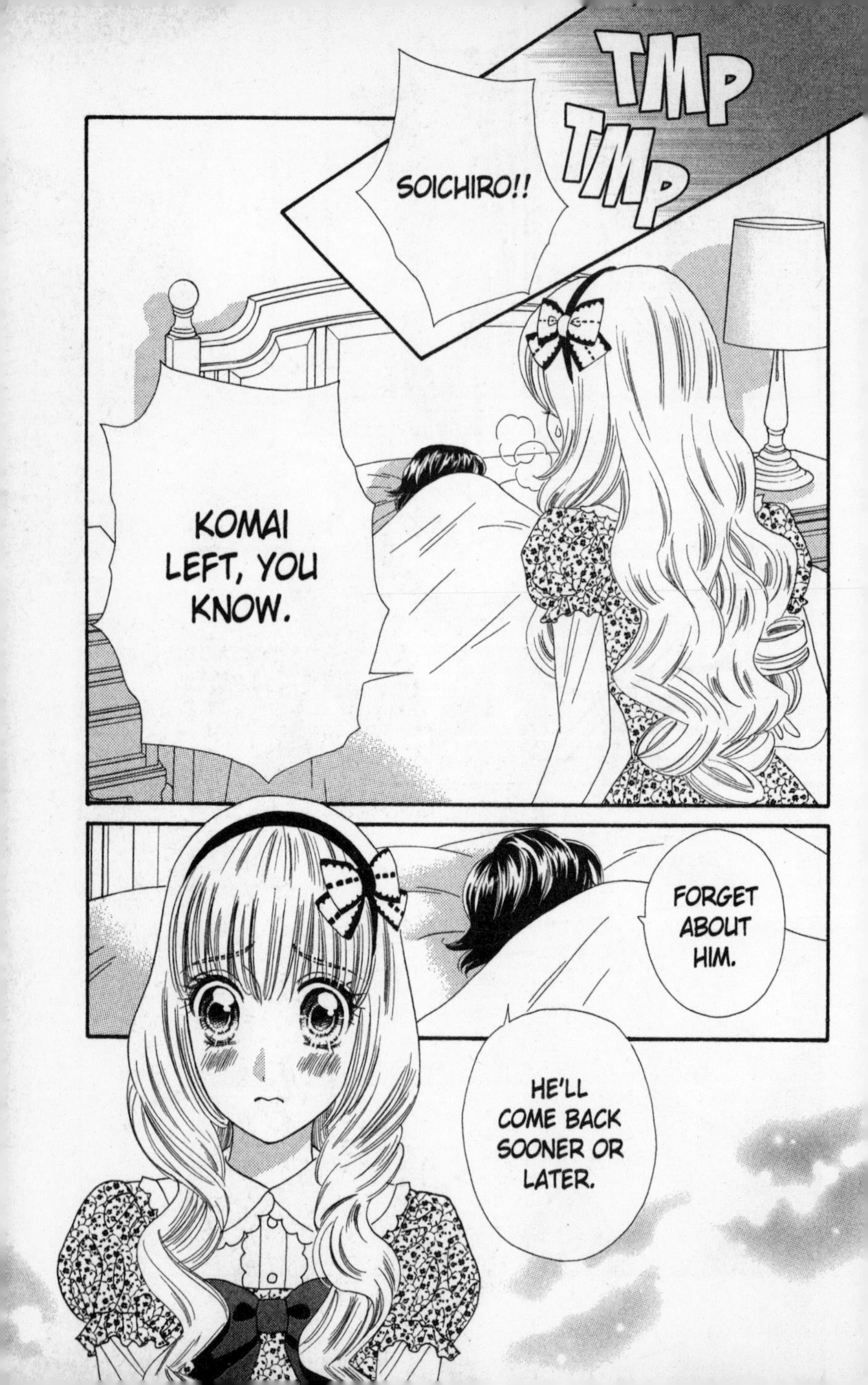
TMP TMP
SOICHIRO!!
KOMAI LEFT, YOU KNOW.
FORGET ABOUT HIM.
HE'LL COME BACK SOONER OR LATER.

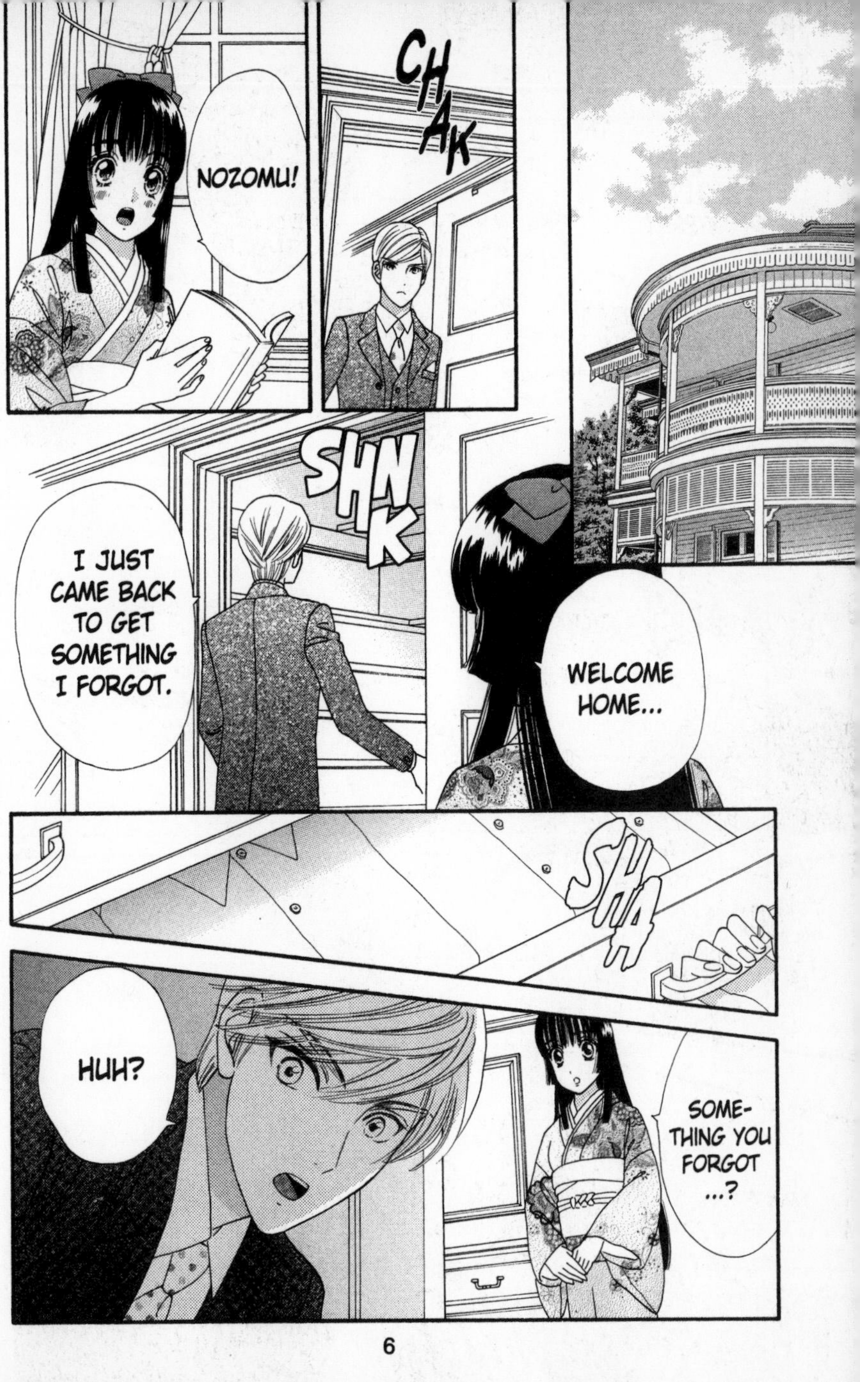
CHAK
NOZOMU!
SHNK
WELCOME HOME...
I JUST CAME BACK TO GET SOMETHING I FORGOT.
SHA
SOME-THING YOU FORGOT ...?
HUH?

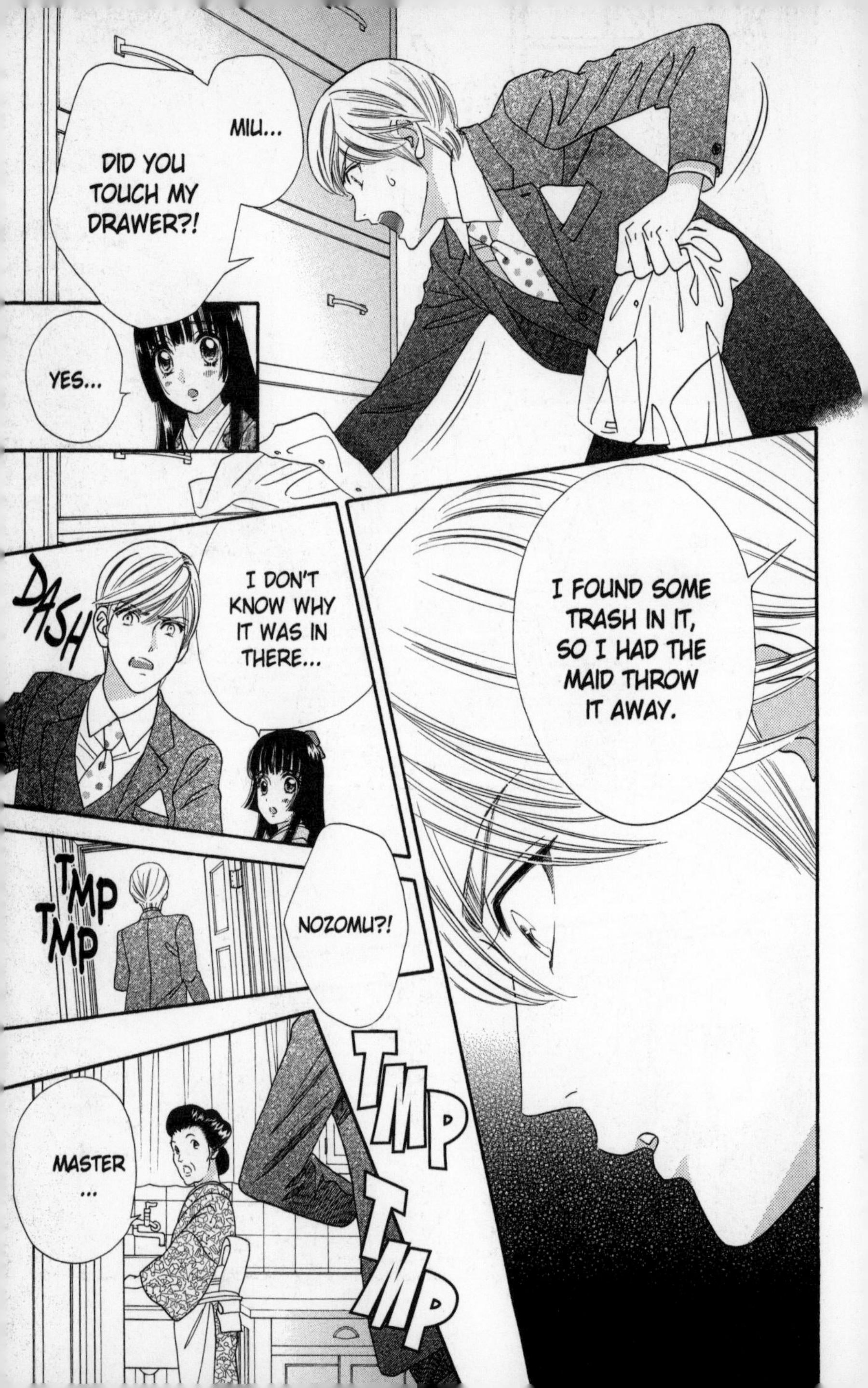
MIU...
DID YOU TOUCH MY DRAWER?!
YES...
I FOUND SOME TRASH IN IT, SO I HAD THE MAID THROW IT AWAY.
DASH
I DON'T KNOW WHY IT WAS IN THERE...
TMP TMP
NOZOMU?!
TMP TMP
MASTER ...

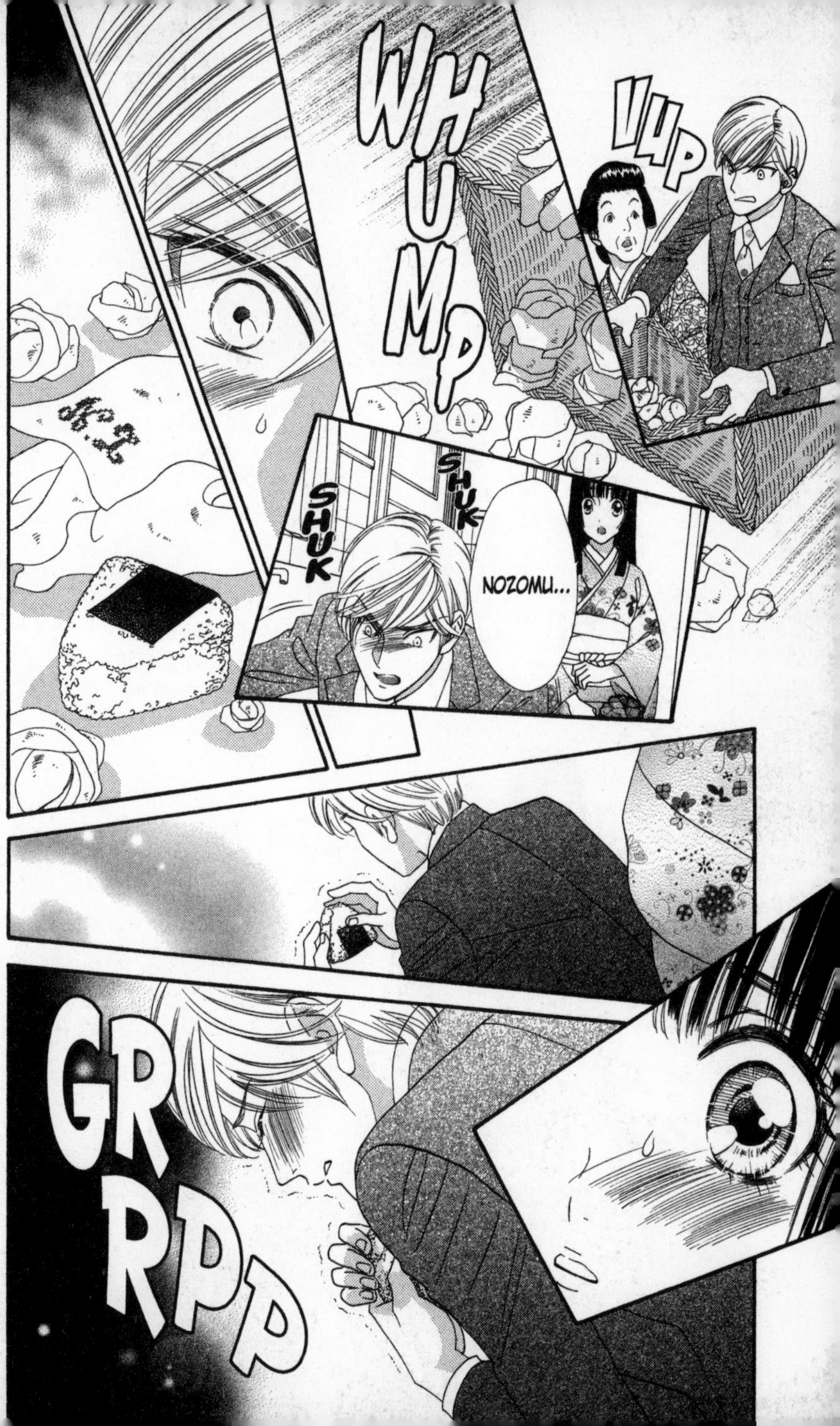
VUP
WHUMP
SHUK SHUK
NOZOMU...
GR RPP

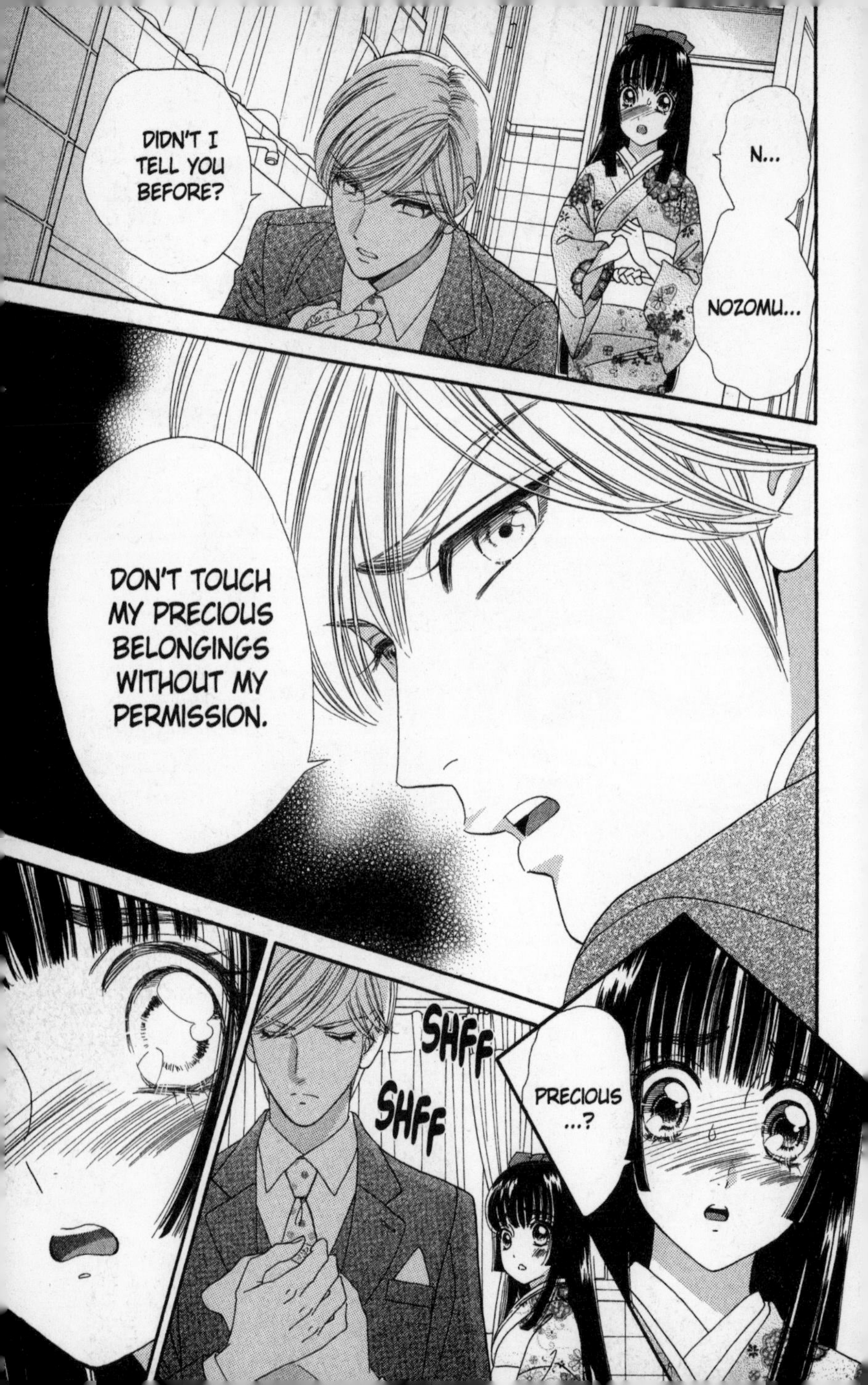
N...
NOZOMU...
DIDN'T I TELL YOU BEFORE?
DON'T TOUCH MY PRECIOUS BELONGINGS WITHOUT MY PERMISSION.
SHFF
SHFF
PRECIOUS ...?

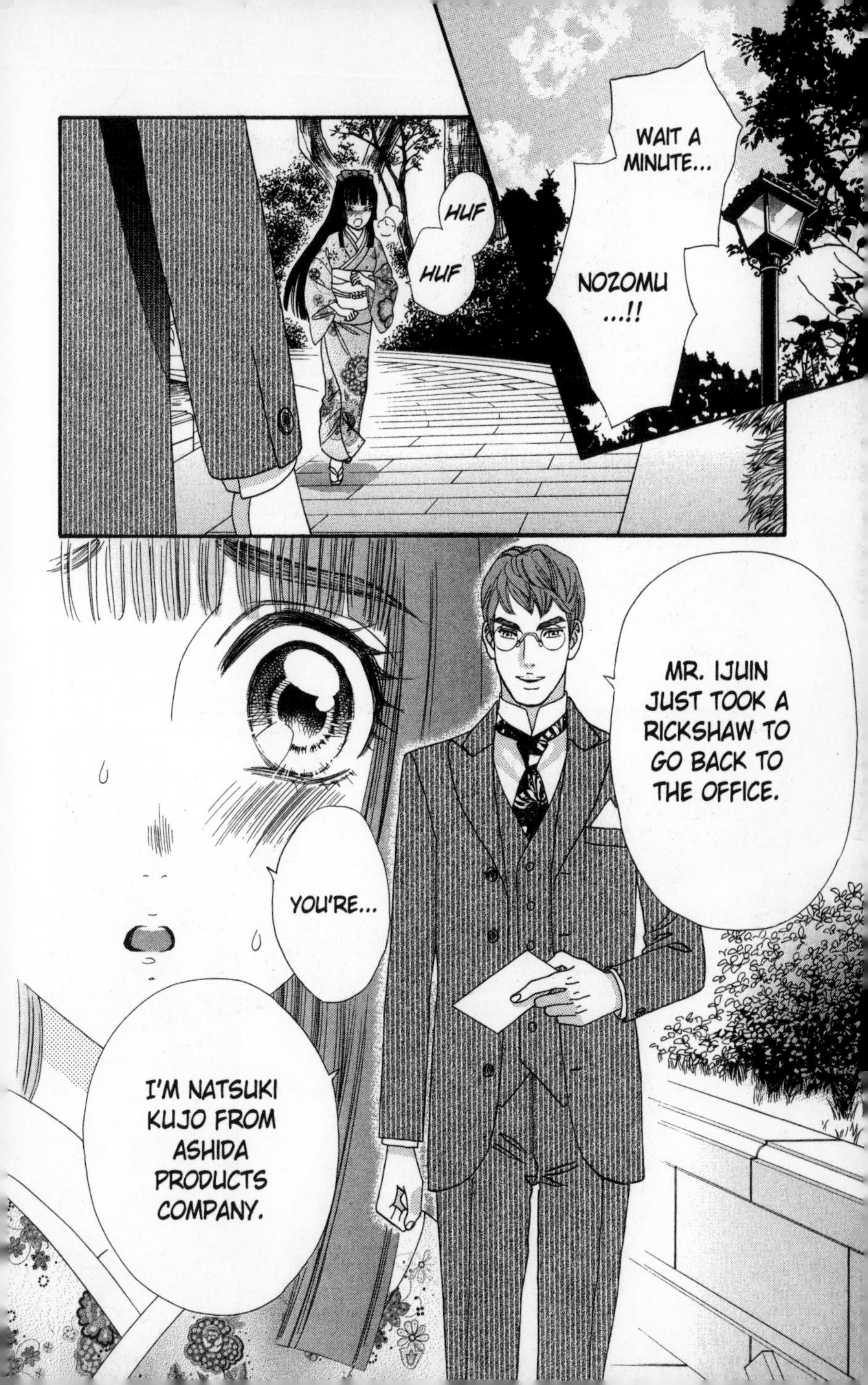
WAIT A MINUTE...
NOZOMU ...!!
HUF
HUF
MR. IJUIN JUST TOOK A RICKSHAW TO GO BACK TO THE OFFICE.
YOU'RE...
I'M NATSUKI KUJO FROM ASHIDA PRODUCTS COMPANY.

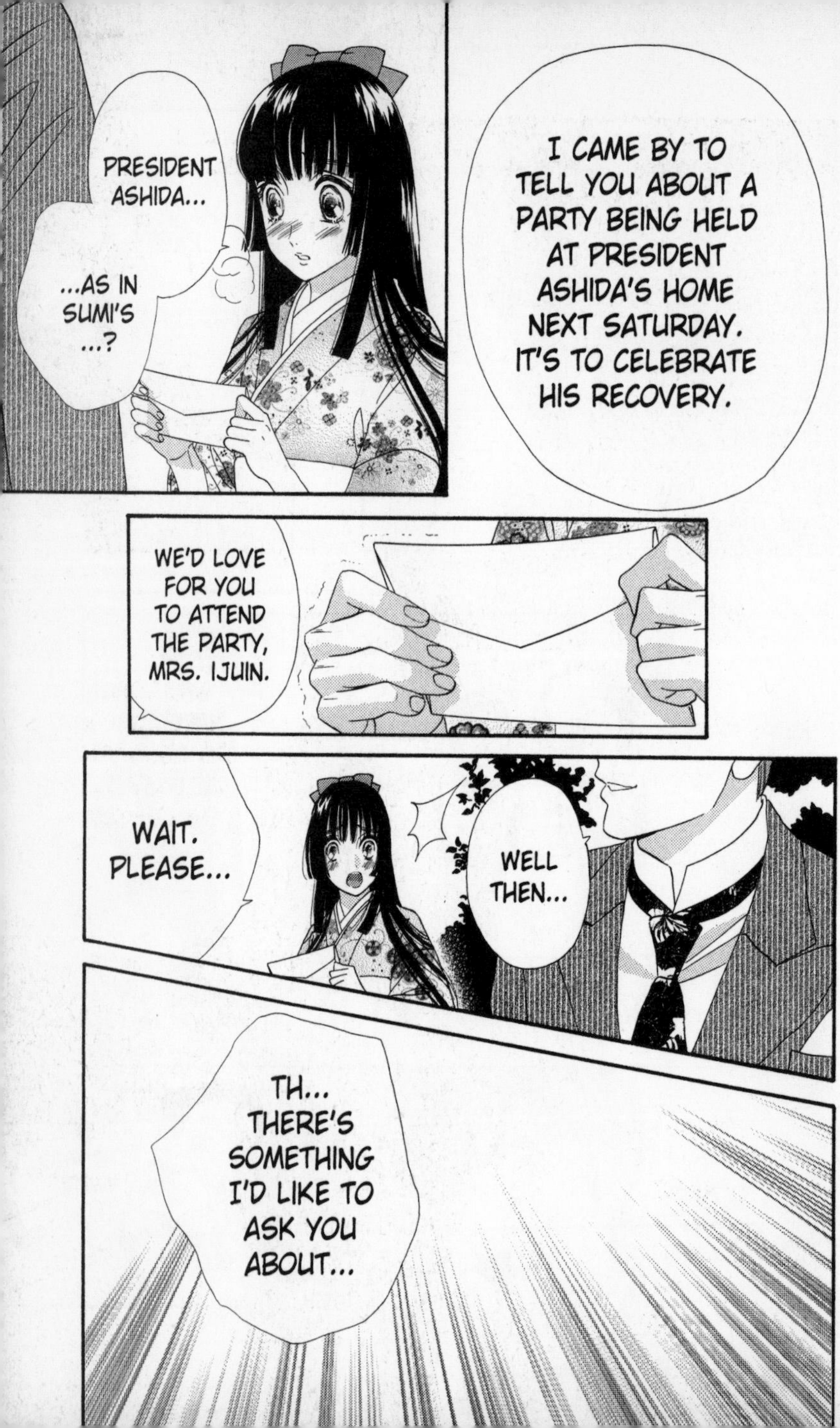
I CAME BY TO TELL YOU ABOUT A PARTY BEING HELD AT PRESIDENT ASHIDA'S HOME NEXT SATURDAY. IT'S TO CELEBRATE HIS RECOVERY.
PRESIDENT ASHIDA...
...AS IN SUMI'S ...?
WE'D LOVE FOR YOU TO ATTEND THE PARTY, MRS. IJUIN.
WELL THEN...
WAIT. PLEASE...
TH... THERE'S SOMETHING I'D LIKE TO ASK YOU ABOUT...

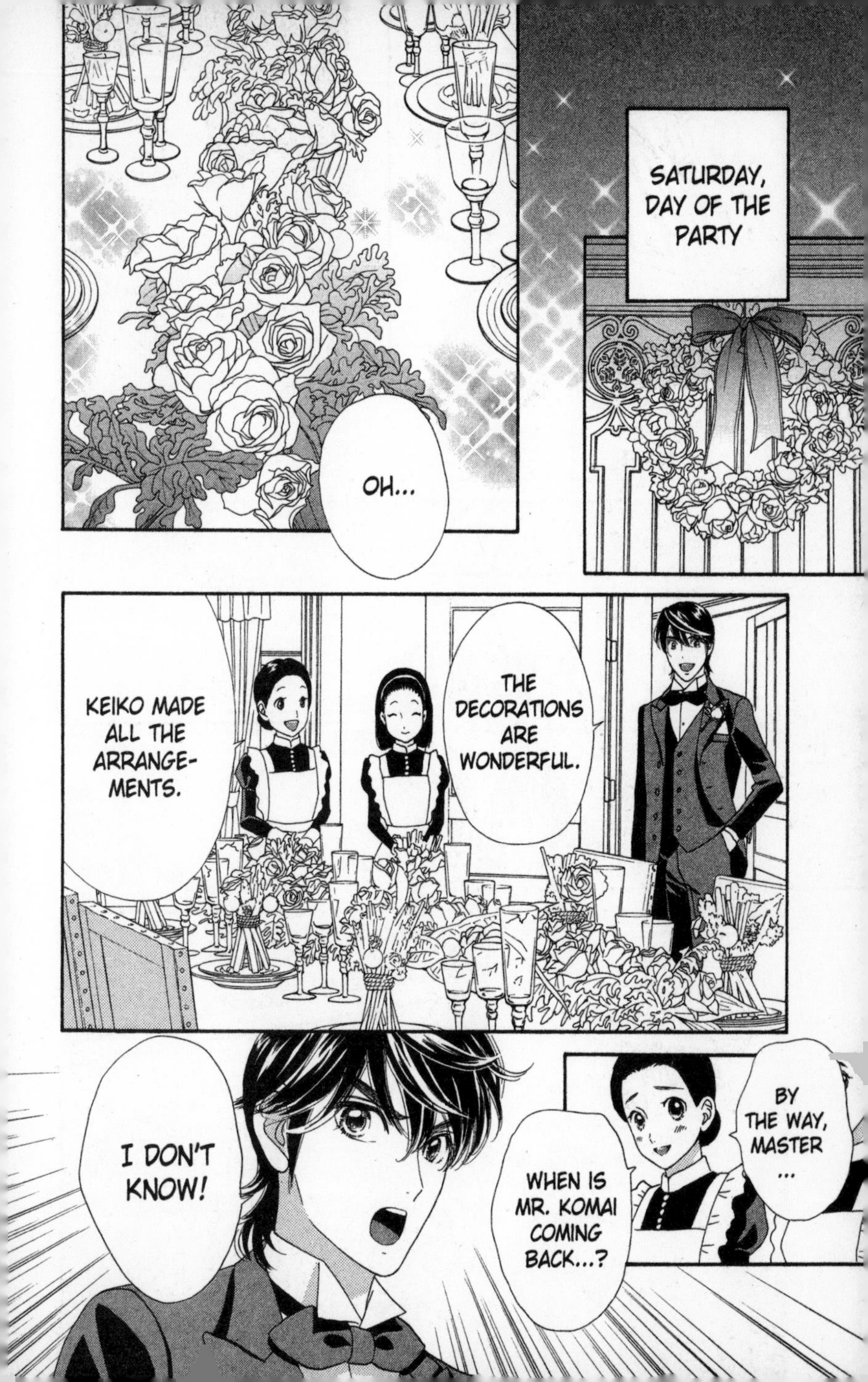
SATURDAY, DAY OF THE PARTY
OH...
THE DECORATIONS ARE WONDERFUL.
KEIKO MADE ALL THE ARRANGE-MENTS.
BY THE WAY, MASTER ...
WHEN IS MR. KOMAI COMING BACK...?
I DON'T KNOW!

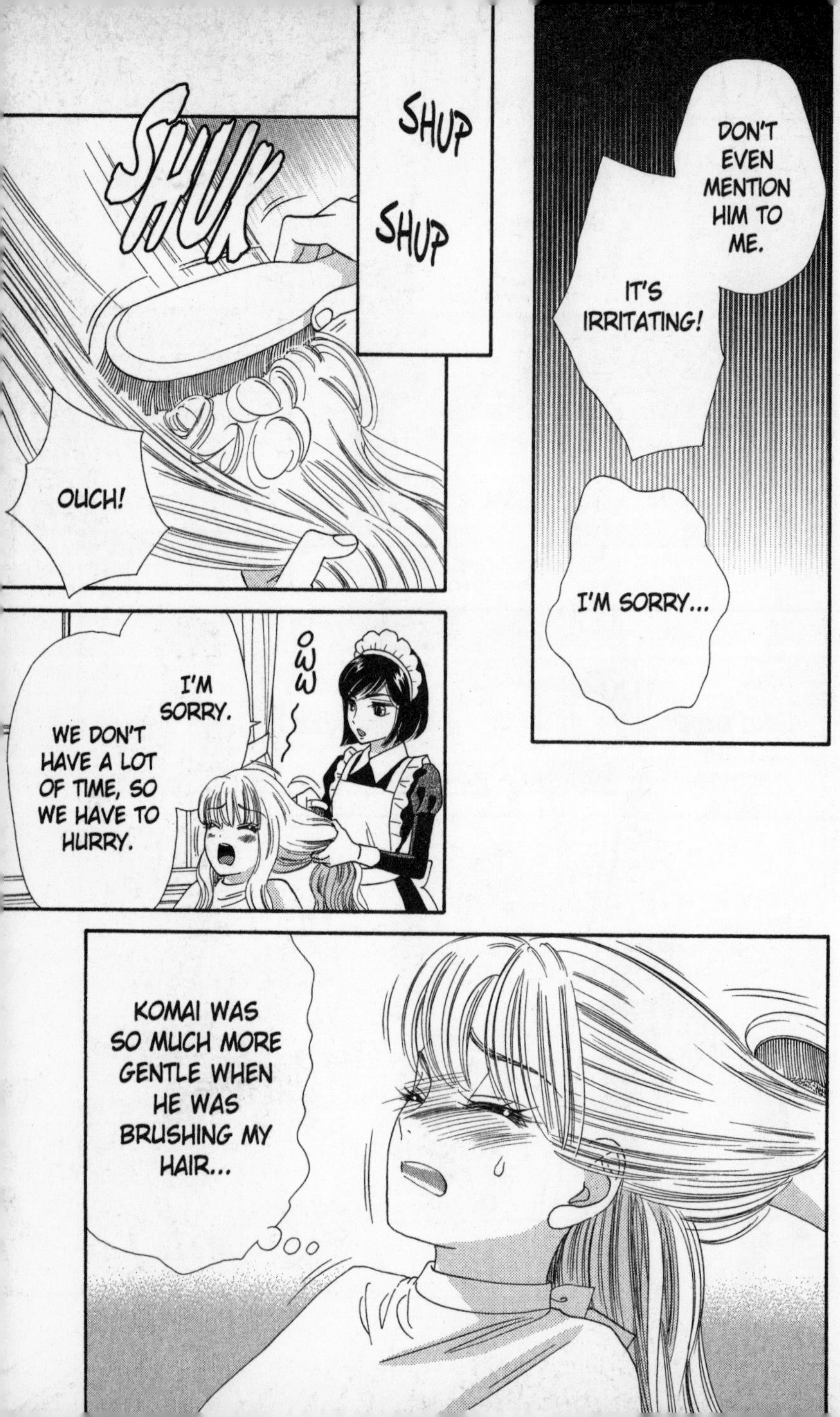
DON'T EVEN MENTION HIM TO ME.
IT'S IRRITATING!
I'M SORRY...
SHUP
SHUP
SHUK
OUCH!
OWW~
I'M SORRY.
WE DON'T HAVE A LOT OF TIME, SO WE HAVE TO HURRY.
KOMAI WAS SO MUCH MORE GENTLE WHEN HE WAS BRUSHING MY HAIR...

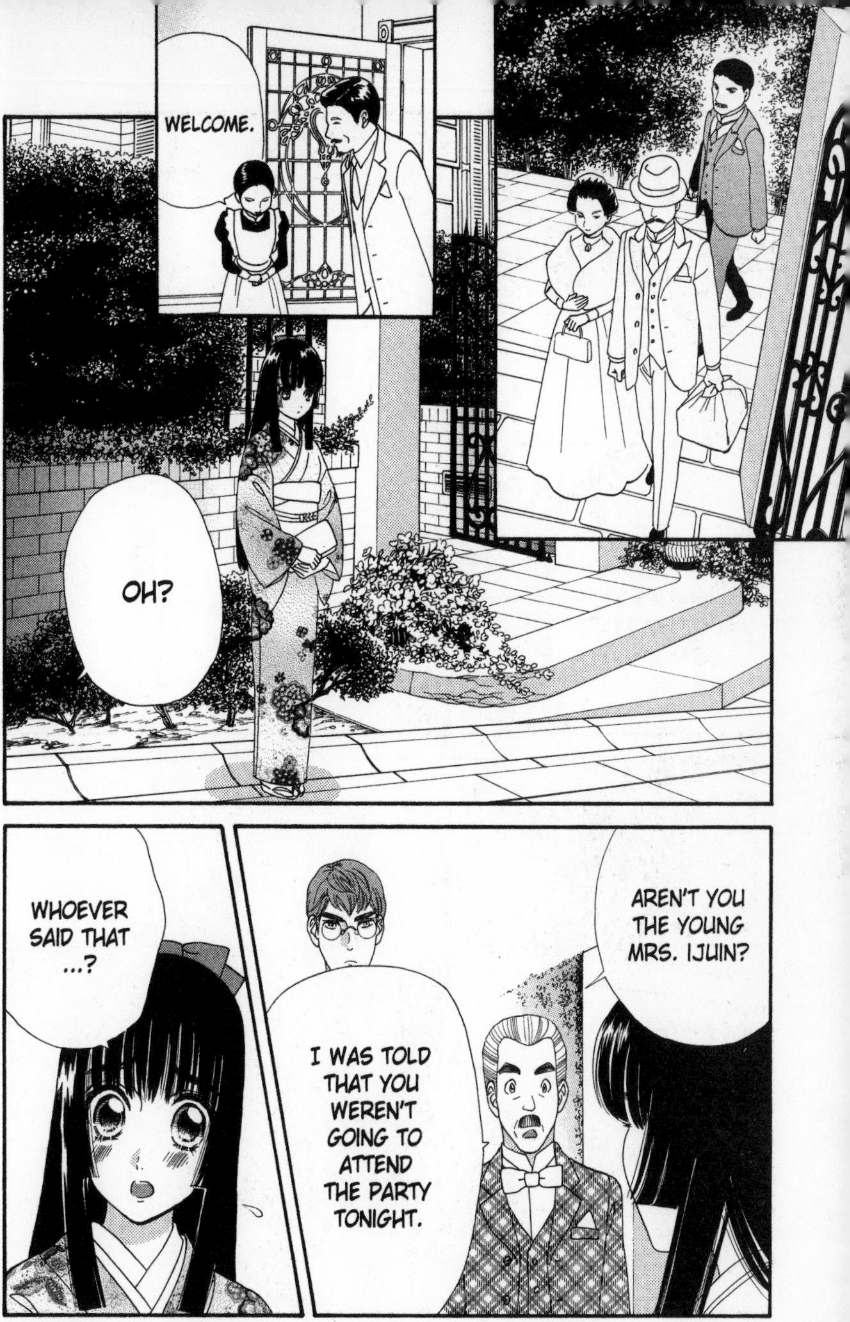
WELCOME.
OH?
AREN'T YOU THE YOUNG MRS. IJUIN?
I WAS TOLD THAT YOU WEREN'T GOING TO ATTEND THE PARTY TONIGHT.
WHOEVER SAID THAT ...?

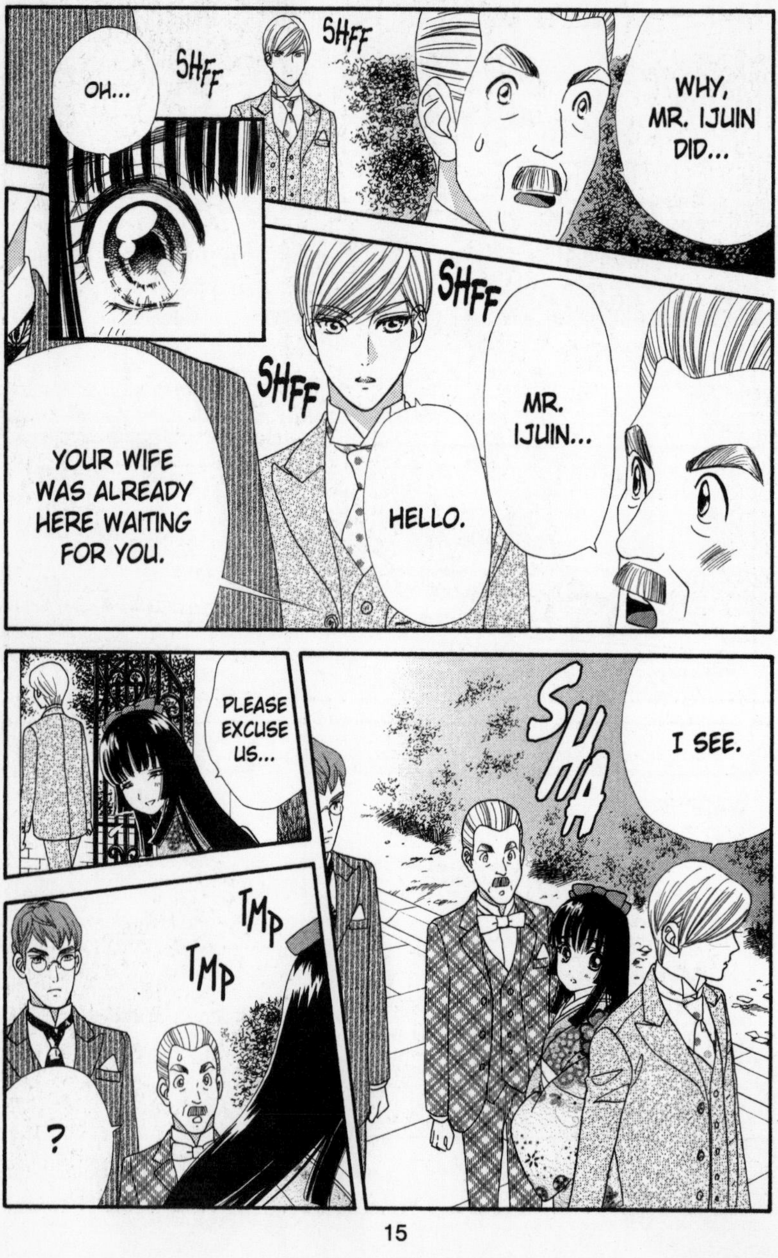
WHY, MR. IJUIN DID...
SHFF
SHFF
OH...
SHFF
MR. IJUIN...
HELLO.
SHFF
YOUR WIFE WAS ALREADY HERE WAITING FOR YOU.
I SEE.
SHA
PLEASE EXCUSE US...
TMP
TMP
?

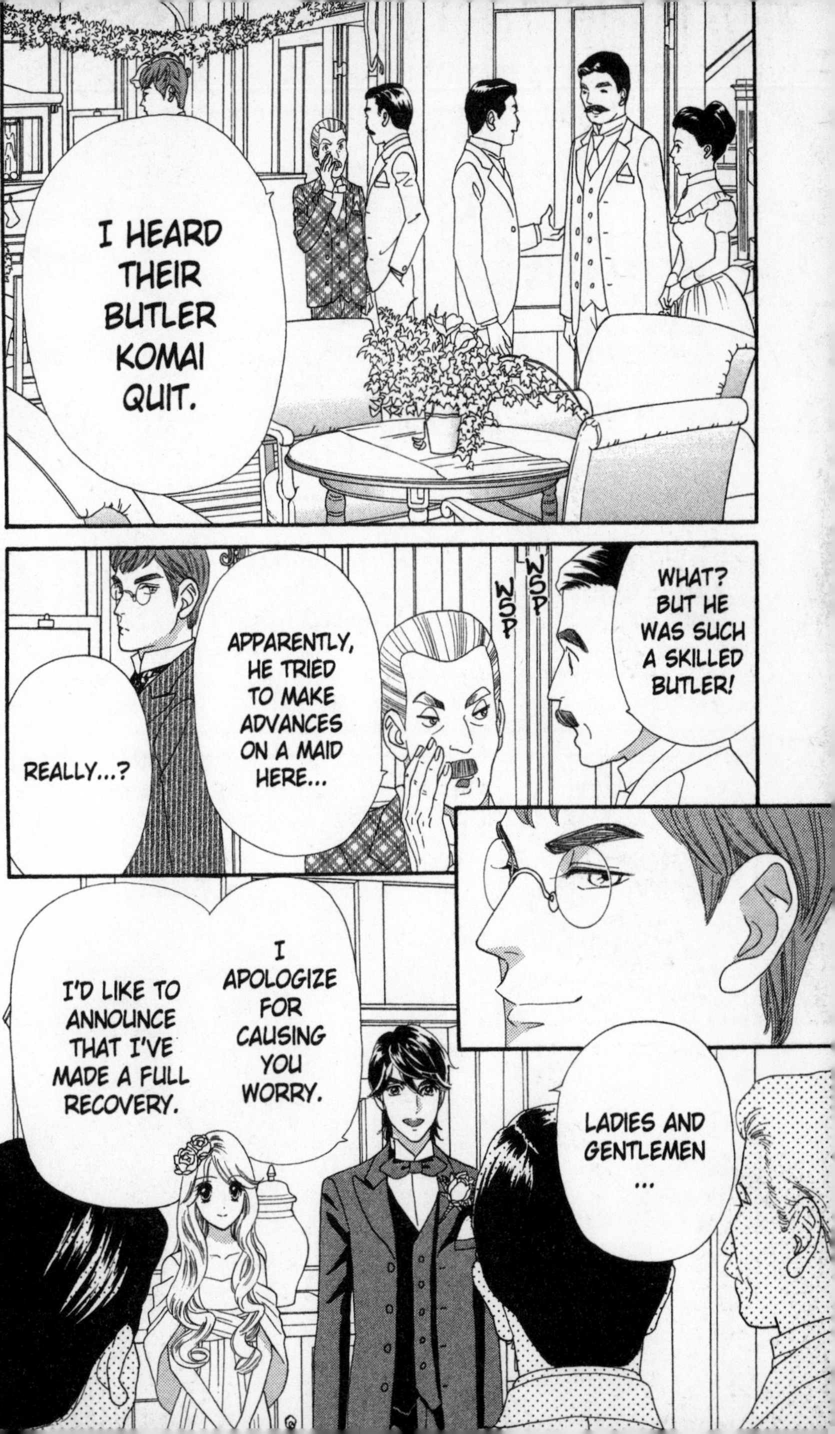
I HEARD THEIR BUTLER KOMAI QUIT.
WSP WSP
WHAT? BUT HE WAS SUCH A SKILLED BUTLER!
APPARENTLY, HE TRIED TO MAKE ADVANCES ON A MAID HERE...
REALLY...?
LADIES AND GENTLEMEN ...
I APOLOGIZE FOR CAUSING YOU WORRY.
I'D LIKE TO ANNOUNCE THAT I'VE MADE A FULL RECOVERY.

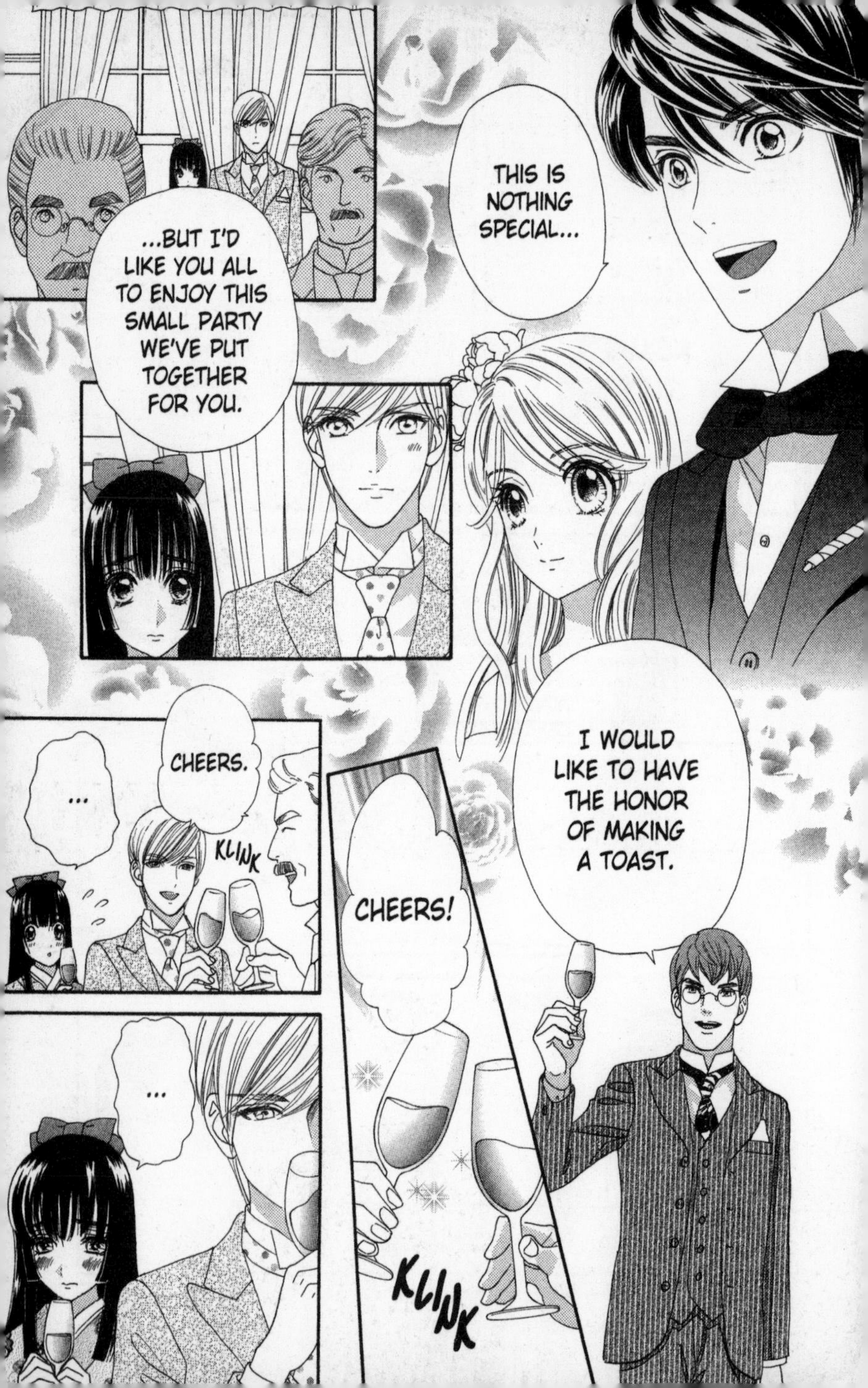
THIS IS NOTHING SPECIAL...
...BUT I'D LIKE YOU ALL TO ENJOY THIS SMALL PARTY WE'VE PUT TOGETHER FOR YOU.
I WOULD LIKE TO HAVE THE HONOR OF MAKING A TOAST.
CHEERS!
KLINK
CHEERS.
KLINK
...
...

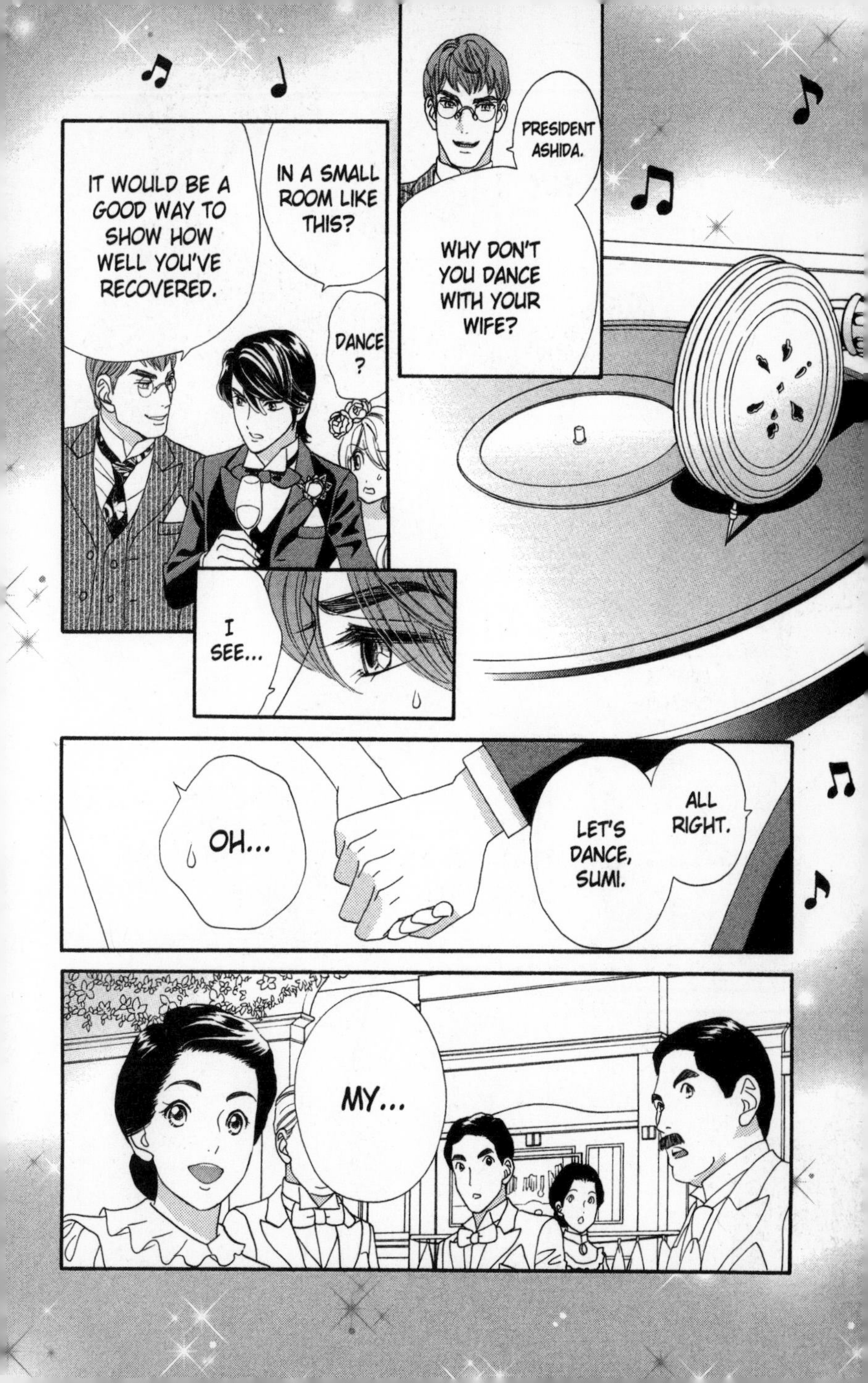
PRESIDENT ASHIDA.
WHY DON'T YOU DANCE WITH YOUR WIFE?
DANCE?
IN A SMALL ROOM LIKE THIS?
IT WOULD BE A GOOD WAY TO SHOW HOW WELL YOU'VE RECOVERED.
I SEE...
ALL RIGHT.
LET'S DANCE, SUMI.
OH...
MY...

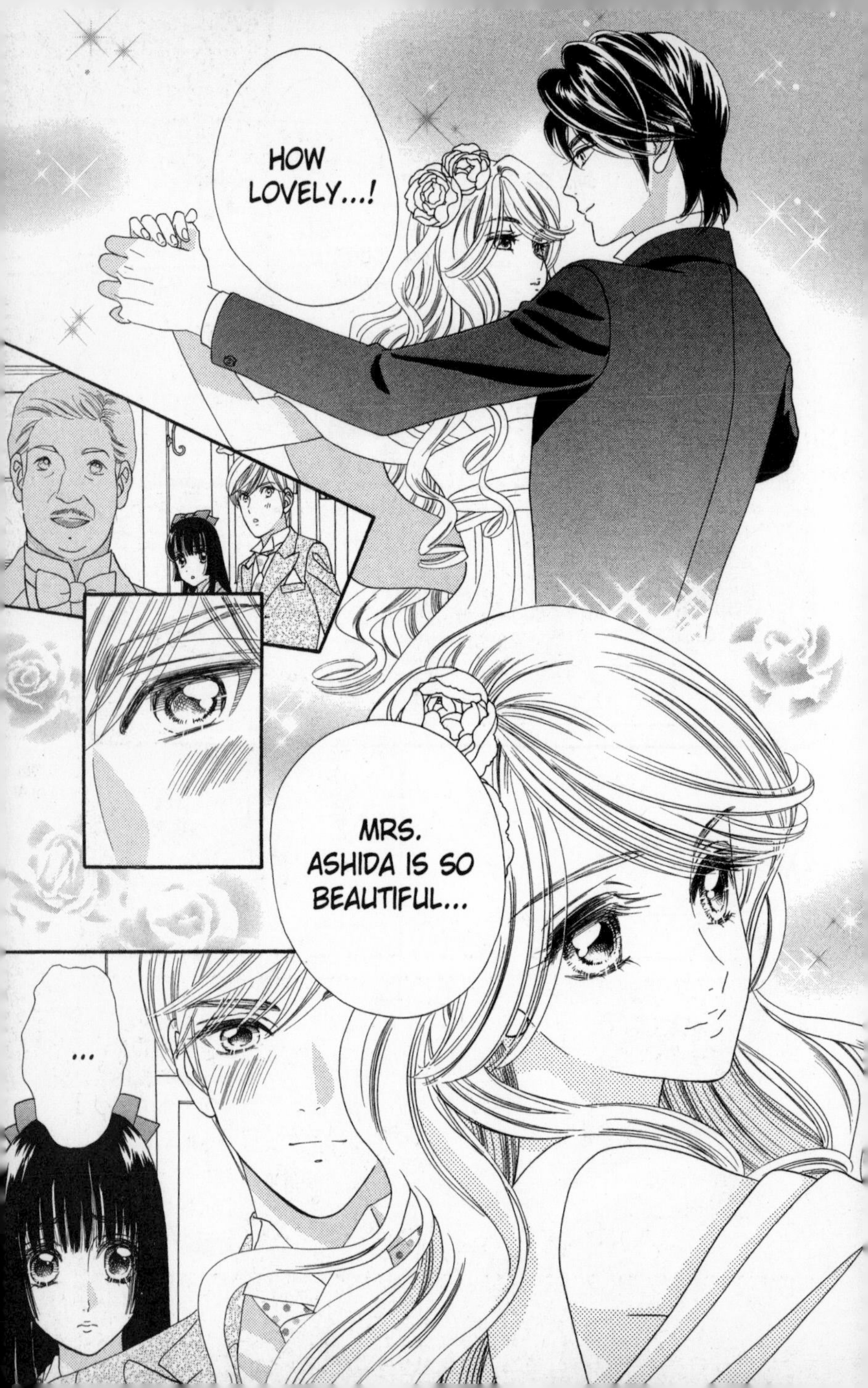
HOW LOVELY...!
MRS. ASHIDA IS SO BEAUTIFUL...
...

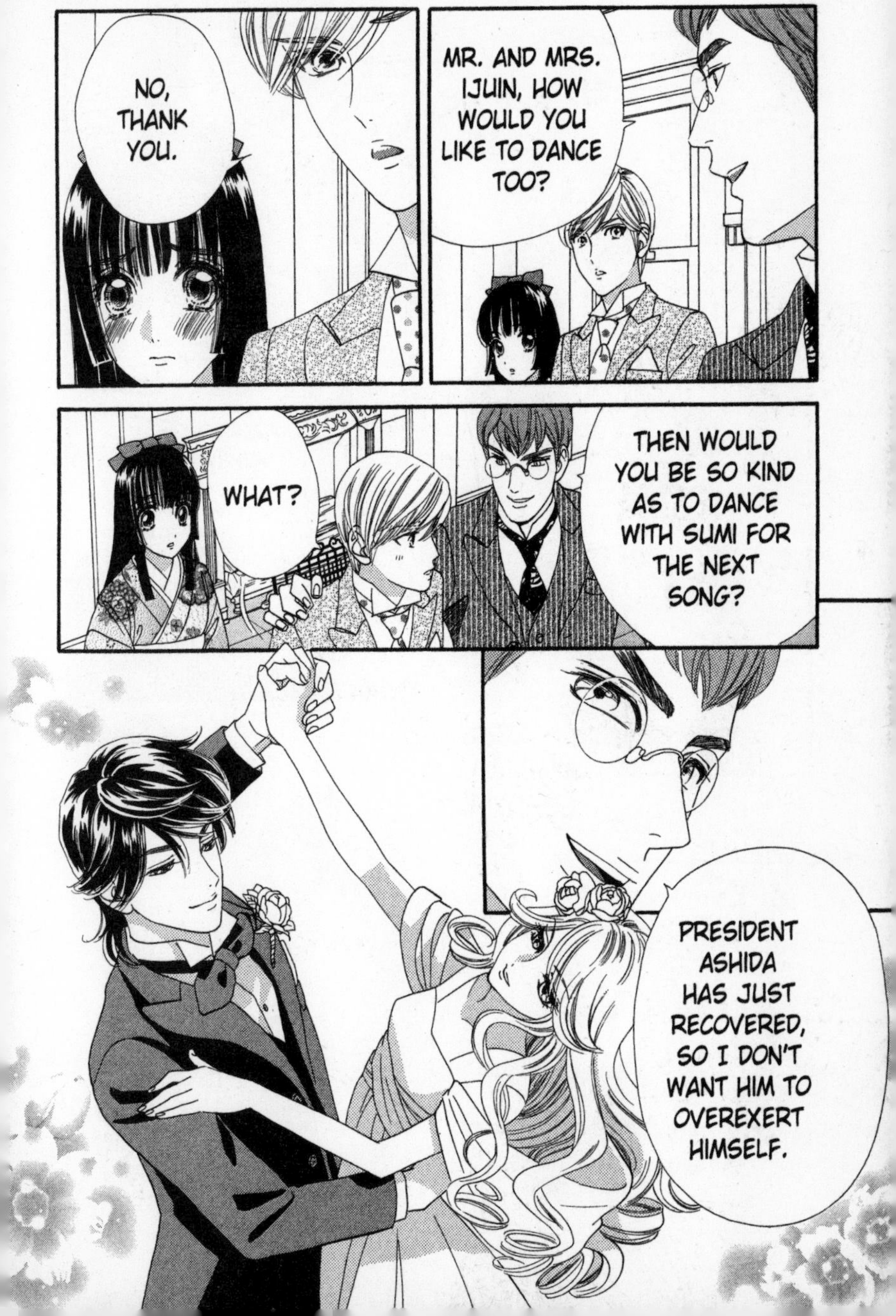
MR. AND MRS. IJUIN, HOW WOULD YOU LIKE TO DANCE TOO?
NO, THANK YOU.
THEN WOULD YOU BE SO KIND AS TO DANCE WITH SUMI FOR THE NEXT SONG?
WHAT?
PRESIDENT ASHIDA HAS JUST RECOVERED, SO I DON'T WANT HIM TO OVEREXERT HIMSELF.

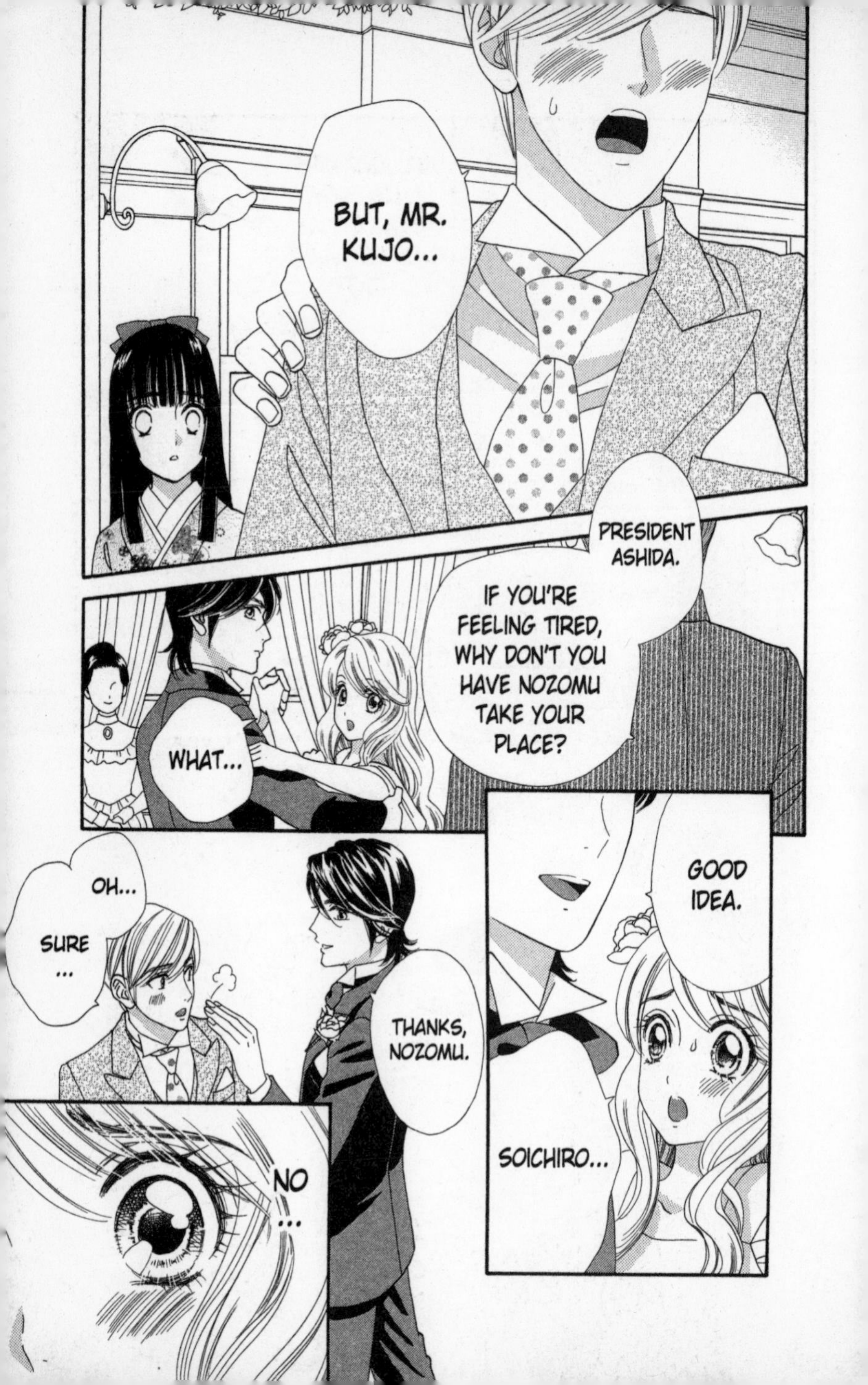
BUT, MR. KUJO...
PRESIDENT ASHIDA.
IF YOU'RE FEELING TIRED, WHY DON'T YOU HAVE NOZOMU TAKE YOUR PLACE?
WHAT...
GOOD IDEA.
SOICHIRO...
THANKS, NOZOMU.
OH...
SURE...
NO...

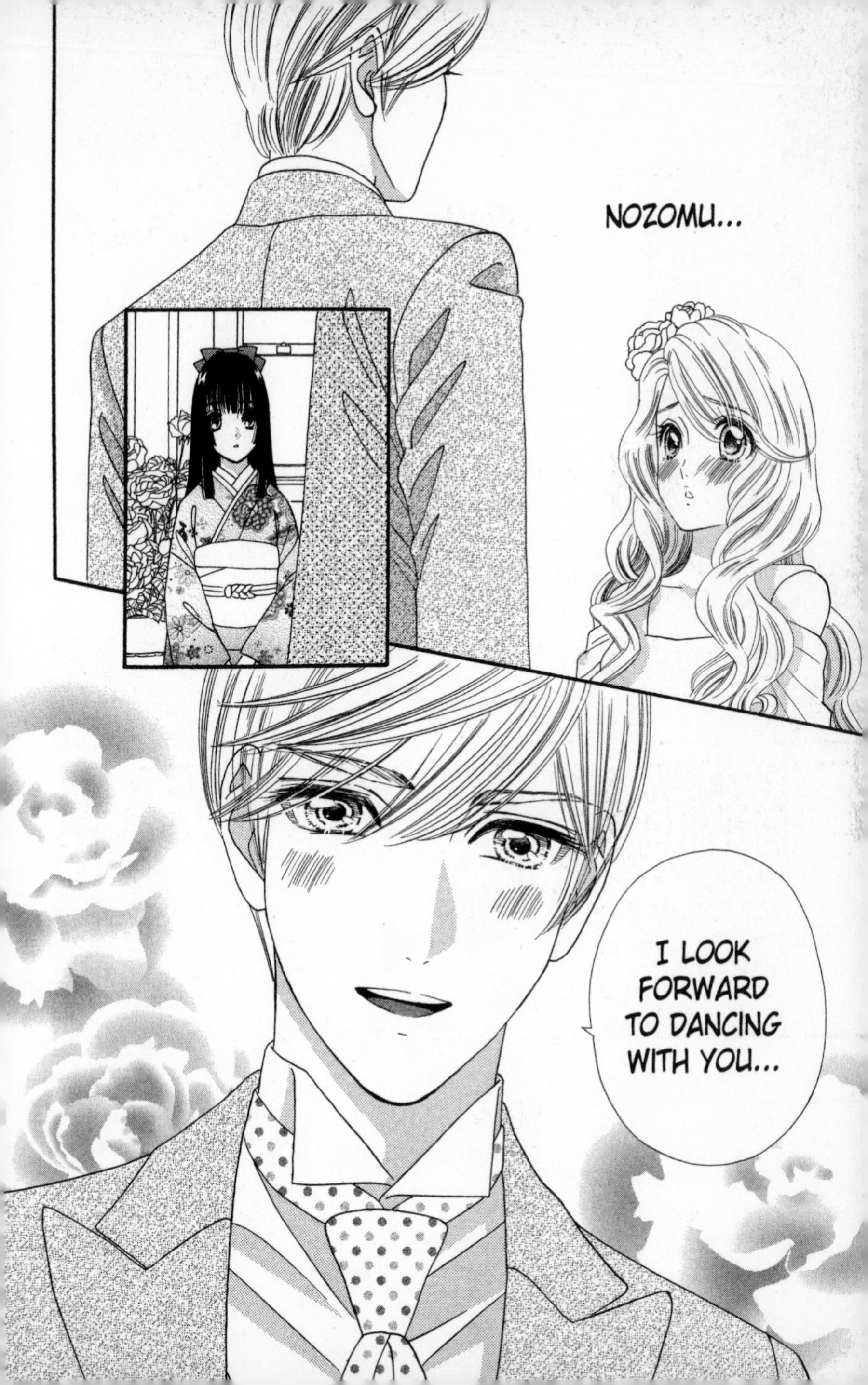
NOZOMU...
I LOOK FORWARD TO DANCING WITH YOU...

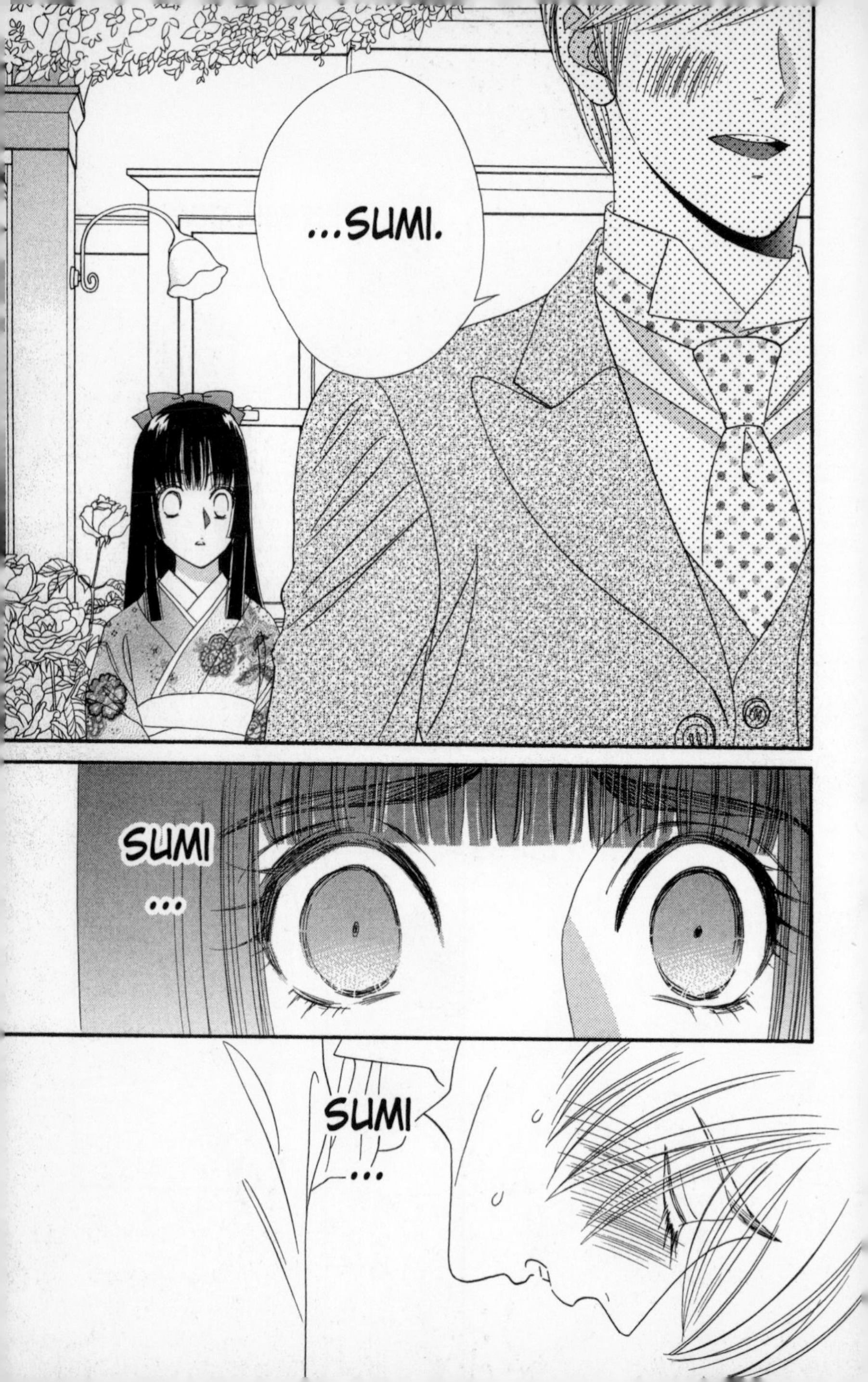
...SUMI.
SUMI ...
SUMI ...

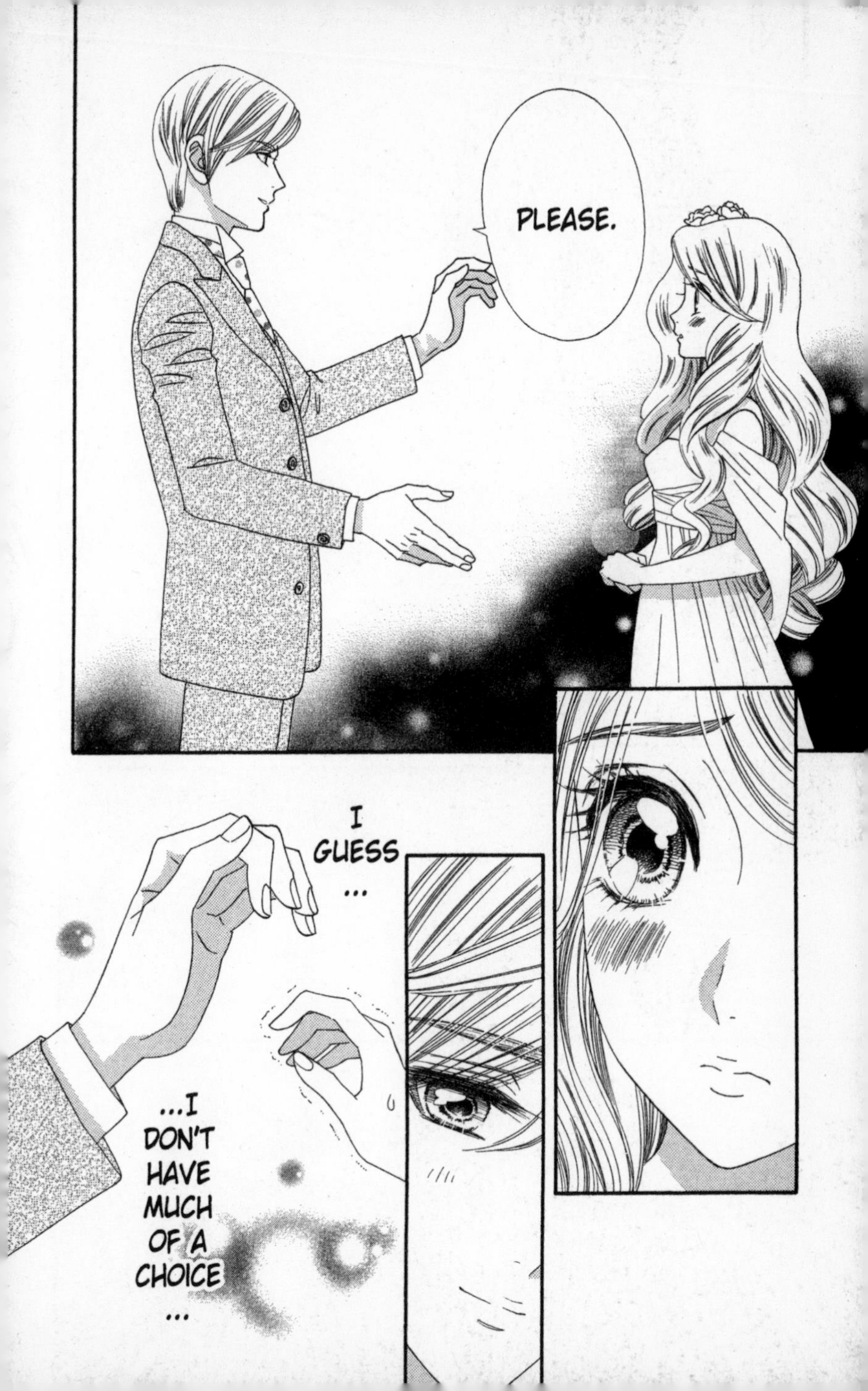
PLEASE.
I GUESS...
...I DON'T HAVE MUCH OF A CHOICE...

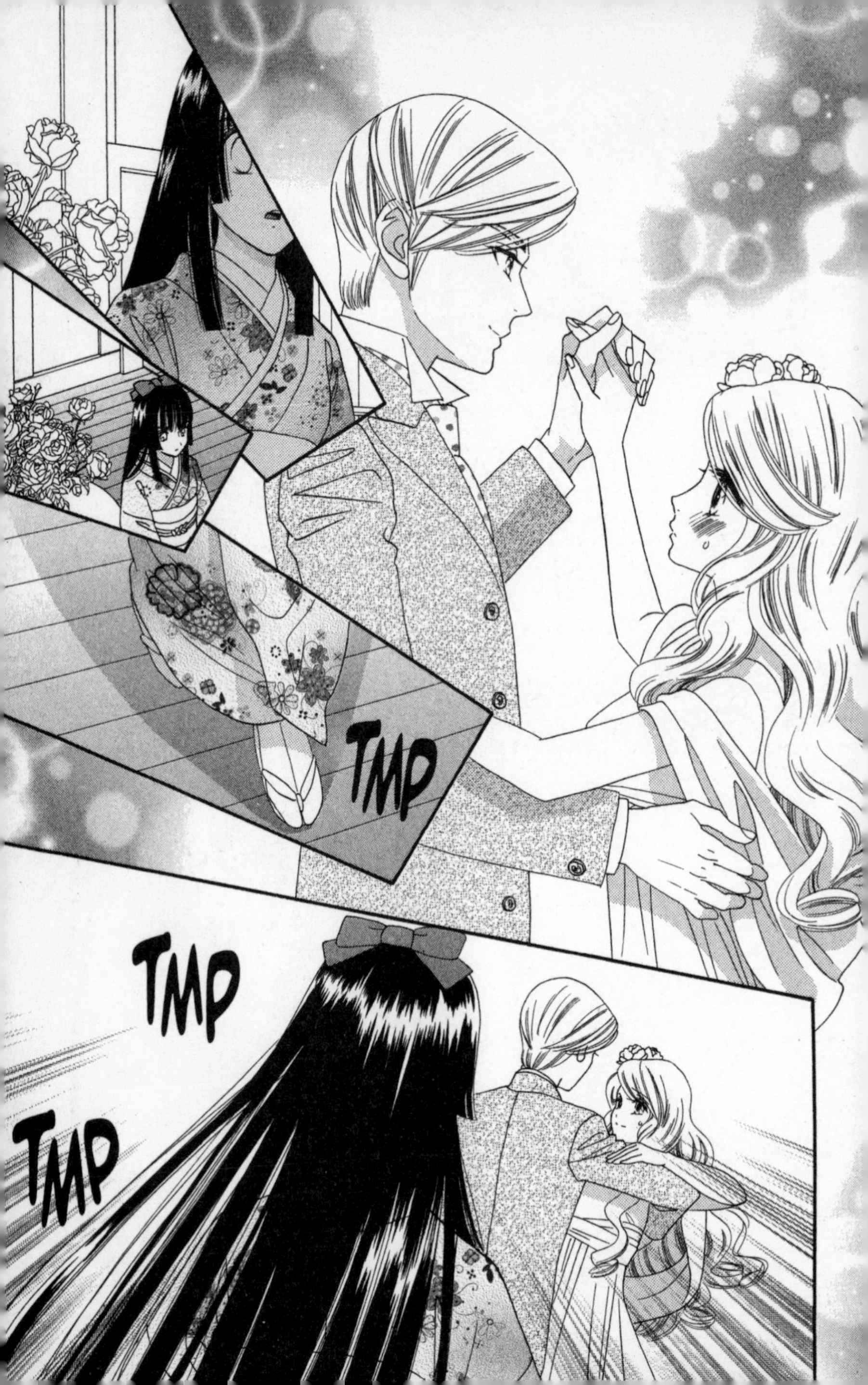
TMP
TMP
TMP

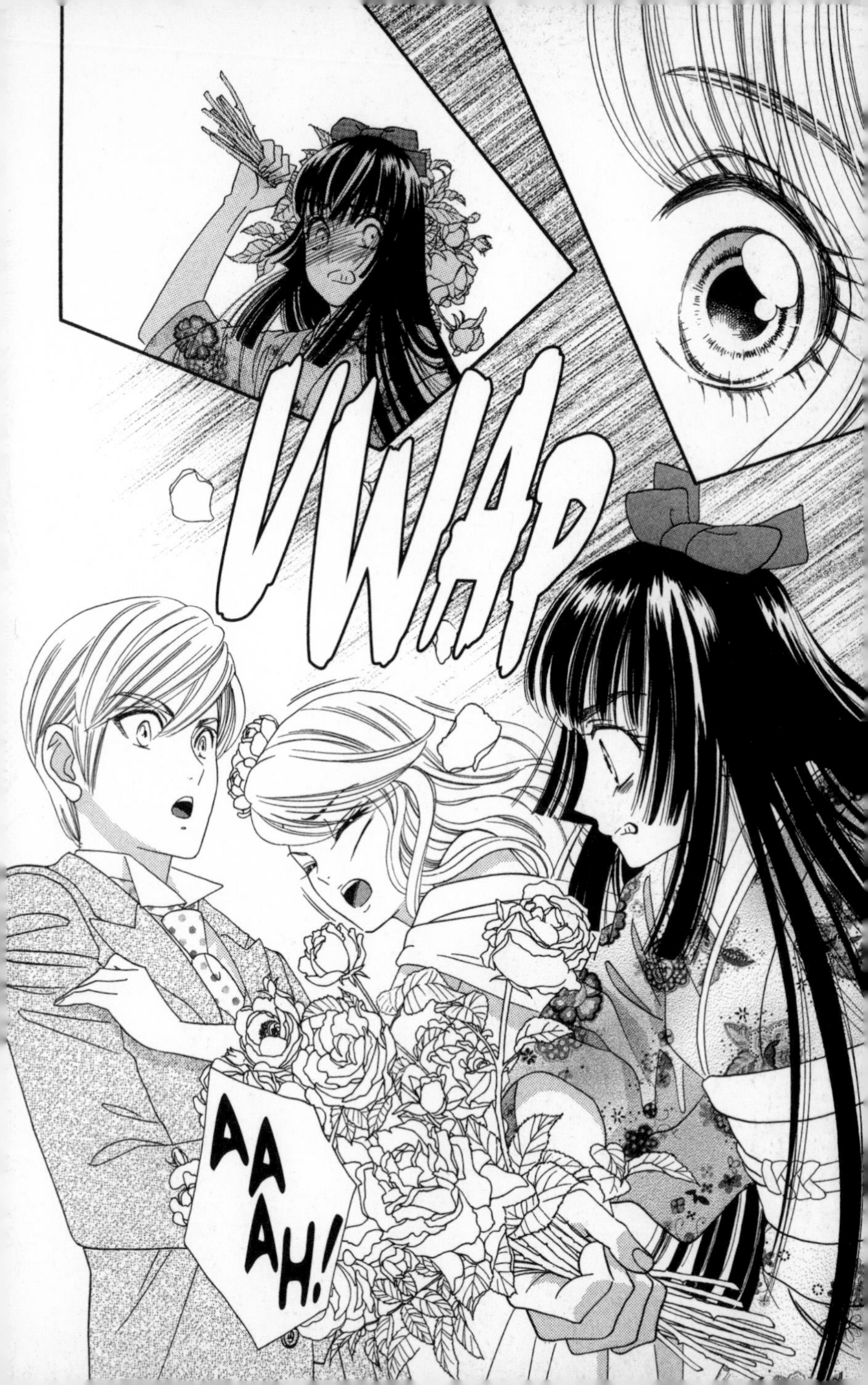
WHAP
AAAAH!

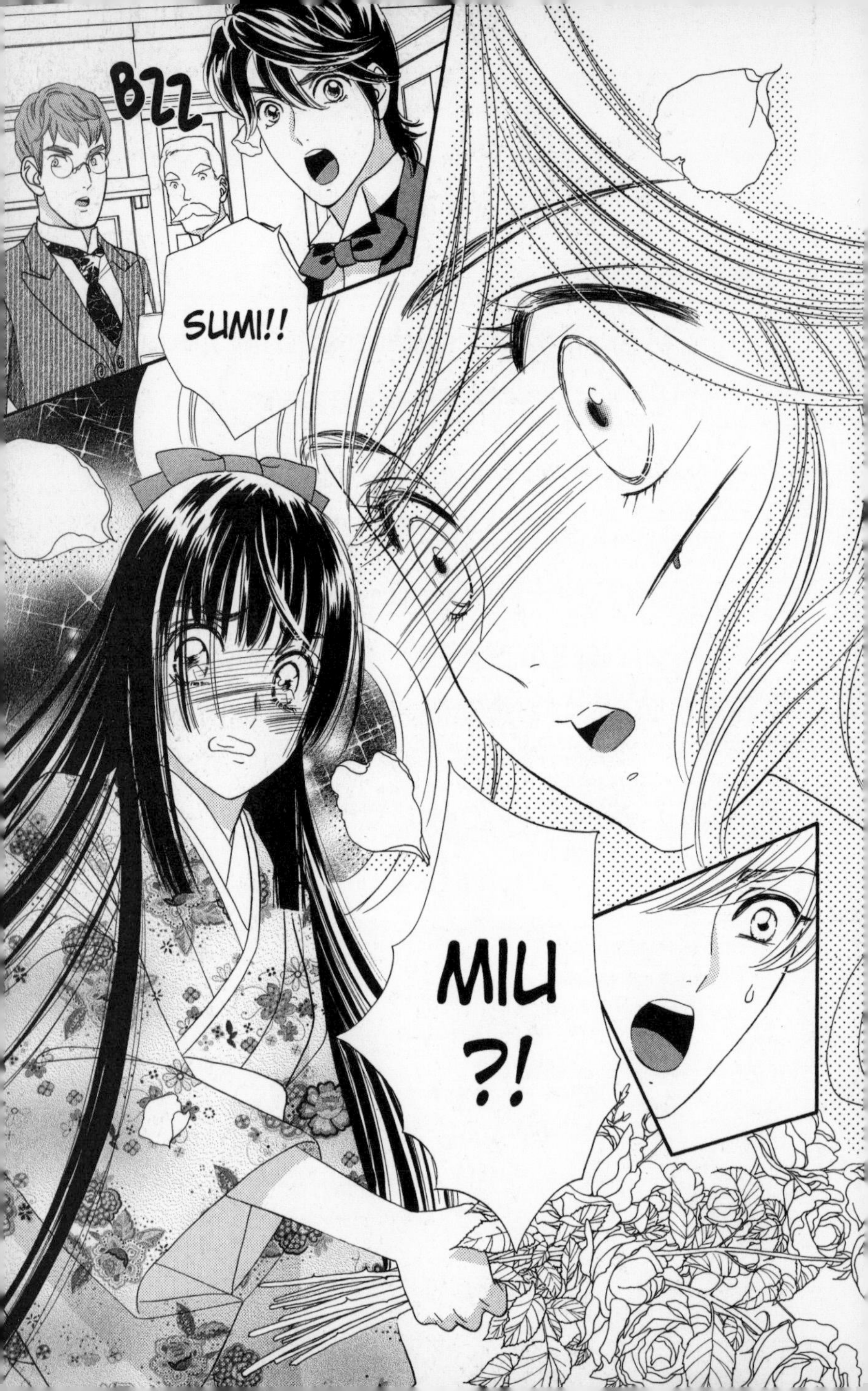
BZZ
SUMI!!
MIU ?!

No. 1

Date

RANDOM CHITCHAT

❀ HELLO, IT'S UE-RIN.

I'M SO SORRY VOLUME 5 TOOK SO LONG TO GET PUBLISHED. TO TELL YOU THE TRUTH, I GAVE BIRTH TO A DAUGHTER AT THE END OF JUNE 2009, SO I TOOK A HALF-YEAR OFF FOR MY MATERNITY LEAVE. NOW I'M BACK AT WORK AND LOOKING AFTER MY CHILD AT THE SAME TIME.

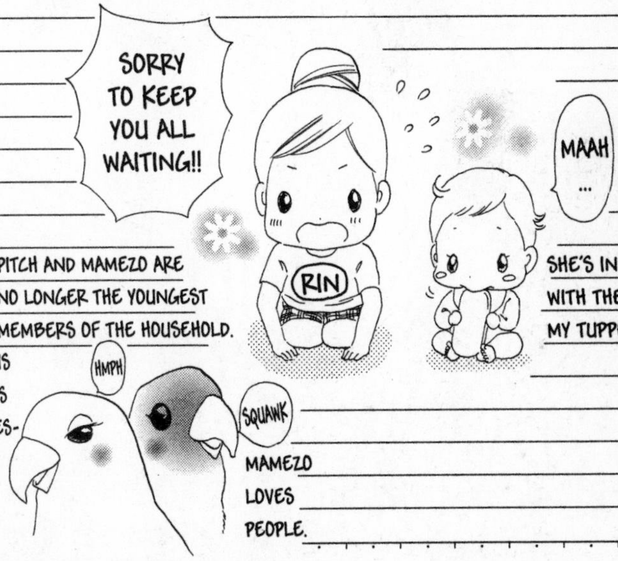

SORRY TO KEEP YOU ALL WAITING!!
RIN
MAAH ...
HMPH
SQUAWK

SHE'S IN LOVE WITH THE LID OF MY TUPPERWARE.

❀ PITCH AND MAMEZO ARE NO LONGER THE YOUNGEST MEMBERS OF THE HOUSEHOLD.

PITCH IS ALWAYS AGGRES-SIVE.

MAMEZO LOVES PEOPLE.

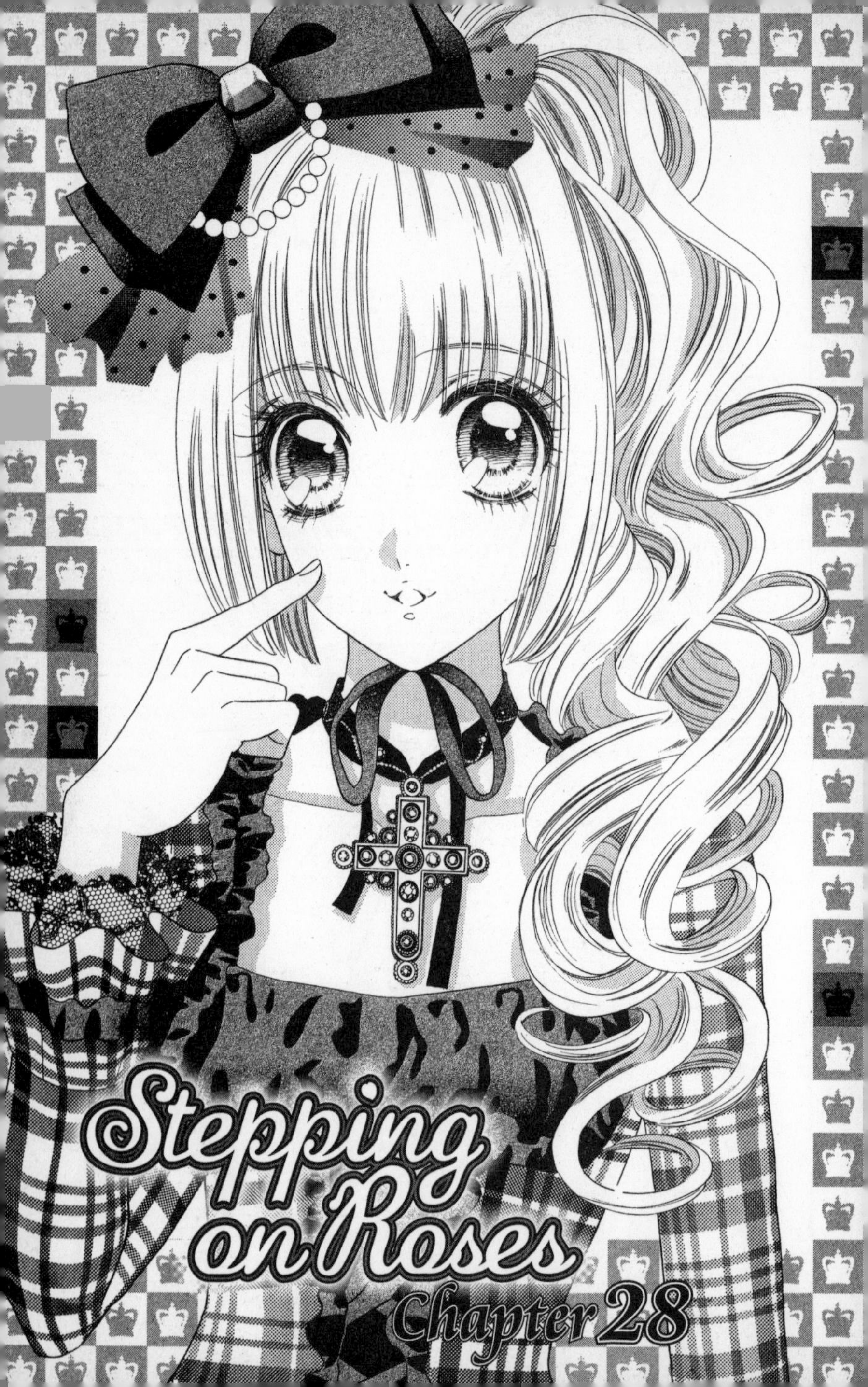
Stepping on Roses
Chapter 28

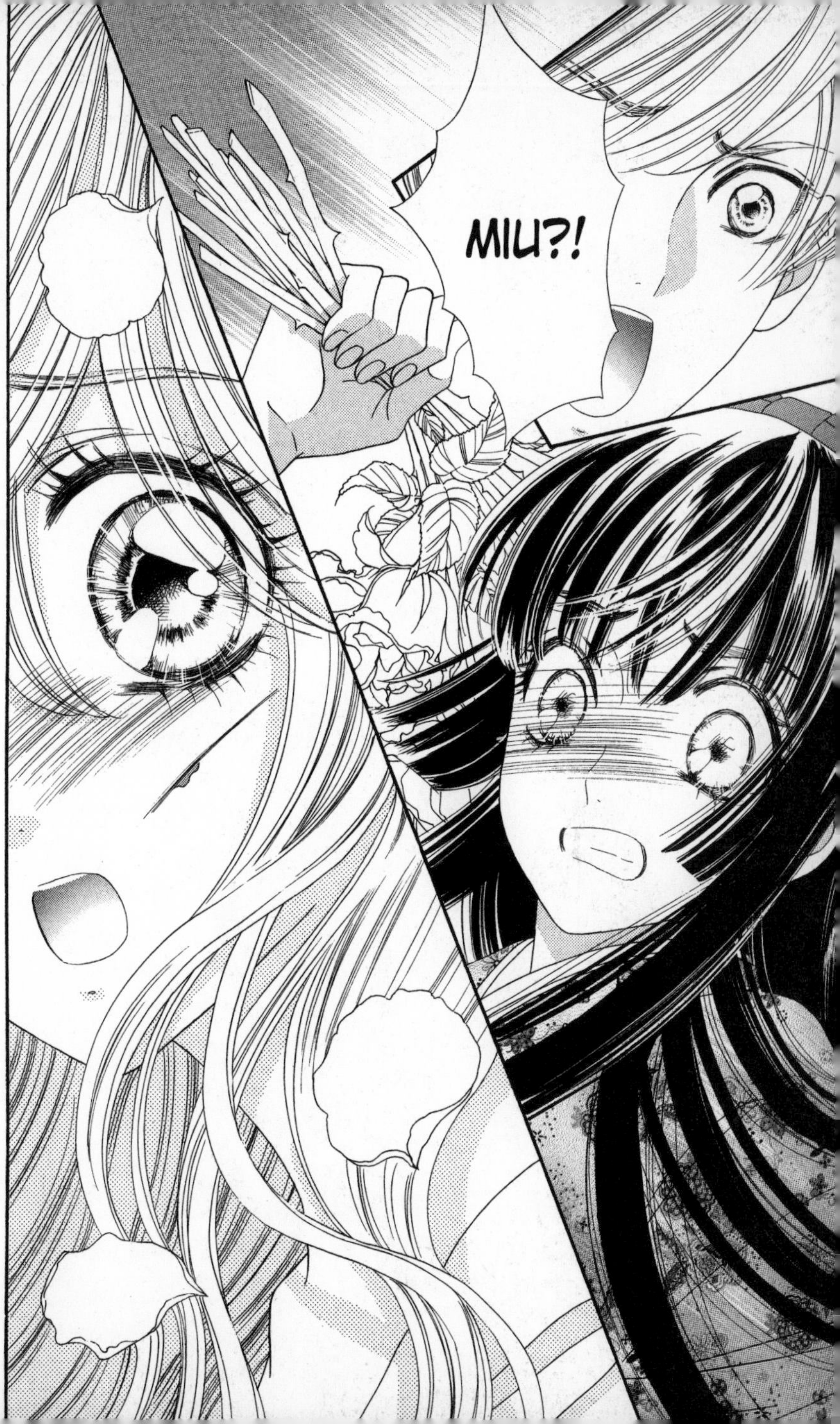
MIU?!

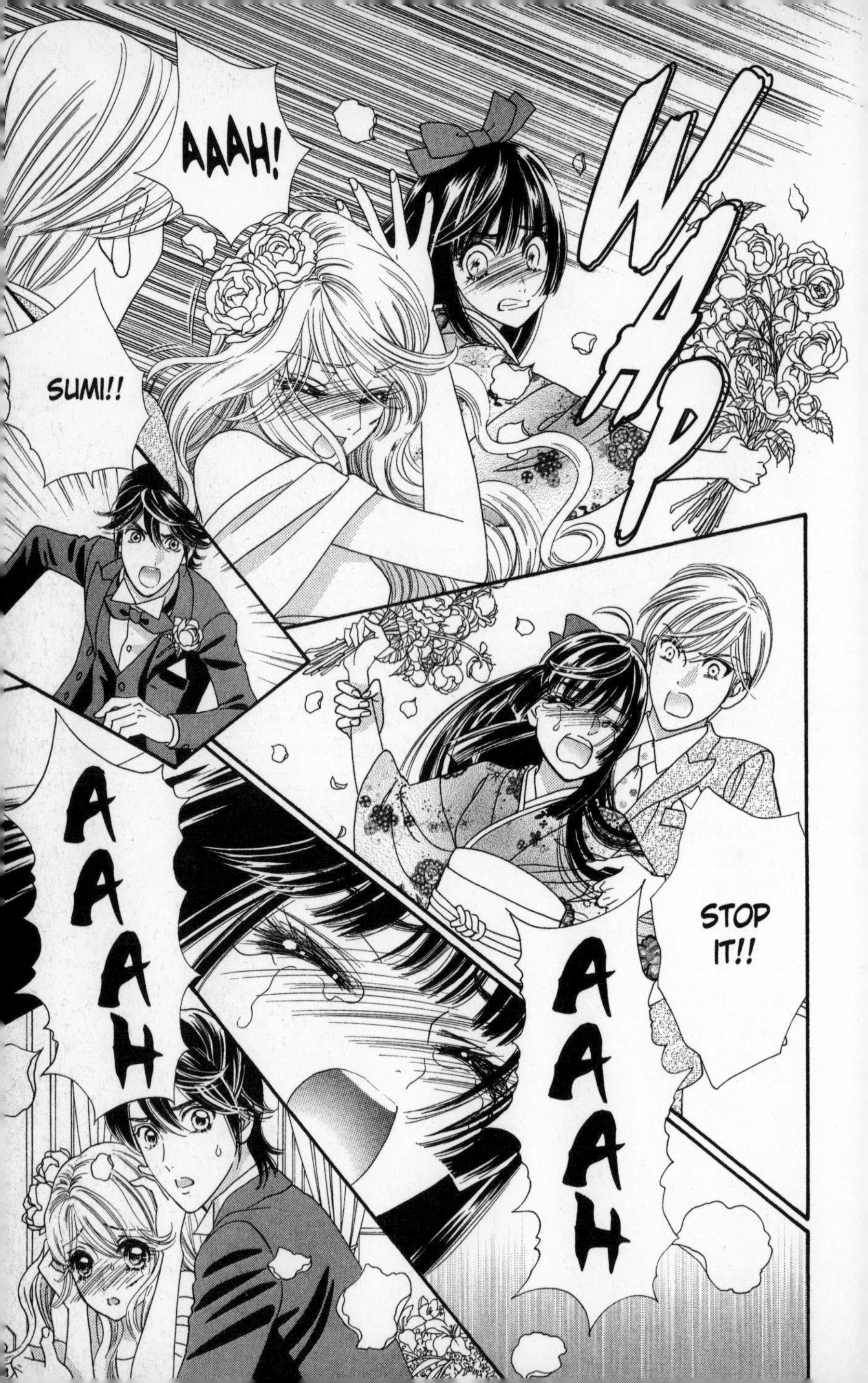
WHAP
AAAH!
SUMI!!
STOP IT!!
AAAAH
AAAH

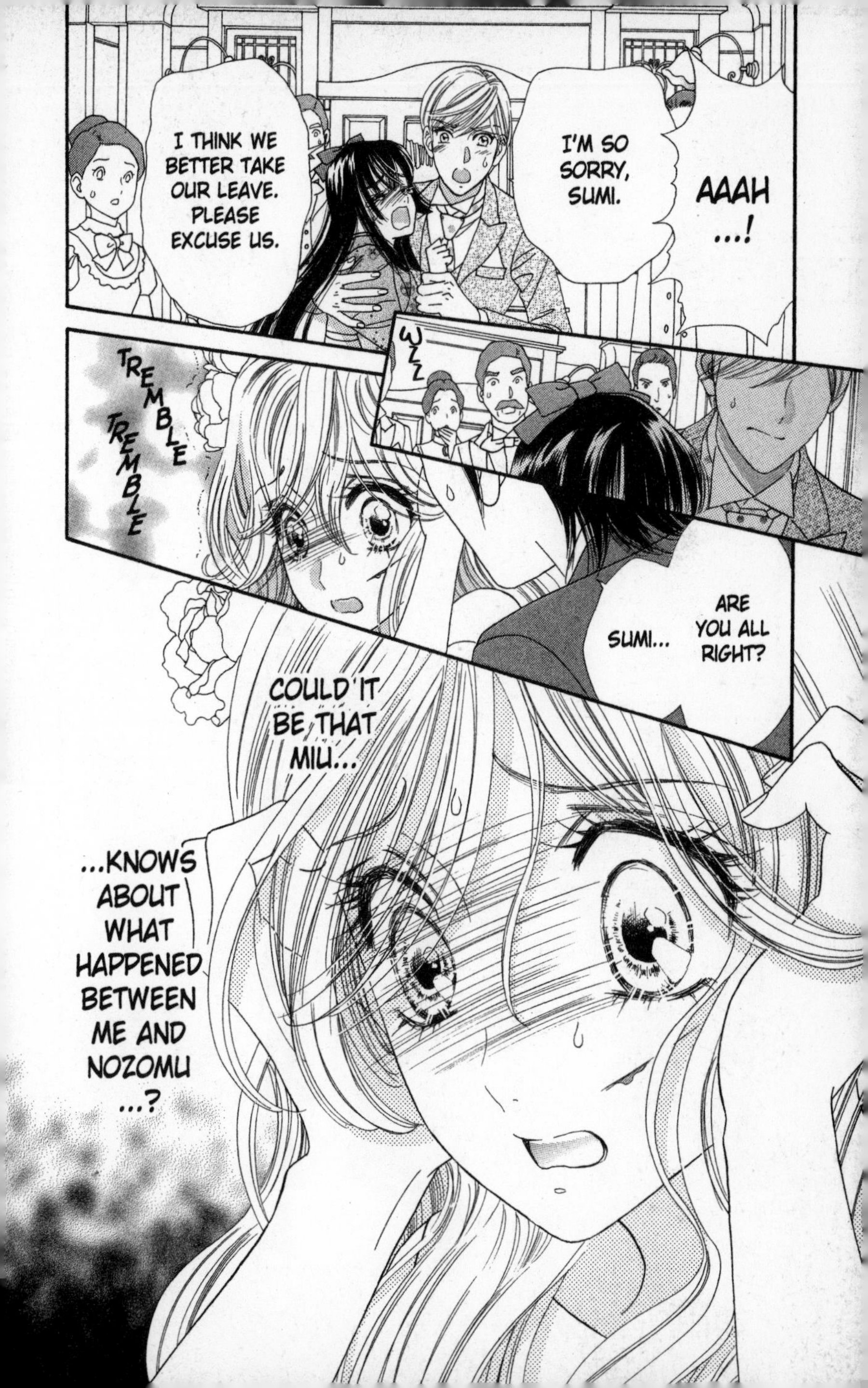
AAAH ...!
I'M SO SORRY, SUMI.
I THINK WE BETTER TAKE OUR LEAVE. PLEASE EXCUSE US.
WZZ
TREMBLE TREMBLE
ARE YOU ALL RIGHT?
SUMI...
COULD IT BE THAT MIU...
...KNOWS ABOUT WHAT HAPPENED BETWEEN ME AND NOZOMU ...?

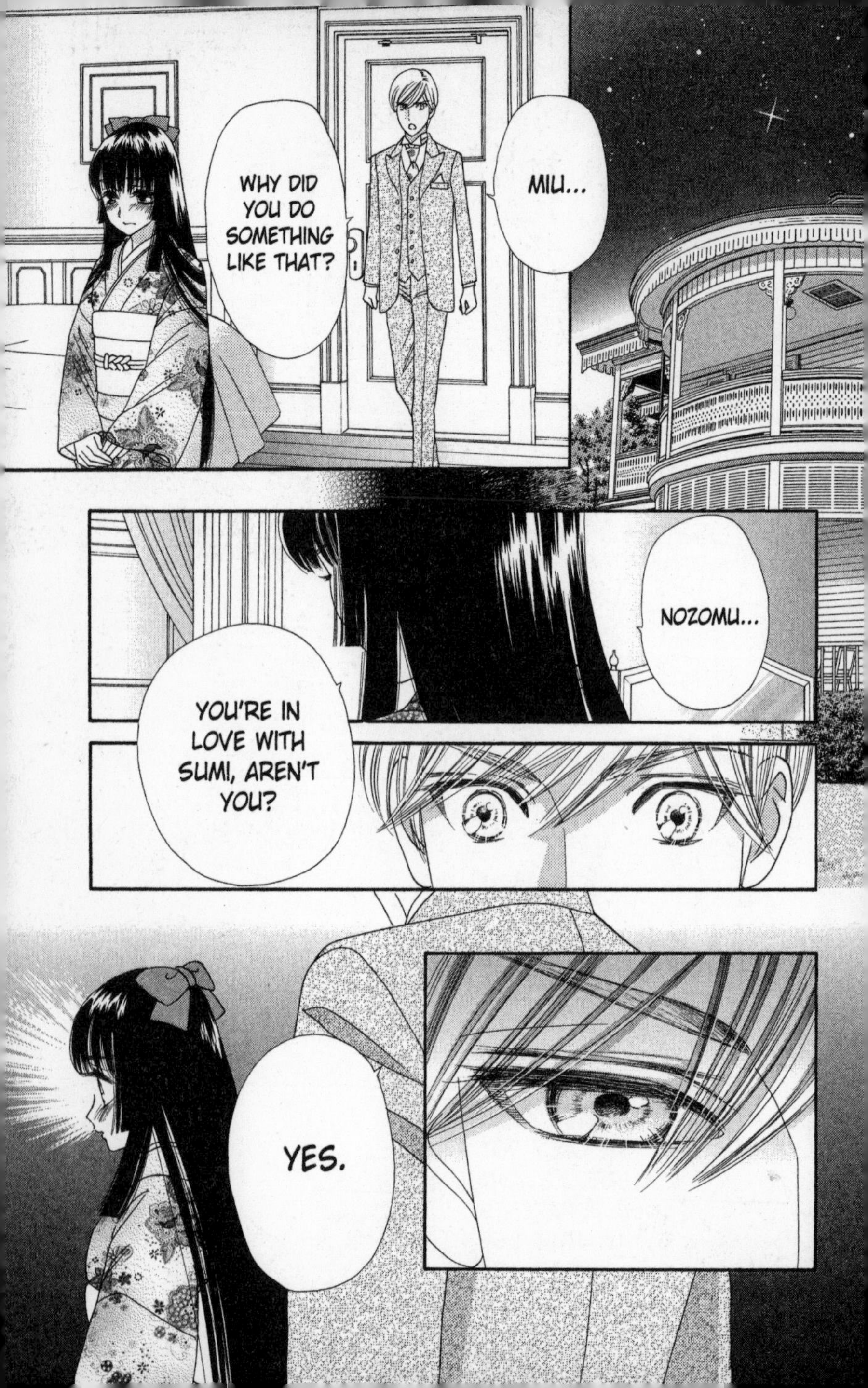
MIU...
WHY DID YOU DO SOMETHING LIKE THAT?
NOZOMU...
YOU'RE IN LOVE WITH SUMI, AREN'T YOU?
YES.

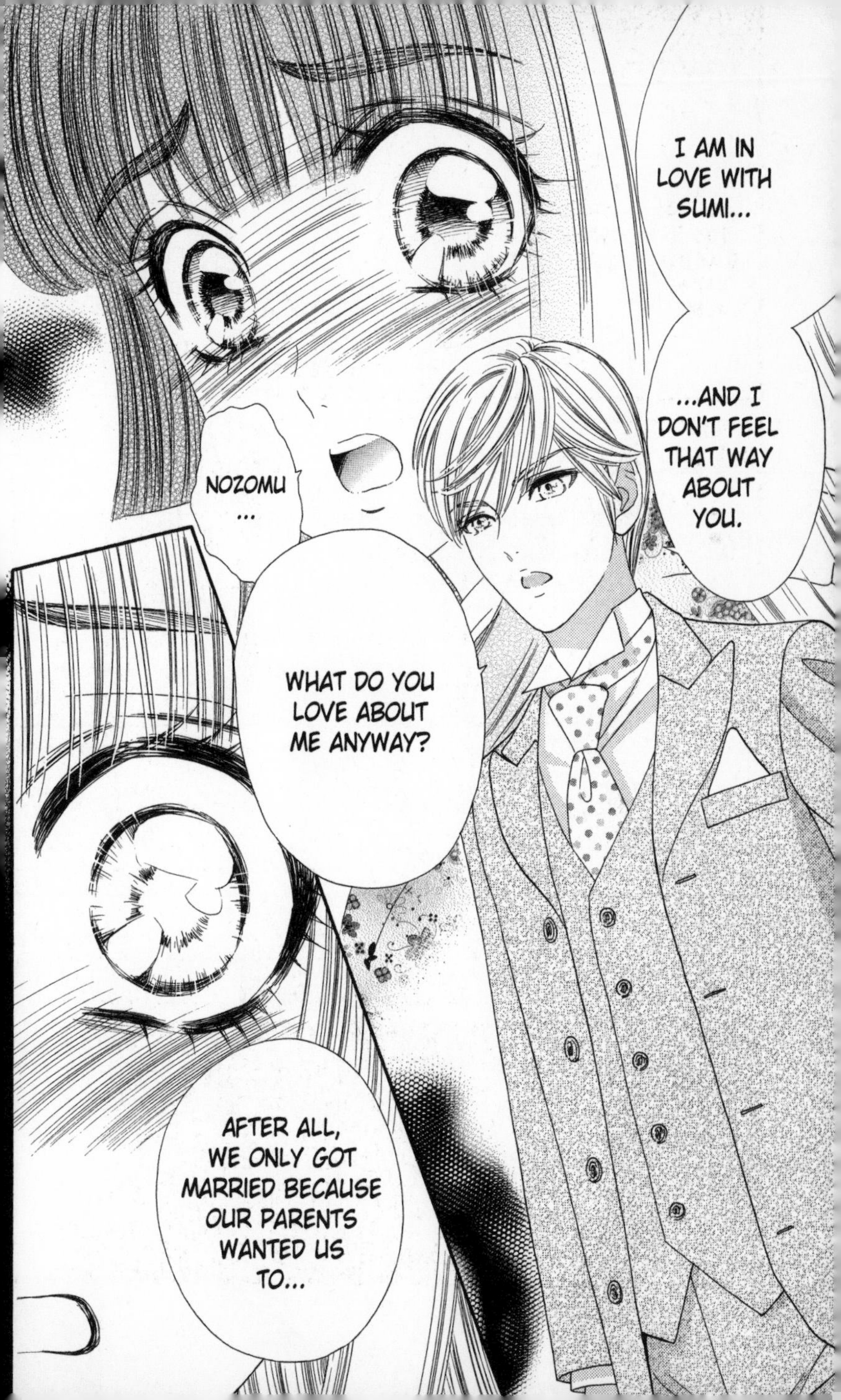
I AM IN LOVE WITH SUMI...
...AND I DON'T FEEL THAT WAY ABOUT YOU.
NOZOMU...
WHAT DO YOU LOVE ABOUT ME ANYWAY?
AFTER ALL, WE ONLY GOT MARRIED BECAUSE OUR PARENTS WANTED US TO...

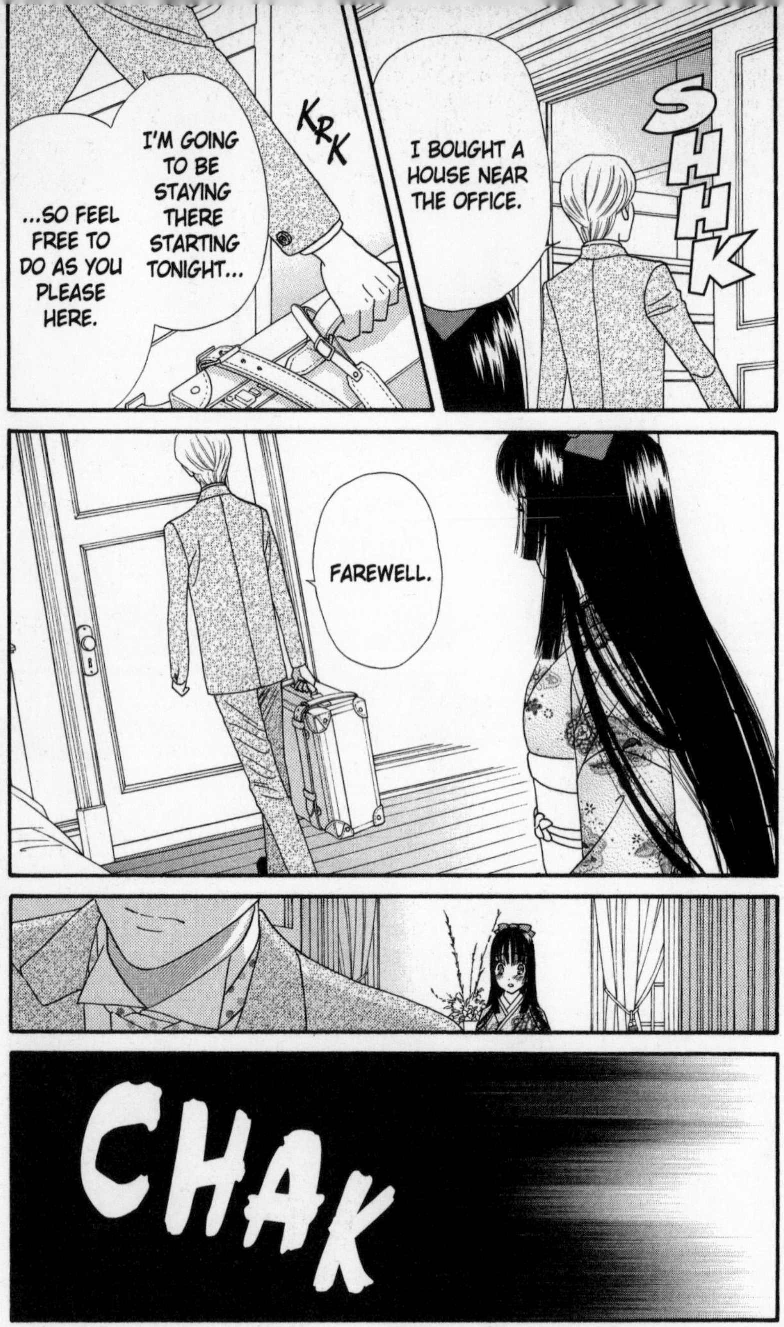
SHHHK
I BOUGHT A HOUSE NEAR THE OFFICE.
KRK
I'M GOING TO BE STAYING THERE STARTING TONIGHT...
...SO FEEL FREE TO DO AS YOU PLEASE HERE.
FAREWELL.
CHAK

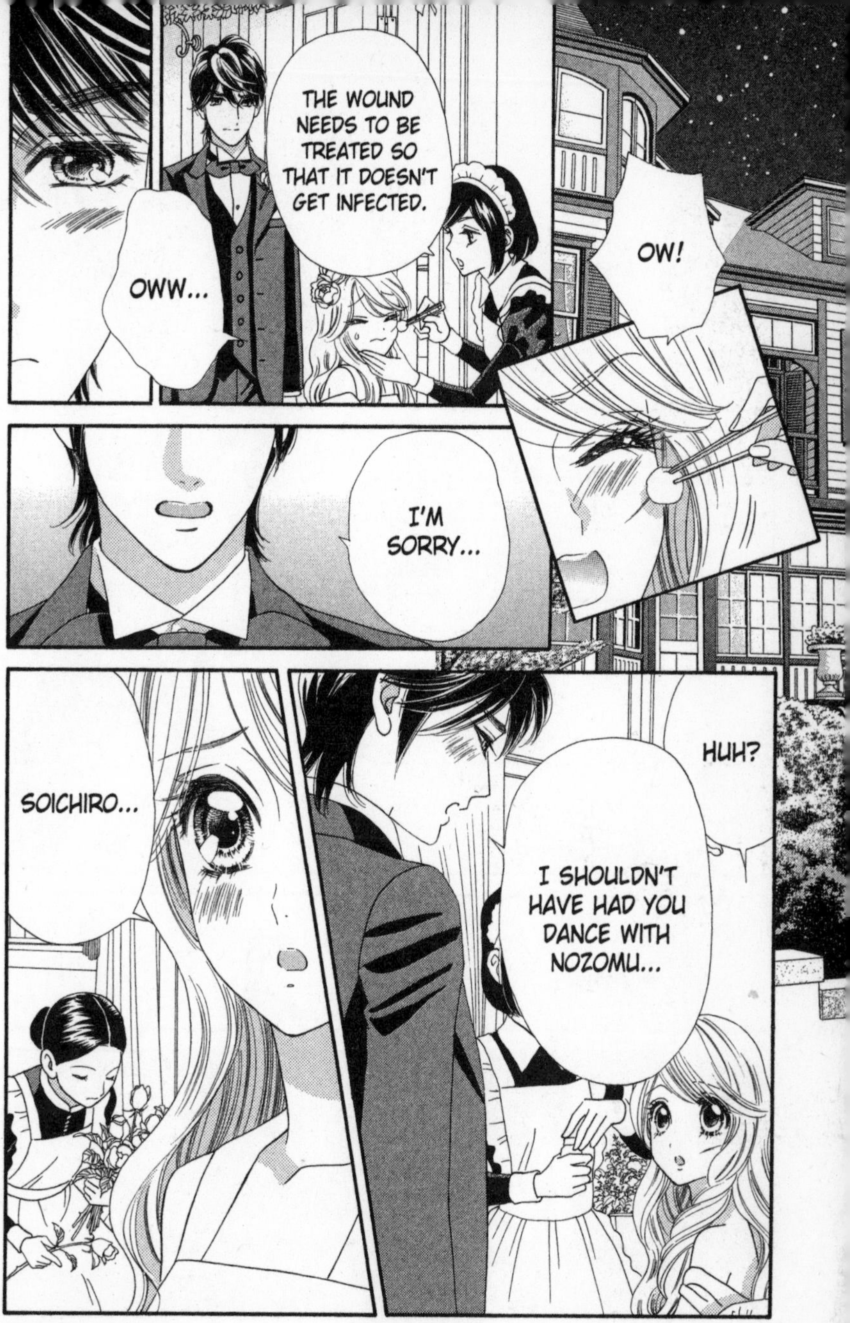
OW!
THE WOUND NEEDS TO BE TREATED SO THAT IT DOESN'T GET INFECTED.
OWW...
I'M SORRY...
HUH?
I SHOULDN'T HAVE HAD YOU DANCE WITH NOZOMU...
SOICHIRO...

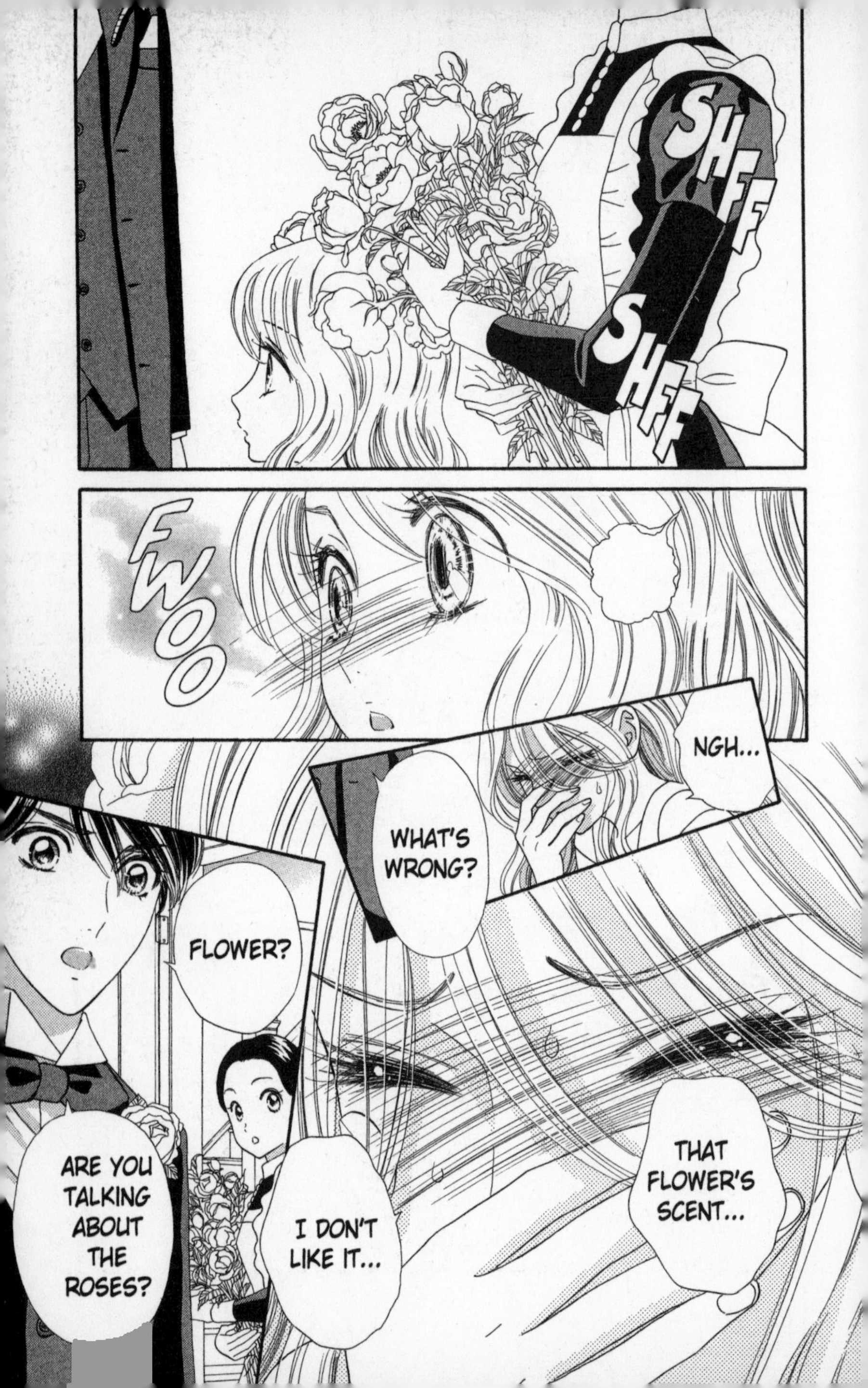
SHEFF
SHEFF
FWOO
NGH...
WHAT'S WRONG?
THAT FLOWER'S SCENT...
I DON'T LIKE IT...
FLOWER?
ARE YOU TALKING ABOUT THE ROSES?

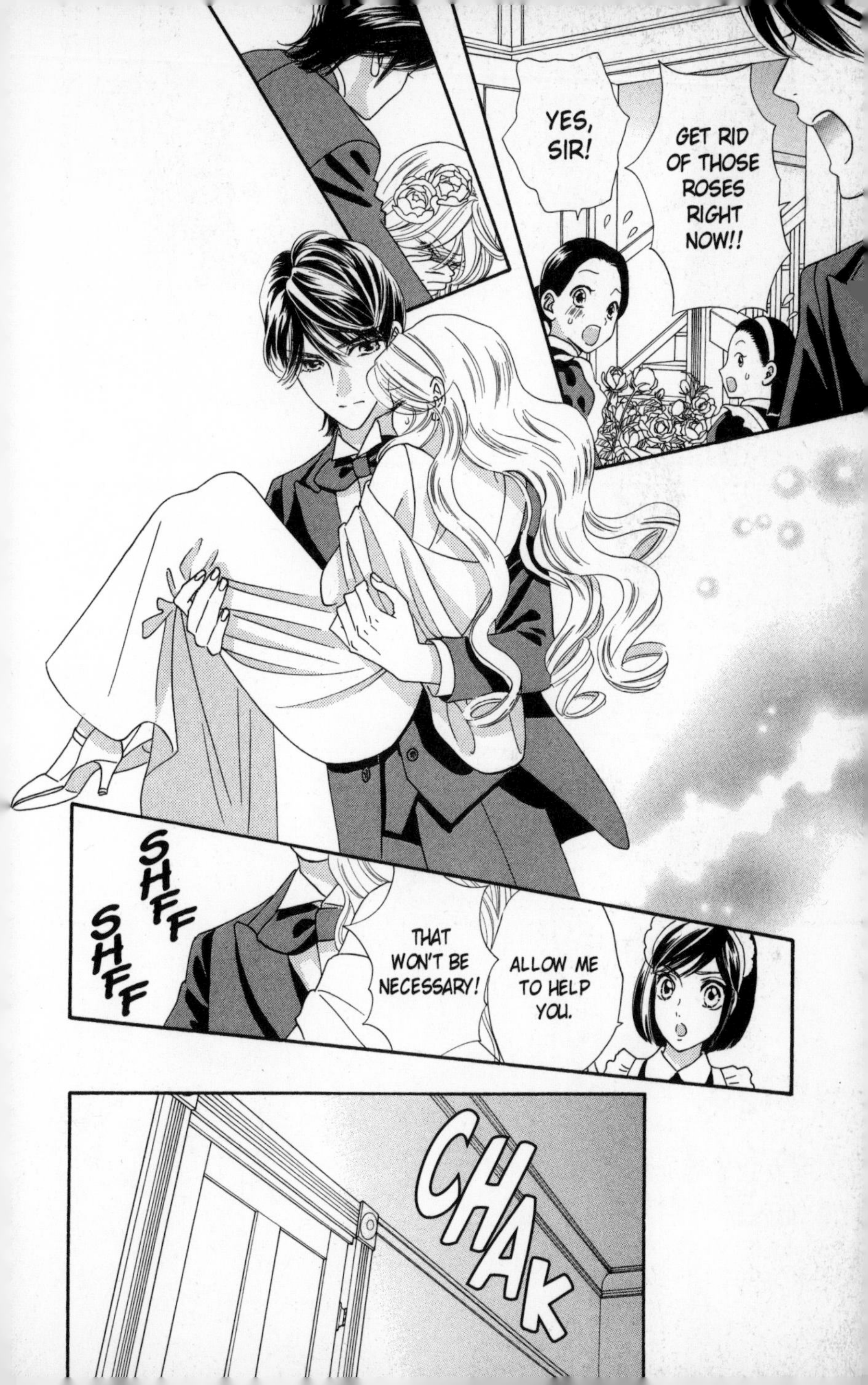
GET RID OF THOSE ROSES RIGHT NOW!!
YES, SIR!
ALLOW ME TO HELP YOU.
THAT WON'T BE NECESSARY!
SHFF SHFF
CHAK

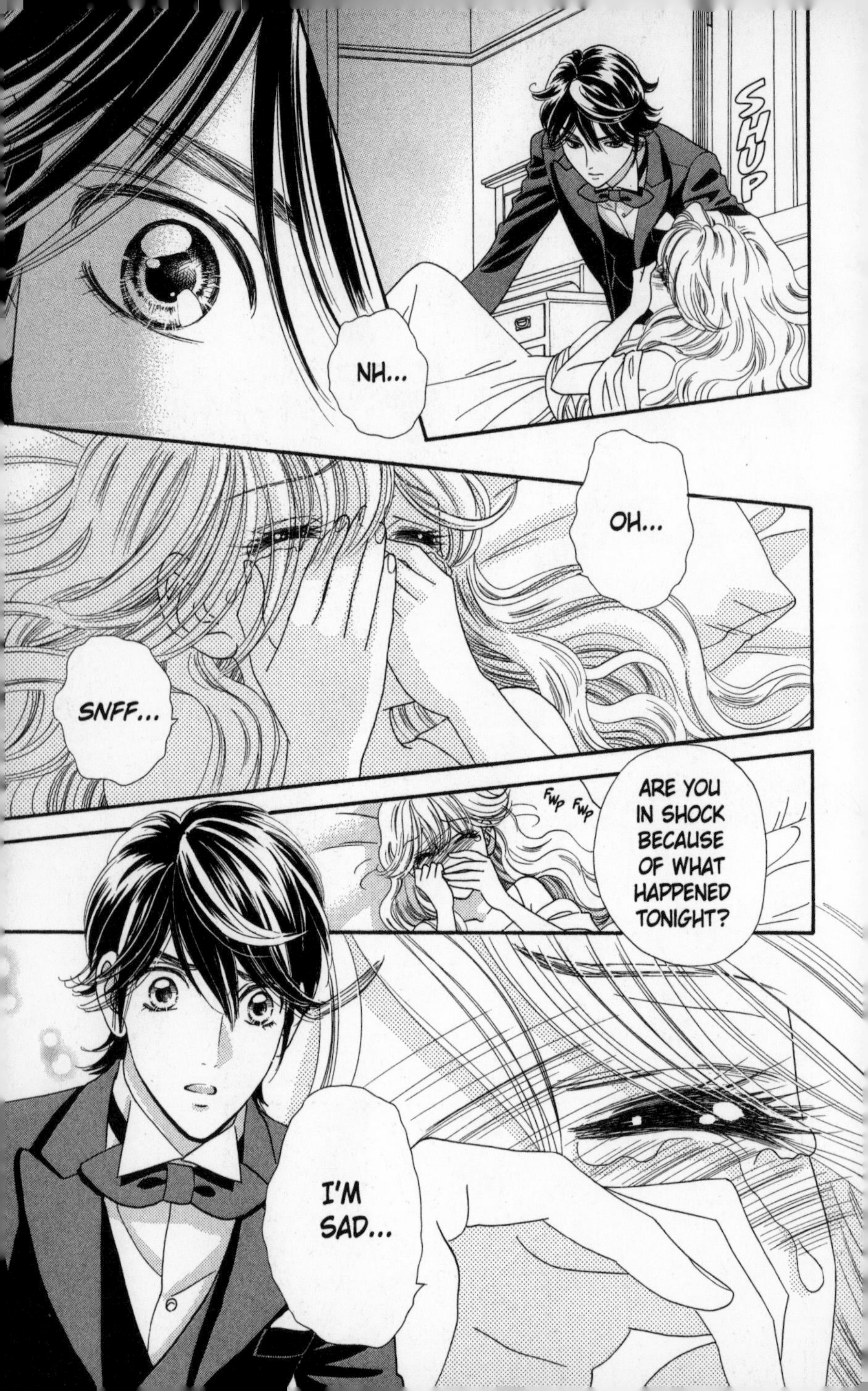
SHUP
NH...
OH...
SNFF...
FWP FWP
ARE YOU IN SHOCK BECAUSE OF WHAT HAPPENED TONIGHT?
I'M SAD...

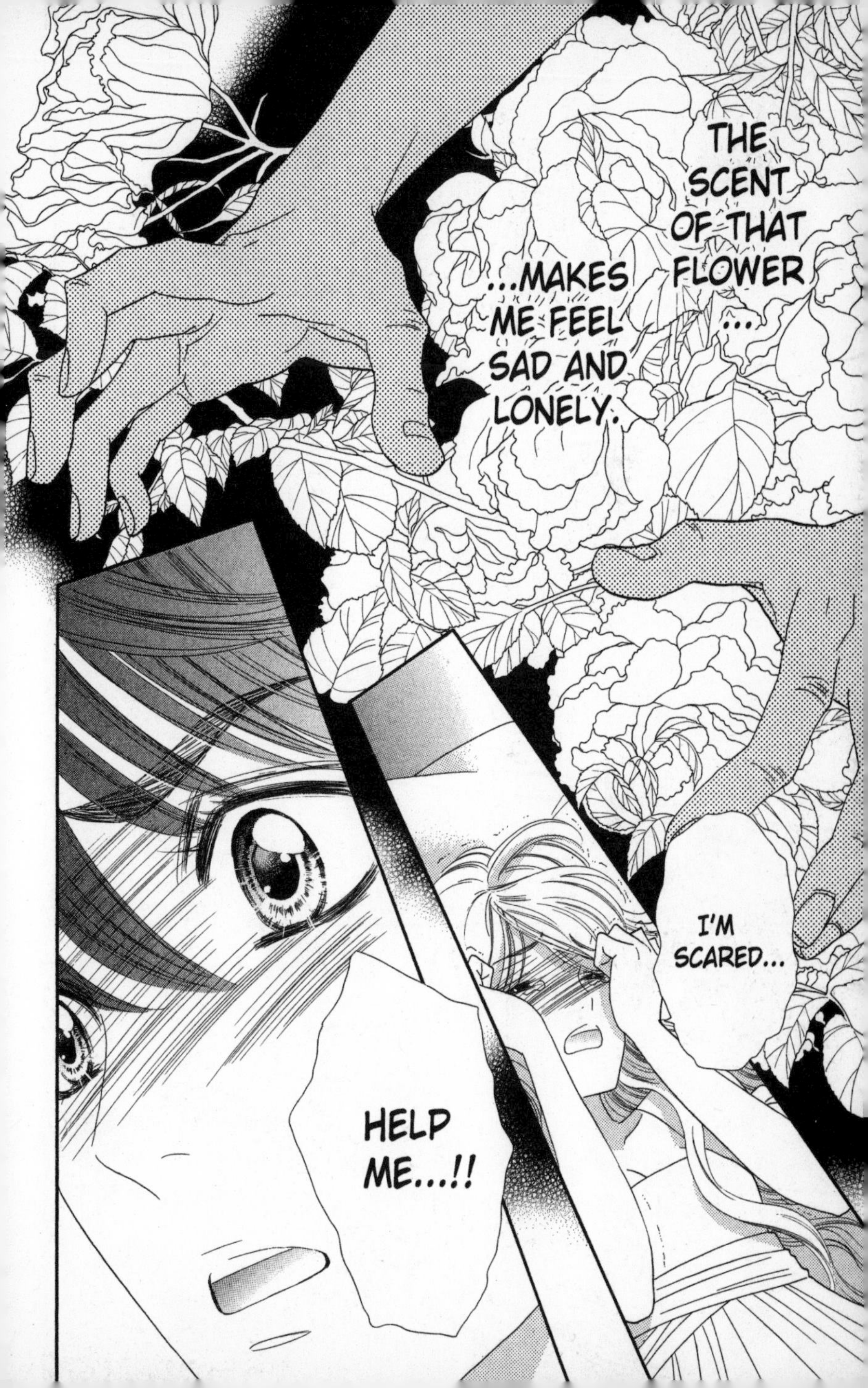
THE SCENT OF THAT FLOWER ...
...MAKES ME FEEL SAD AND LONELY.
I'M SCARED...
HELP ME...!!

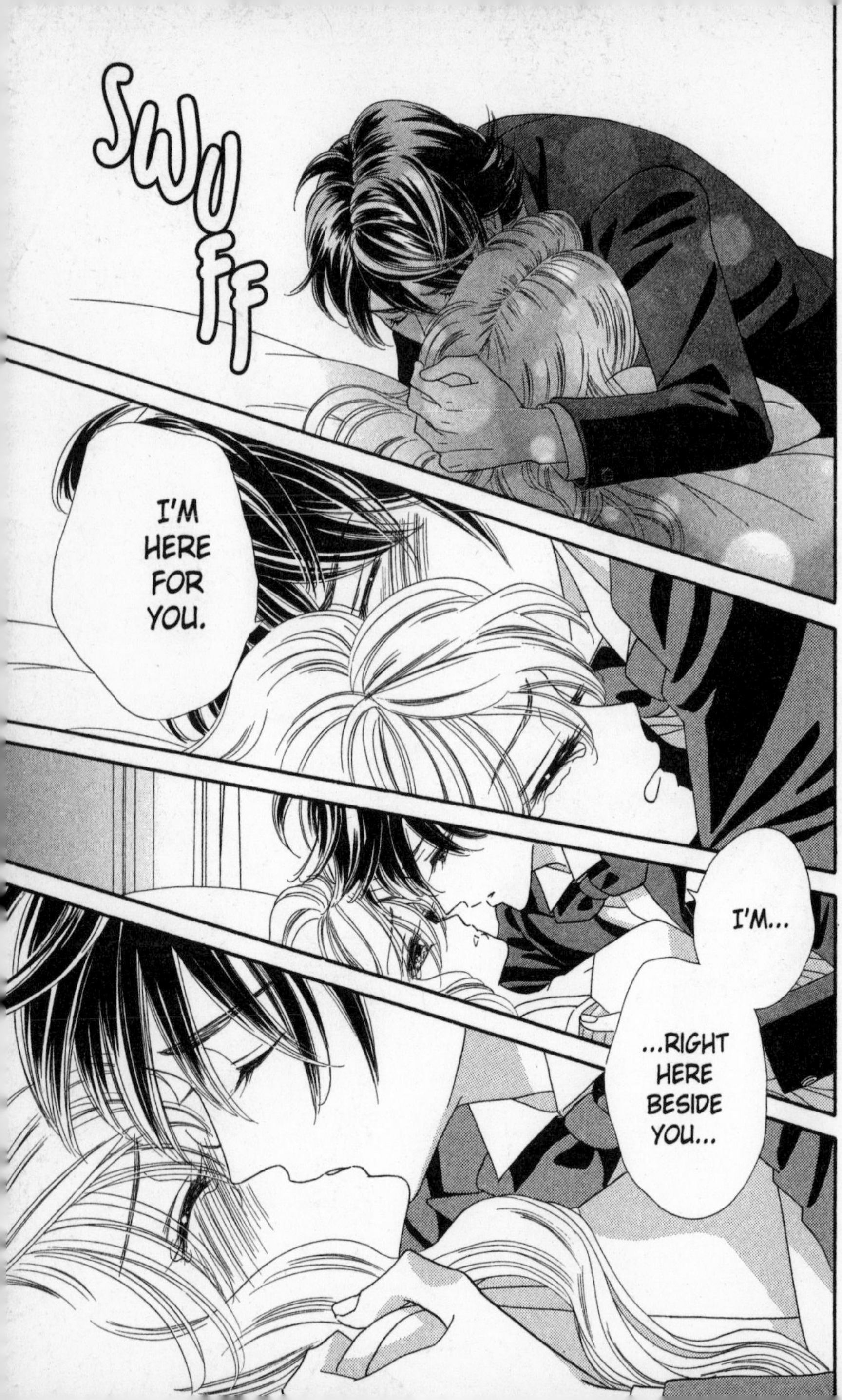
SWUFF
I'M HERE FOR YOU.
I'M...
...RIGHT HERE BESIDE YOU...

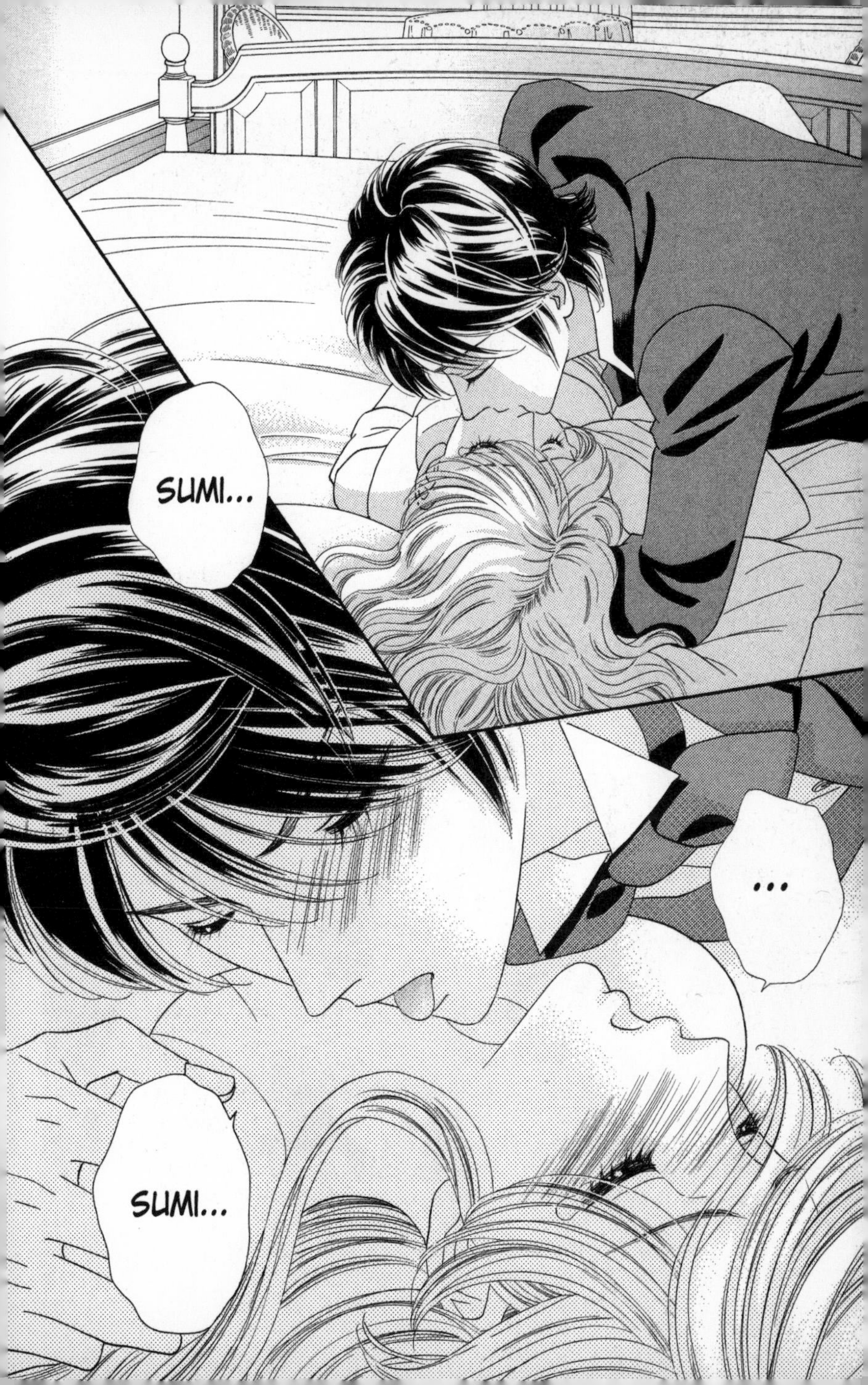
SUMI...
...
SUMI...

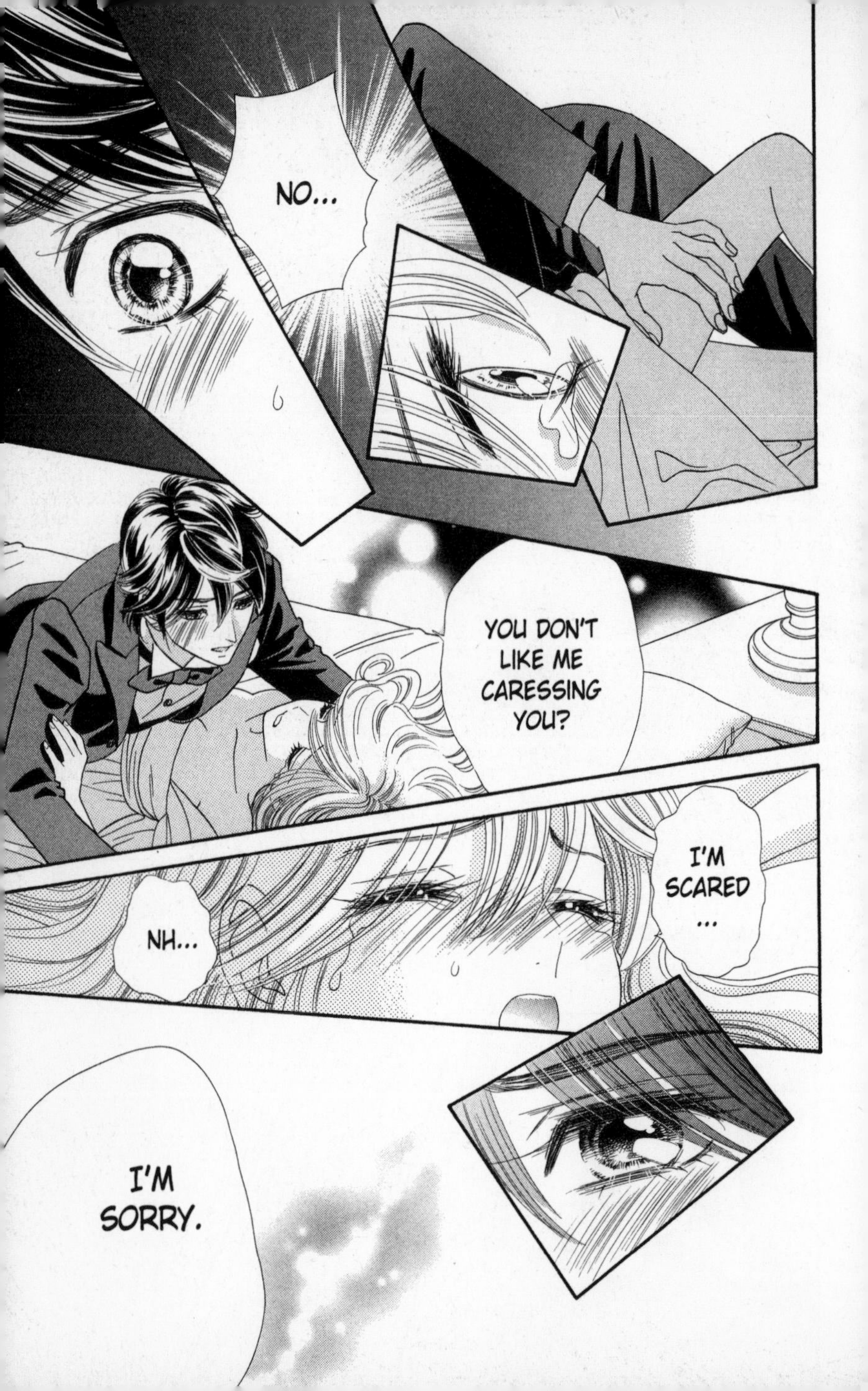
NO...
YOU DON'T LIKE ME CARESSING YOU?
I'M SCARED ...
NH...
I'M SORRY.

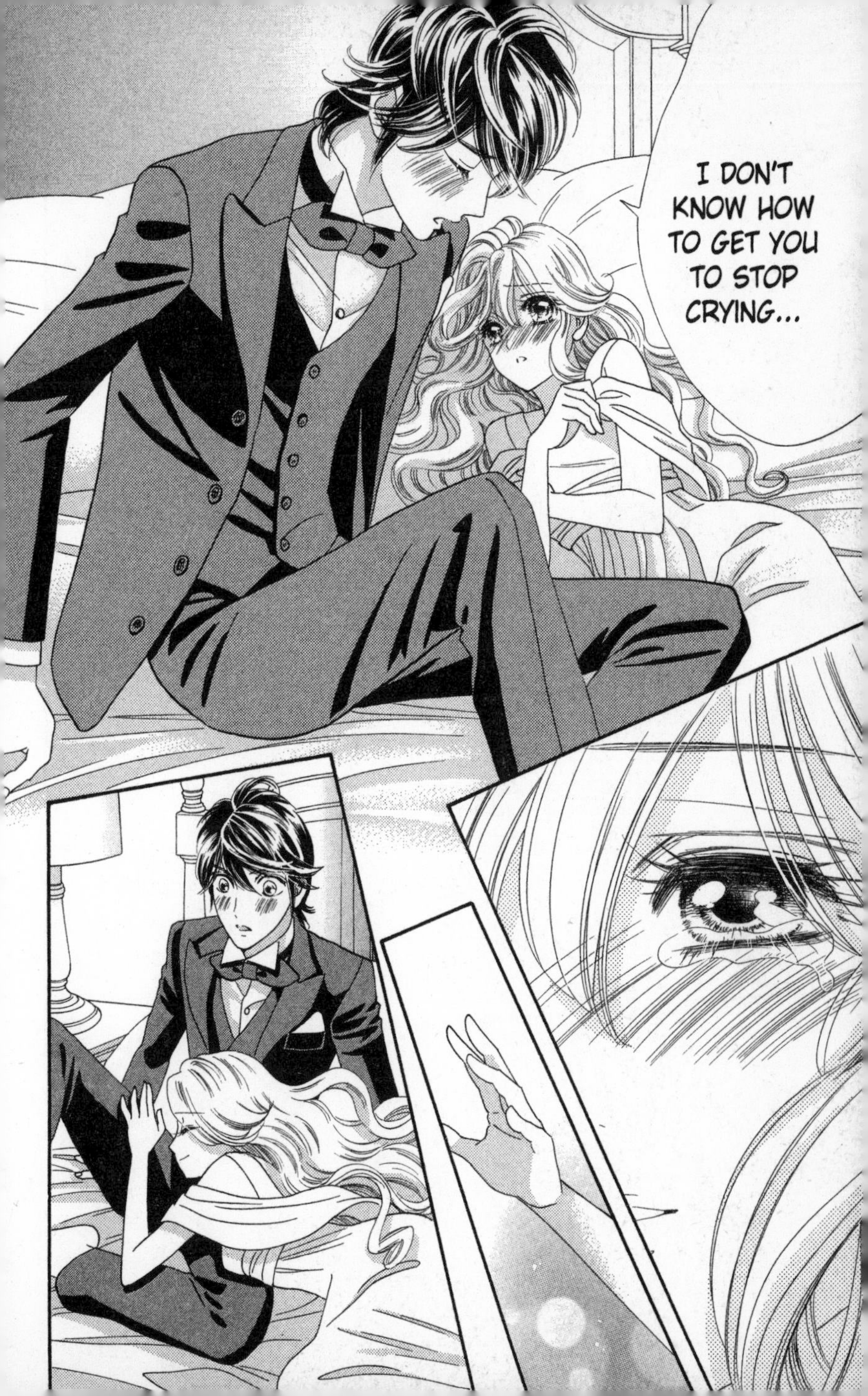
I DON'T KNOW HOW TO GET YOU TO STOP CRYING...

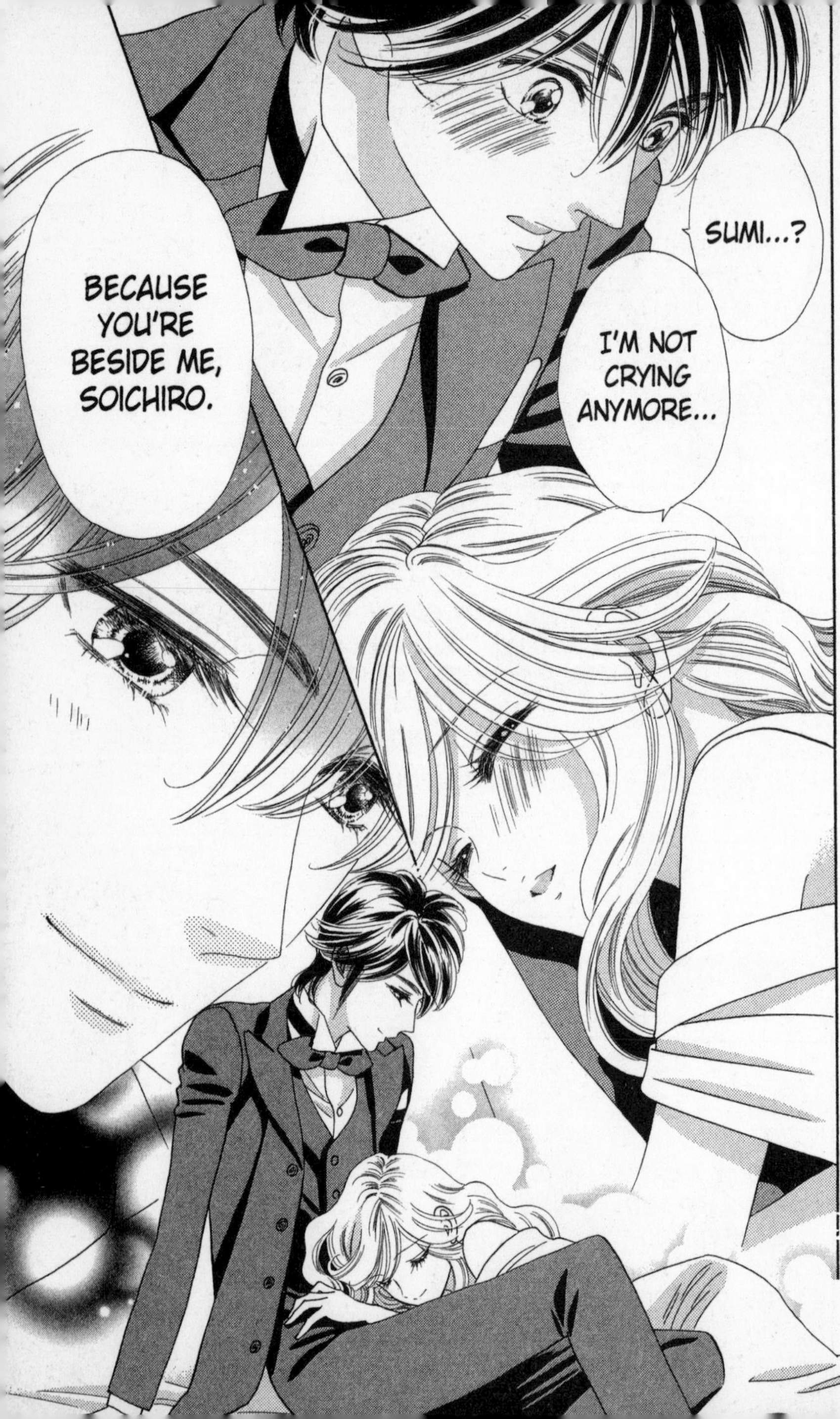
SUMI...?
I'M NOT CRYING ANYMORE...
BECAUSE YOU'RE BESIDE ME, SOICHIRO.

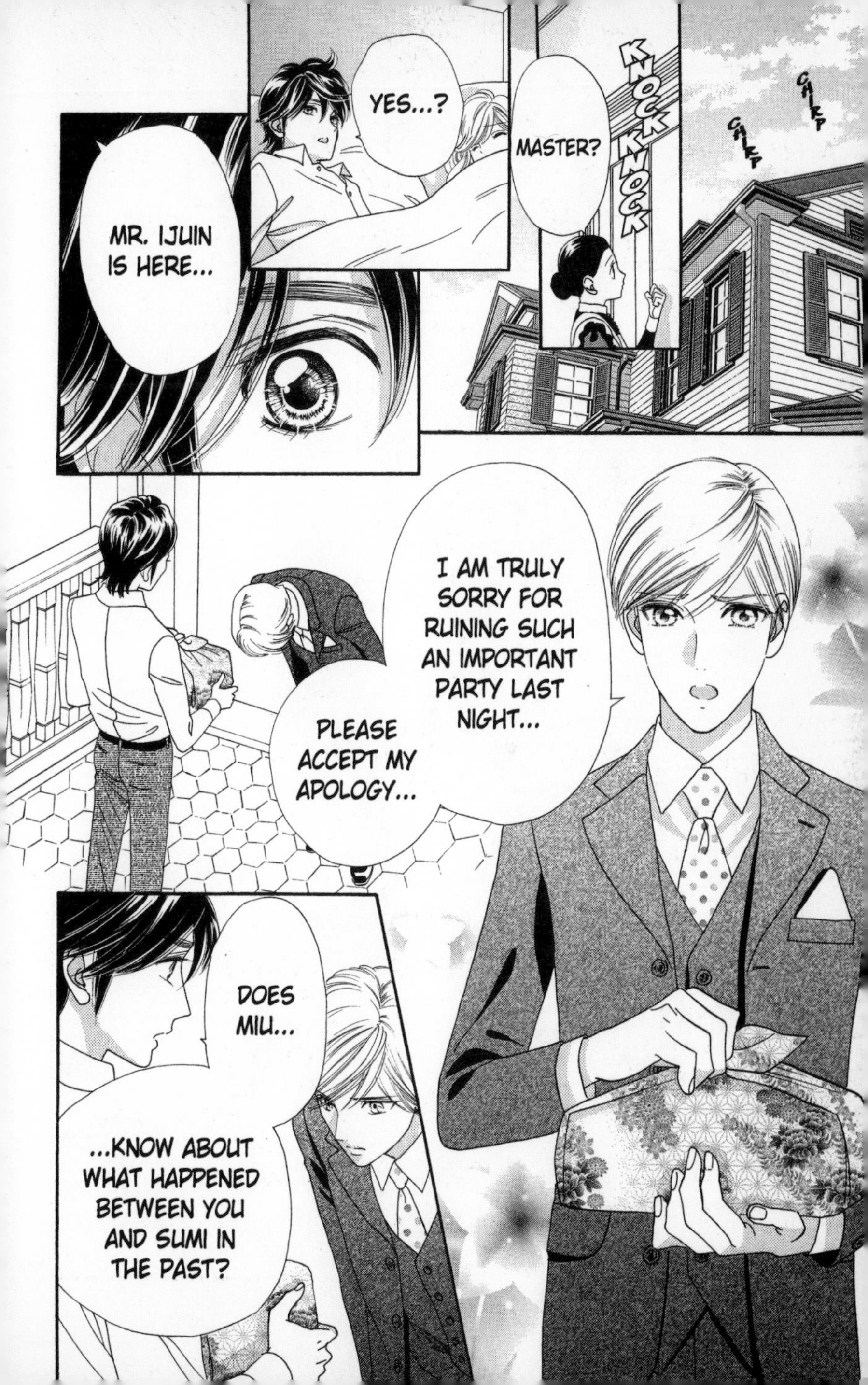
CHIRP
CHIRP
KNOCK KNOCK
MASTER?
YES...?
MR. IJUIN IS HERE...
I AM TRULY SORRY FOR RUINING SUCH AN IMPORTANT PARTY LAST NIGHT...
PLEASE ACCEPT MY APOLOGY...
DOES MIU...
...KNOW ABOUT WHAT HAPPENED BETWEEN YOU AND SUMI IN THE PAST?

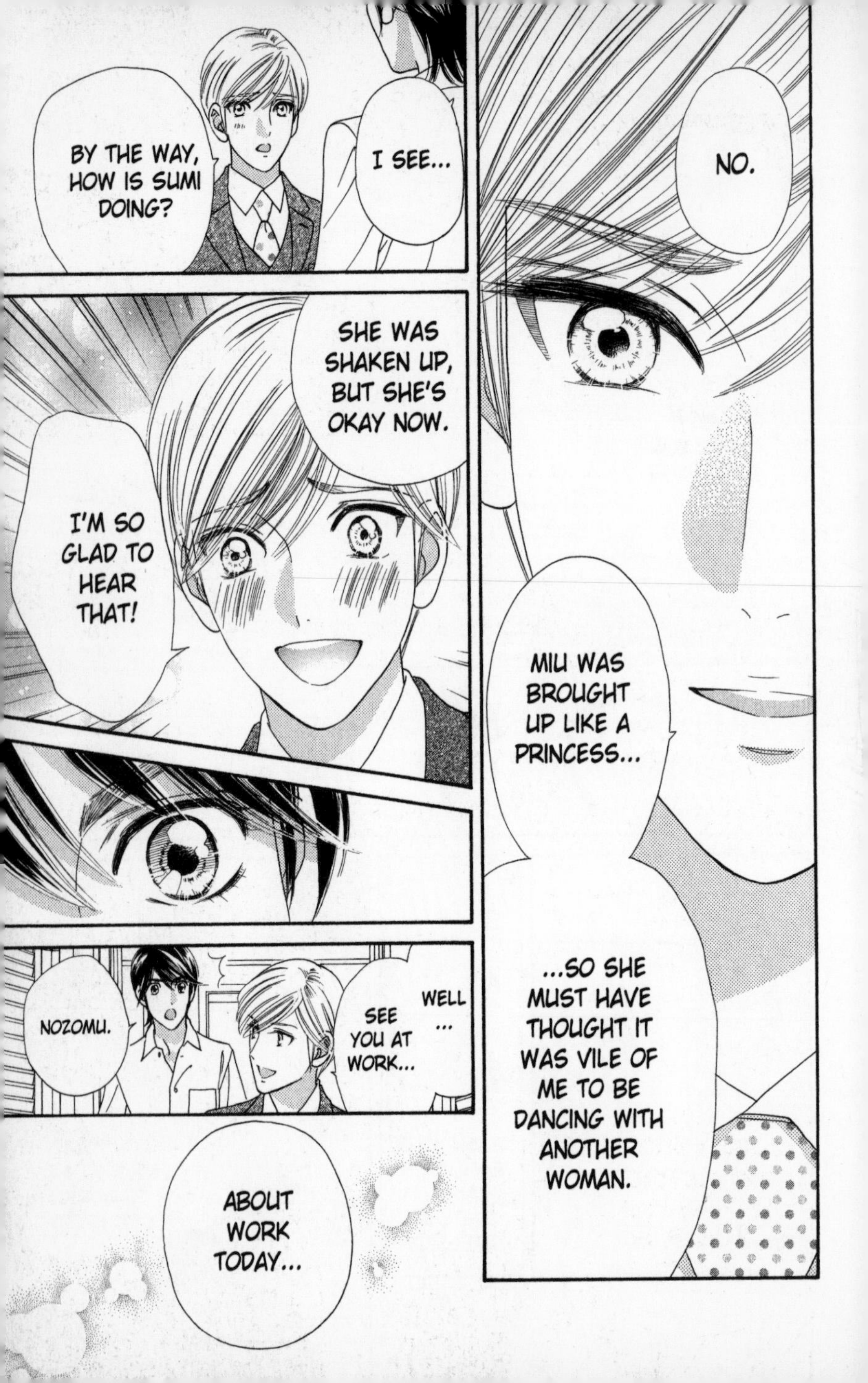
NO.
MIU WAS BROUGHT UP LIKE A PRINCESS...
...SO SHE MUST HAVE THOUGHT IT WAS VILE OF ME TO BE DANCING WITH ANOTHER WOMAN.
I SEE...
BY THE WAY, HOW IS SUMI DOING?
SHE WAS SHAKEN UP, BUT SHE'S OKAY NOW.
I'M SO GLAD TO HEAR THAT!
WELL ...
SEE YOU AT WORK...
NOZOMU.
ABOUT WORK TODAY...

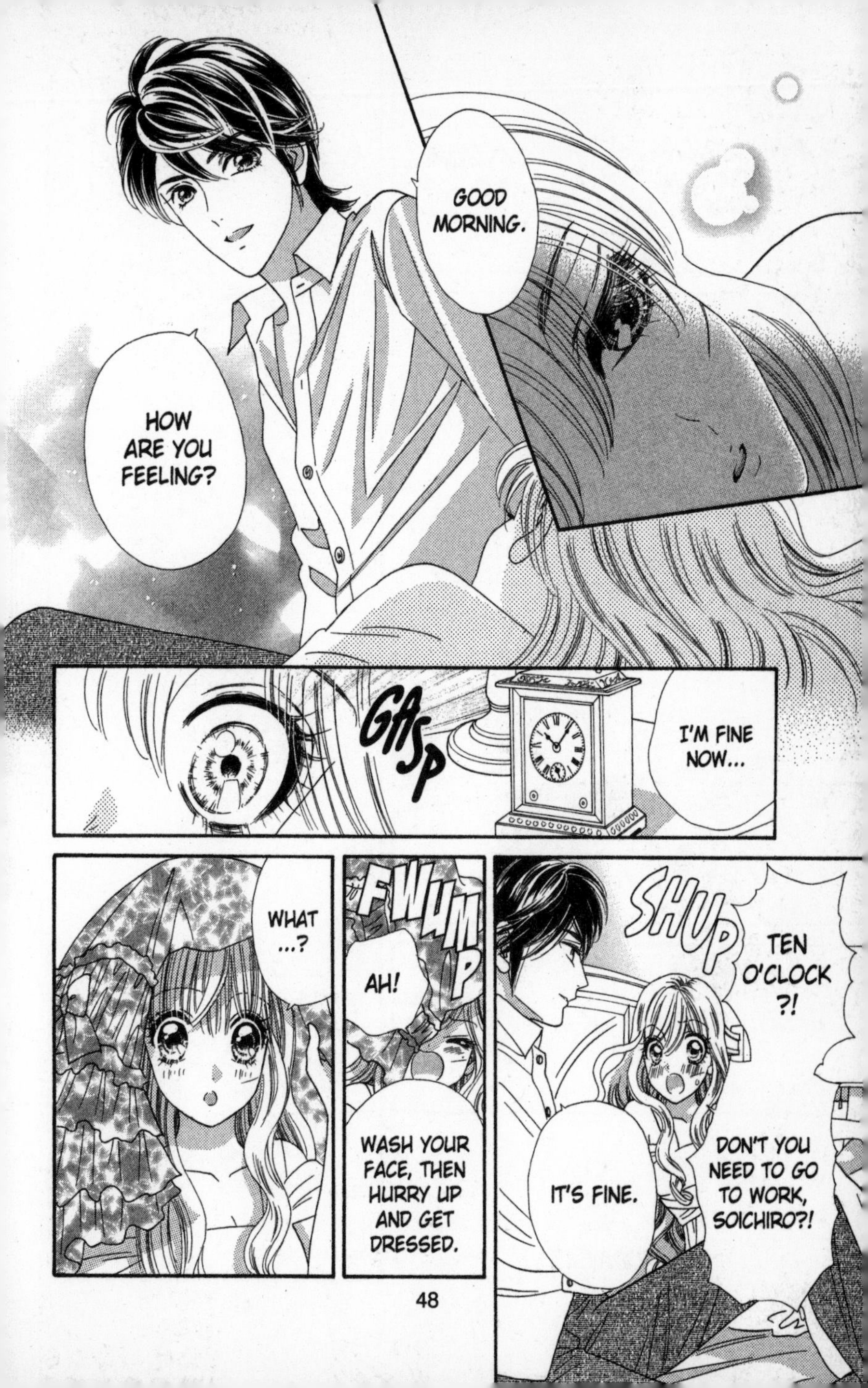
GOOD MORNING.
HOW ARE YOU FEELING?
I'M FINE NOW...
GASP
TEN O'CLOCK ?!
SHUP
DON'T YOU NEED TO GO TO WORK, SOICHIRO?!
IT'S FINE.
FWUMP
AH!
WASH YOUR FACE, THEN HURRY UP AND GET DRESSED.
WHAT ...?

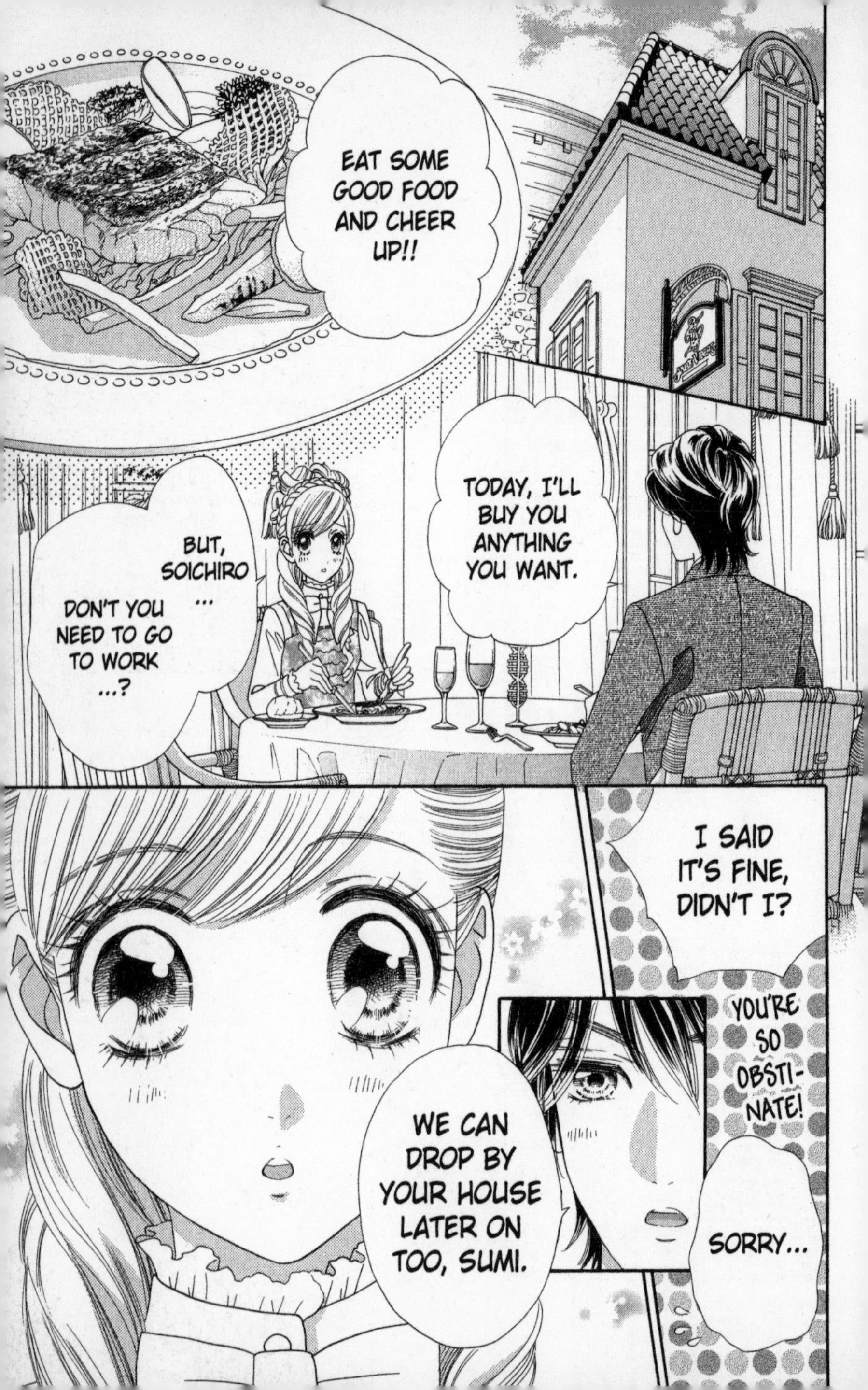
EAT SOME GOOD FOOD AND CHEER UP!!
TODAY, I'LL BUY YOU ANYTHING YOU WANT.
BUT, SOICHIRO ...
DON'T YOU NEED TO GO TO WORK ...?
I SAID IT'S FINE, DIDN'T I?
YOU'RE SO OBSTI-NATE!
SORRY...
WE CAN DROP BY YOUR HOUSE LATER ON TOO, SUMI.

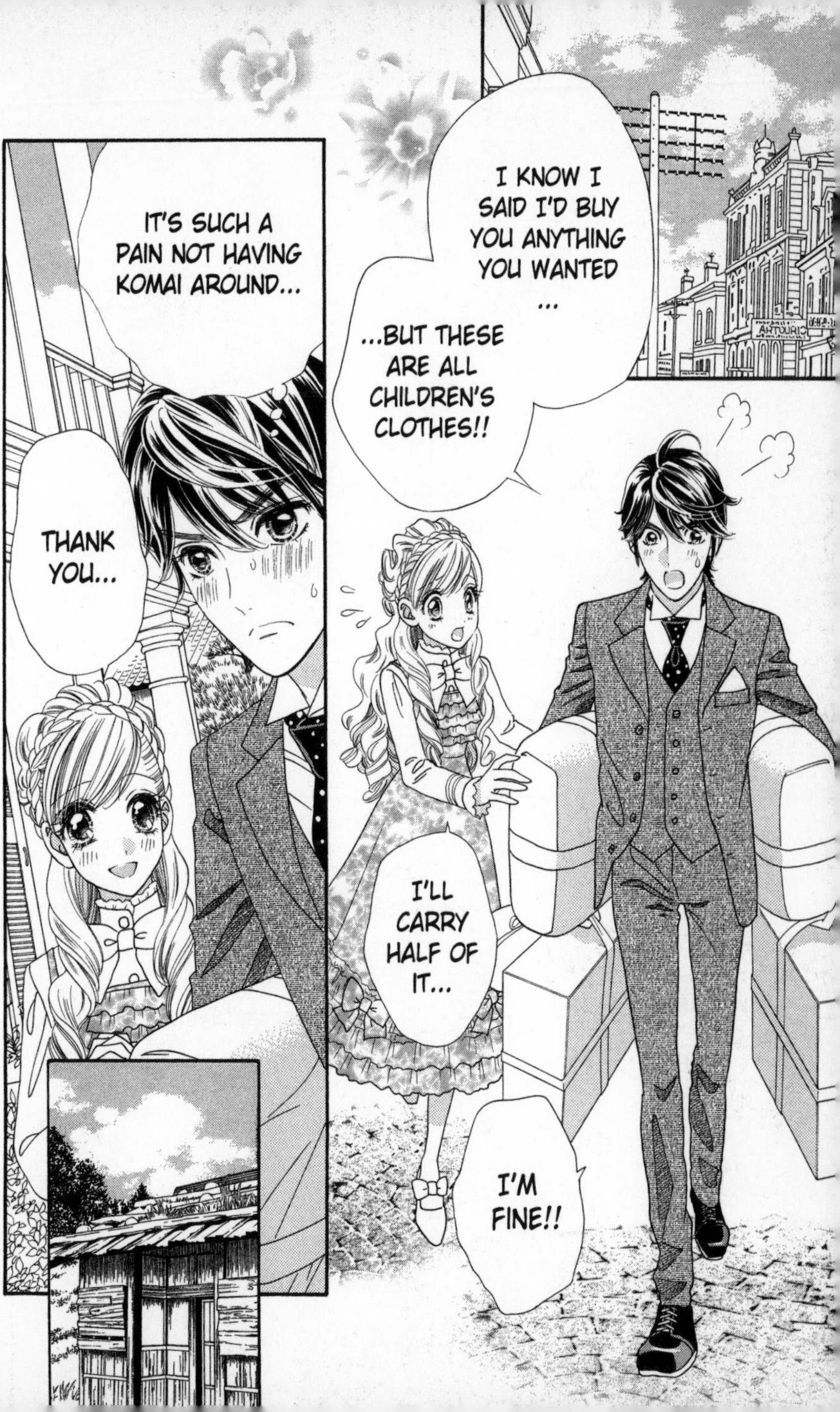
I KNOW I SAID I'D BUY YOU ANYTHING YOU WANTED ...
...BUT THESE ARE ALL CHILDREN'S CLOTHES!!
I'LL CARRY HALF OF IT...
I'M FINE!!
IT'S SUCH A PAIN NOT HAVING KOMAI AROUND...
THANK YOU...

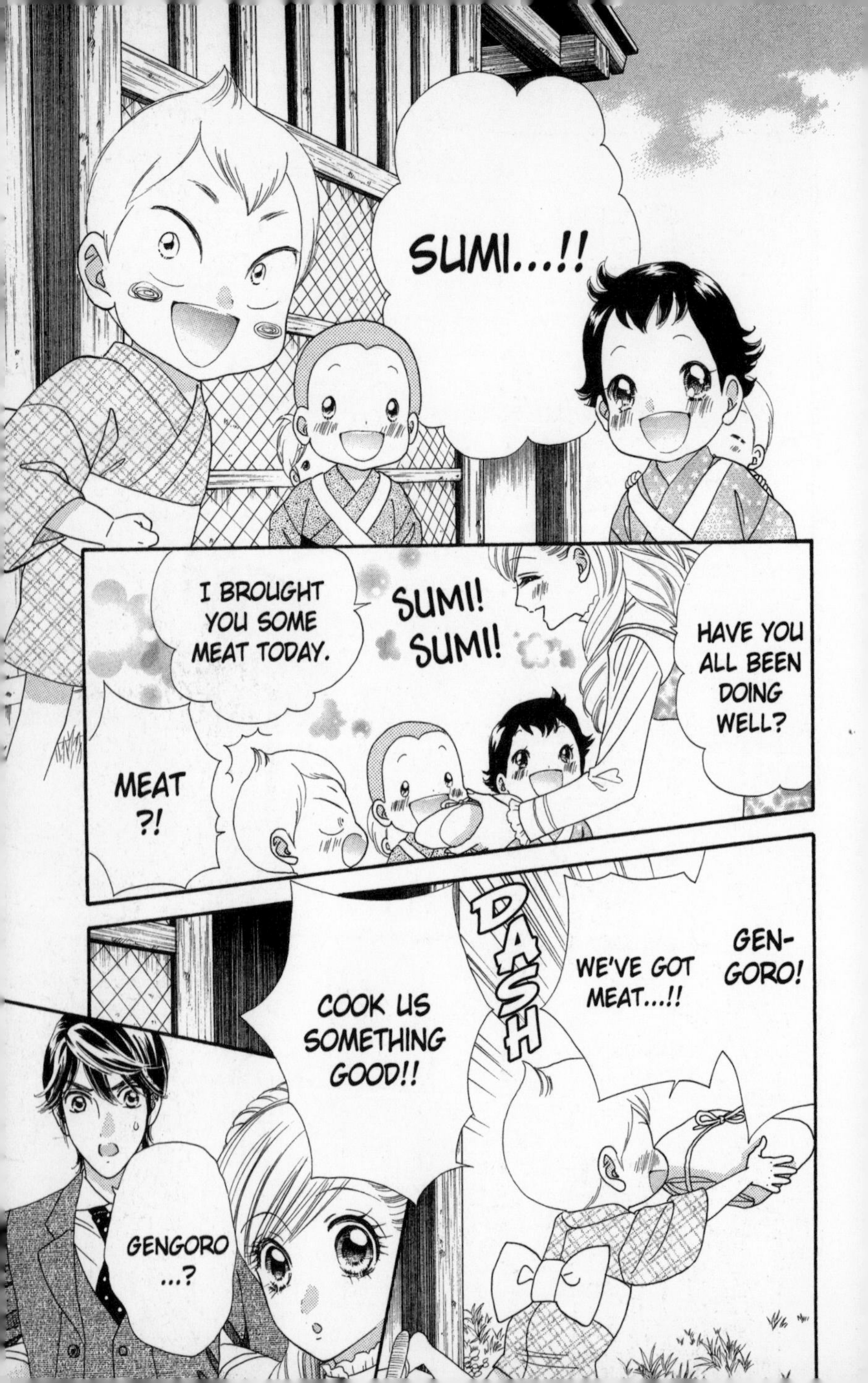
SUMI...!!
HAVE YOU ALL BEEN DOING WELL?
SUMI! SUMI!
I BROUGHT YOU SOME MEAT TODAY.
MEAT ?!
GEN-GORO!
WE'VE GOT MEAT...!!
DASH
COOK US SOMETHING GOOD!!
GENGORO ...?

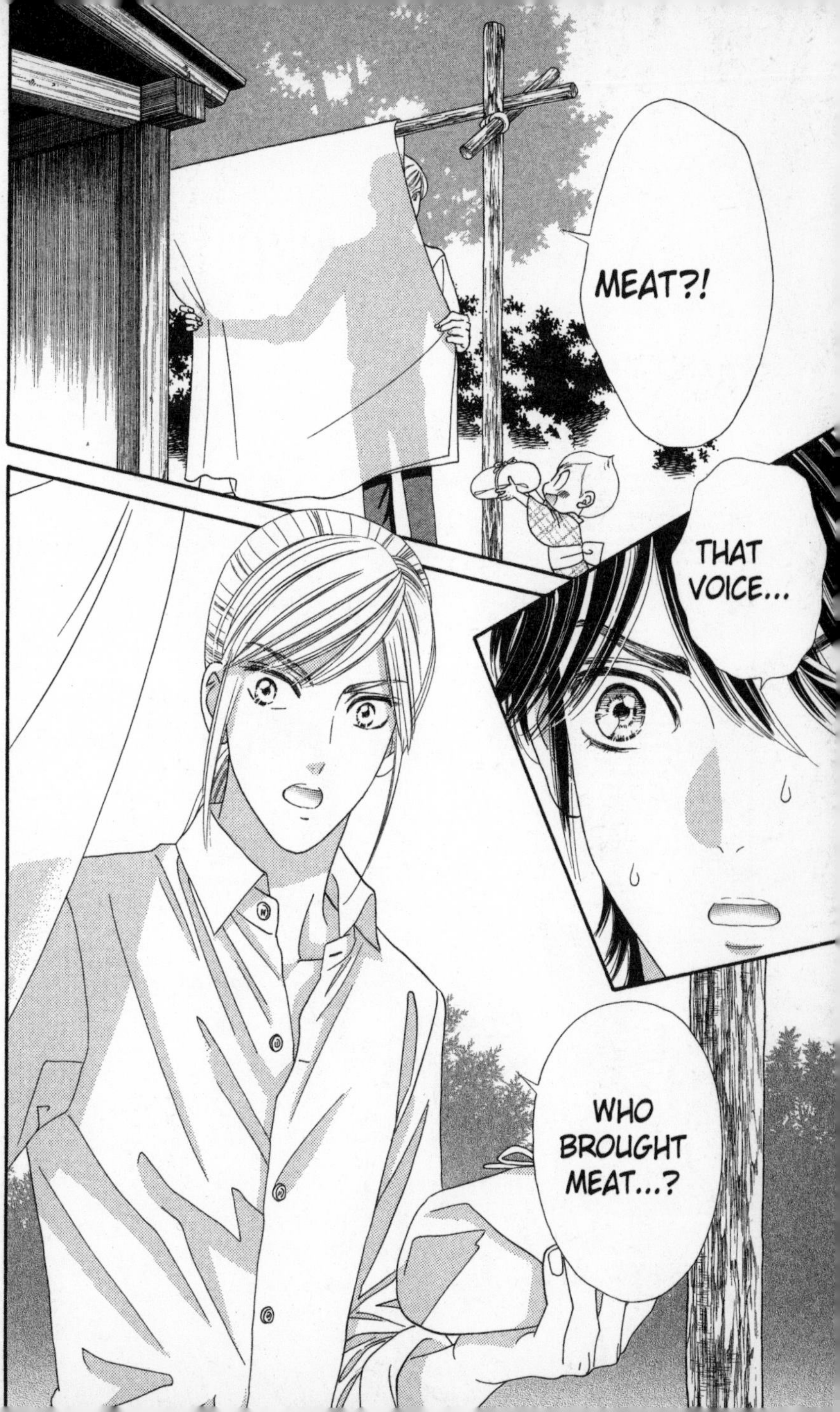
MEAT?!
THAT VOICE...
WHO BROUGHT MEAT...?

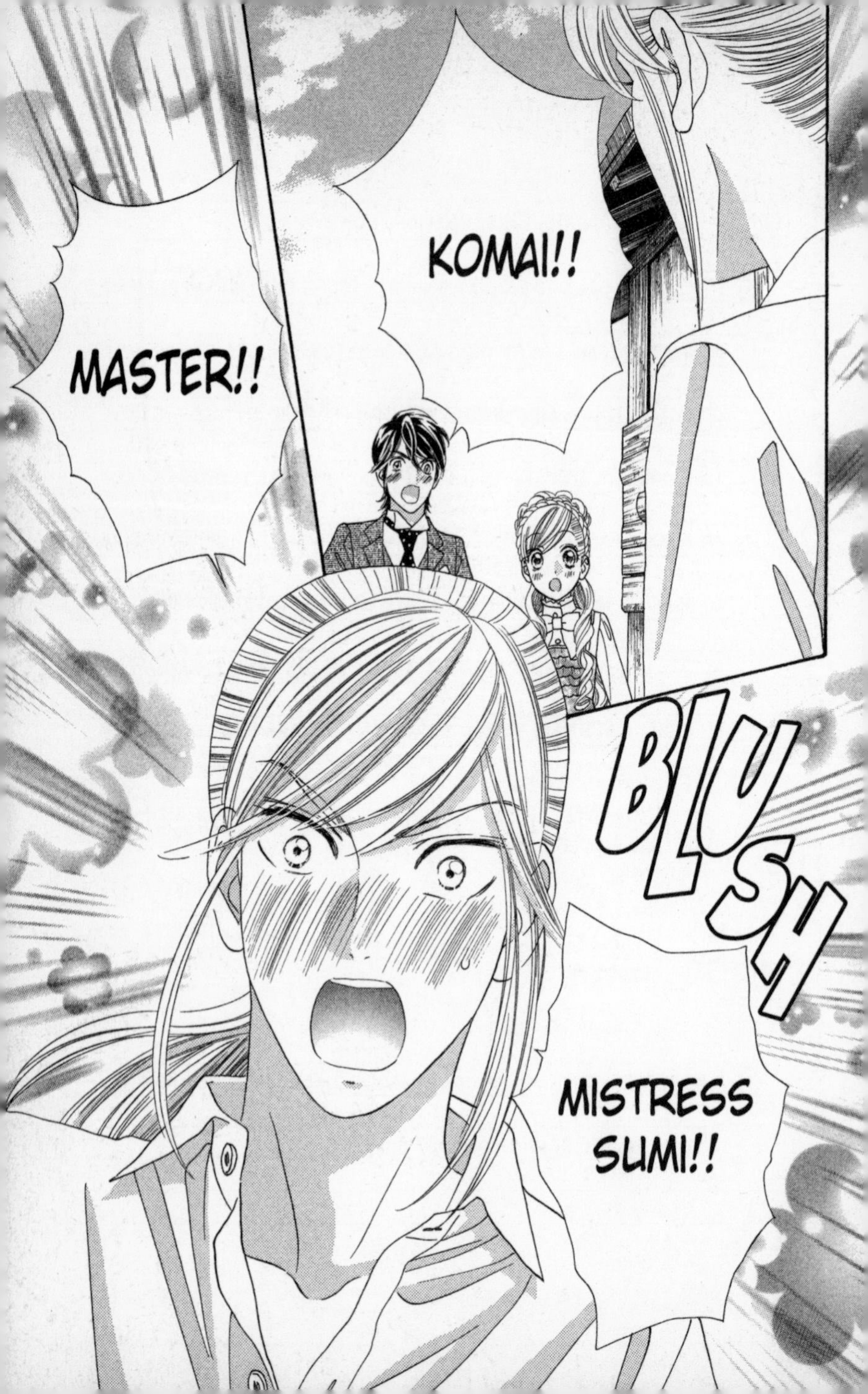
KOMAI!!
MASTER!!
BLUSH
MISTRESS SUMI!!

No. 2

RANDOM CHITCHAT

Date . .

✿ IT ALL GOES BACK TO FALL 2008 WHEN I FOUND OUT I WAS PREGNANT. IT WAS THE SAME DAY AS THE RECORDING FOR VOMIC [A TYPE OF MOTION COMIC], SO IT WAS LIKE HAVING THE BON FESTIVAL AND NEW YEAR'S TOGETHER. I'M SHOCKED TO REALIZE THAT THAT WAS TWO YEARS AGO...

✿ I'M A HUGE FAN OF DRAMA CDS, SO I WAS EXTREMELY HAPPY TO BE ABLE TO HEAR MY WORK ACTED OUT. NOW I'D LIKE TO INTRODUCE THE VOICE ACTORS WHO ADDED DEPTH TO THE WORLD OF *STEPPING ON ROSES*.

REI MATSUZAKI PLAYED SUMI KITAMURA, THE MAIN CHARACTER.

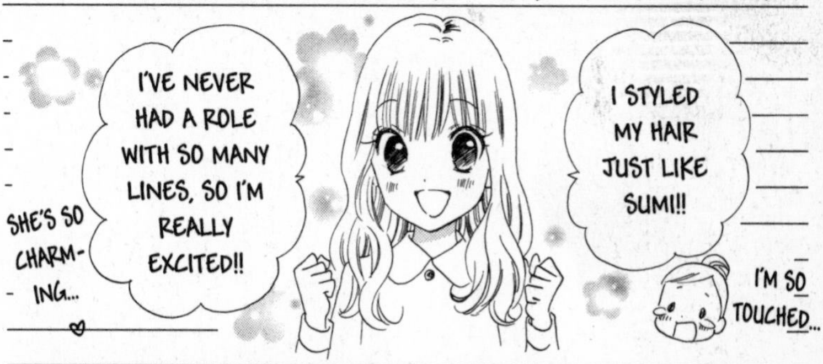

I STYLED MY HAIR JUST LIKE SUMI!!
I'M SO TOUCHED...
I'VE NEVER HAD A ROLE WITH SO MANY LINES, SO I'M REALLY EXCITED!!
SHE'S SO CHARMING...

✿ SHE PERFORMED SUMI JUST AS I IMAGINED HER TO BE. HER HONESTY AND DILIGENCE REMINDED ME OF SUMI TOO.

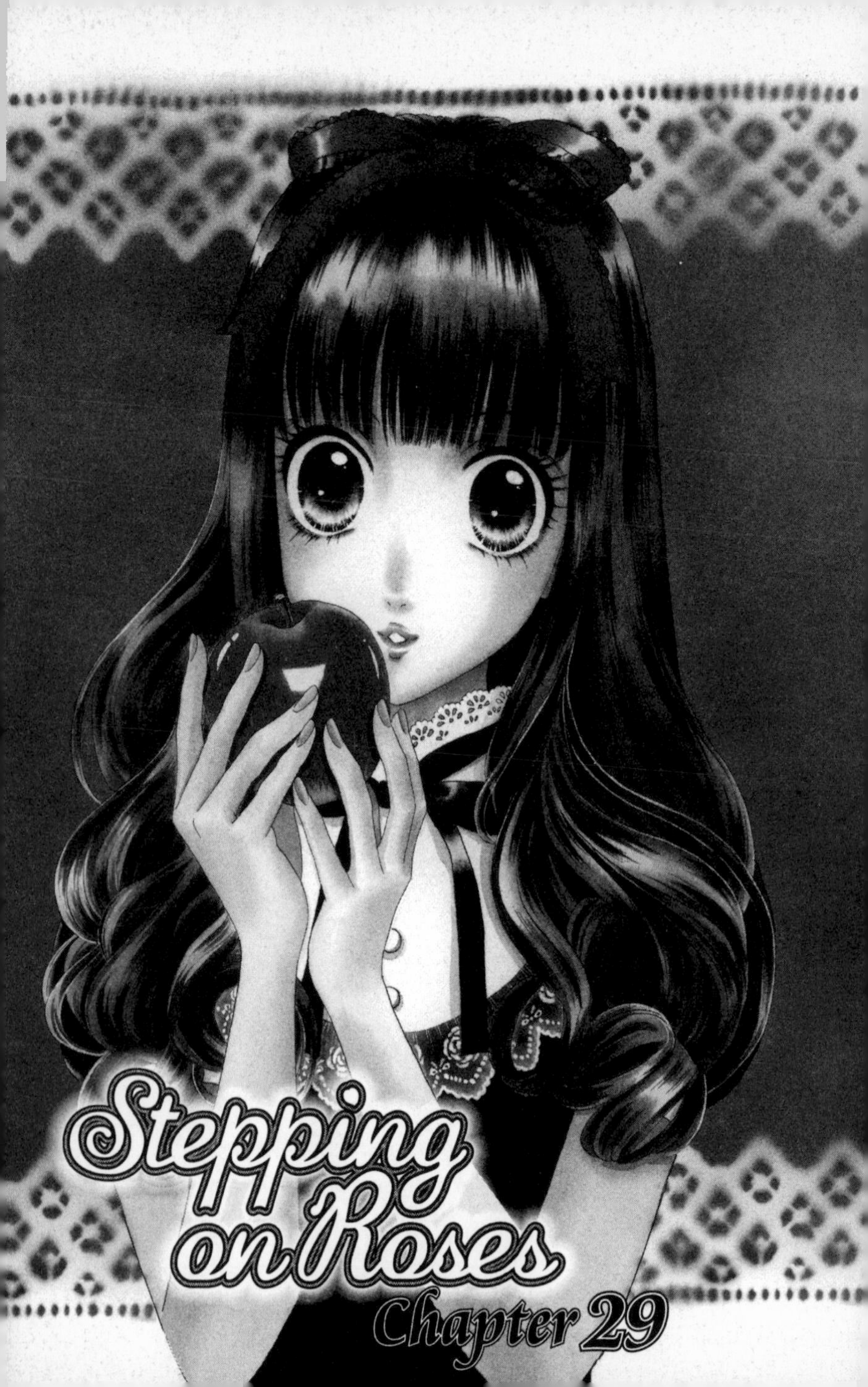
Stepping on Roses
Chapter 29

Stepping on Roses

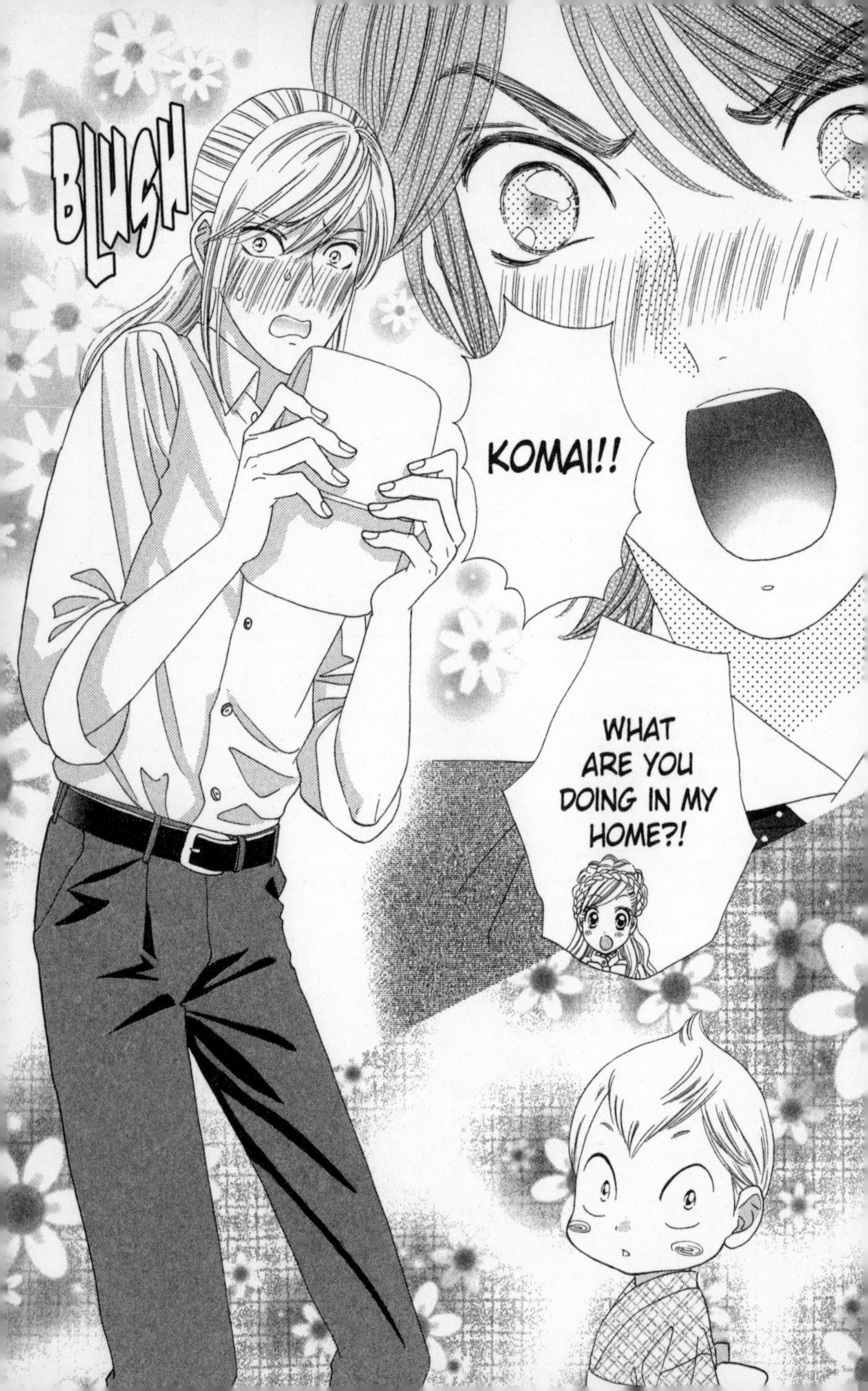
KOMAI!!
WHAT ARE YOU DOING IN MY HOME?!
BLUSH

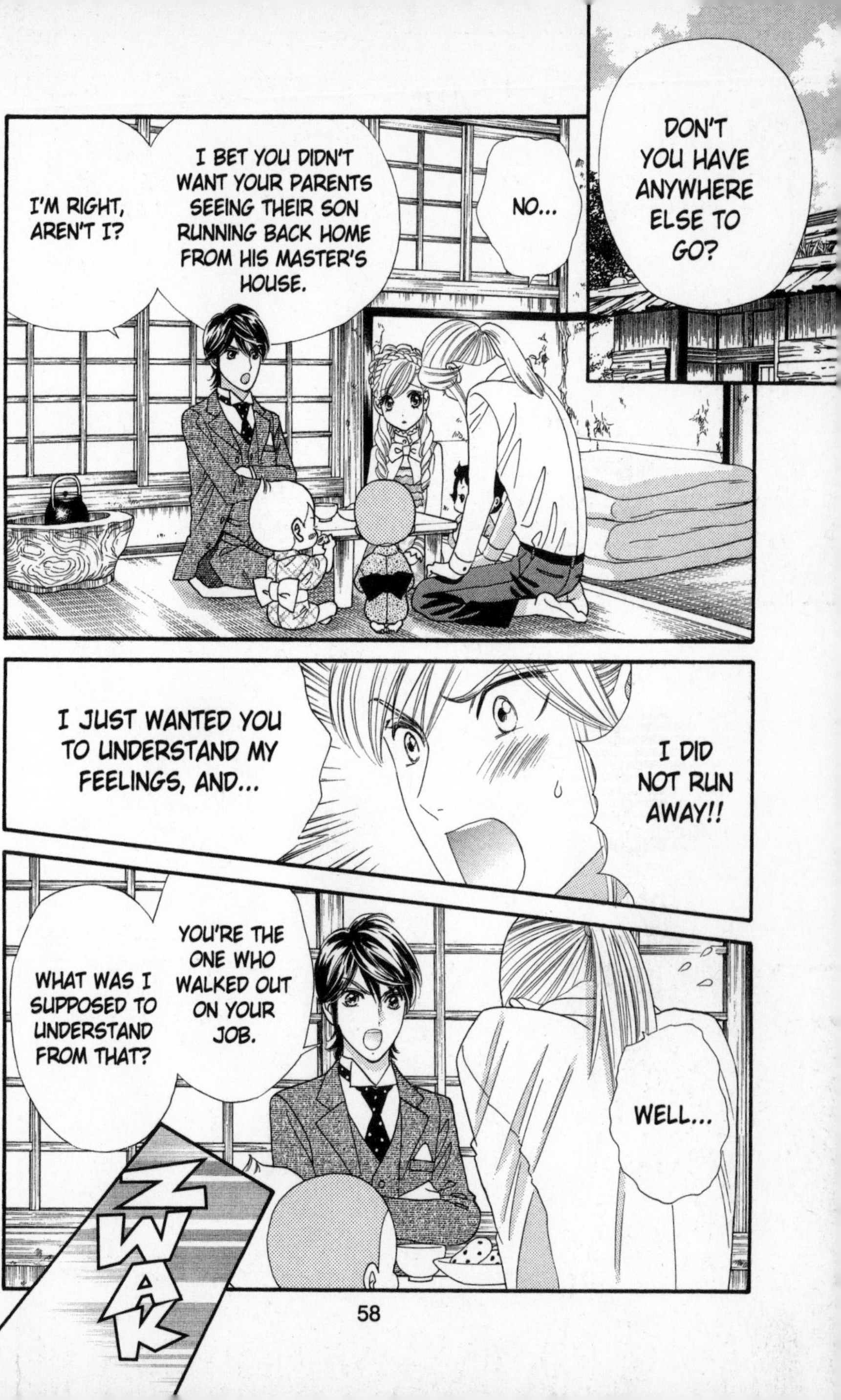
DON'T YOU HAVE ANYWHERE ELSE TO GO?
NO...
I BET YOU DIDN'T WANT YOUR PARENTS SEEING THEIR SON RUNNING BACK HOME FROM HIS MASTER'S HOUSE.
I'M RIGHT, AREN'T I?
I DID NOT RUN AWAY!!
I JUST WANTED YOU TO UNDERSTAND MY FEELINGS, AND...
WELL...
YOU'RE THE ONE WHO WALKED OUT ON YOUR JOB.
WHAT WAS I SUPPOSED TO UNDERSTAND FROM THAT?
ZWAK

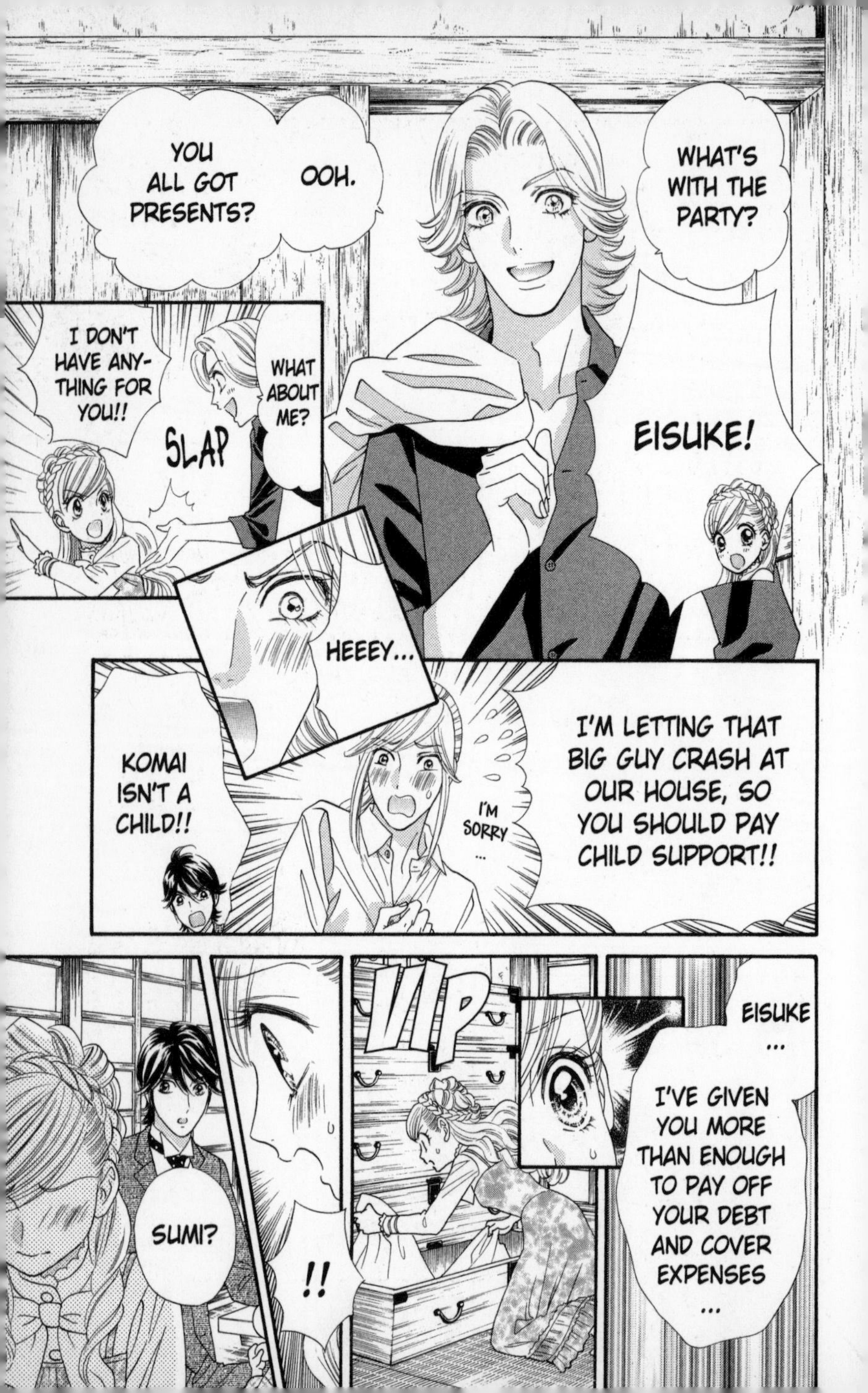
WHAT'S WITH THE PARTY?
OOH.
YOU ALL GOT PRESENTS?
EISUKE!
WHAT ABOUT ME?
I DON'T HAVE ANY-THING FOR YOU!!
SLAP
HEEEY...
I'M LETTING THAT BIG GUY CRASH AT OUR HOUSE, SO YOU SHOULD PAY CHILD SUPPORT!!
I'M SORRY ...
KOMAI ISN'T A CHILD!!
EISUKE ...
I'VE GIVEN YOU MORE THAN ENOUGH TO PAY OFF YOUR DEBT AND COVER EXPENSES ...
VIP
!!
SUMI?

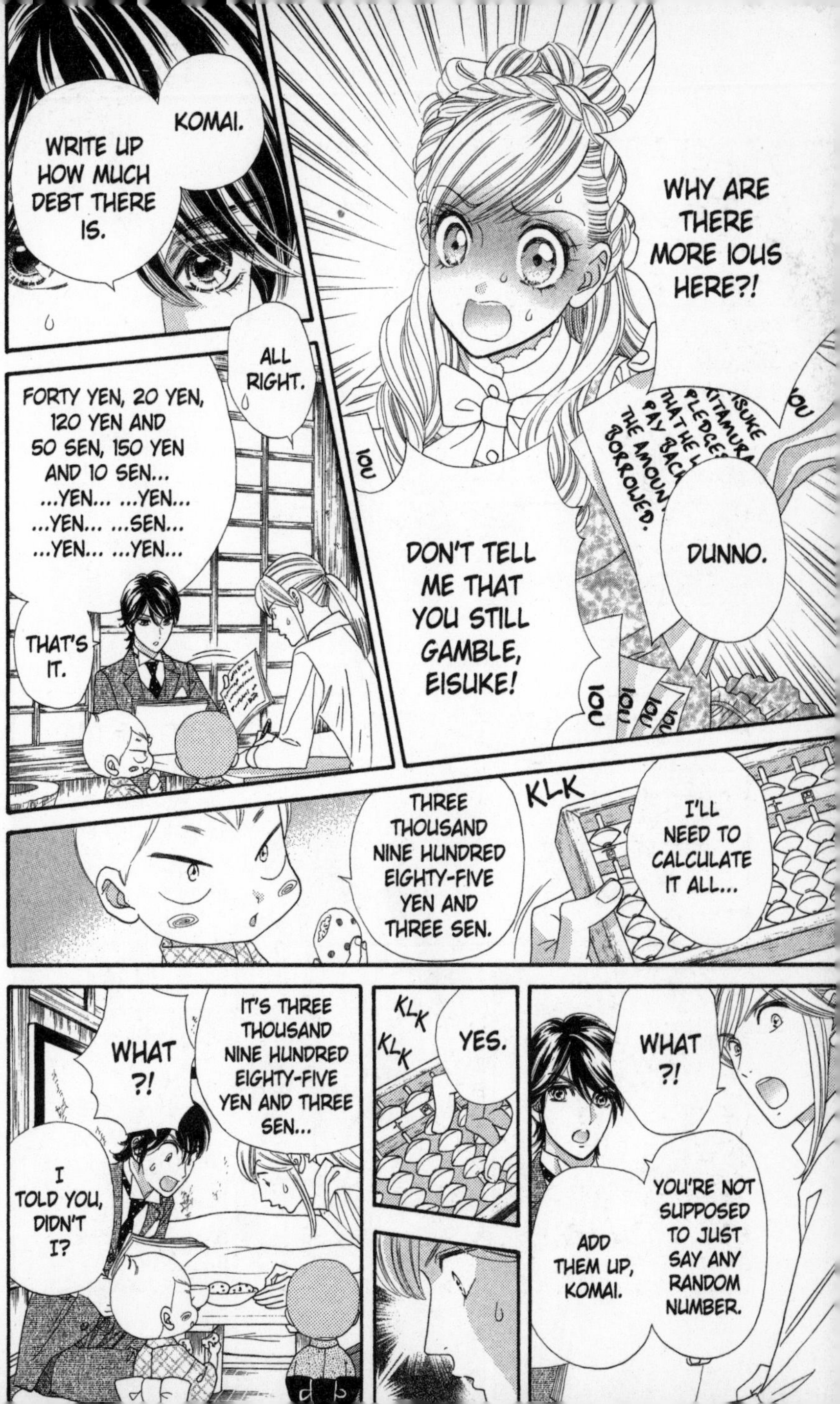
WHY ARE THERE MORE IOUS HERE?!
IOU
IOU
IOU
DON'T TELL ME THAT YOU STILL GAMBLE, EISUKE!
DUNNO.
IOU
IOU
IOU
IOU
KOMAI.
WRITE UP HOW MUCH DEBT THERE IS.
ALL RIGHT.
FORTY YEN, 20 YEN, 120 YEN AND 50 SEN, 150 YEN AND 10 SEN... ...YEN... ...YEN... ...YEN... ...SEN... ...YEN... ...YEN...
THAT'S IT.
I'LL NEED TO CALCULATE IT ALL...
KLK
THREE THOUSAND NINE HUNDRED EIGHTY-FIVE YEN AND THREE SEN.
WHAT ?!
KLK
KLK
YES.
YOU'RE NOT SUPPOSED TO JUST SAY ANY RANDOM NUMBER.
ADD THEM UP, KOMAI.
IT'S THREE THOUSAND NINE HUNDRED EIGHTY-FIVE YEN AND THREE SEN...
WHAT ?!
I TOLD YOU, DIDN'T I?

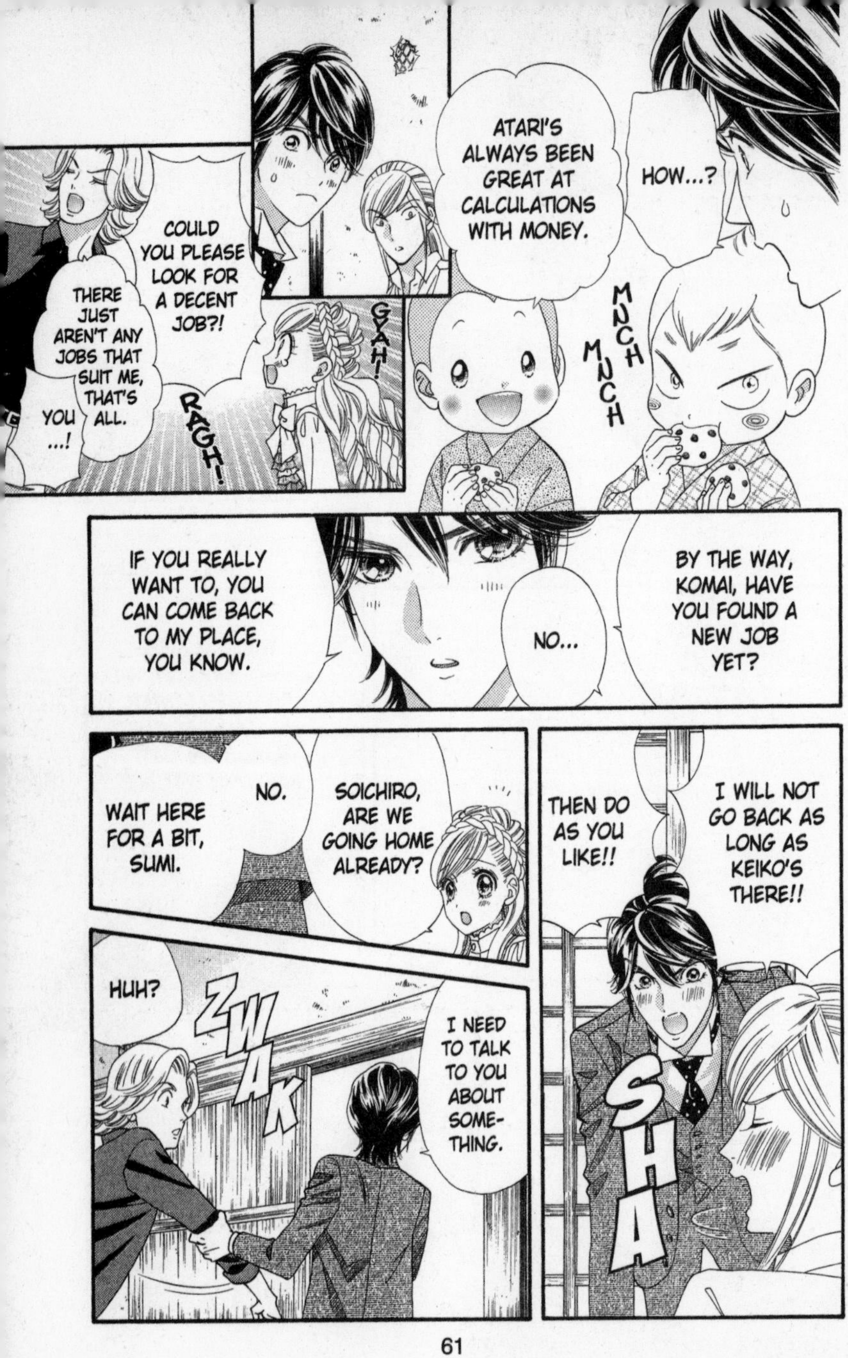
HOW...?
MUNCH MUNCH
ATARI'S ALWAYS BEEN GREAT AT CALCULATIONS WITH MONEY.
GYAH!
COULD YOU PLEASE LOOK FOR A DECENT JOB?!
RAGH!
THERE JUST AREN'T ANY JOBS THAT SUIT ME, THAT'S ALL.
YOU ...!
BY THE WAY, KOMAI, HAVE YOU FOUND A NEW JOB YET?
NO...
IF YOU REALLY WANT TO, YOU CAN COME BACK TO MY PLACE, YOU KNOW.
I WILL NOT GO BACK AS LONG AS KEIKO'S THERE!!
THEN DO AS YOU LIKE!!
SHA
SOICHIRO, ARE WE GOING HOME ALREADY?
NO.
WAIT HERE FOR A BIT, SUMI.
I NEED TO TALK TO YOU ABOUT SOME-THING.
ZWAK
HUH?

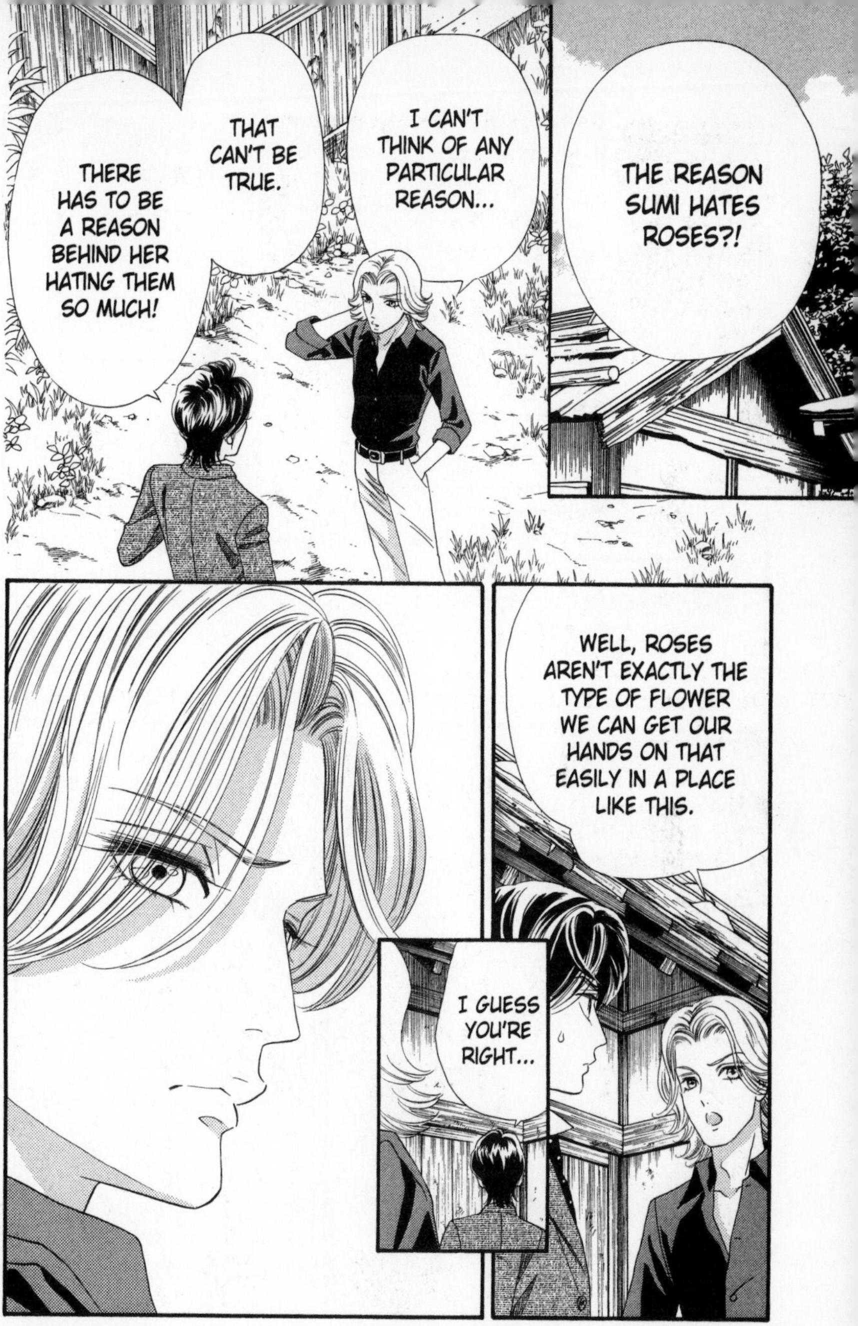
THE REASON SUMI HATES ROSES?!
I CAN'T THINK OF ANY PARTICULAR REASON...
THAT CAN'T BE TRUE.
THERE HAS TO BE A REASON BEHIND HER HATING THEM SO MUCH!
WELL, ROSES AREN'T EXACTLY THE TYPE OF FLOWER WE CAN GET OUR HANDS ON THAT EASILY IN A PLACE LIKE THIS.
I GUESS YOU'RE RIGHT...

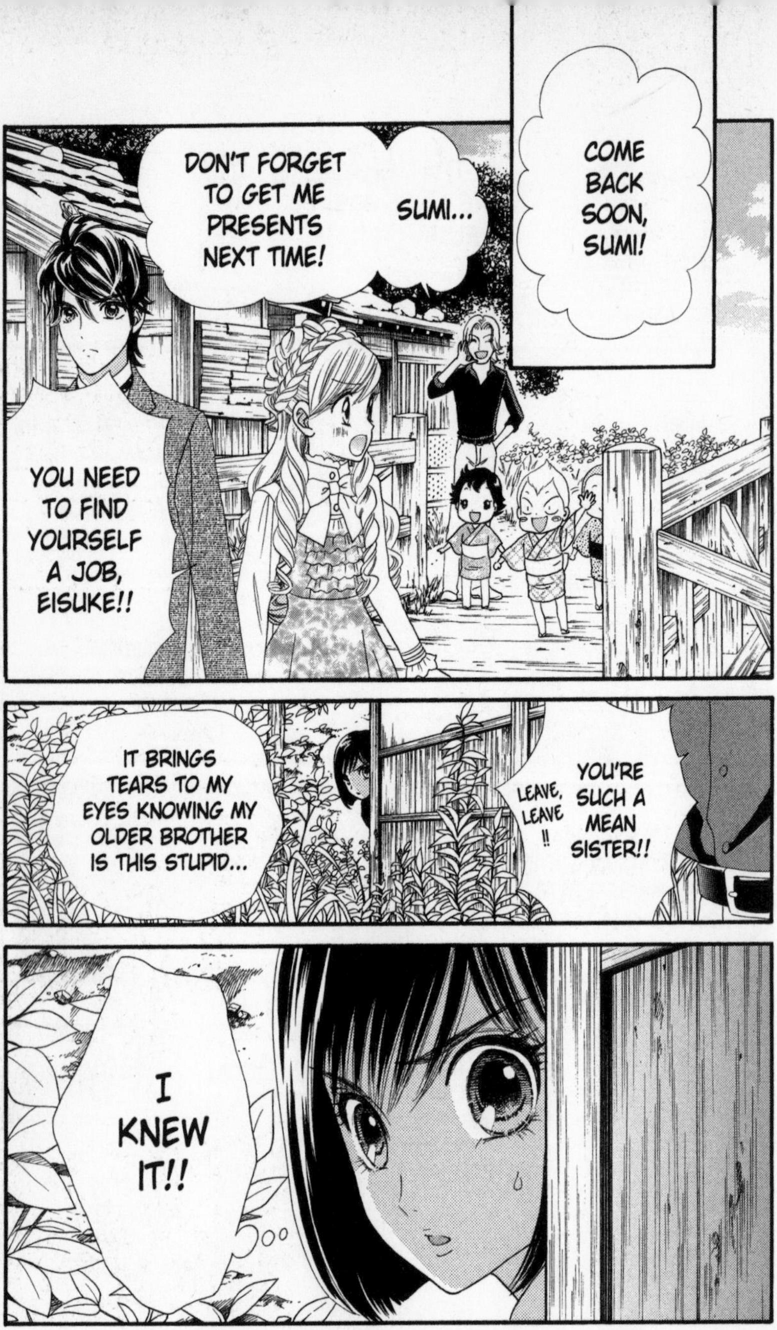
COME BACK SOON, SUMI!
SUMI...
DON'T FORGET TO GET ME PRESENTS NEXT TIME!
YOU NEED TO FIND YOURSELF A JOB, EISUKE!!
YOU'RE SUCH A MEAN SISTER!!
LEAVE, LEAVE !!
IT BRINGS TEARS TO MY EYES KNOWING MY OLDER BROTHER IS THIS STUPID...
I KNEW IT!!

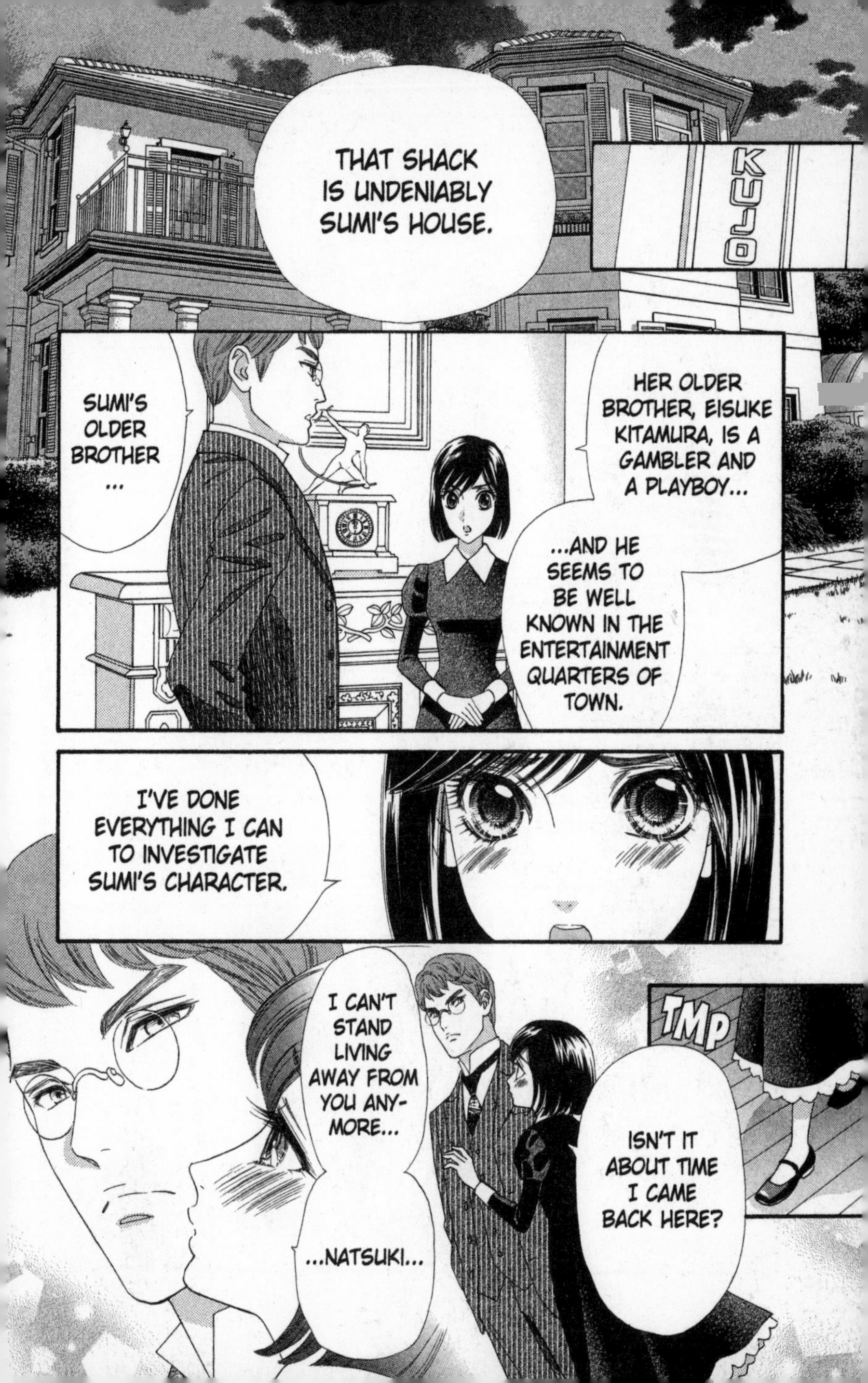
KUJO
THAT SHACK IS UNDENIABLY SUMI'S HOUSE.
HER OLDER BROTHER, EISUKE KITAMURA, IS A GAMBLER AND A PLAYBOY...
...AND HE SEEMS TO BE WELL KNOWN IN THE ENTERTAINMENT QUARTERS OF TOWN.
SUMI'S OLDER BROTHER ...
I'VE DONE EVERYTHING I CAN TO INVESTIGATE SUMI'S CHARACTER.
TMP
ISN'T IT ABOUT TIME I CAME BACK HERE?
I CAN'T STAND LIVING AWAY FROM YOU ANY-MORE...
...NATSUKI...

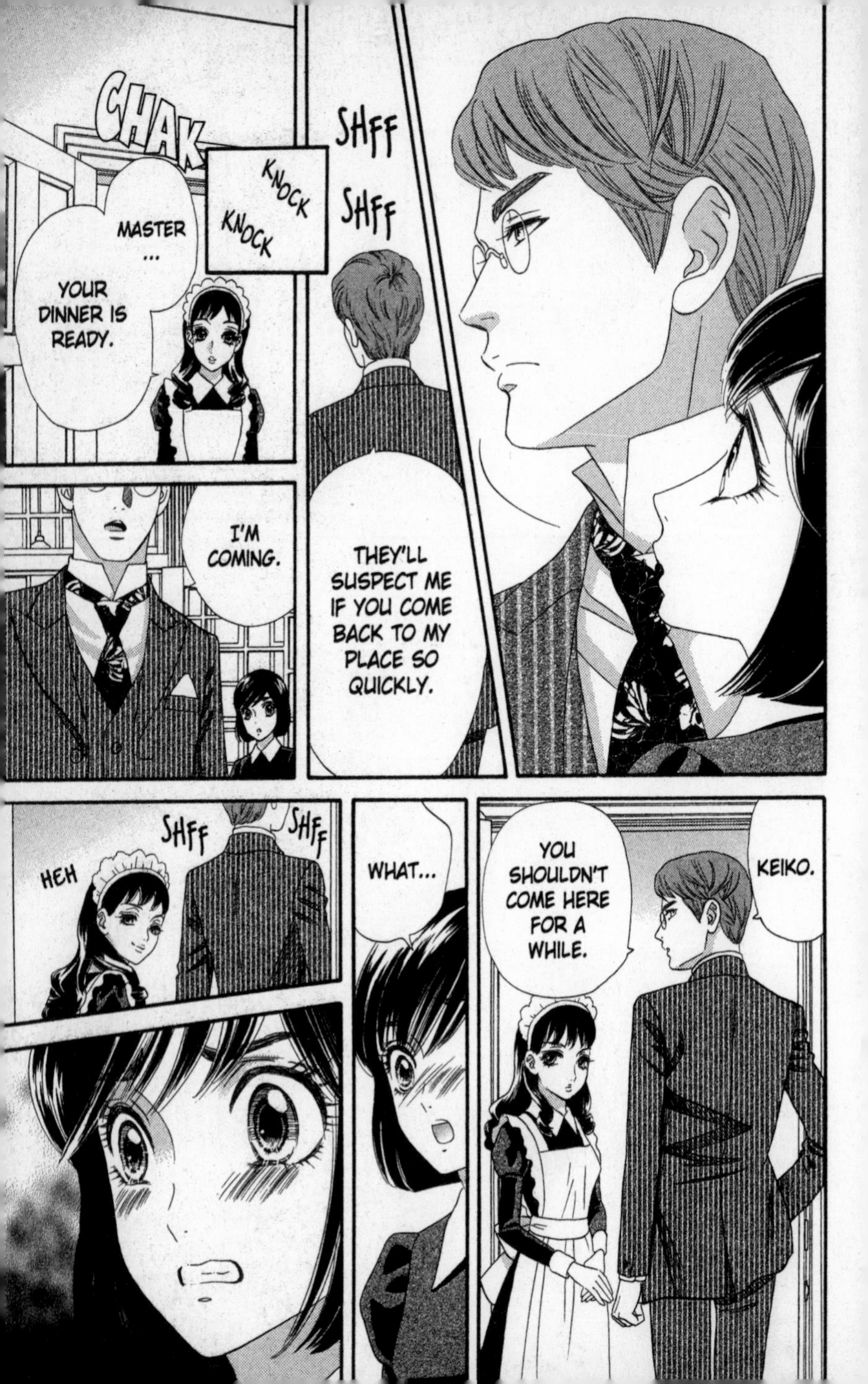
SHFF
SHFF
THEY'LL SUSPECT ME IF YOU COME BACK TO MY PLACE SO QUICKLY.
KNOCK
KNOCK
CHAK
MASTER ... YOUR DINNER IS READY.
I'M COMING.
KEIKO.
YOU SHOULDN'T COME HERE FOR A WHILE.
WHAT...
SHFF
SHFF
HEH

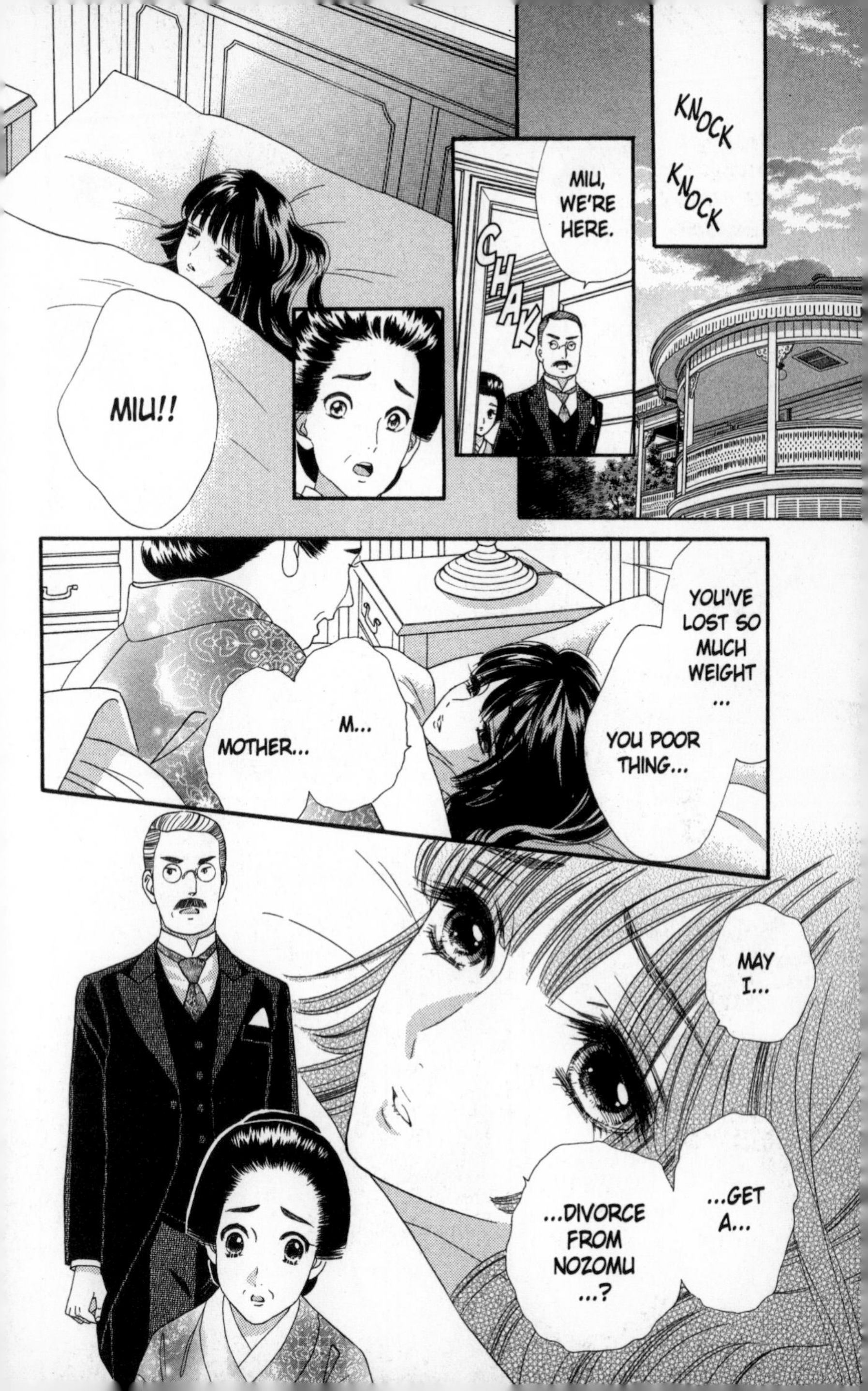
KNOCK
KNOCK
MIU, WE'RE HERE.
CHAK
MIU!!
YOU'VE LOST SO MUCH WEIGHT...
YOU POOR THING...
M... MOTHER...
MAY I...
...GET A...
...DIVORCE FROM NOZOMU...?

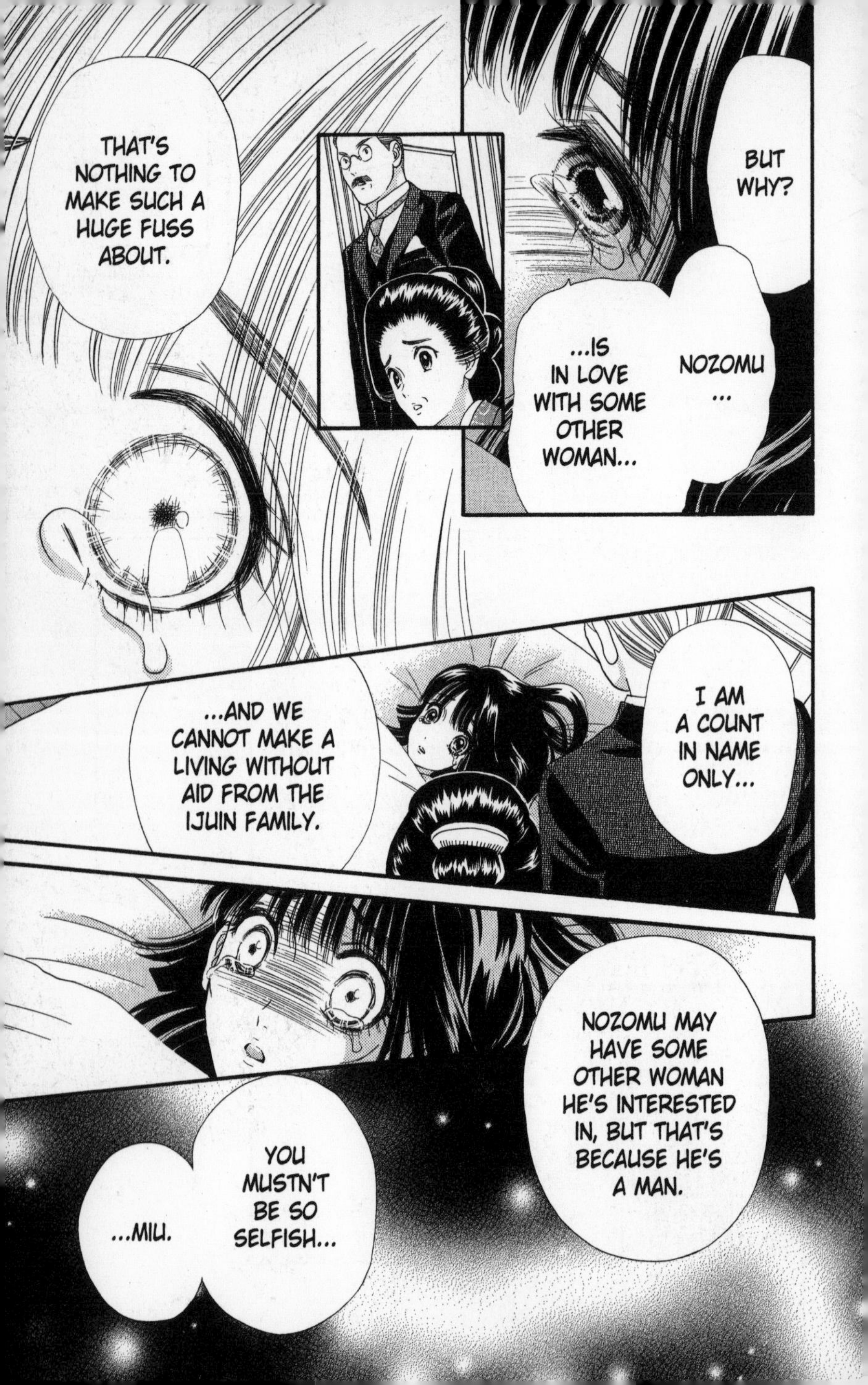
BUT WHY?
NOZOMU ...
...IS IN LOVE WITH SOME OTHER WOMAN...
THAT'S NOTHING TO MAKE SUCH A HUGE FUSS ABOUT.
I AM A COUNT IN NAME ONLY...
...AND WE CANNOT MAKE A LIVING WITHOUT AID FROM THE IJUIN FAMILY.
NOZOMU MAY HAVE SOME OTHER WOMAN HE'S INTERESTED IN, BUT THAT'S BECAUSE HE'S A MAN.
YOU MUSTN'T BE SO SELFISH...
...MIU.

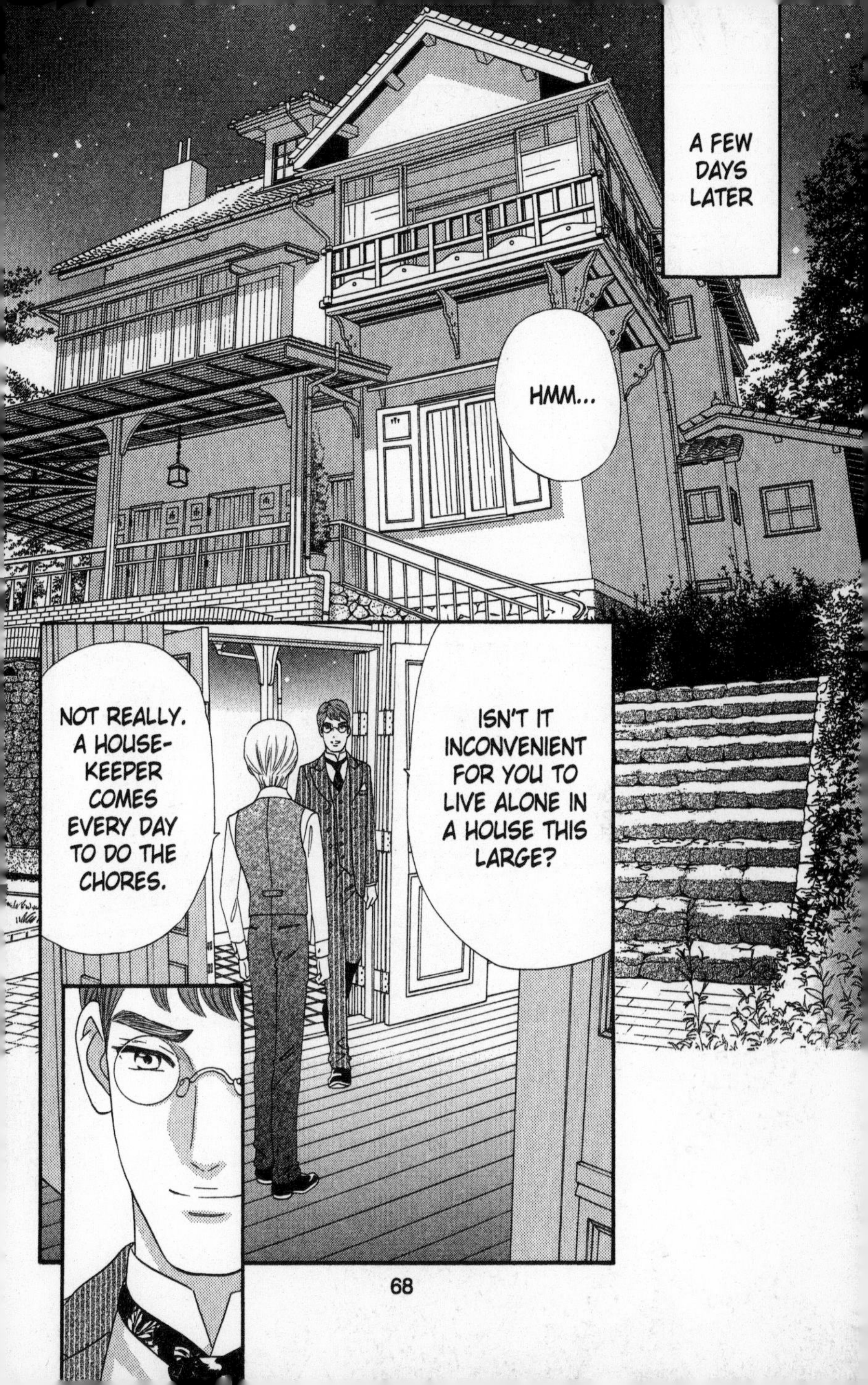
A FEW DAYS LATER
HMM...
ISN'T IT INCONVENIENT FOR YOU TO LIVE ALONE IN A HOUSE THIS LARGE?
NOT REALLY. A HOUSE-KEEPER COMES EVERY DAY TO DO THE CHORES.

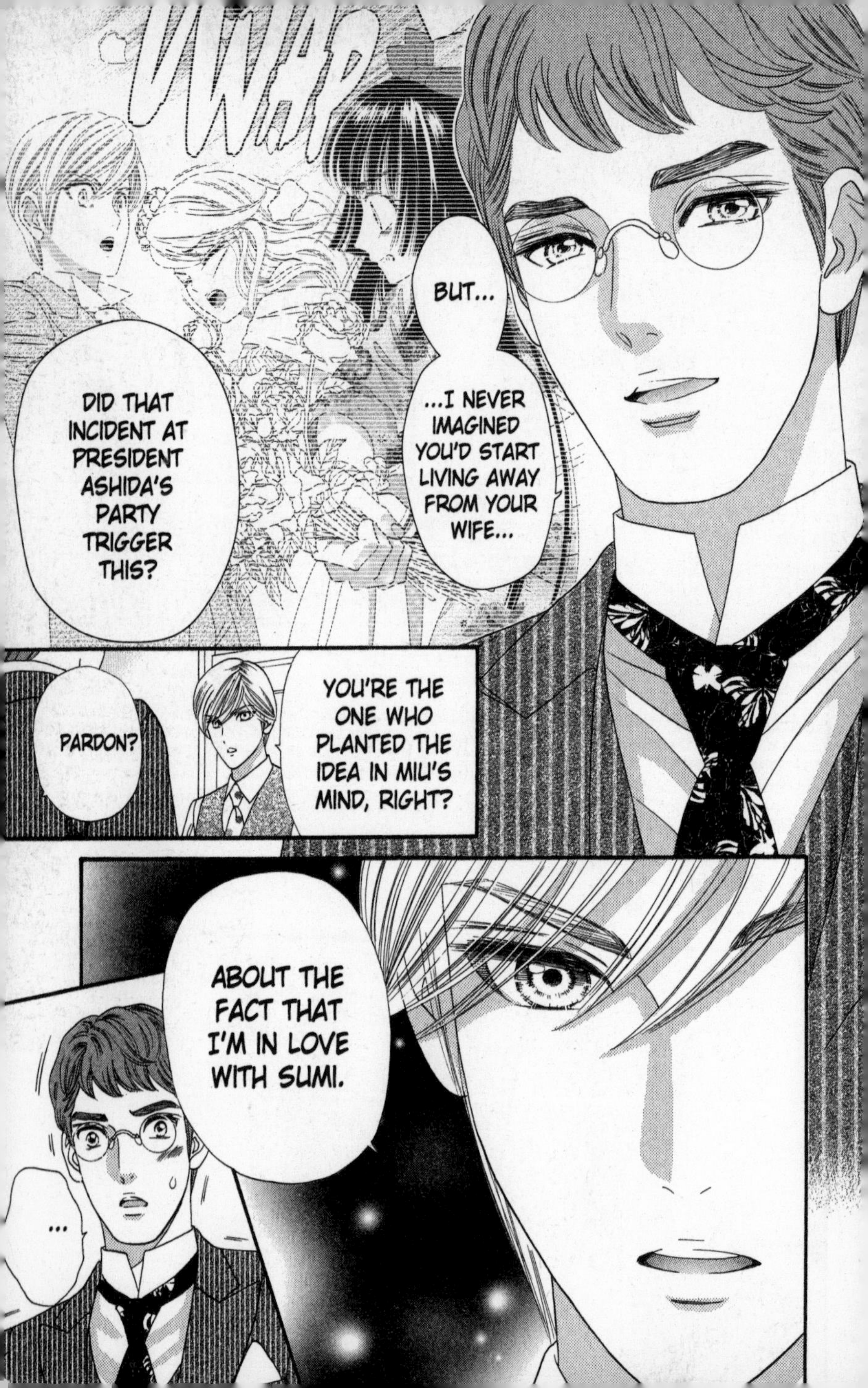
UNWRAP
BUT...
...I NEVER IMAGINED YOU'D START LIVING AWAY FROM YOUR WIFE...
DID THAT INCIDENT AT PRESIDENT ASHIDA'S PARTY TRIGGER THIS?
YOU'RE THE ONE WHO PLANTED THE IDEA IN MIU'S MIND, RIGHT?
PARDON?
ABOUT THE FACT THAT I'M IN LOVE WITH SUMI.
...

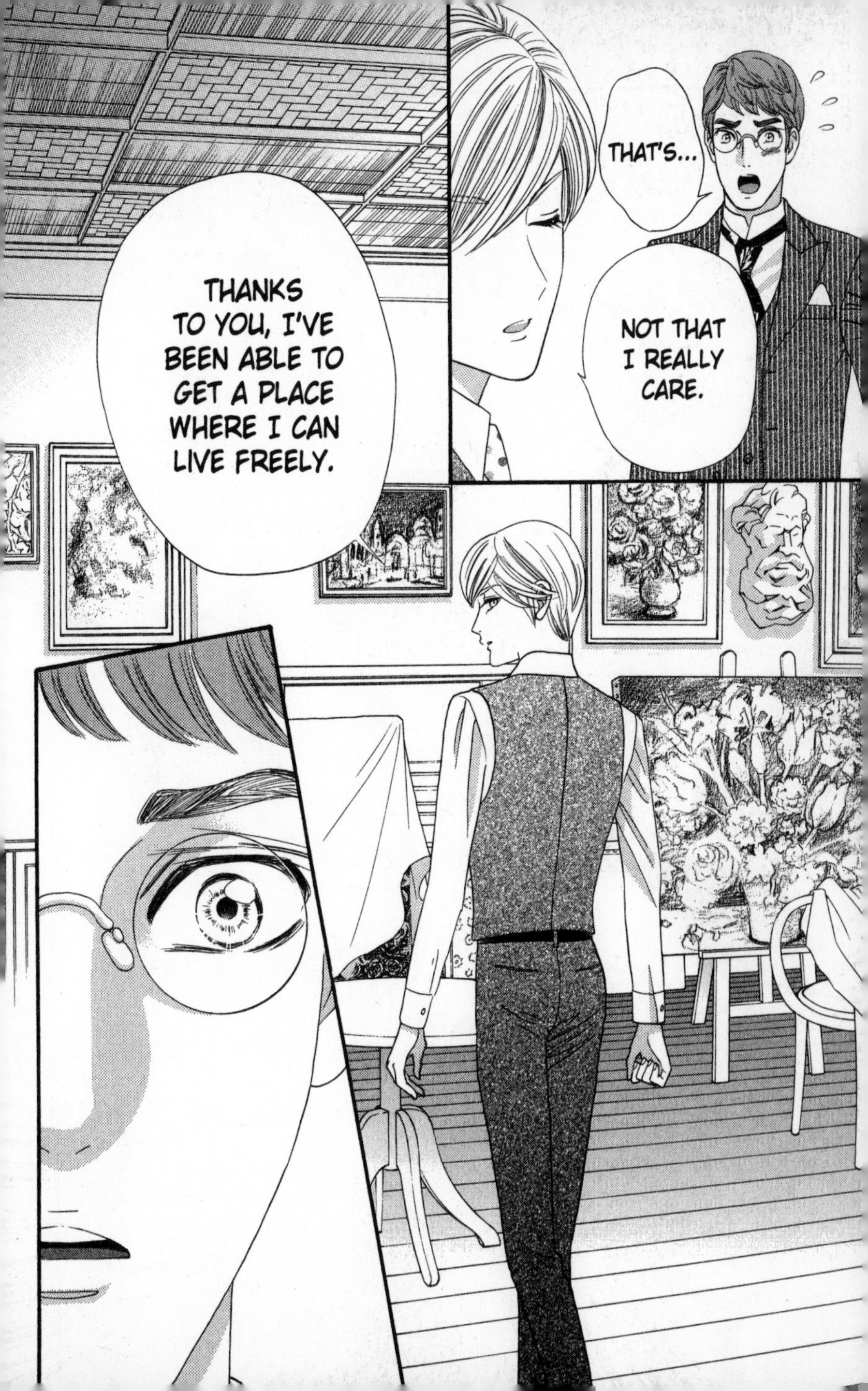
THAT'S...
NOT THAT I REALLY CARE.
THANKS TO YOU, I'VE BEEN ABLE TO GET A PLACE WHERE I CAN LIVE FREELY.

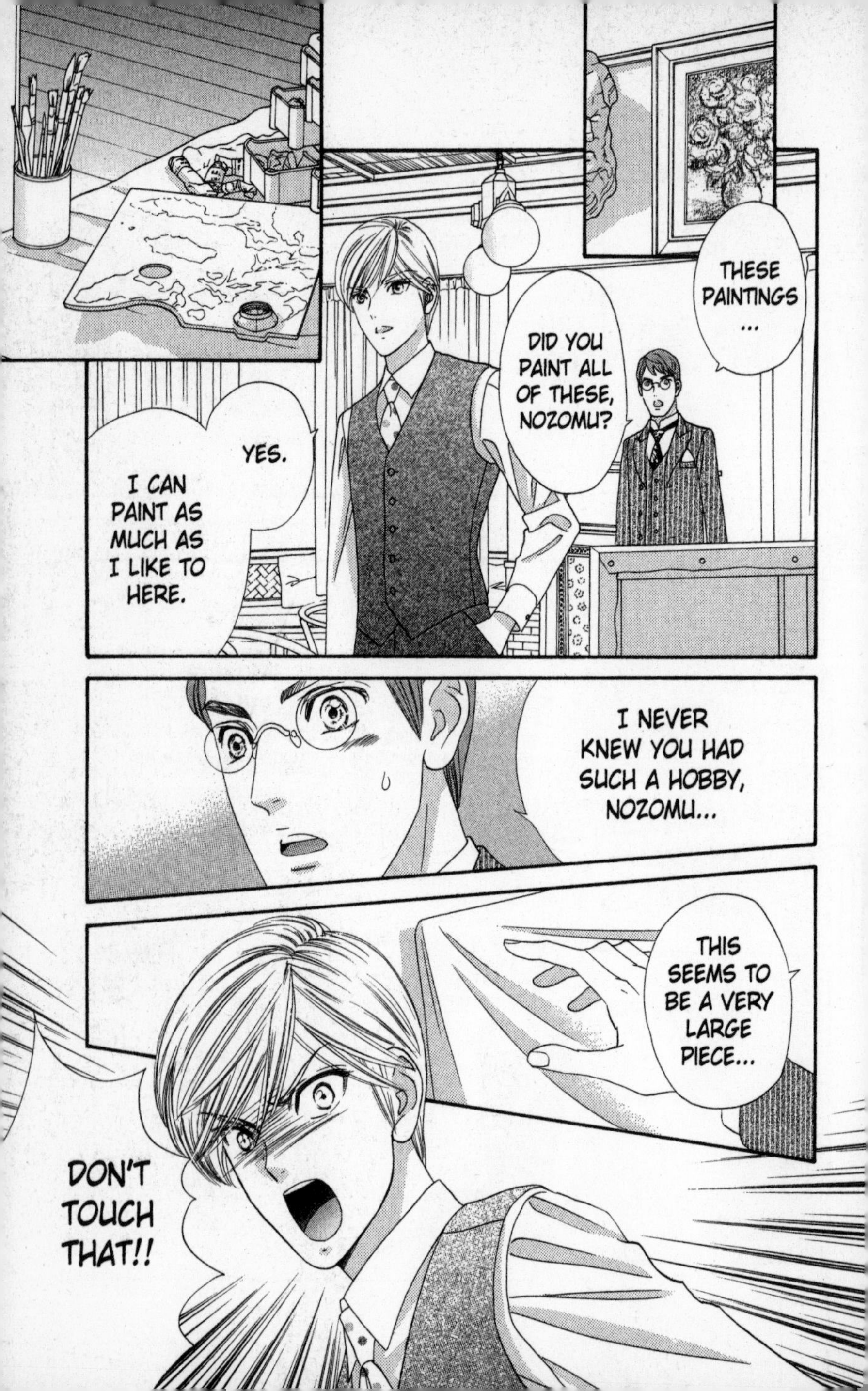
THESE PAINTINGS ...
DID YOU PAINT ALL OF THESE, NOZOMU?
YES.
I CAN PAINT AS MUCH AS I LIKE TO HERE.
I NEVER KNEW YOU HAD SUCH A HOBBY, NOZOMU...
THIS SEEMS TO BE A VERY LARGE PIECE...
DON'T TOUCH THAT!!

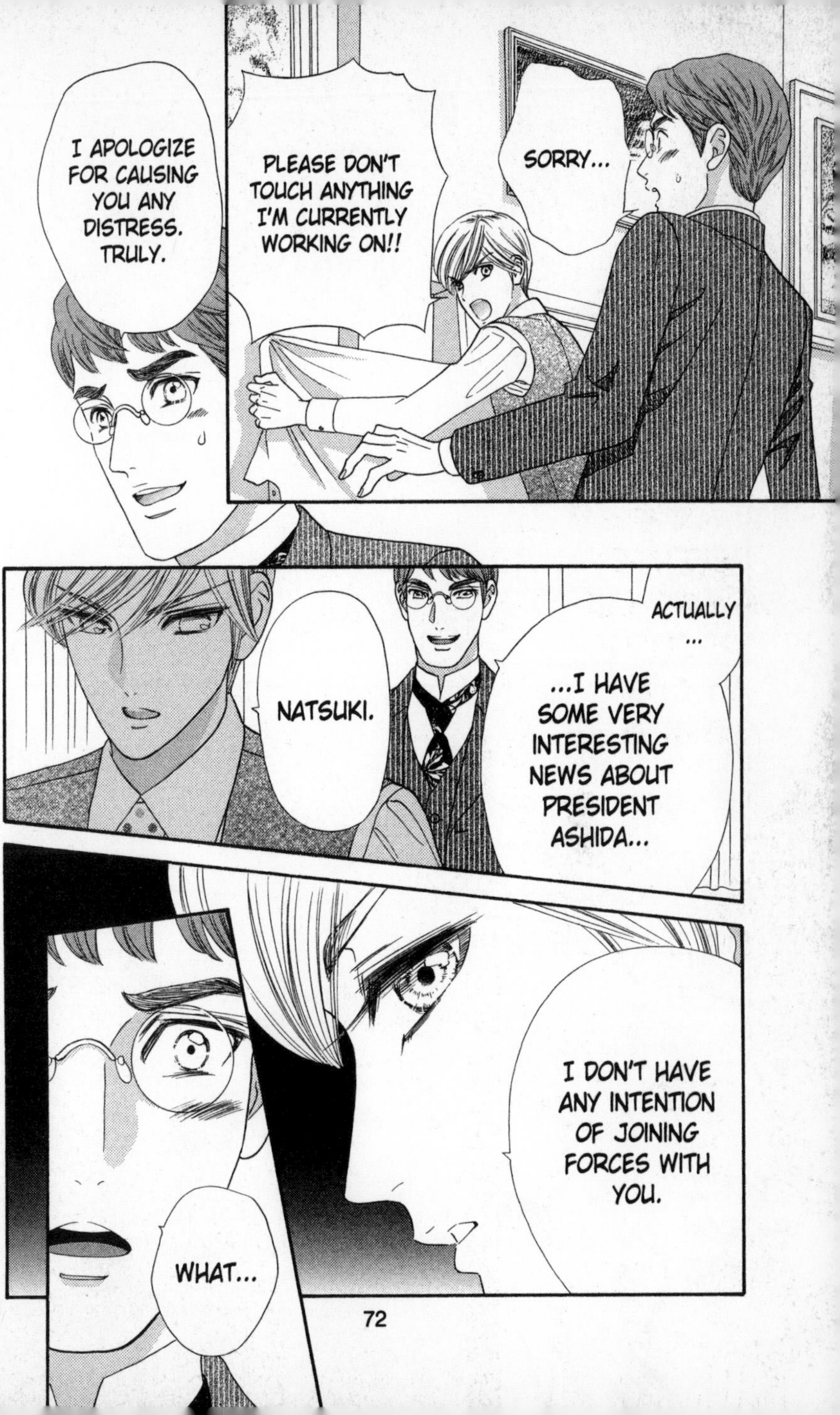
SORRY...
PLEASE DON'T TOUCH ANYTHING I'M CURRENTLY WORKING ON!!
I APOLOGIZE FOR CAUSING YOU ANY DISTRESS. TRULY.
ACTUALLY... ...I HAVE SOME VERY INTERESTING NEWS ABOUT PRESIDENT ASHIDA...
NATSUKI.
I DON'T HAVE ANY INTENTION OF JOINING FORCES WITH YOU.
WHAT...

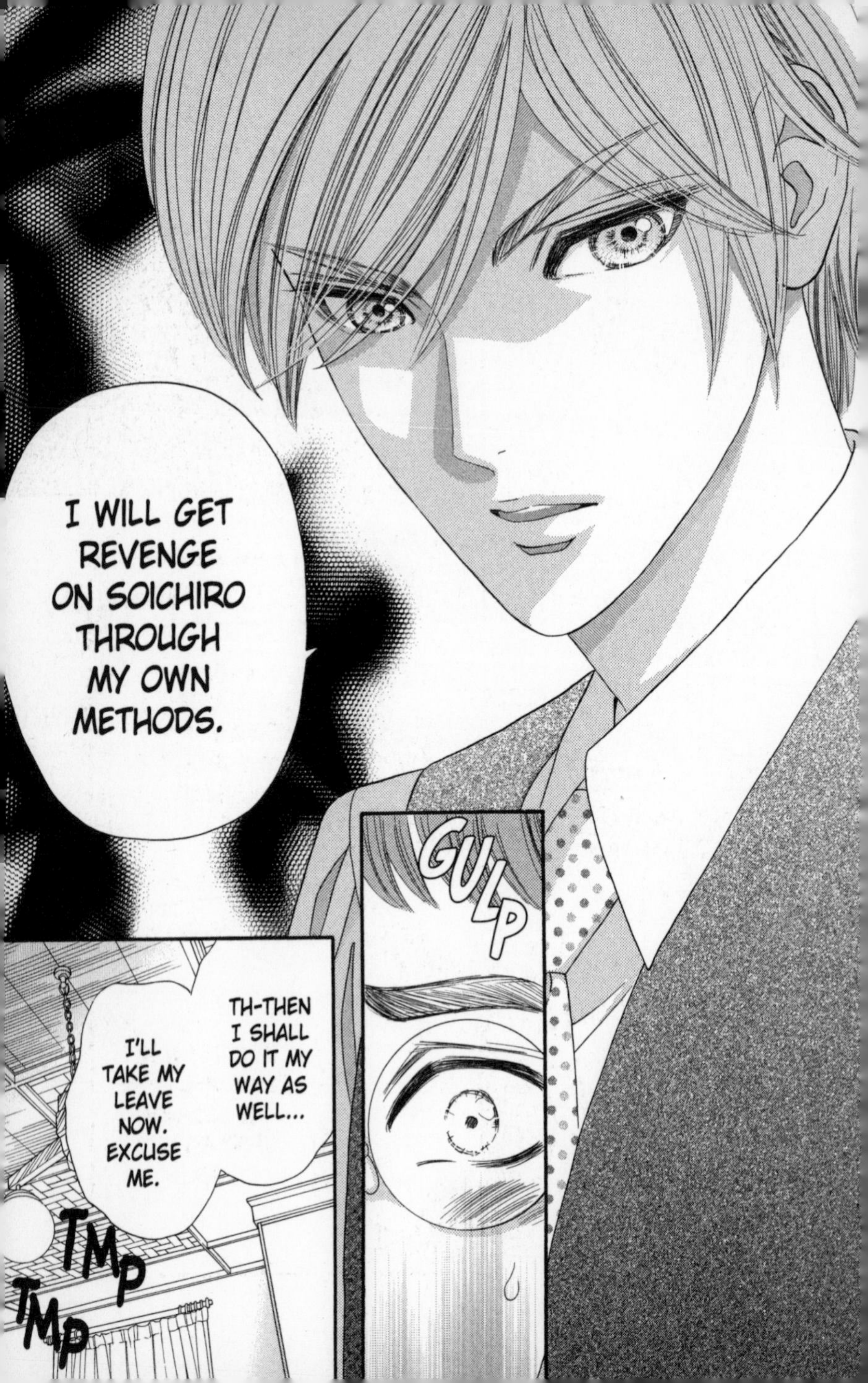
I WILL GET REVENGE ON SOICHIRO THROUGH MY OWN METHODS.
GULP
TH-THEN I SHALL DO IT MY WAY AS WELL...
I'LL TAKE MY LEAVE NOW. EXCUSE ME.
TMP
TMP

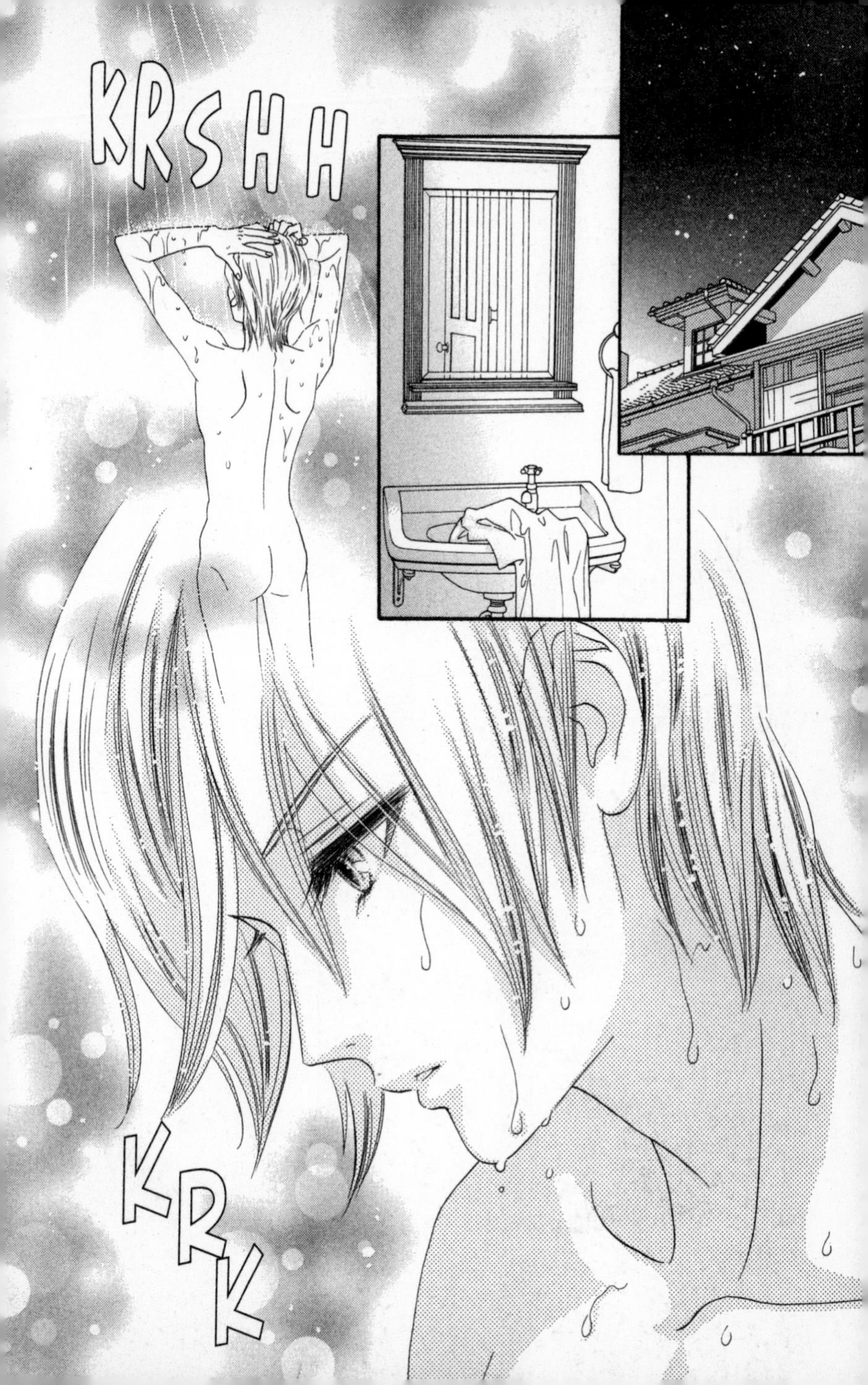
KRSHH
KRK

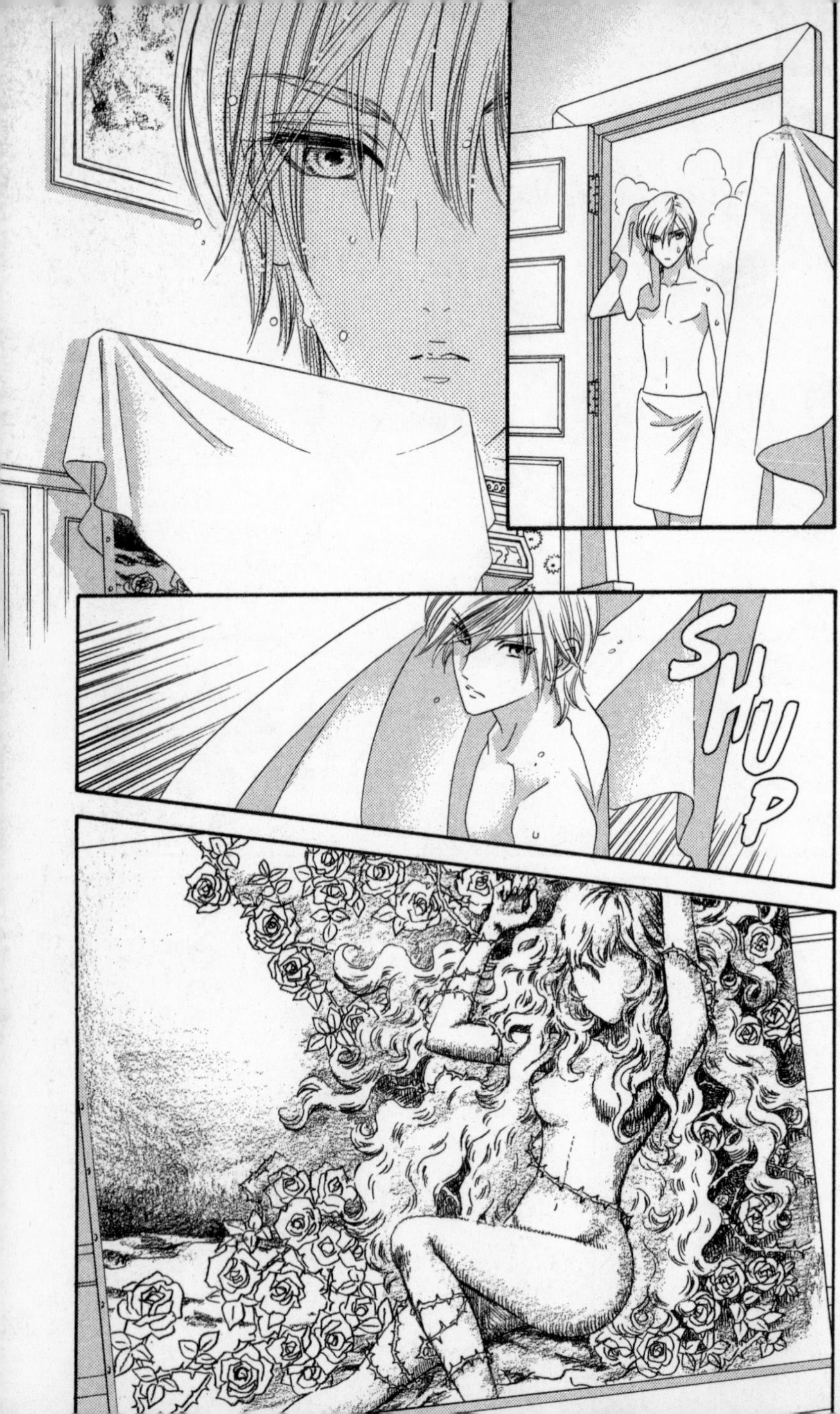
SHUP

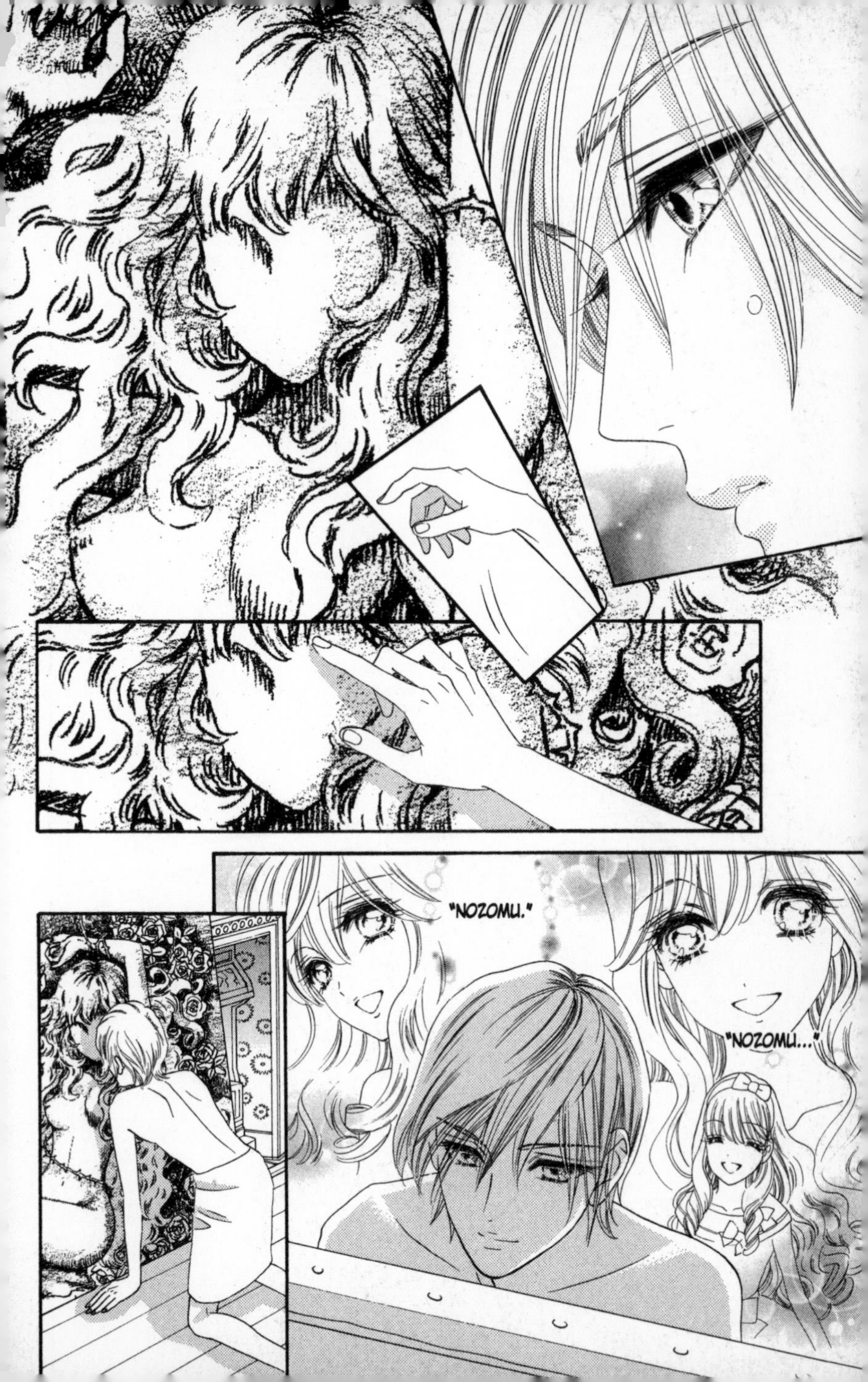
"NOZOMU."
"NOZOMU..."

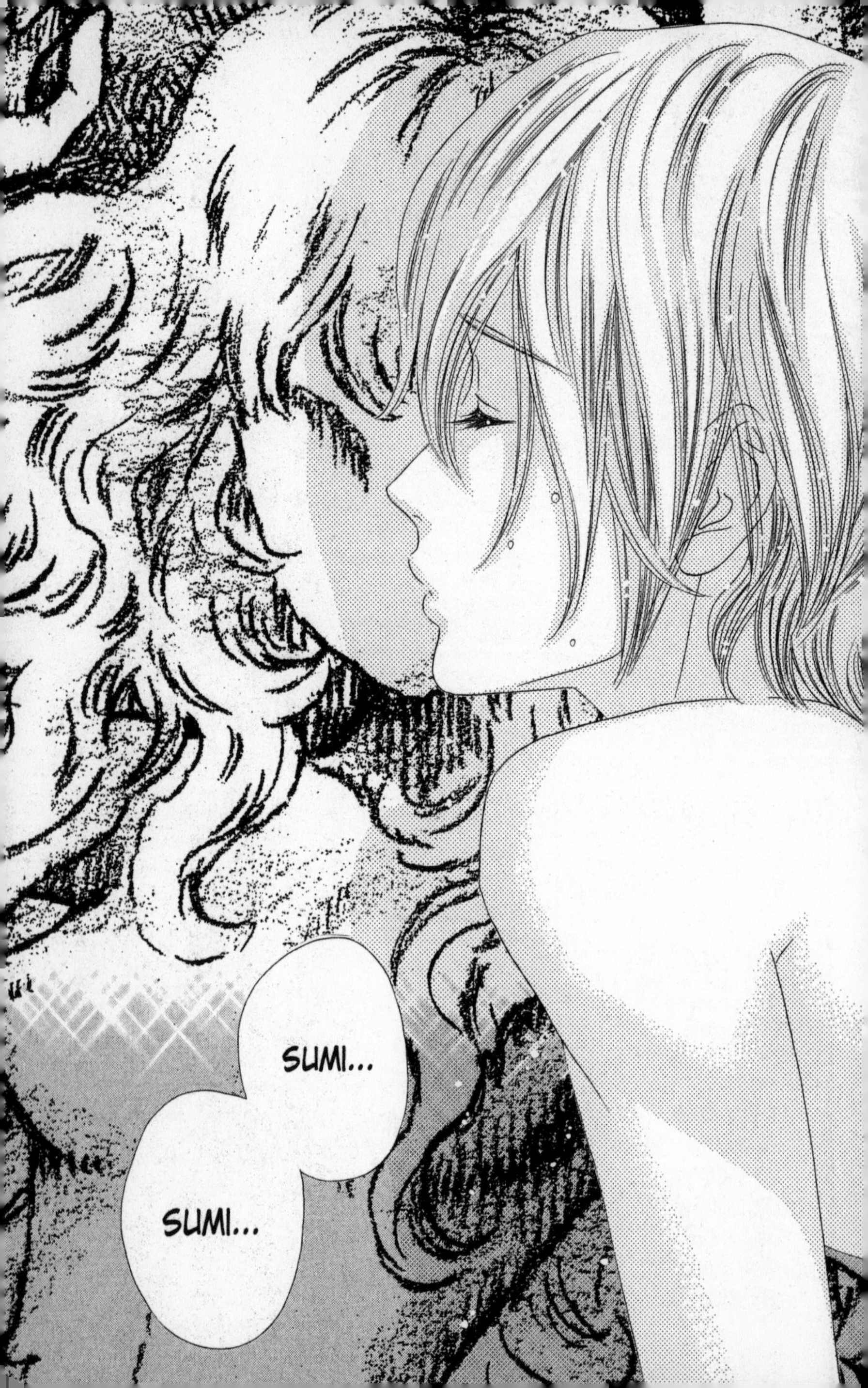
SUMI...
SUMI...

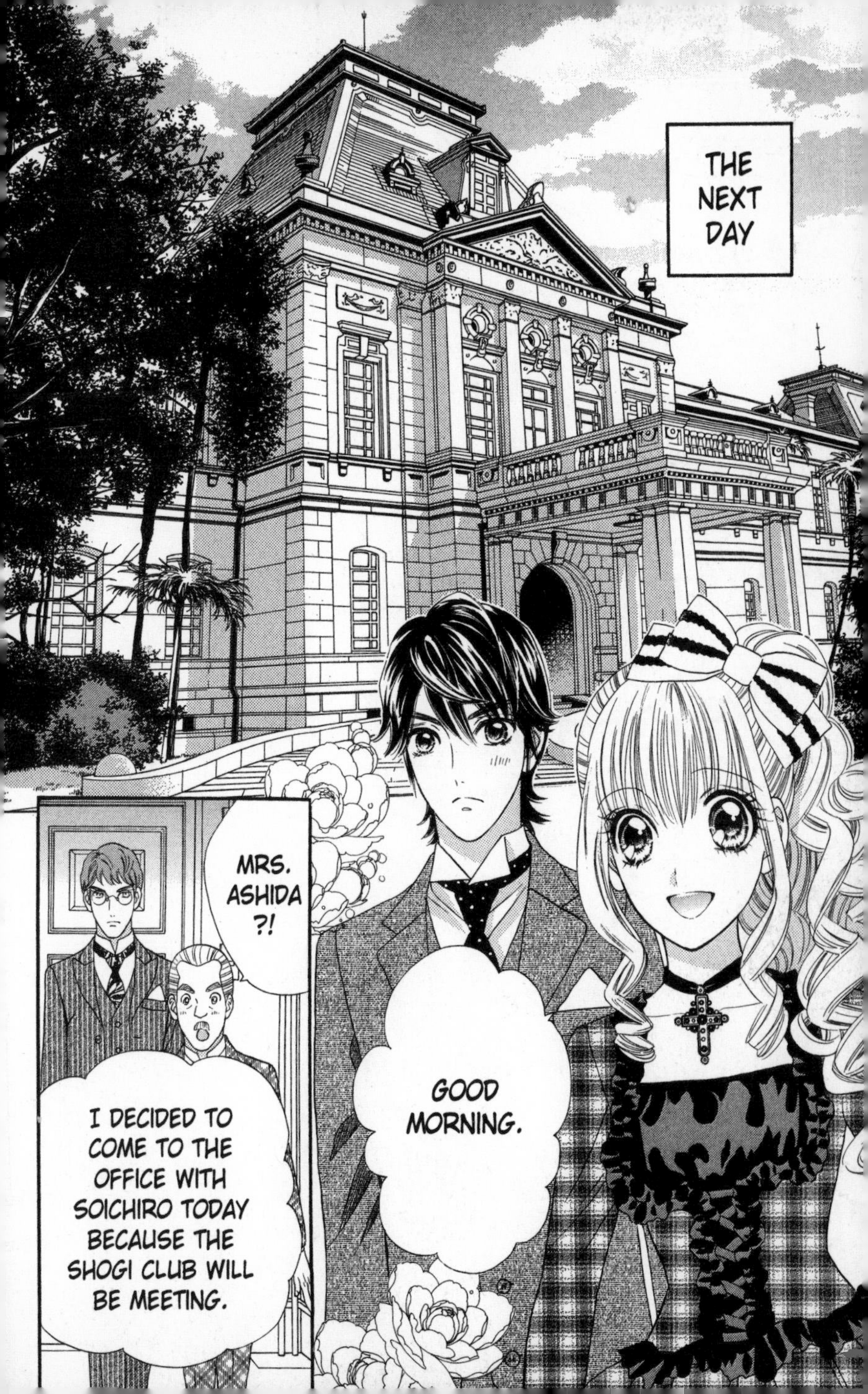
THE NEXT DAY
GOOD MORNING.
MRS. ASHIDA ?!
I DECIDED TO COME TO THE OFFICE WITH SOICHIRO TODAY BECAUSE THE SHOGI CLUB WILL BE MEETING.

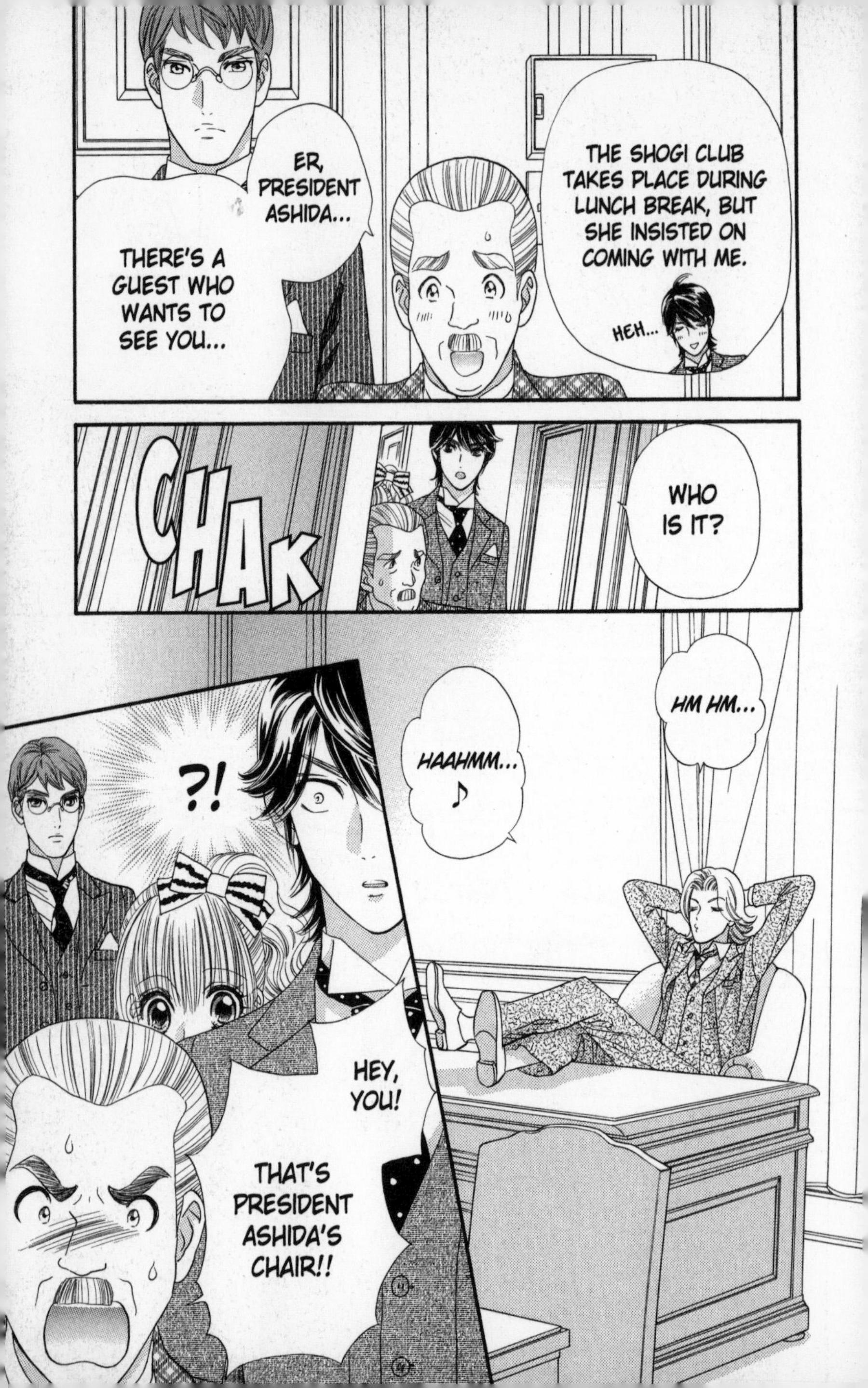
THE SHOGI CLUB TAKES PLACE DURING LUNCH BREAK, BUT SHE INSISTED ON COMING WITH ME.
HEH...
ER, PRESIDENT ASHIDA...
THERE'S A GUEST WHO WANTS TO SEE YOU...
WHO IS IT?
CHAK
HM HM...
HAAHMM... ♪
?!
HEY, YOU!
THAT'S PRESIDENT ASHIDA'S CHAIR!!

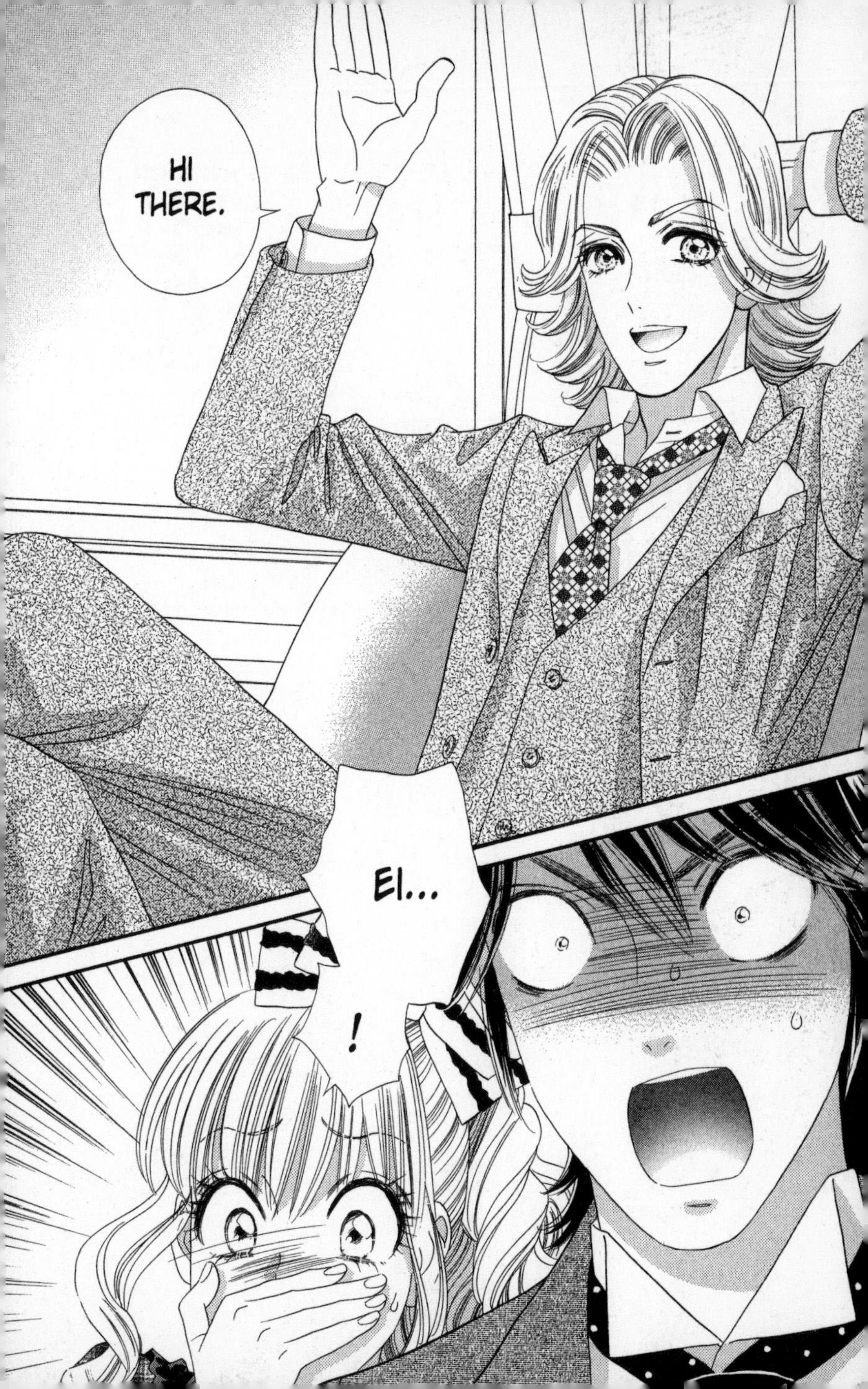
HI THERE.
EI...
!

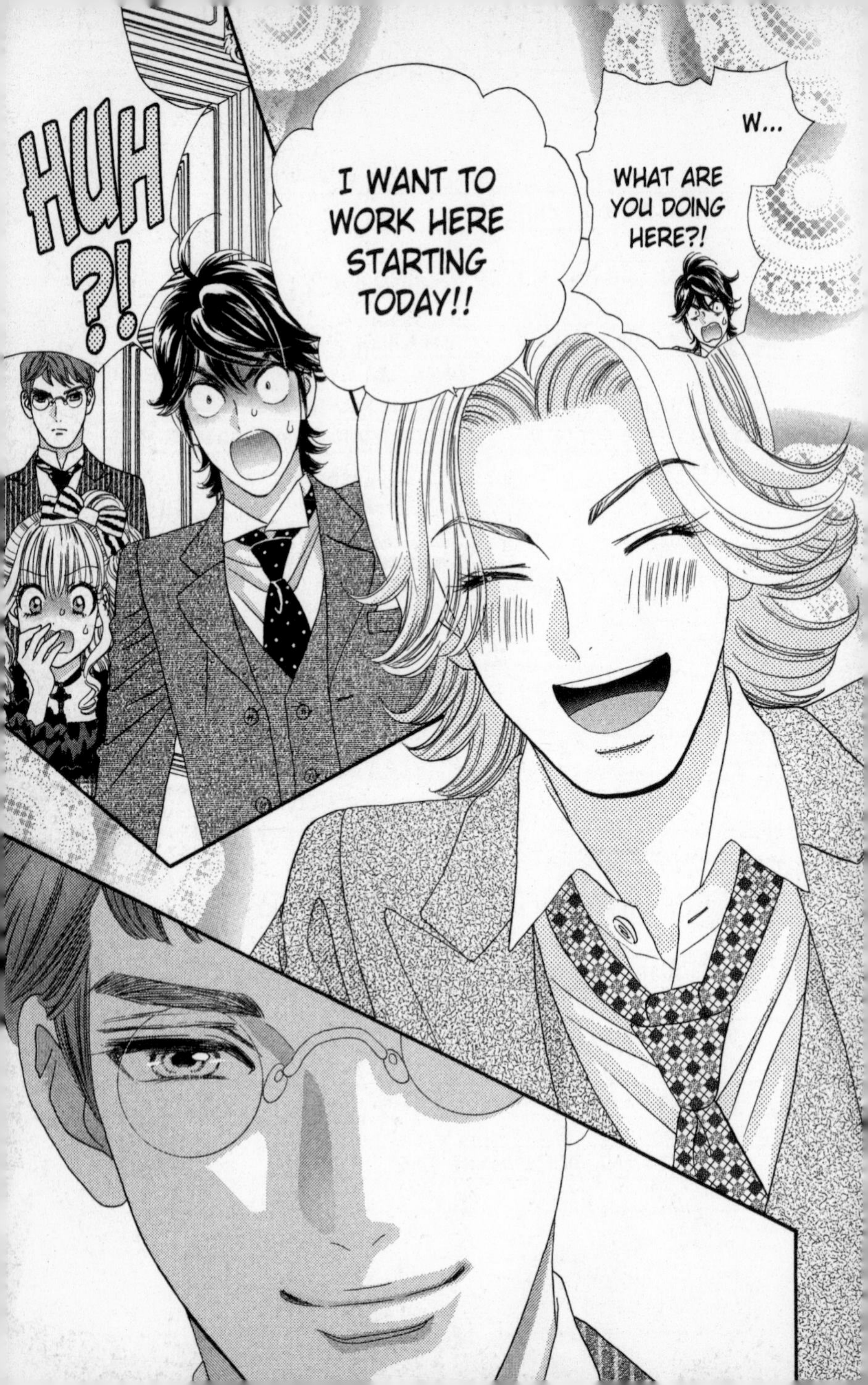
W...
WHAT ARE YOU DOING HERE?!
I WANT TO WORK HERE STARTING TODAY!!
HUH ?!

No. 3

RANDOM CHITCHAT

Date . .

DAISUKE ONO PLAYED SOICHIRO ASHIDA.

HE'S REALLY GOOD-LOOKING!!

AND HIS PHYSIQUE...IT'S AS IF HE REALLY CAME OUT OF A SHOJO MANGA!!

I'M A HUGE FAN OF THE GIRLS' VIDEO GAME *FULL HOUSE KISS*.* I'VE ATTENDED ALL ITS RELATED EVENTS, SO I'M SO DELIGHTED TO BE ABLE TO MEET YOU!!

MY HEAD WAS IN A TIZZY, BUT I TOLD HIM THAT AND...

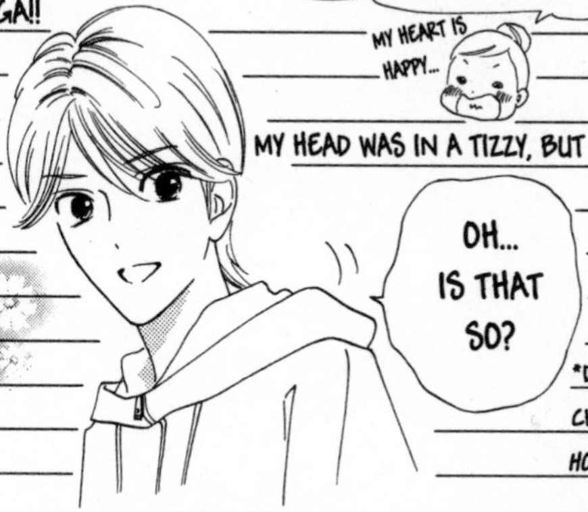
MY HEART IS HAPPY...
OH... IS THAT SO?

*DAISUKE ONO PLAYS A CHARACTER IN THE *FULL HOUSE KISS* SERIES.

I WANTED TO PRESENT MYSELF AS THE CALM AUTHOR OF THE SERIES, BUT I JUST COULDN'T HOLD BACK MY PASSION.

SOICHIRO DOESN'T APPEAR UNTIL THE LAST HALF... I WAITED IMPATIENTLY AND FOUND MYSELF BEING KNOCKED OUT BY SOICHIRO'S SADISTIC-SOUNDING VOICE.

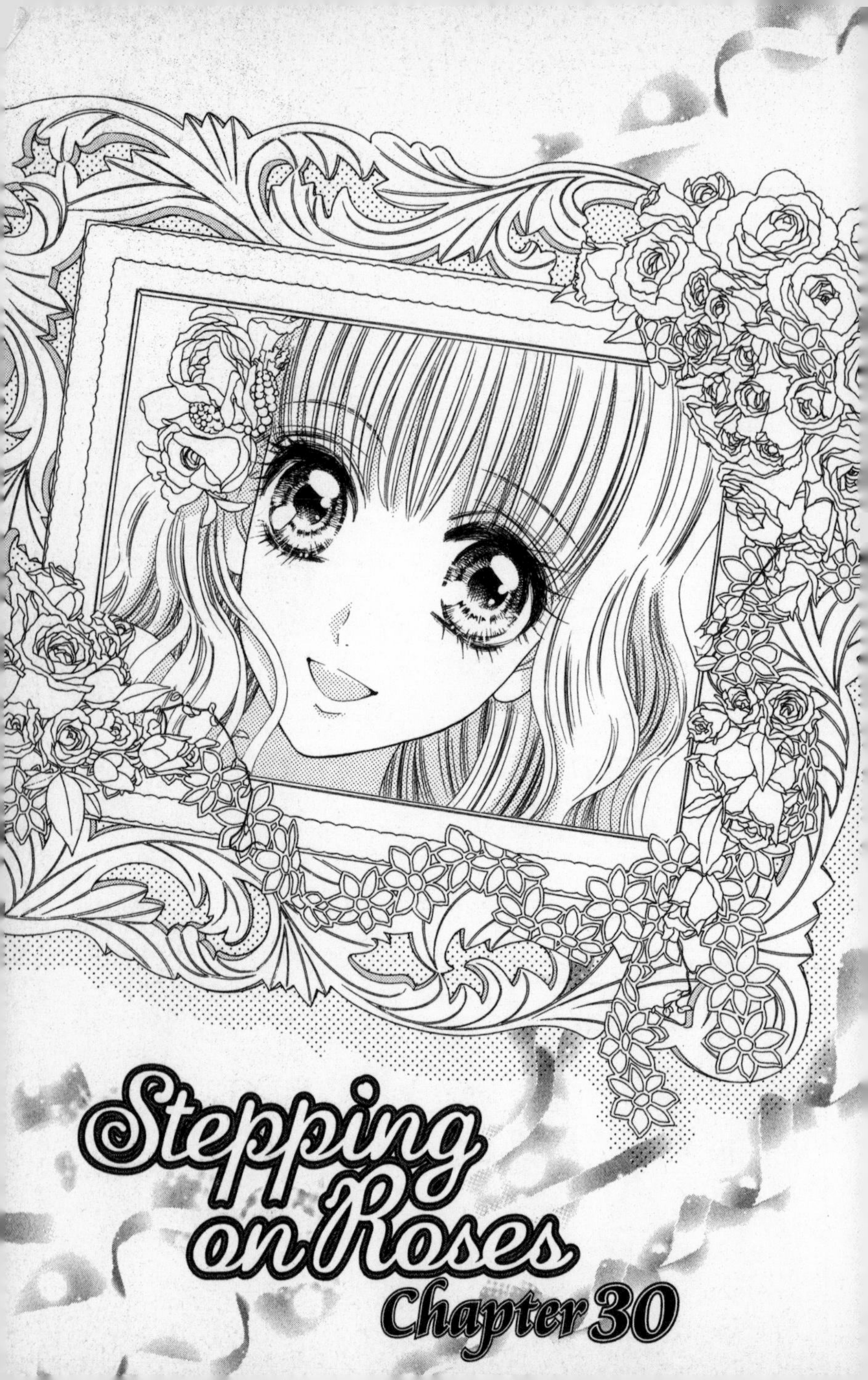
Stepping on Roses
Chapter 30

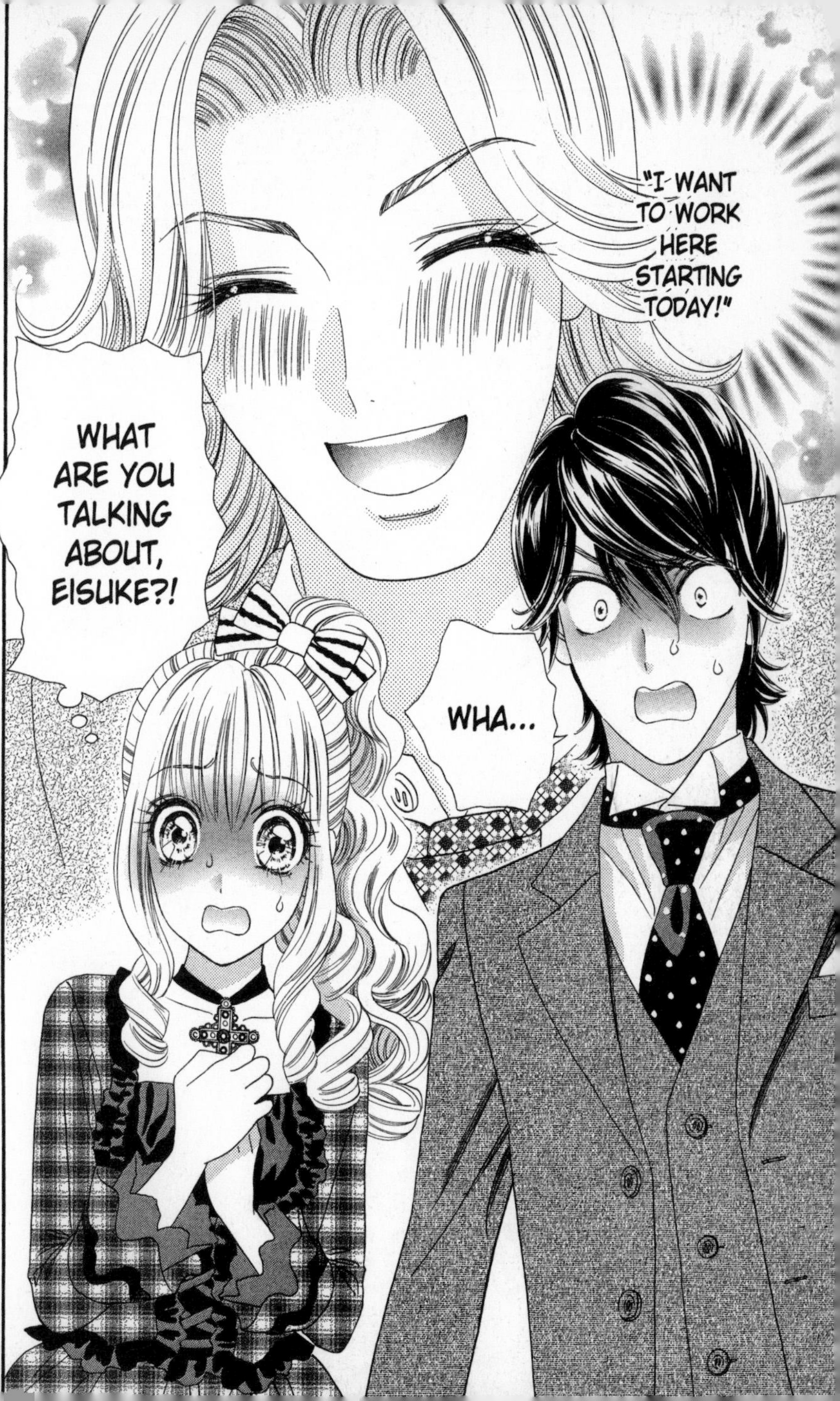
"I WANT TO WORK HERE STARTING TODAY!"
WHAT ARE YOU TALKING ABOUT, EISUKE?!
WHA...

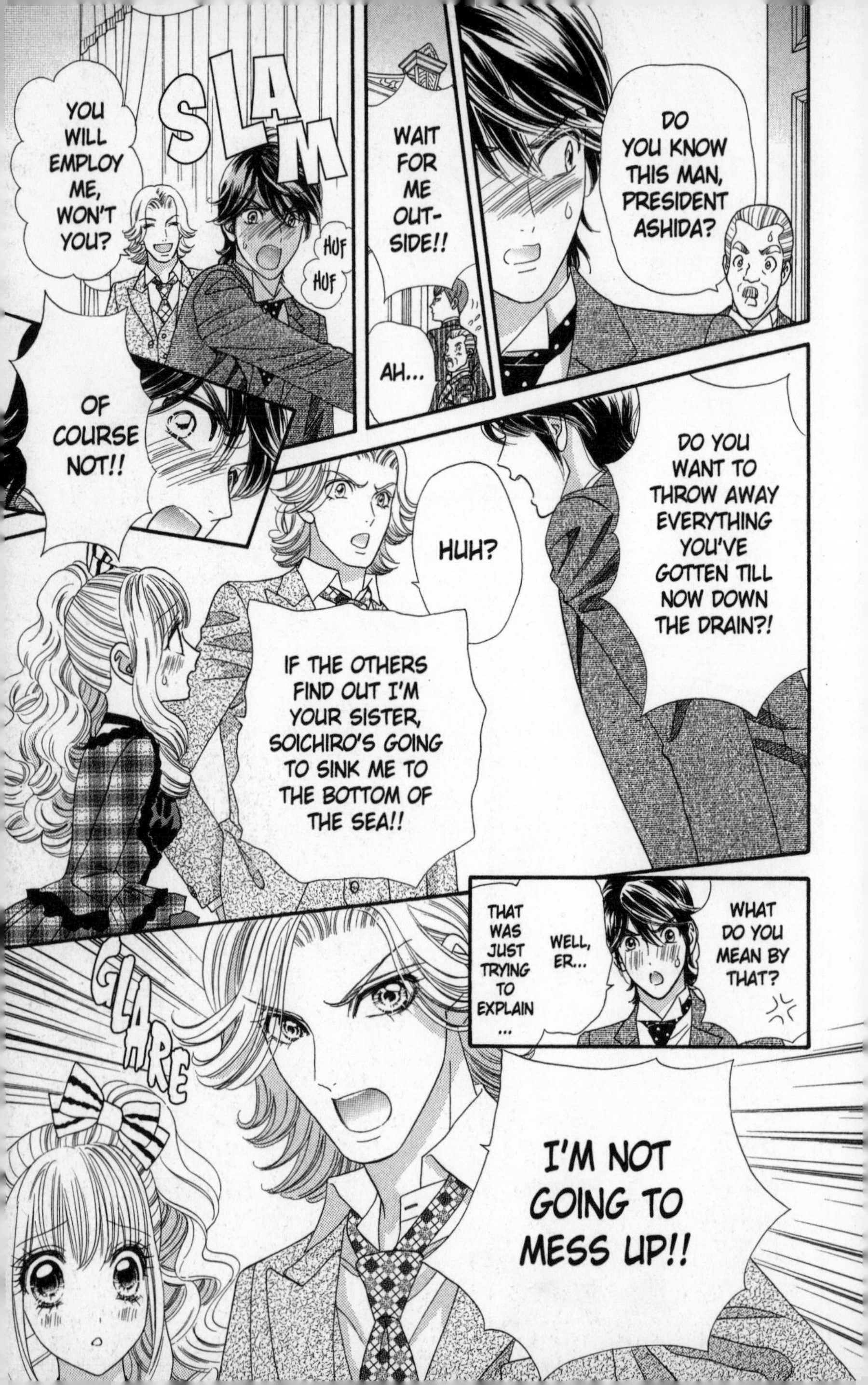
DO YOU KNOW THIS MAN, PRESIDENT ASHIDA?
WAIT FOR ME OUT-SIDE!!
AH...
SLAM
YOU WILL EMPLOY ME, WON'T YOU?
HUF
HUF
OF COURSE NOT!!
DO YOU WANT TO THROW AWAY EVERYTHING YOU'VE GOTTEN TILL NOW DOWN THE DRAIN?!
HUH?
IF THE OTHERS FIND OUT I'M YOUR SISTER, SOICHIRO'S GOING TO SINK ME TO THE BOTTOM OF THE SEA!!
WHAT DO YOU MEAN BY THAT?
WELL, ER...
THAT WAS JUST TRYING TO EXPLAIN ...
I'M NOT GOING TO MESS UP!!
GLARE

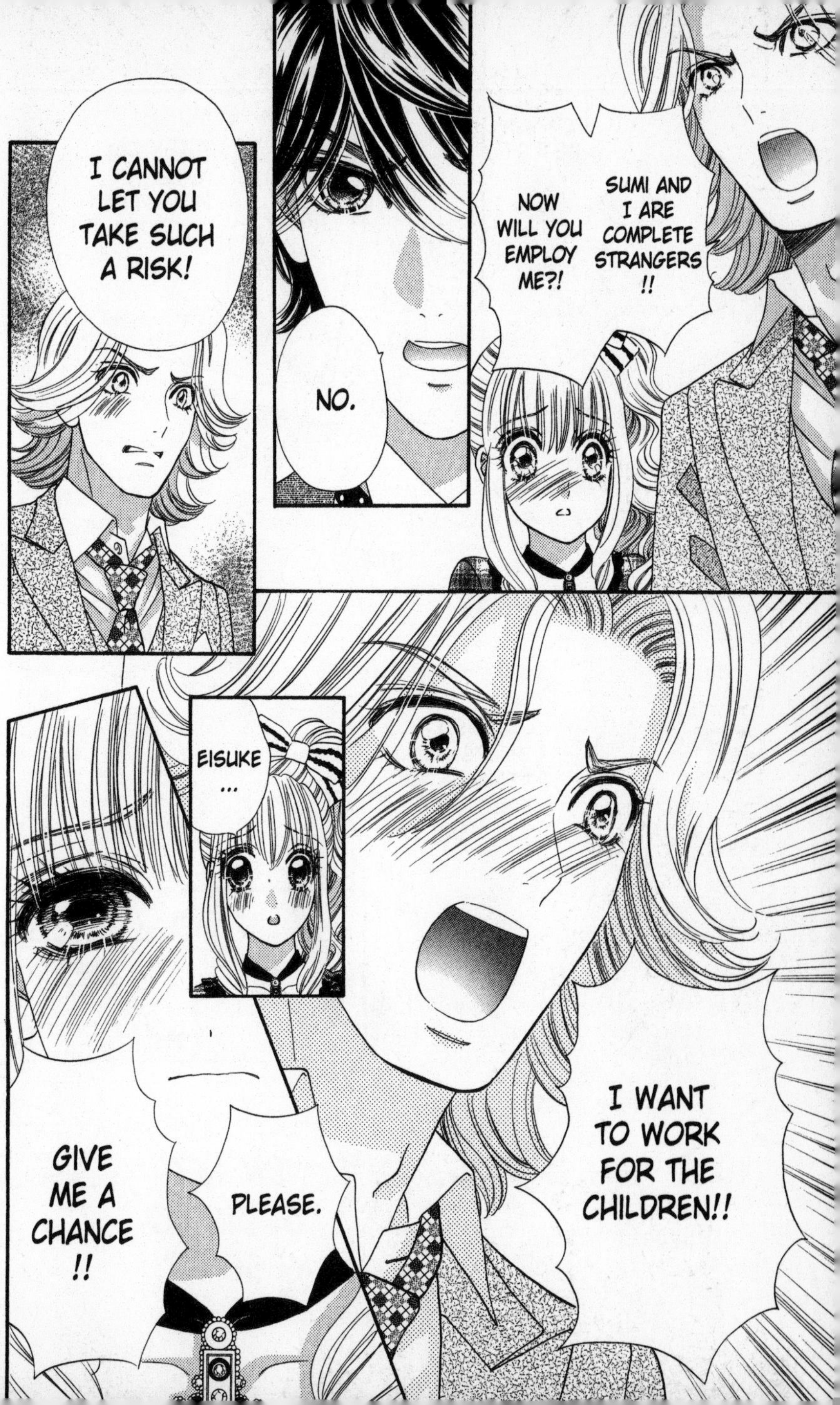
SUMI AND I ARE COMPLETE STRANGERS!!
NOW WILL YOU EMPLOY ME?!
NO.
I CANNOT LET YOU TAKE SUCH A RISK!
I WANT TO WORK FOR THE CHILDREN!!
EISUKE...
PLEASE.
GIVE ME A CHANCE!!

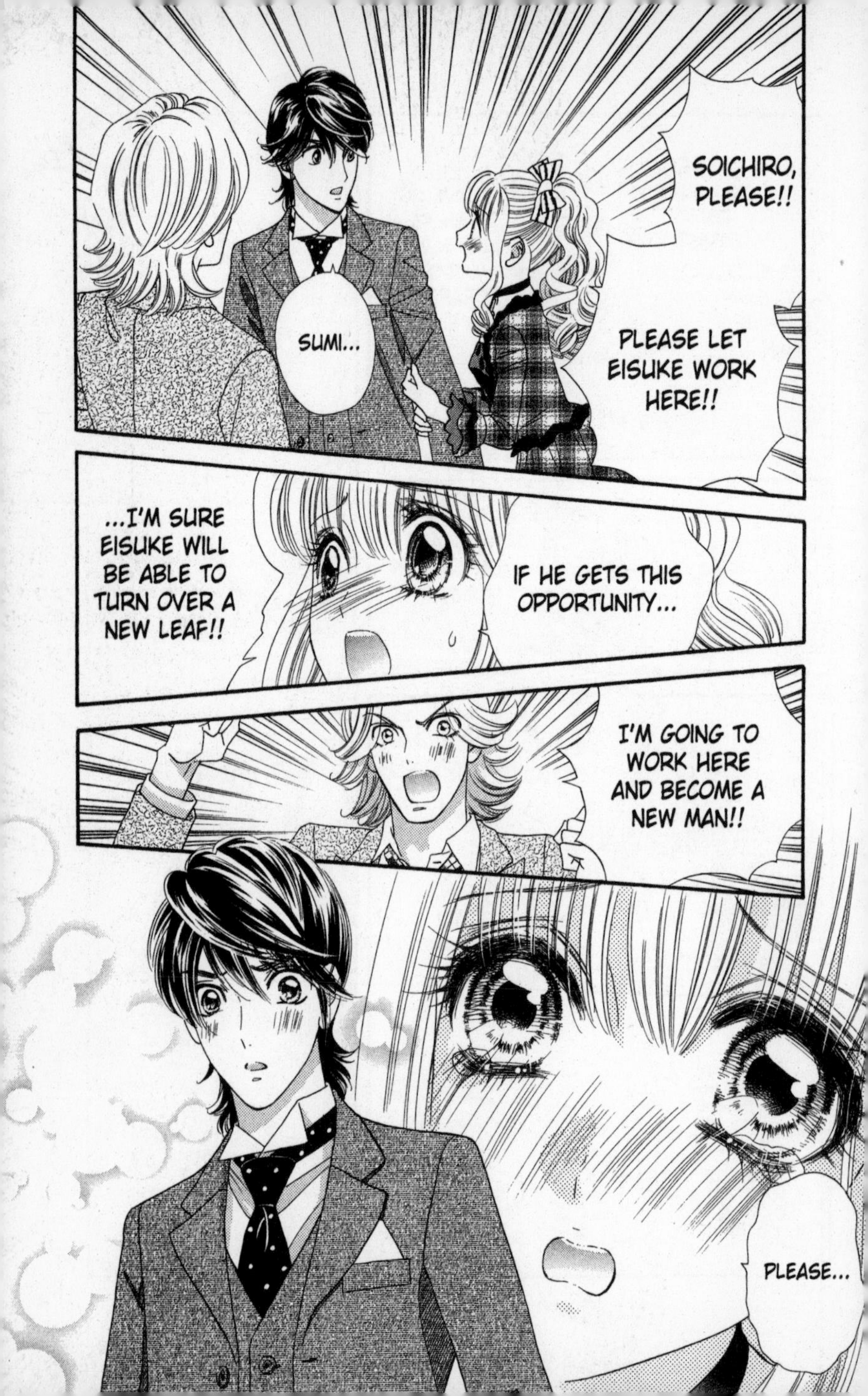
SOICHIRO, PLEASE!!
PLEASE LET EISUKE WORK HERE!!
SUMI...
IF HE GETS THIS OPPORTUNITY...
...I'M SURE EISUKE WILL BE ABLE TO TURN OVER A NEW LEAF!!
I'M GOING TO WORK HERE AND BECOME A NEW MAN!!
PLEASE...

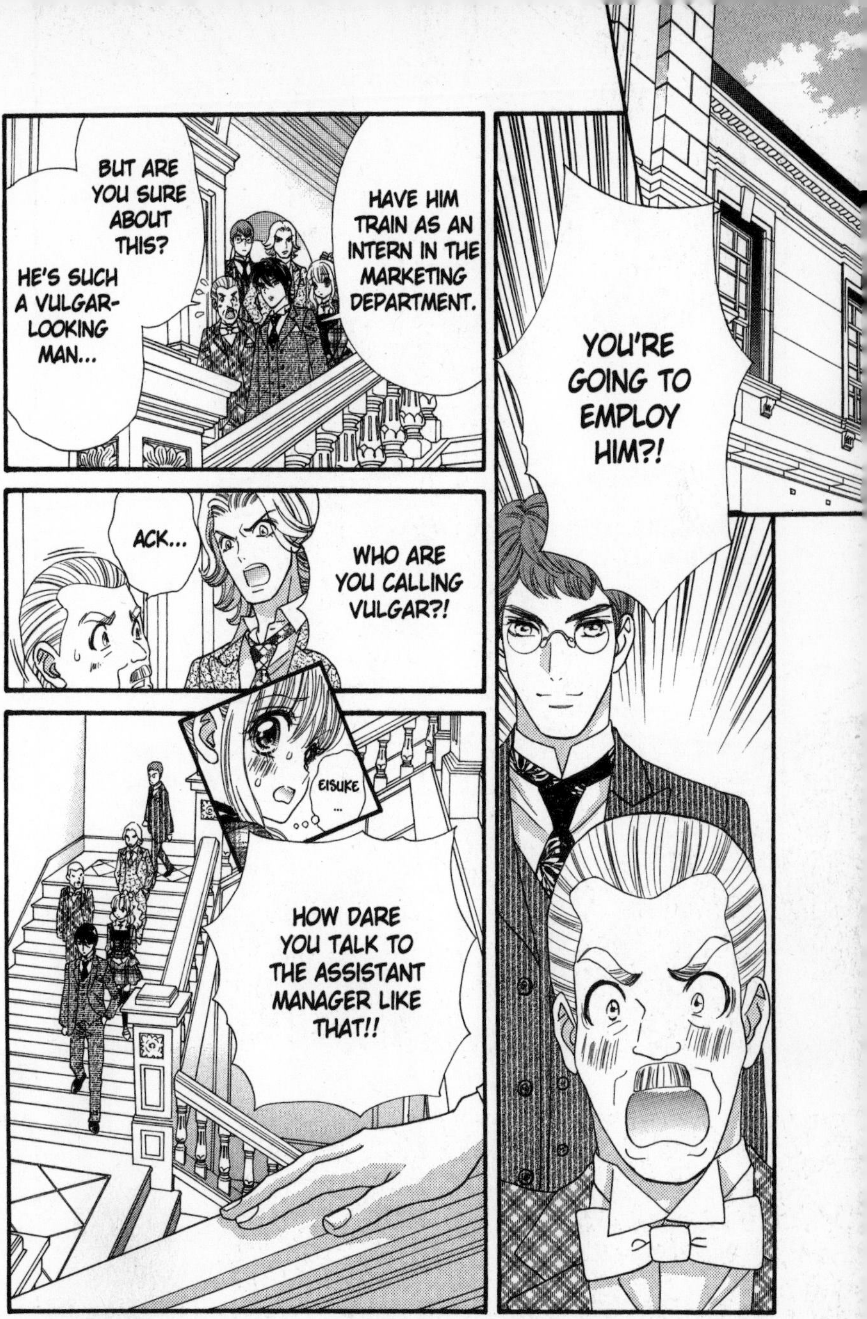
YOU'RE GOING TO EMPLOY HIM?!
HAVE HIM TRAIN AS AN INTERN IN THE MARKETING DEPARTMENT.
BUT ARE YOU SURE ABOUT THIS?
HE'S SUCH A VULGAR-LOOKING MAN...
WHO ARE YOU CALLING VULGAR?!
ACK...
EISUKE ...
HOW DARE YOU TALK TO THE ASSISTANT MANAGER LIKE THAT!!

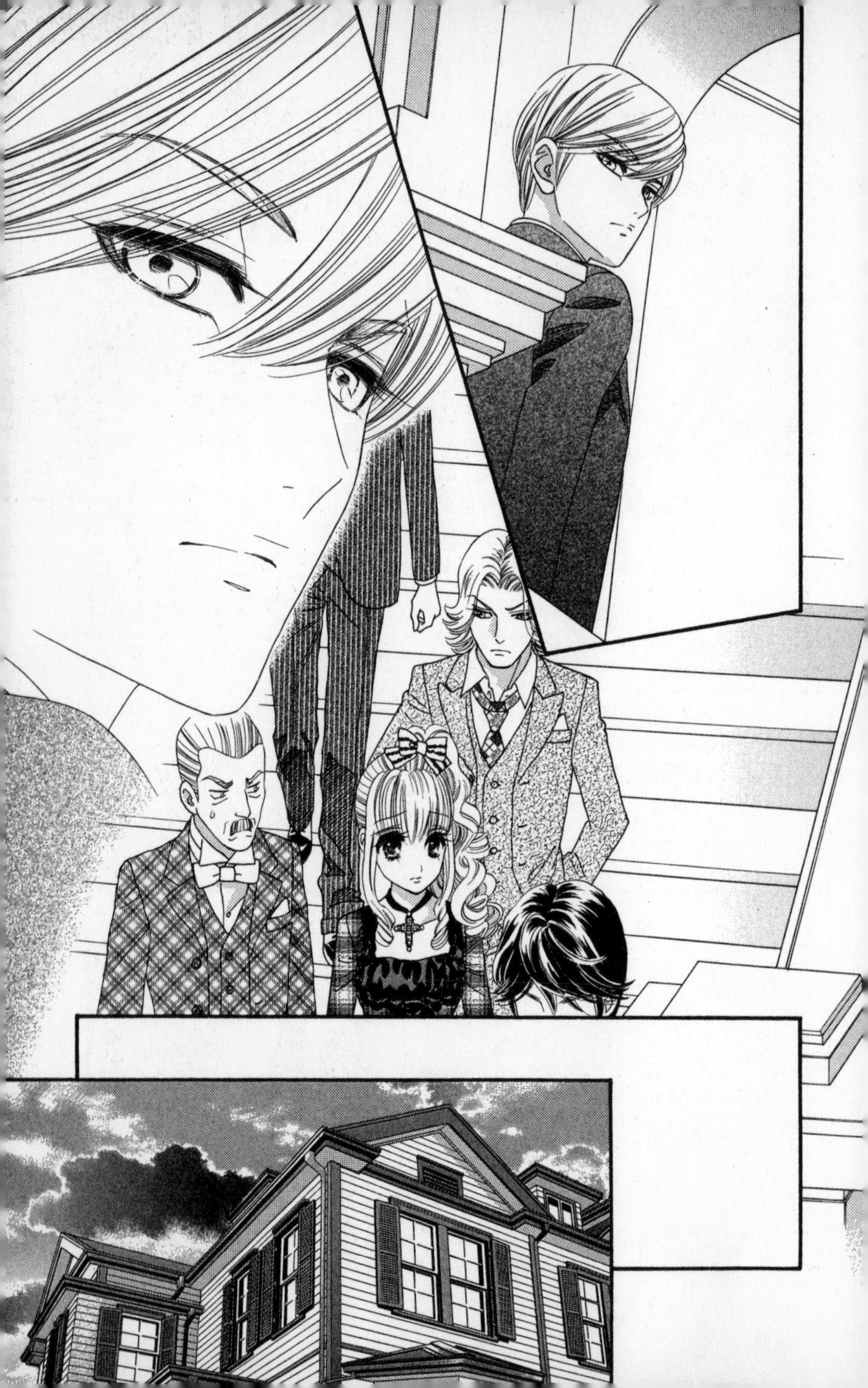

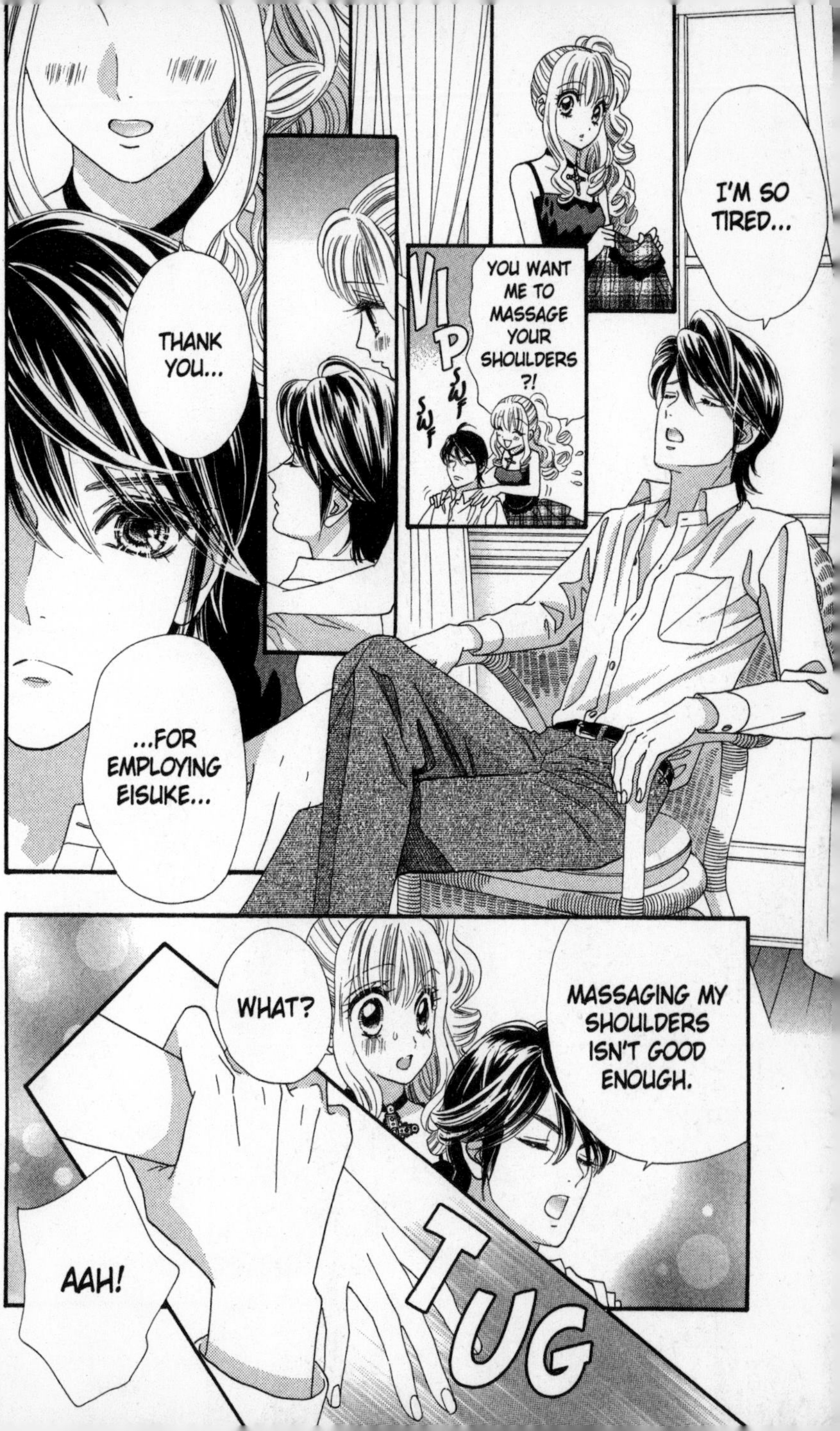
I'M SO TIRED...
VIP
SWF
SWF
YOU WANT ME TO MASSAGE YOUR SHOULDERS ?!
THANK YOU...
...FOR EMPLOYING EISUKE...
MASSAGING MY SHOULDERS ISN'T GOOD ENOUGH.
WHAT?
TUG
AAH!

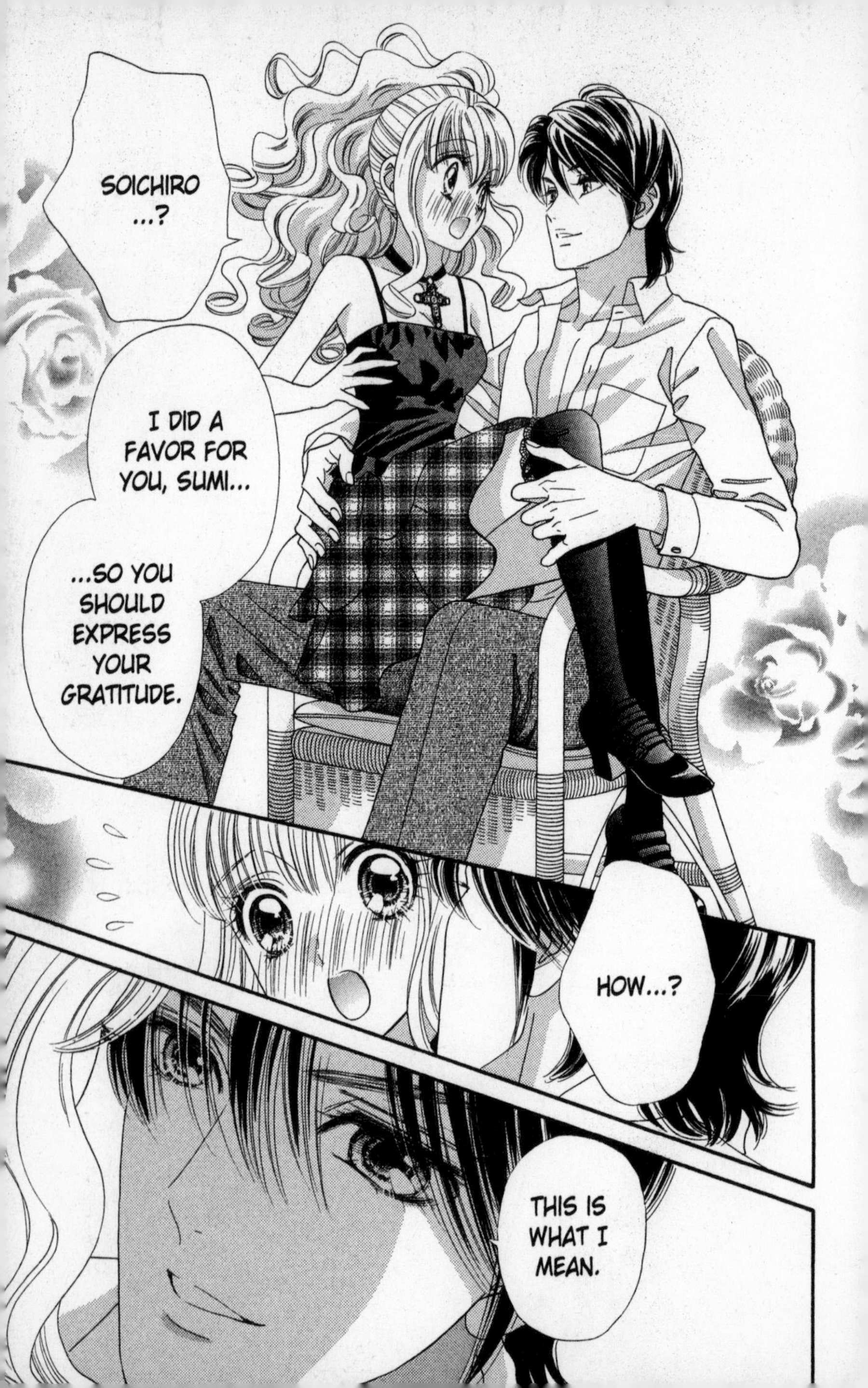
SOICHIRO ...?
I DID A FAVOR FOR YOU, SUMI...
...SO YOU SHOULD EXPRESS YOUR GRATITUDE.
HOW...?
THIS IS WHAT I MEAN.

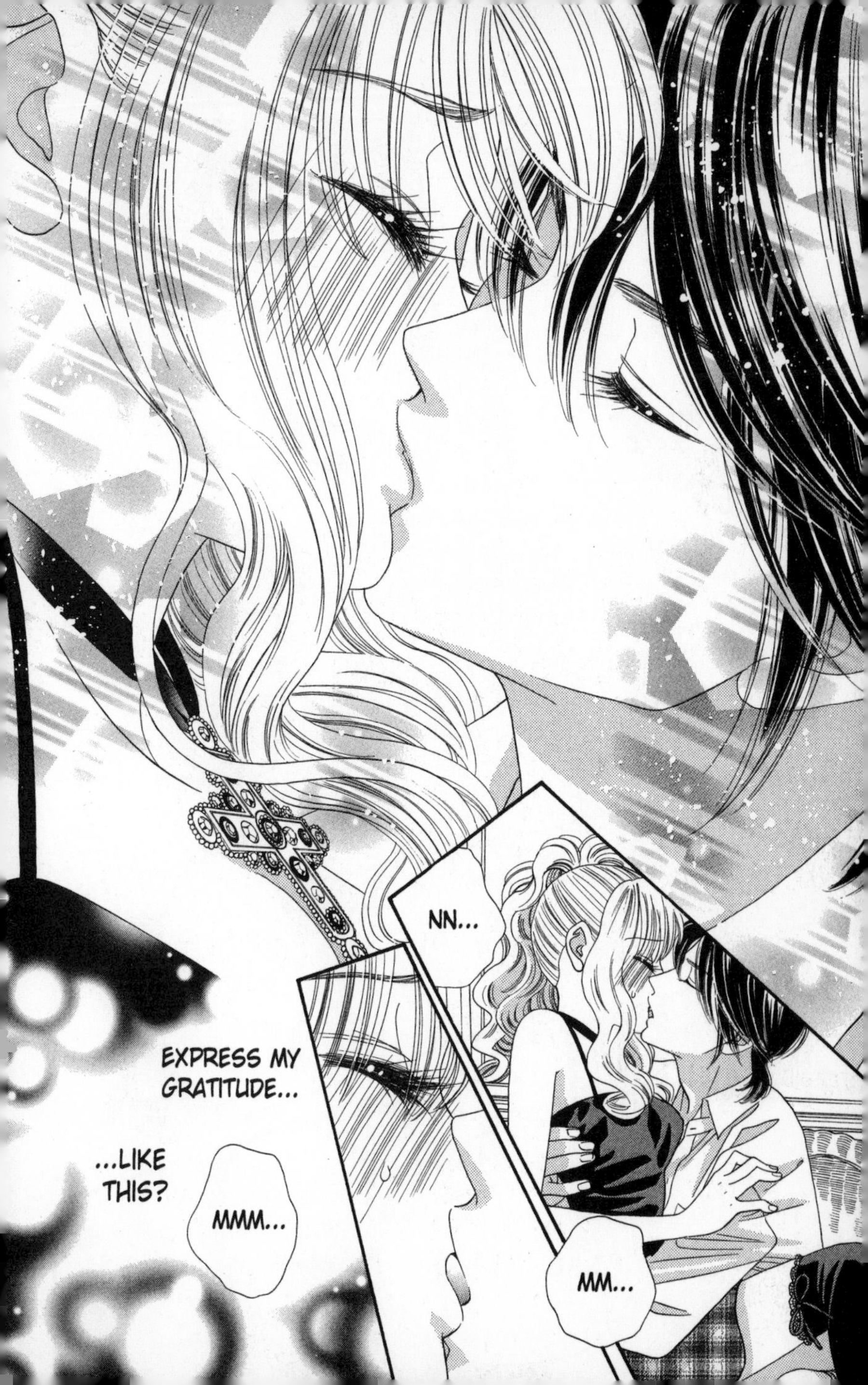

NN...
MM...
EXPRESS MY GRATITUDE...
...LIKE THIS?
MMM...

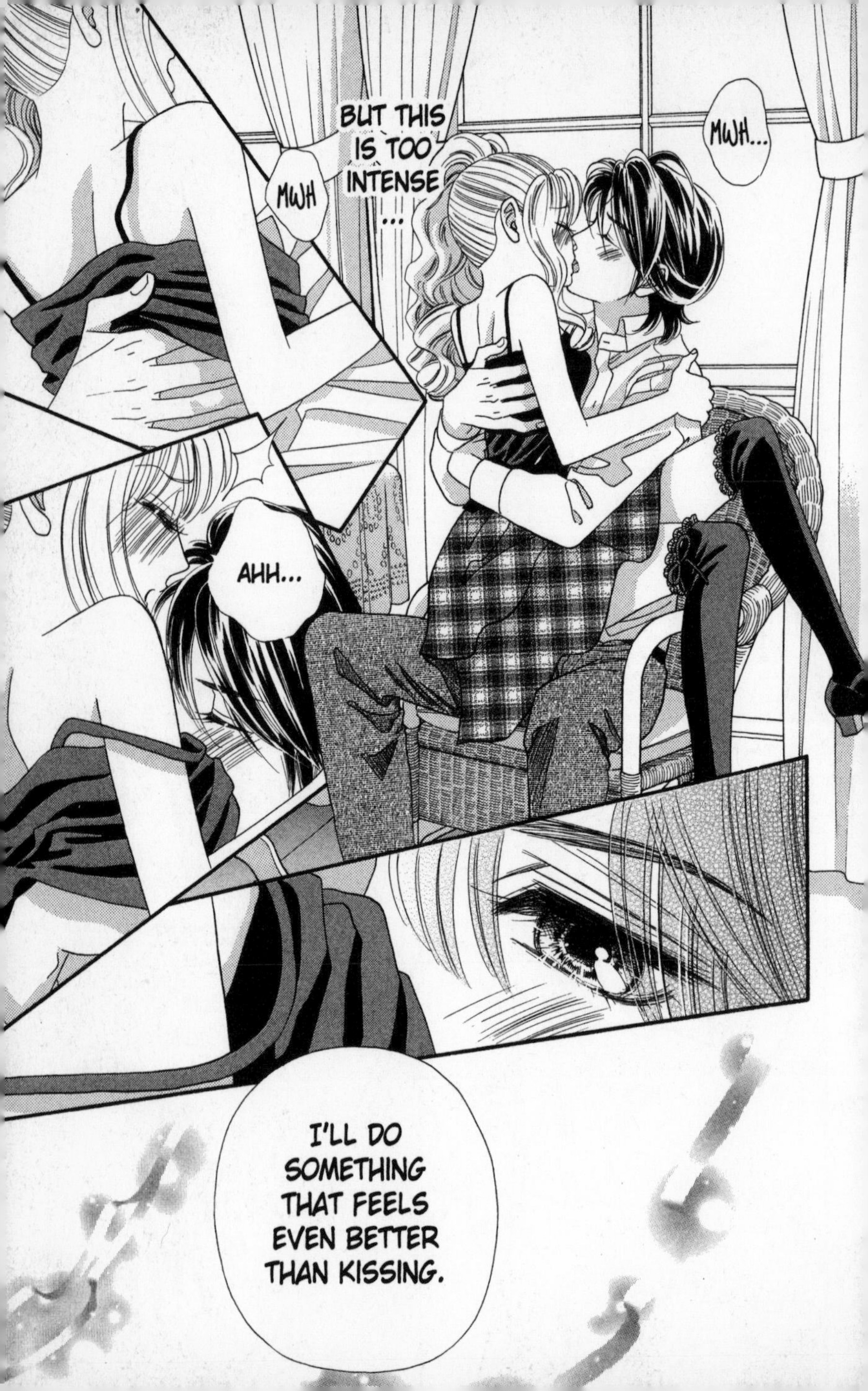
MWH...
BUT THIS IS TOO INTENSE...
MWH
AHH...
I'LL DO SOMETHING THAT FEELS EVEN BETTER THAN KISSING.

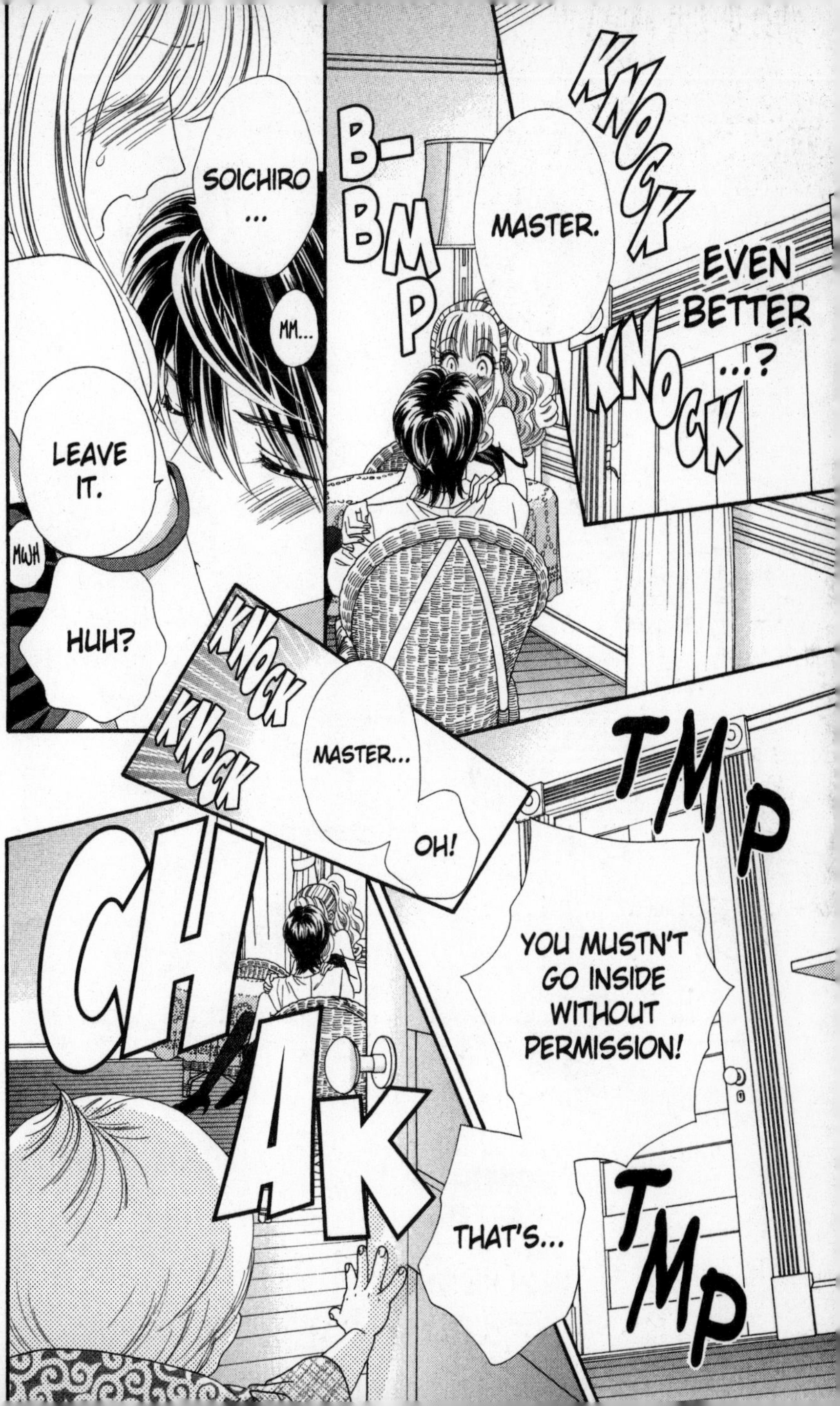
KNOCK
EVEN BETTER ...?
KNOCK
MASTER.
B-BMP
SOICHIRO ...
MM...
LEAVE IT.
MWH
HUH?
KNOCK KNOCK
MASTER...
OH!
TMP
YOU MUSTN'T GO INSIDE WITHOUT PERMISSION!
TMP
THAT'S...
CHAK

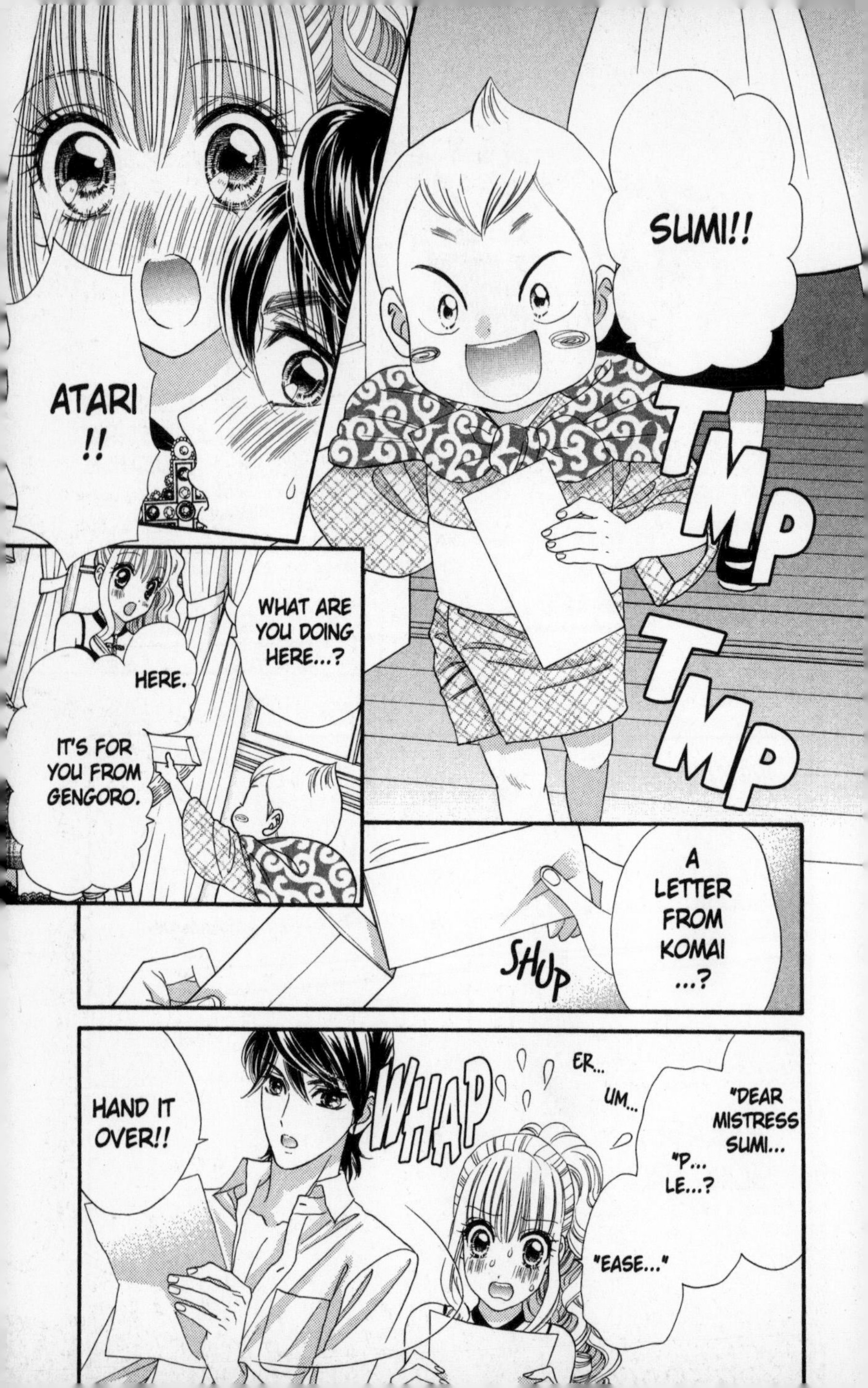
SUMI!!
TMP
TMP
ATARI!!
WHAT ARE YOU DOING HERE...?
HERE.
IT'S FOR YOU FROM GENGORO.
A LETTER FROM KOMAI...?
SHUP
"DEAR MISTRESS SUMI...
"P... LE...?
"EASE..."
ER...
UM...
WHAP
HAND IT OVER!!

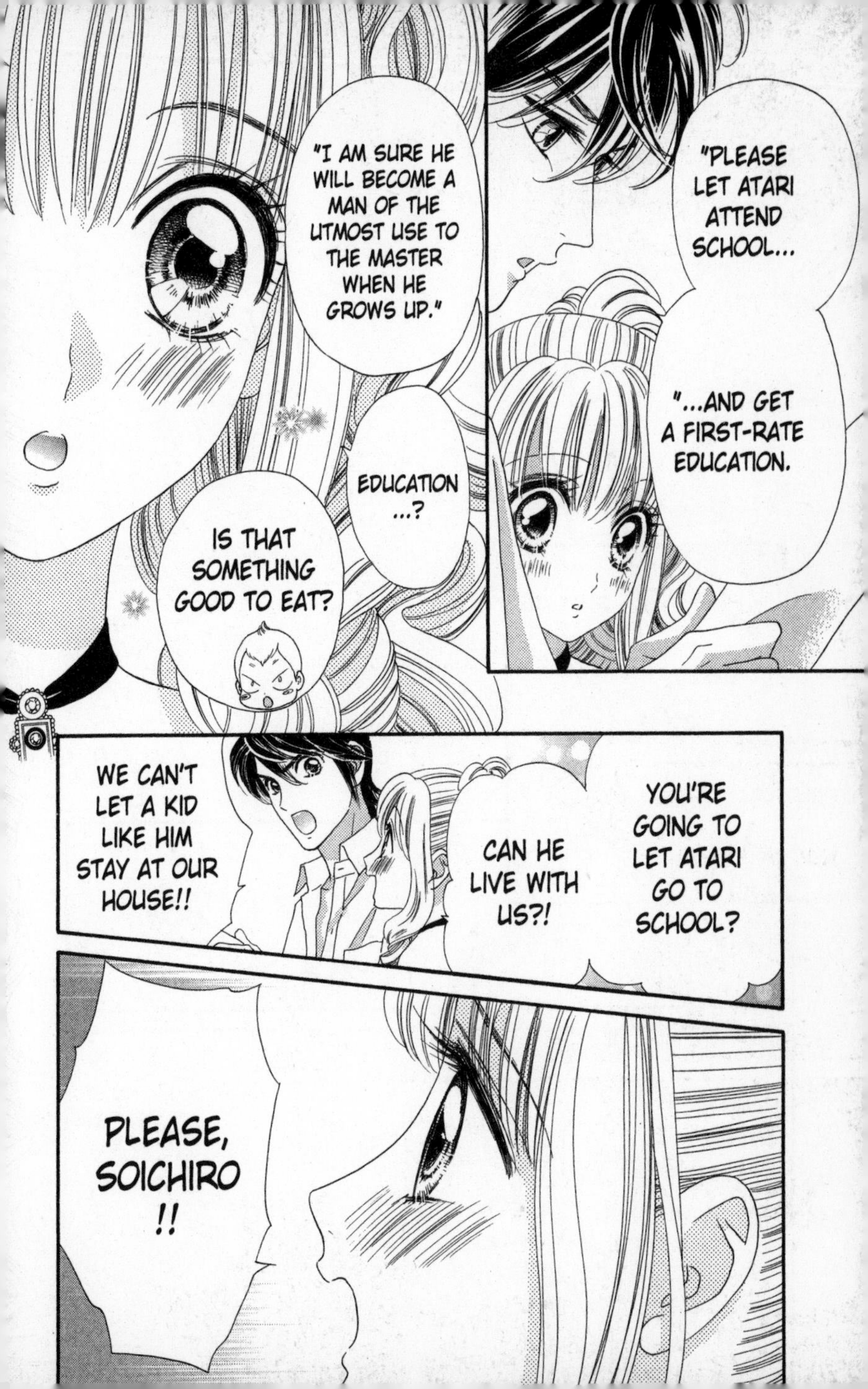
"PLEASE LET ATARI ATTEND SCHOOL...
"...AND GET A FIRST-RATE EDUCATION.
"I AM SURE HE WILL BECOME A MAN OF THE UTMOST USE TO THE MASTER WHEN HE GROWS UP."
EDUCATION ...?
IS THAT SOMETHING GOOD TO EAT?
YOU'RE GOING TO LET ATARI GO TO SCHOOL?
CAN HE LIVE WITH US?!
WE CAN'T LET A KID LIKE HIM STAY AT OUR HOUSE!!
PLEASE, SOICHIRO !!

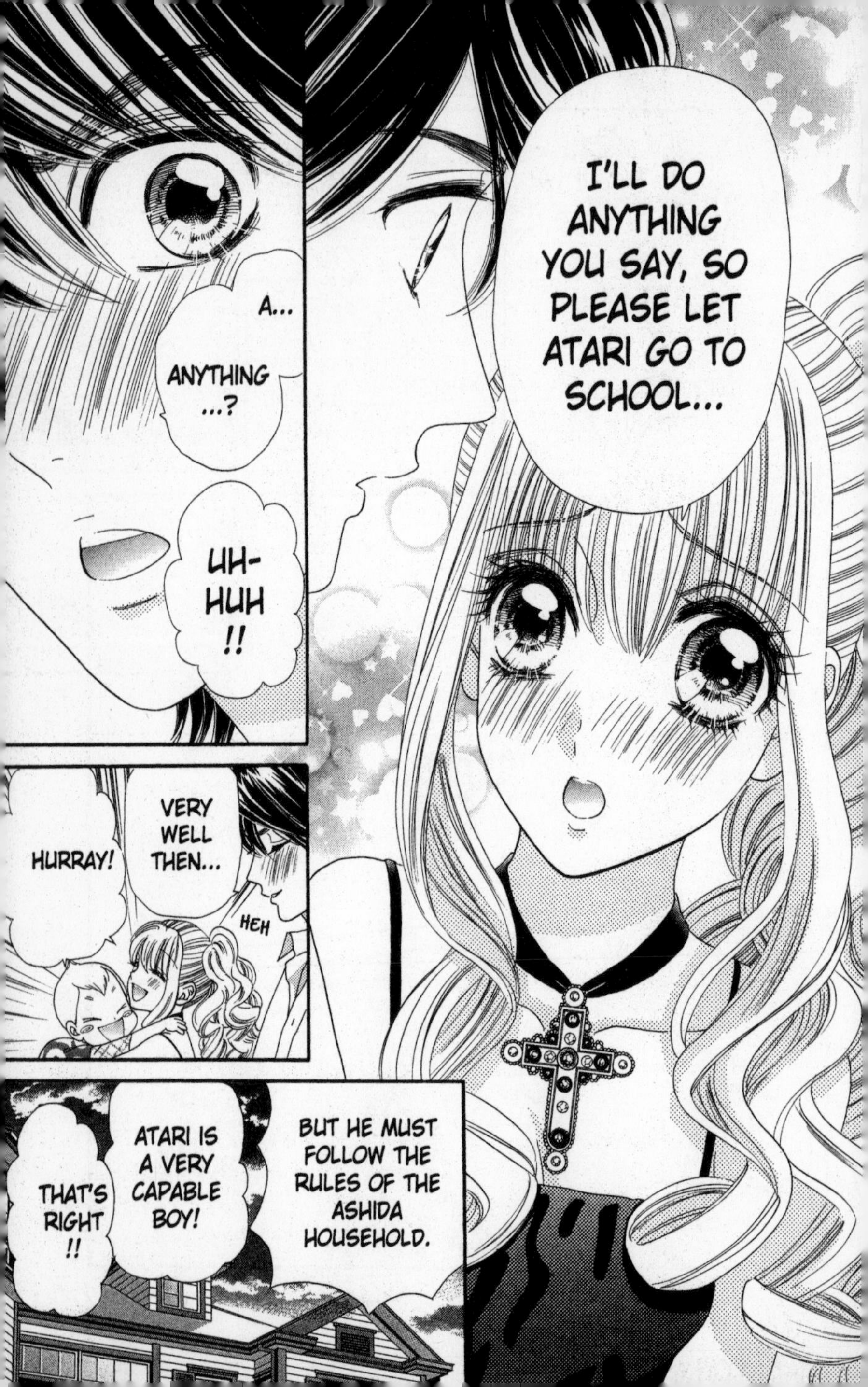
I'LL DO ANYTHING YOU SAY, SO PLEASE LET ATARI GO TO SCHOOL...
A...
ANYTHING ...?
UH-HUH !!
VERY WELL THEN...
HURRAY!
HEH
BUT HE MUST FOLLOW THE RULES OF THE ASHIDA HOUSEHOLD.
ATARI IS A VERY CAPABLE BOY!
THAT'S RIGHT !!

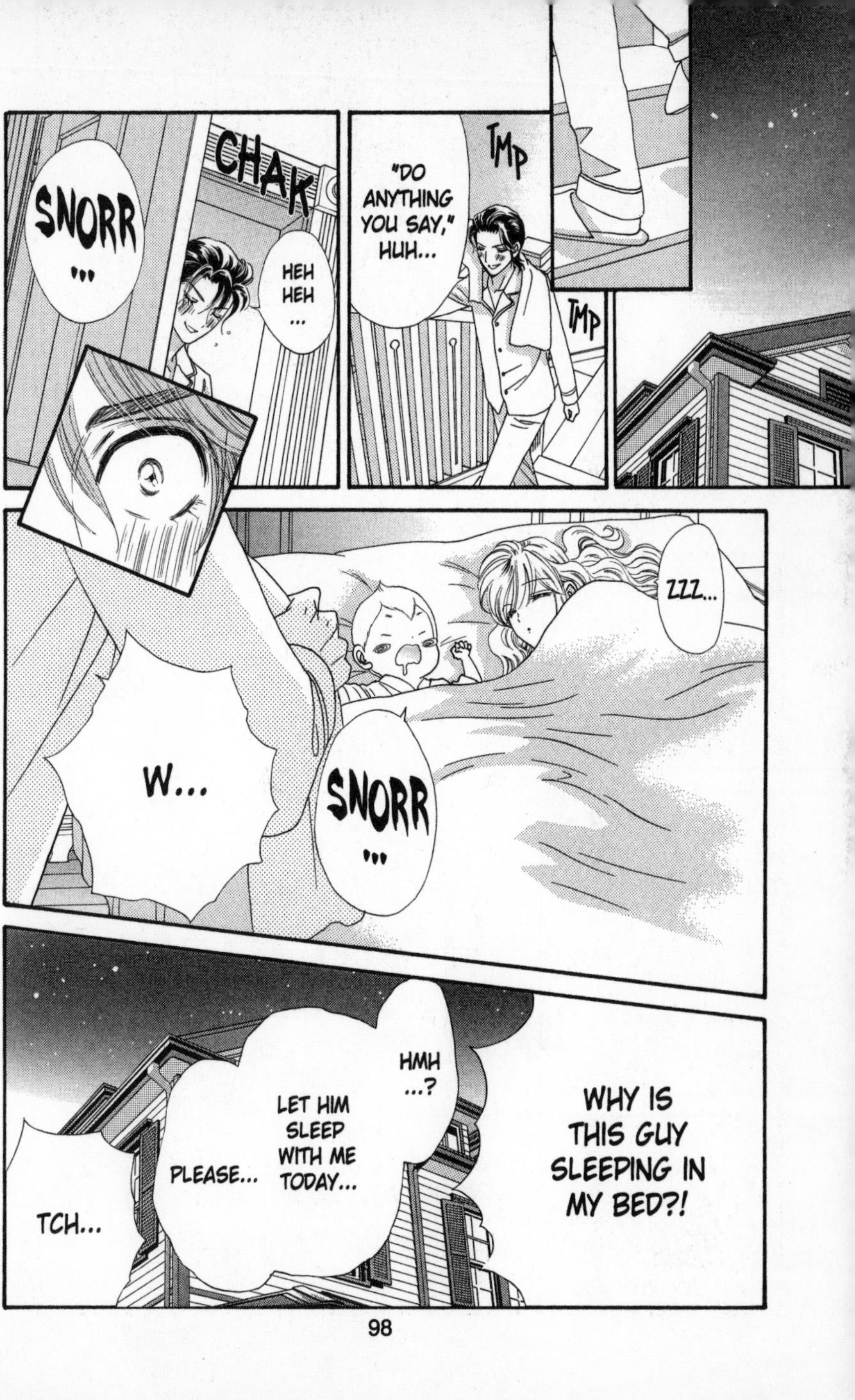
TMP
TMP
TMP
"DO ANYTHING YOU SAY," HUH...
CHAK
HEH HEH ...
SNORR ...
ZZZ...
SNORR ...
W...
WHY IS THIS GUY SLEEPING IN MY BED?!
HMH ...?
LET HIM SLEEP WITH ME TODAY...
PLEASE...
TCH...

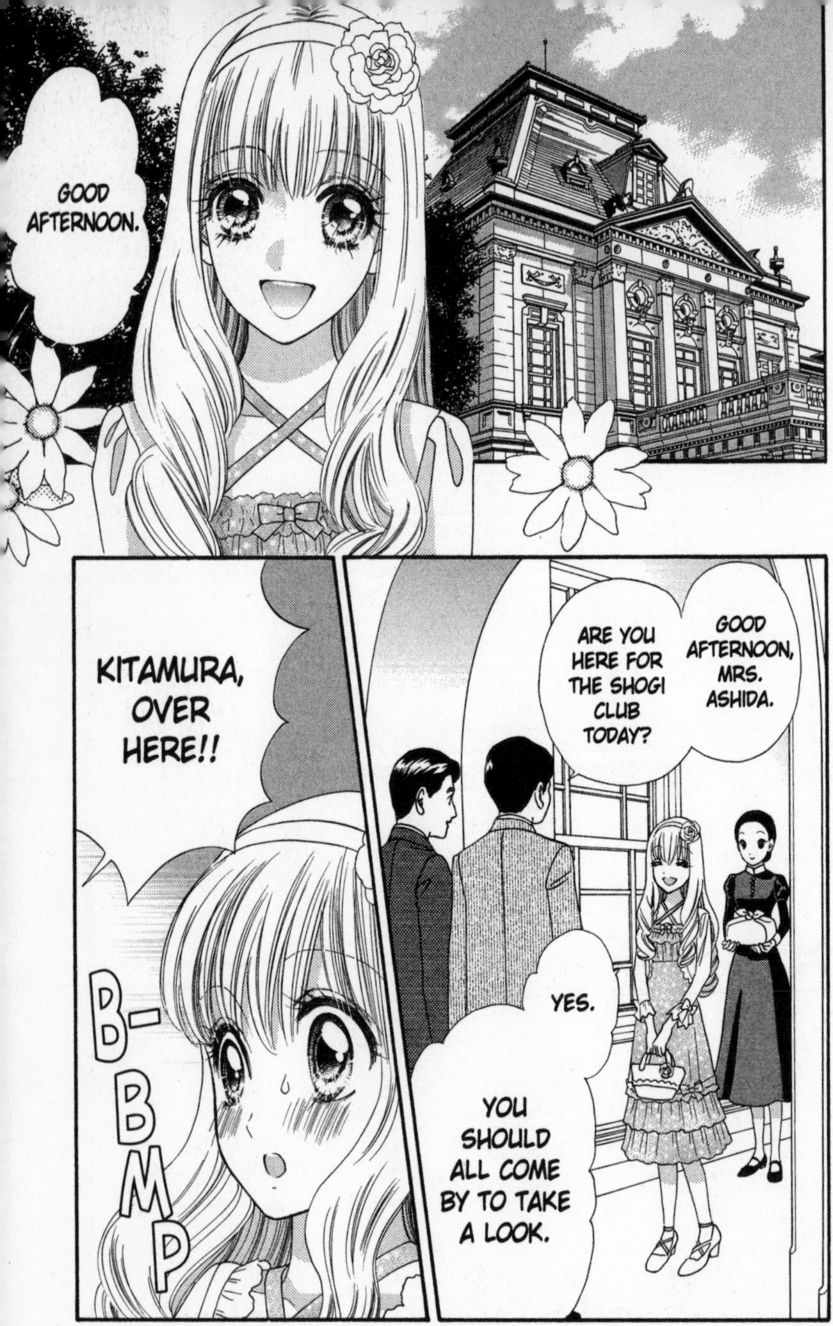
GOOD AFTERNOON.
GOOD AFTERNOON, MRS. ASHIDA.
ARE YOU HERE FOR THE SHOGI CLUB TODAY?
YES.
YOU SHOULD ALL COME BY TO TAKE A LOOK.
KITAMURA, OVER HERE!!
B-BMP

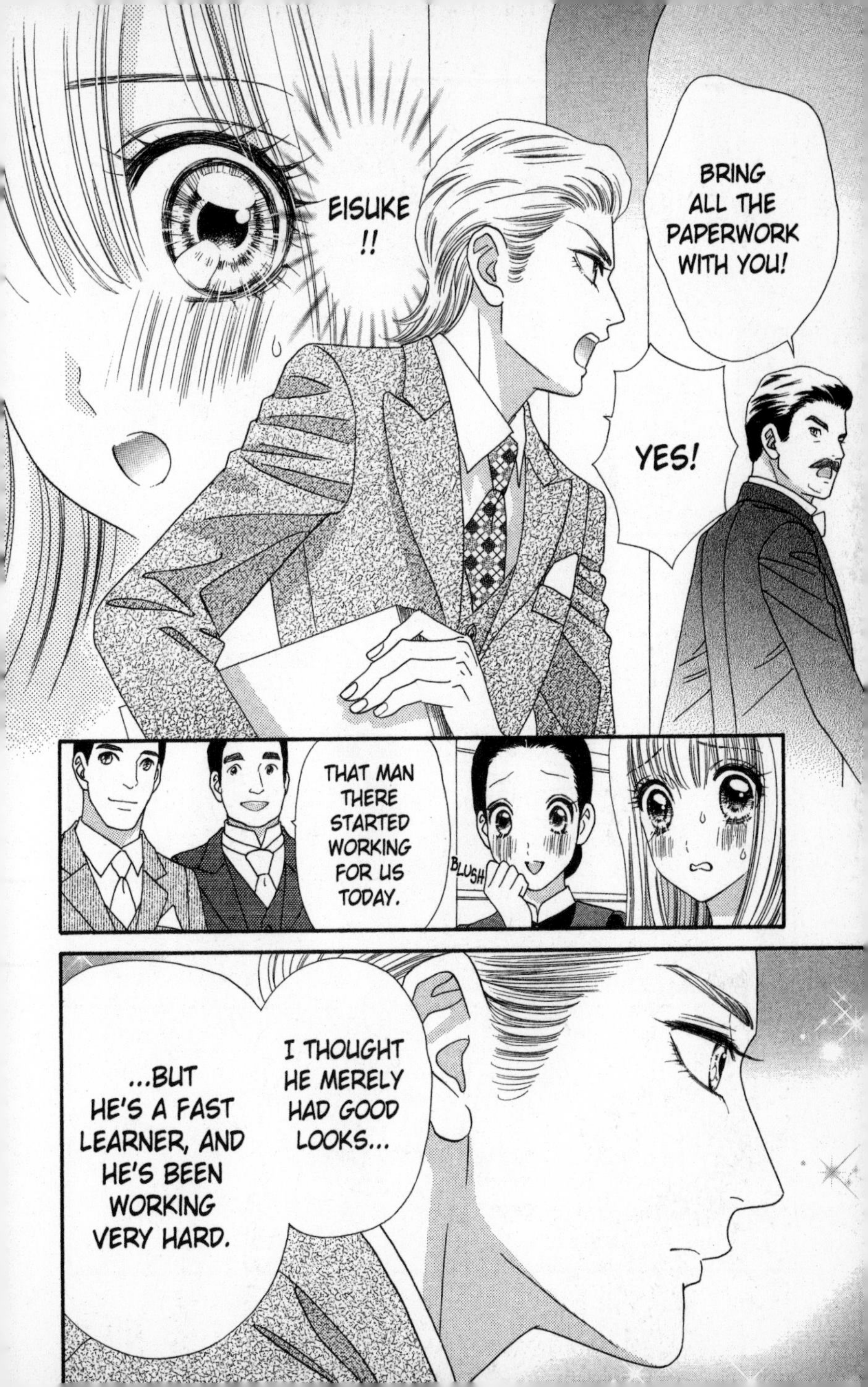

BRING ALL THE PAPERWORK WITH YOU!
YES!
EISUKE !!
THAT MAN THERE STARTED WORKING FOR US TODAY.
BLUSH
I THOUGHT HE MERELY HAD GOOD LOOKS...
...BUT HE'S A FAST LEARNER, AND HE'S BEEN WORKING VERY HARD.

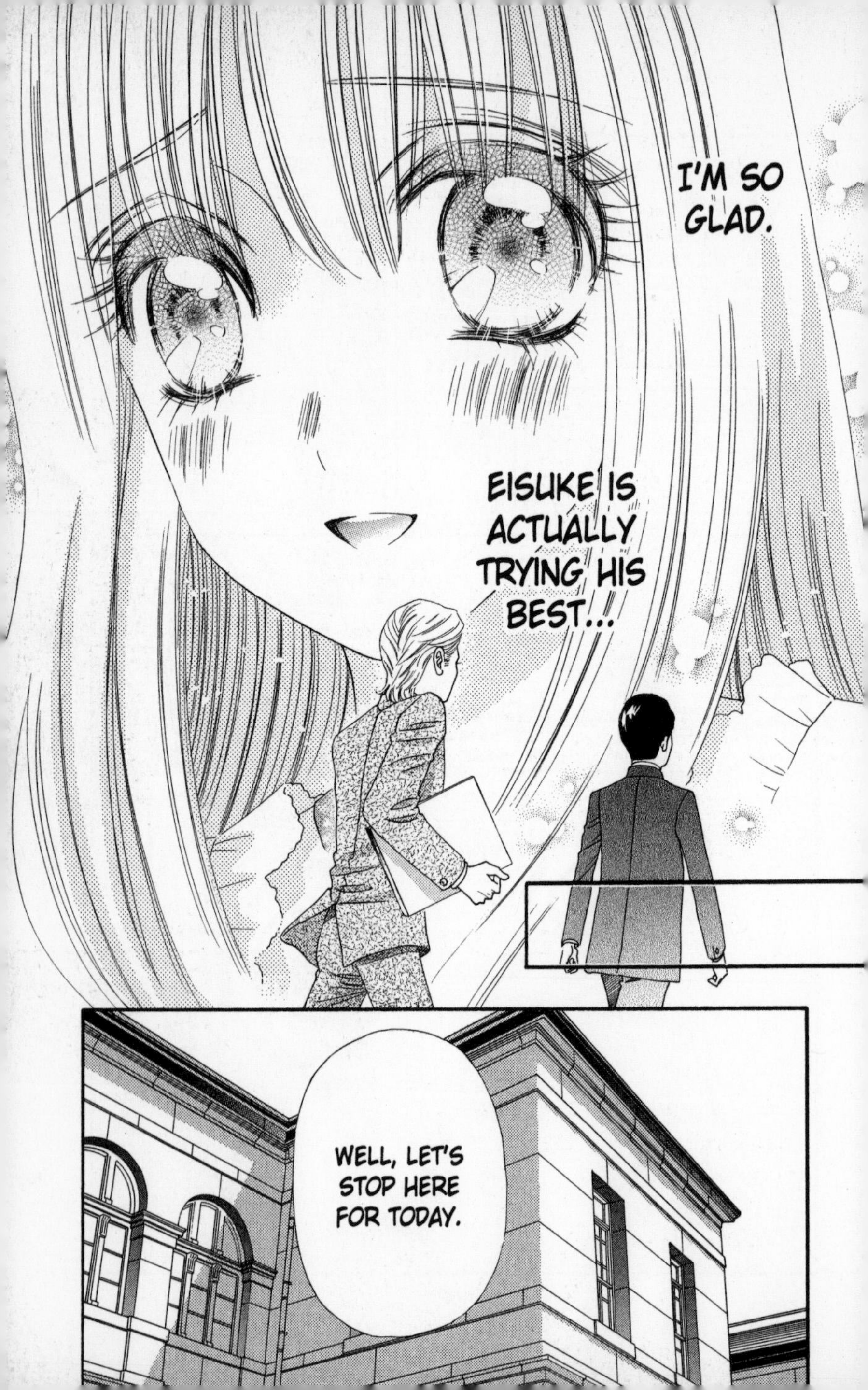
I'M SO GLAD.
EISUKE IS ACTUALLY TRYING HIS BEST...
WELL, LET'S STOP HERE FOR TODAY.

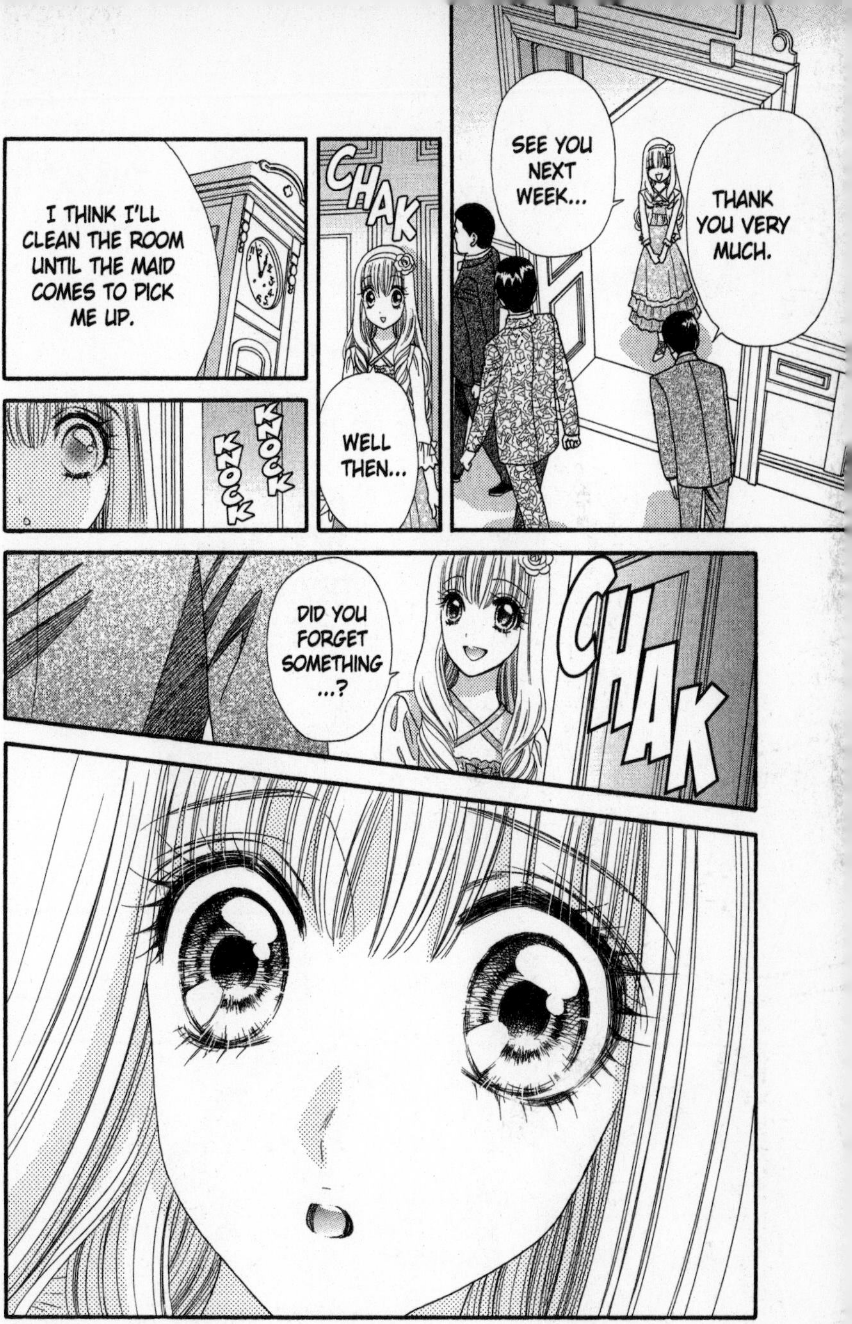
THANK YOU VERY MUCH.
SEE YOU NEXT WEEK...
CHAK
I THINK I'LL CLEAN THE ROOM UNTIL THE MAID COMES TO PICK ME UP.
WELL THEN...
KNOCK KNOCK
CHAK
DID YOU FORGET SOMETHING ...?

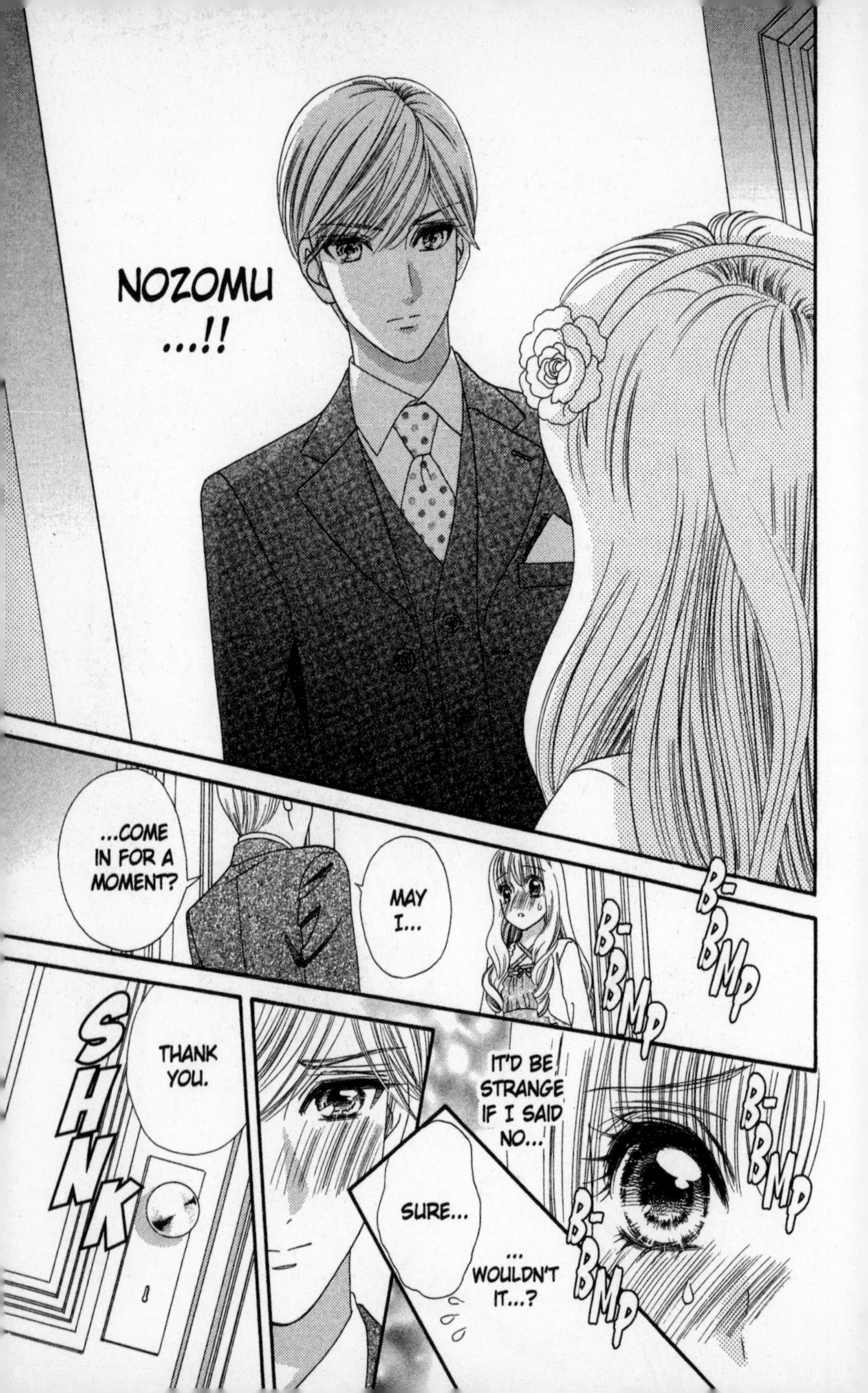
NOZOMU ...!!
B-BMP
B-BMP
MAY I...
...COME IN FOR A MOMENT?
B-BMP
B-BMP
IT'D BE STRANGE IF I SAID NO...
SURE...
...WOULDN'T IT...?
THANK YOU.
SHHNK

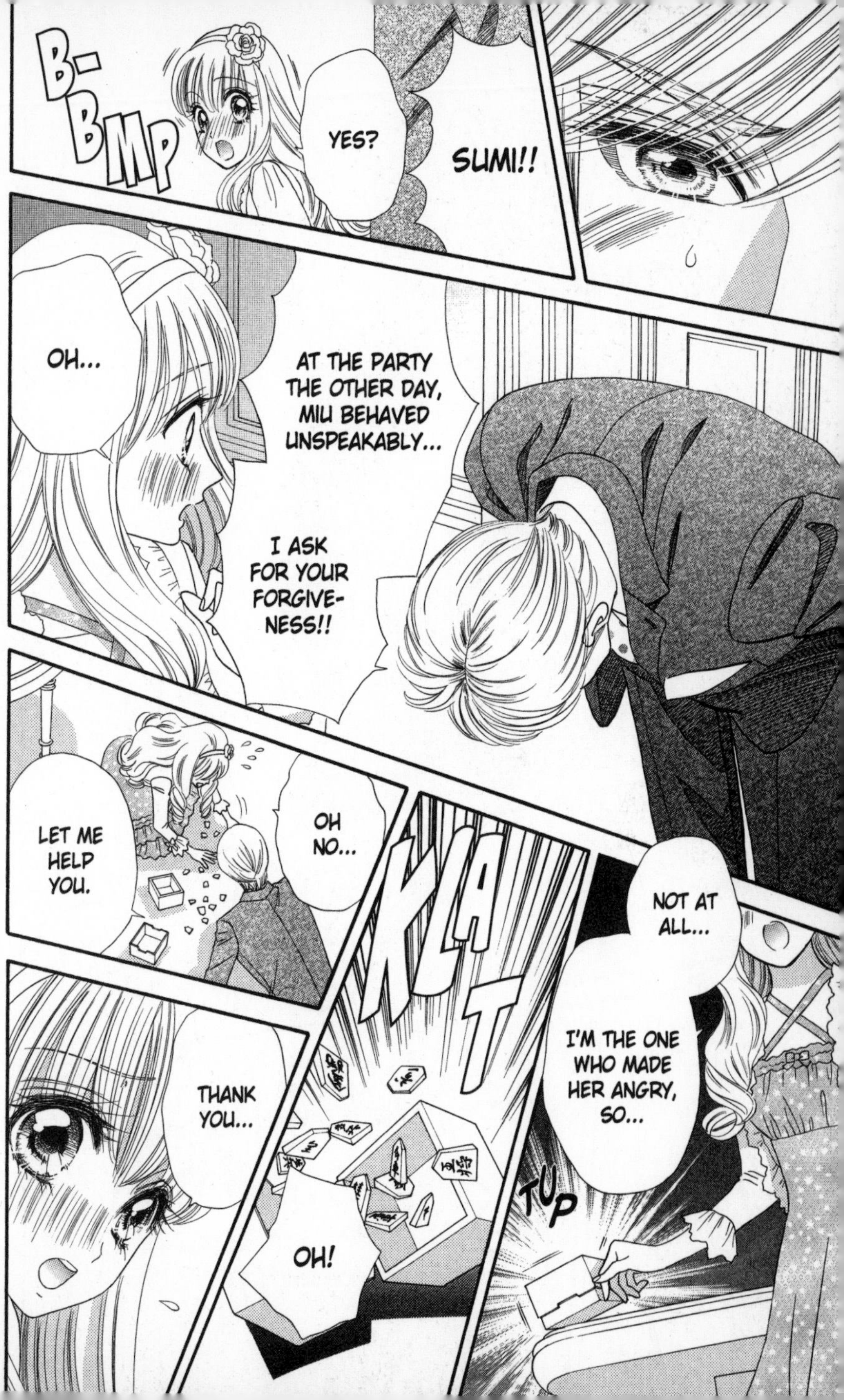
SUMI!!
YES?
B-BMP
AT THE PARTY THE OTHER DAY, MIU BEHAVED UNSPEAKABLY...
I ASK FOR YOUR FORGIVE-NESS!!
OH...
NOT AT ALL...
I'M THE ONE WHO MADE HER ANGRY, SO...
TUP
KLAT
OH!
OH NO...
LET ME HELP YOU.
THANK YOU...

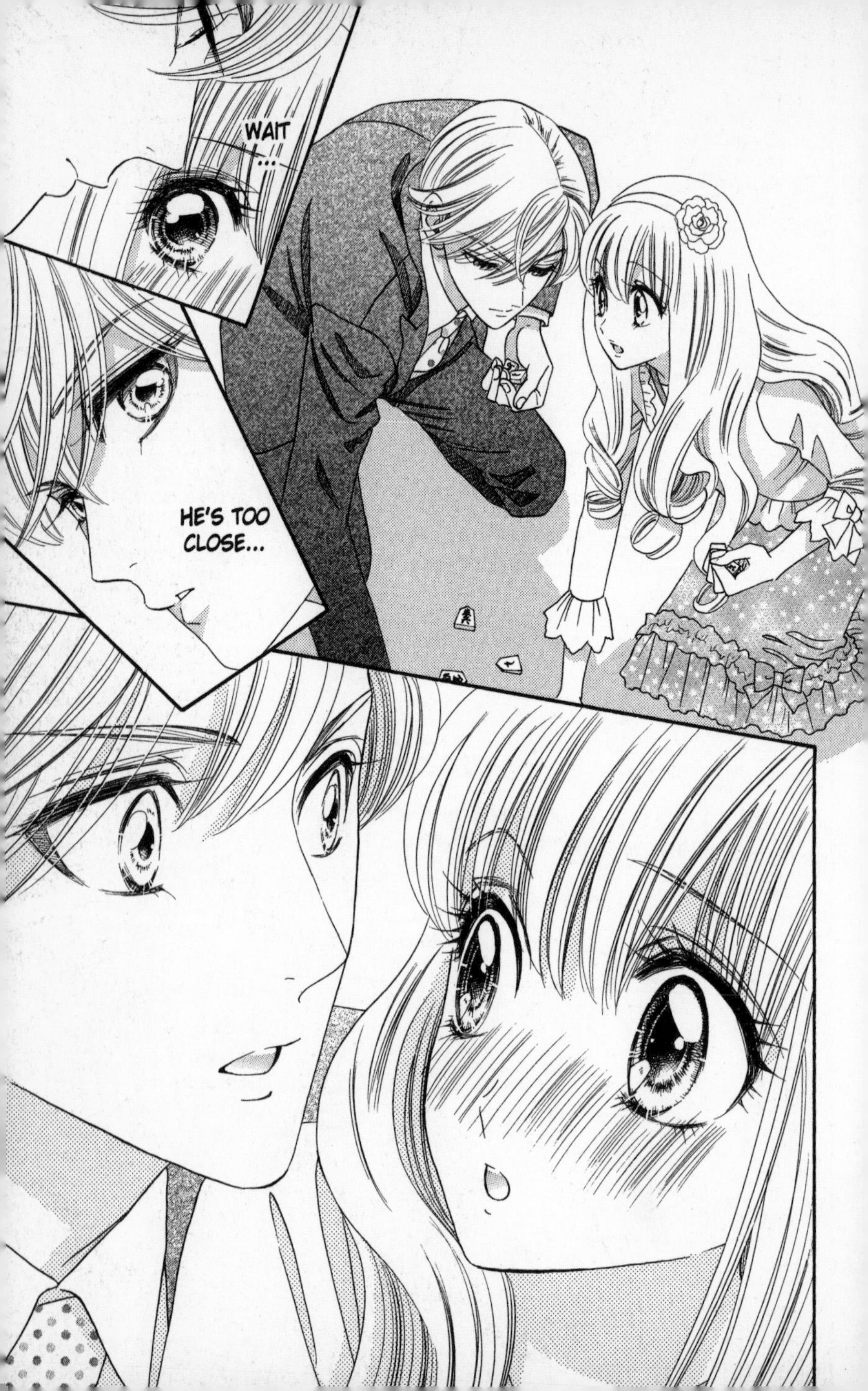
WAIT ...
HE'S TOO CLOSE...

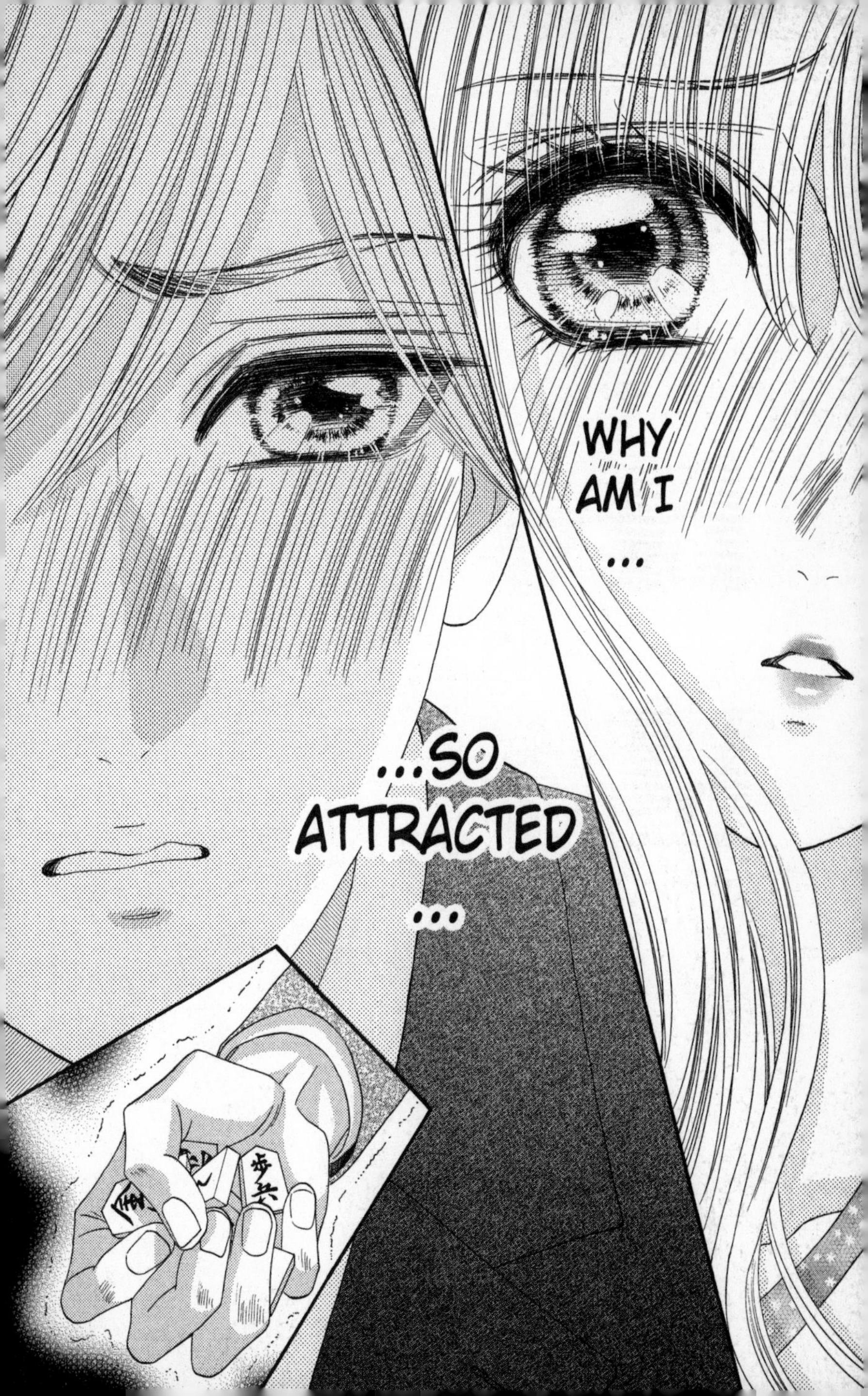
WHY AM I ...
...SO ATTRACTED ...

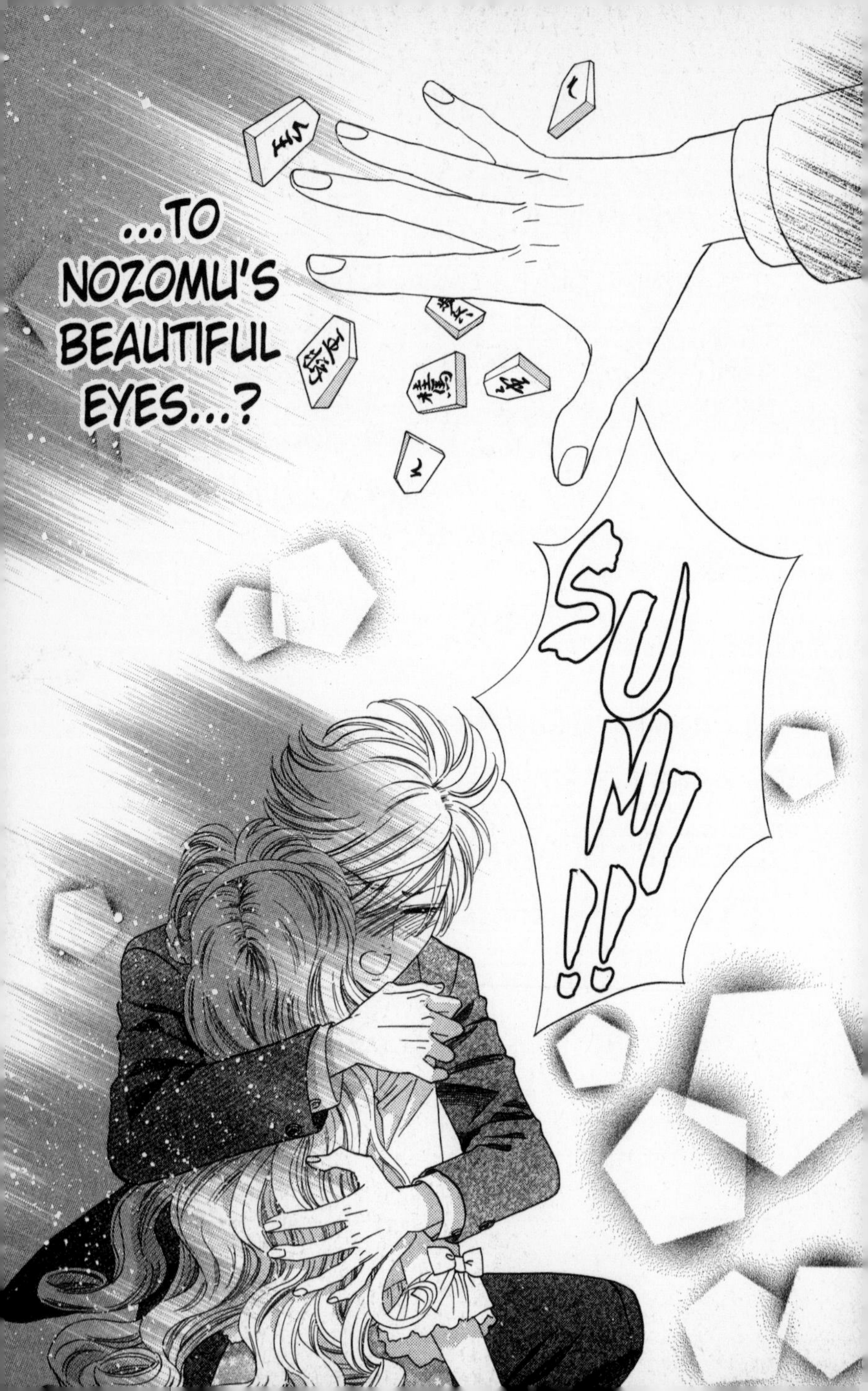
...TO NOZOMU'S BEAUTIFUL EYES...?
SUMI!!

RANDOM CHITCHAT

No. 4
Date . .

DAISUKE KISHIO PLAYED NOZOMU IJUIN.

A VERY NICE AND SMARTLY DRESSED PERSON!!

MR. KISHIO IS IN A GIRLS' VIDEO GAME THAT I AM ALSO VERY FOND OF (HE HAS A COMEDIC ROLE IN THAT GAME), SO IT WAS GREAT TO BE ABLE TO MEET HIM.

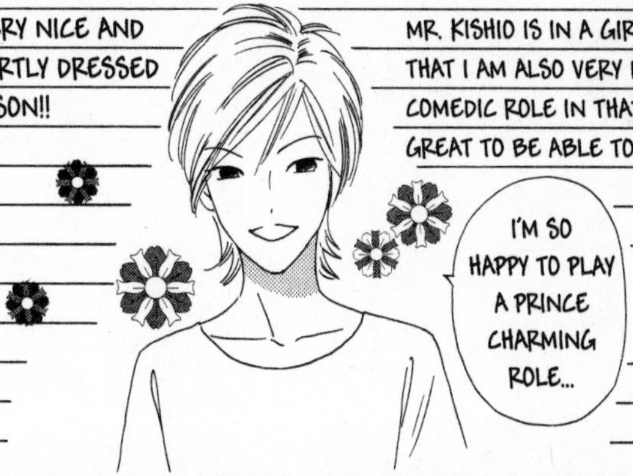
I'M SO HAPPY TO PLAY A PRINCE CHARMING ROLE...

✿ NOZOMU WAS STILL AN INNOCENT PRINCE IN CHAPTER 1...

I WOULD HAVE LOVED TO HEAR HIM READ NOZOMU'S DARK, EVIL LINES FROM VOLUME 2 AND ON.

A CONVERSATION BETWEEN THE VOICE ACTORS WAS RECORDED FOR VOMIC, AND EVERYBODY AT THE STUDIO COULDN'T STOP LAUGHING AT THE CHEERFUL THINGS MR. KISHIO SAID.

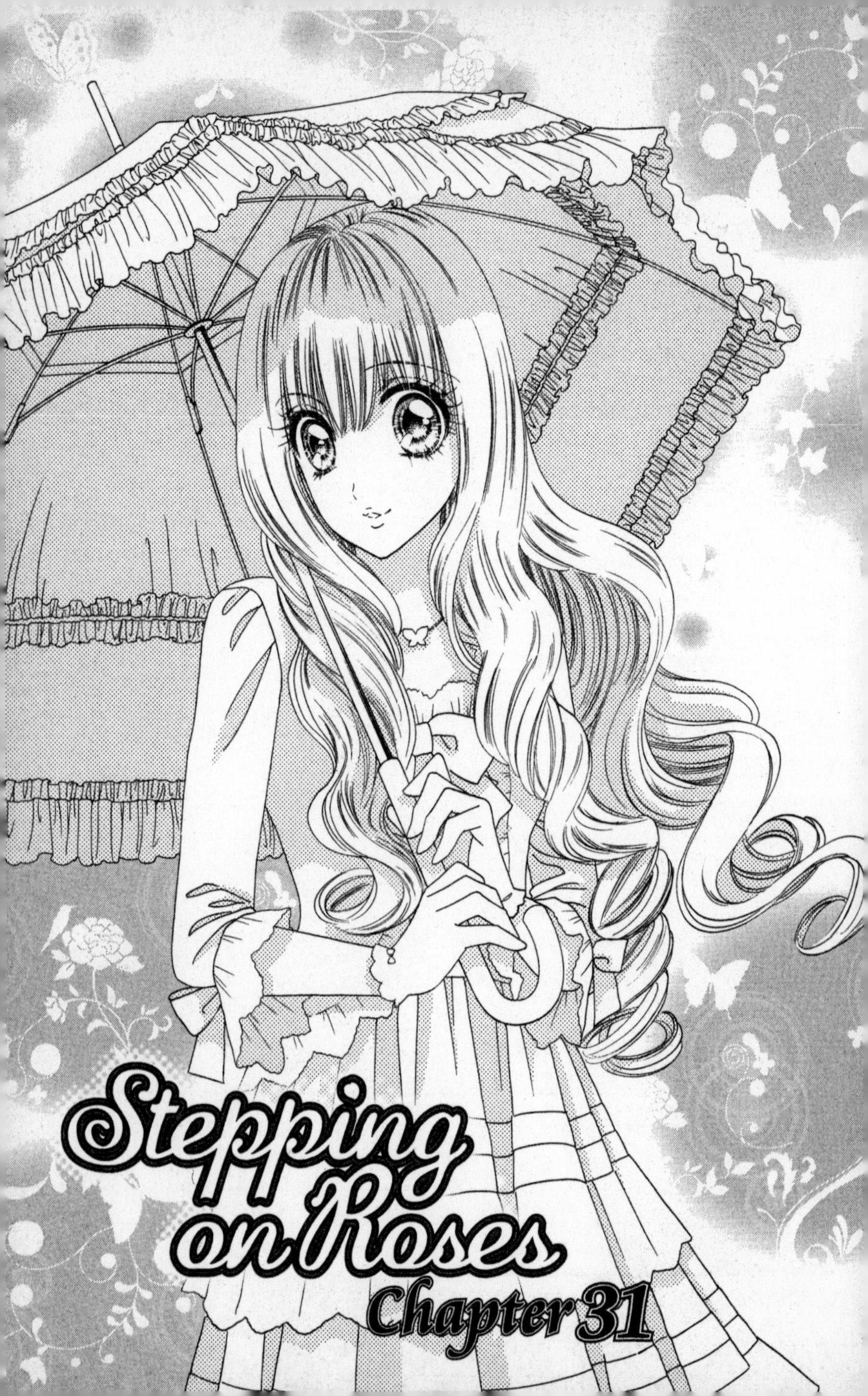
Stepping on Roses
Chapter 31

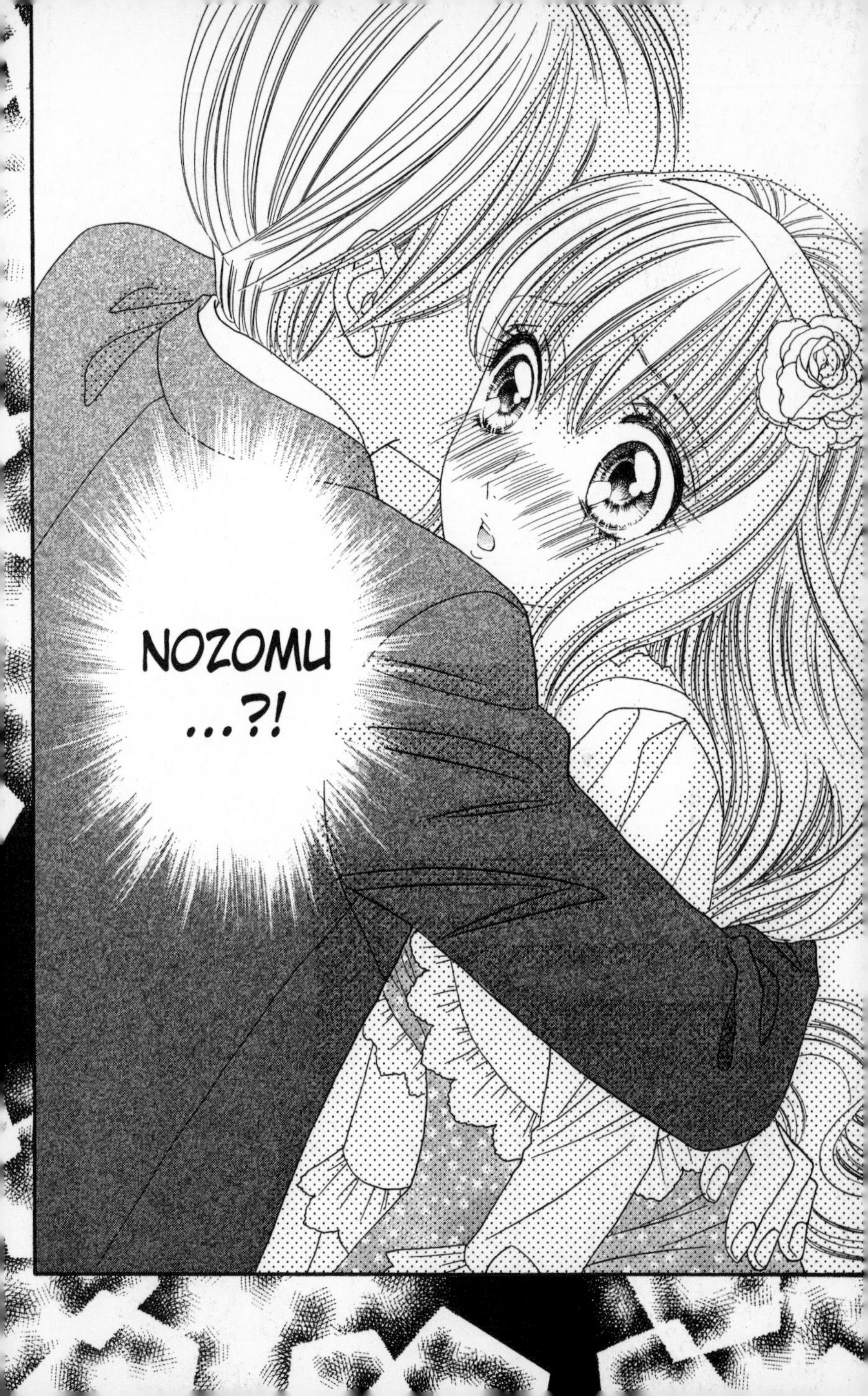
NOZOMU ...?!

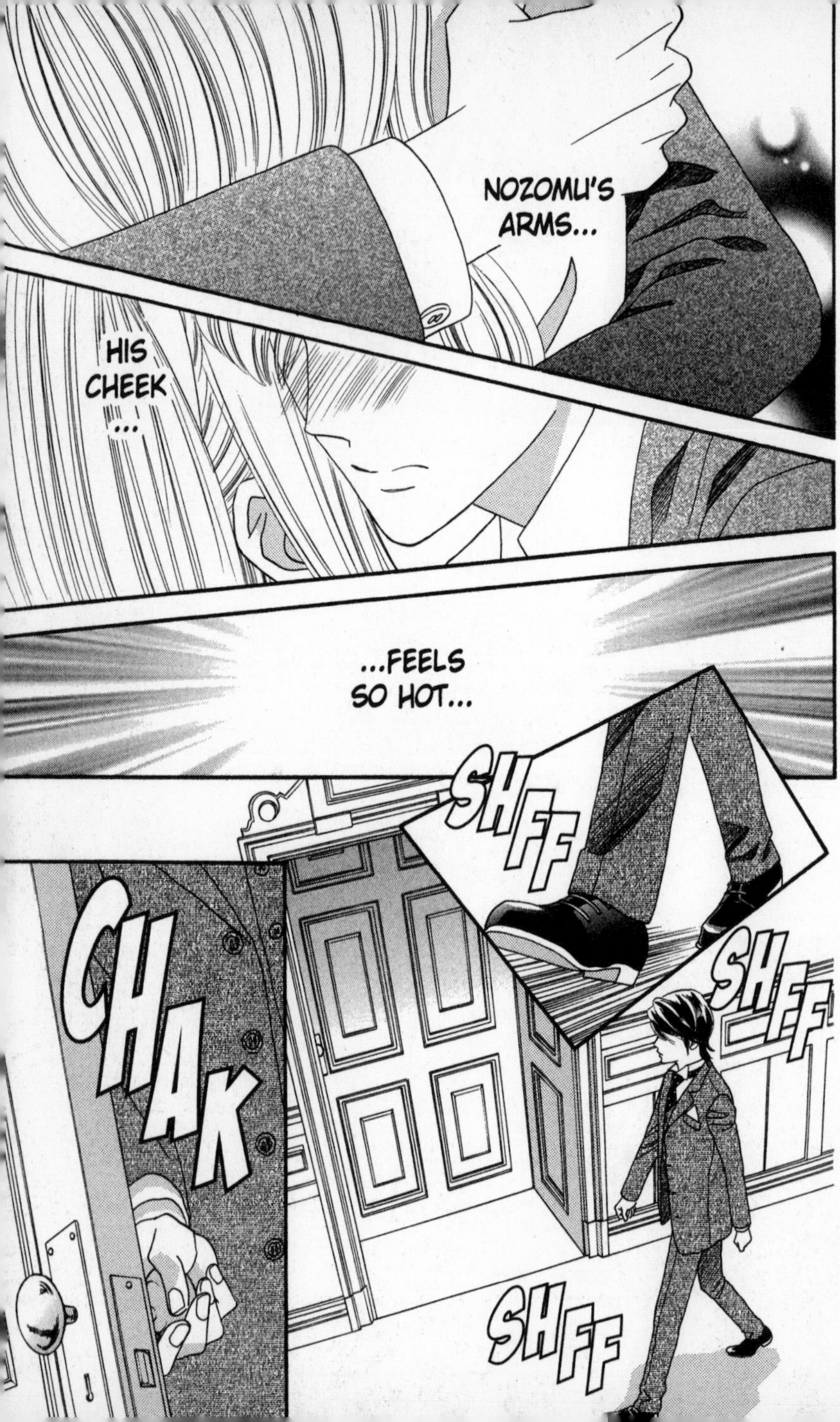
NOZOMU'S ARMS...
HIS CHEEK ...
...FEELS SO HOT...
SHFF
SHFF
CHAK
SHFF

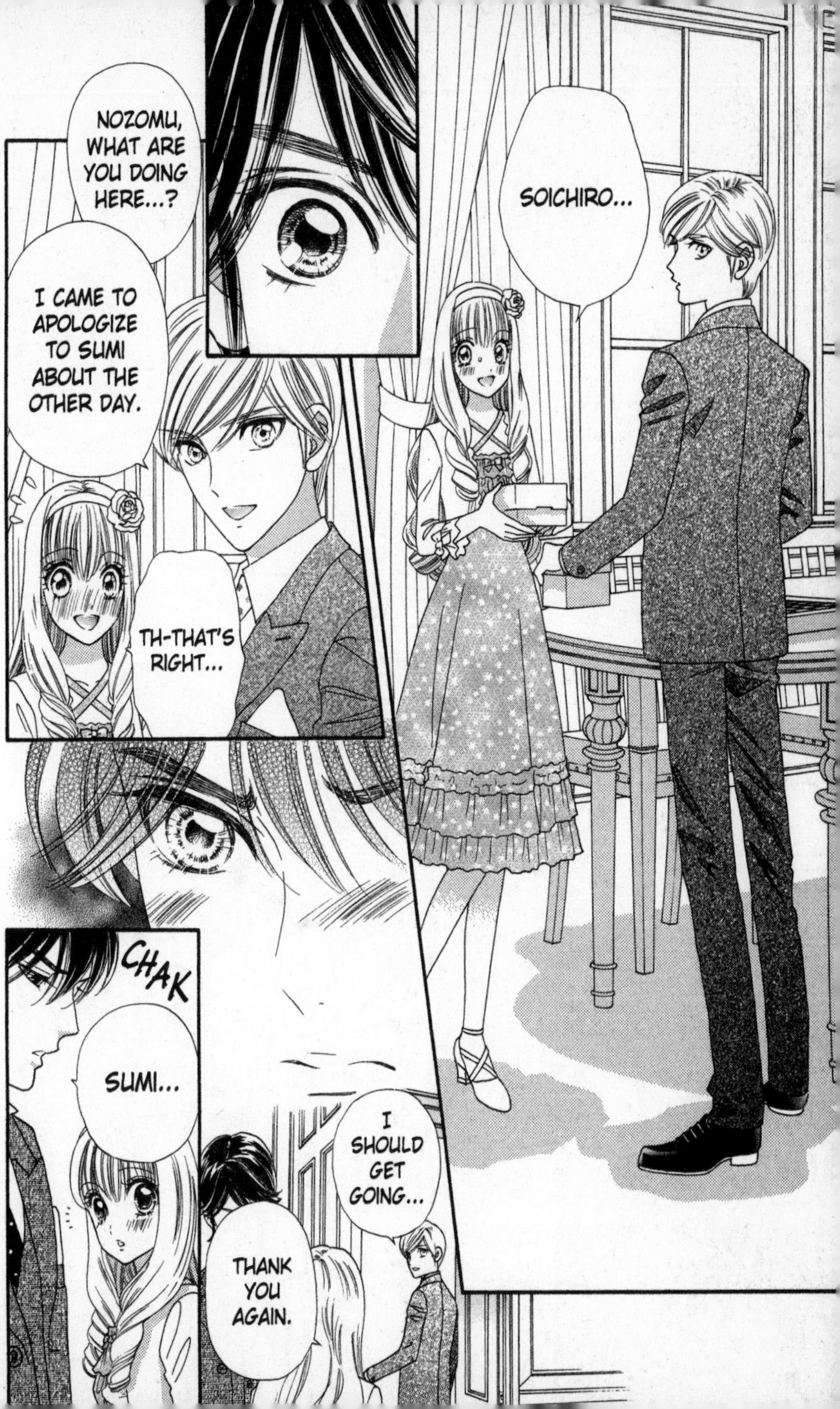
SOICHIRO...
NOZOMU, WHAT ARE YOU DOING HERE...?
I CAME TO APOLOGIZE TO SUMI ABOUT THE OTHER DAY.
TH-THAT'S RIGHT...
CHAK
SUMI...
I SHOULD GET GOING...
THANK YOU AGAIN.

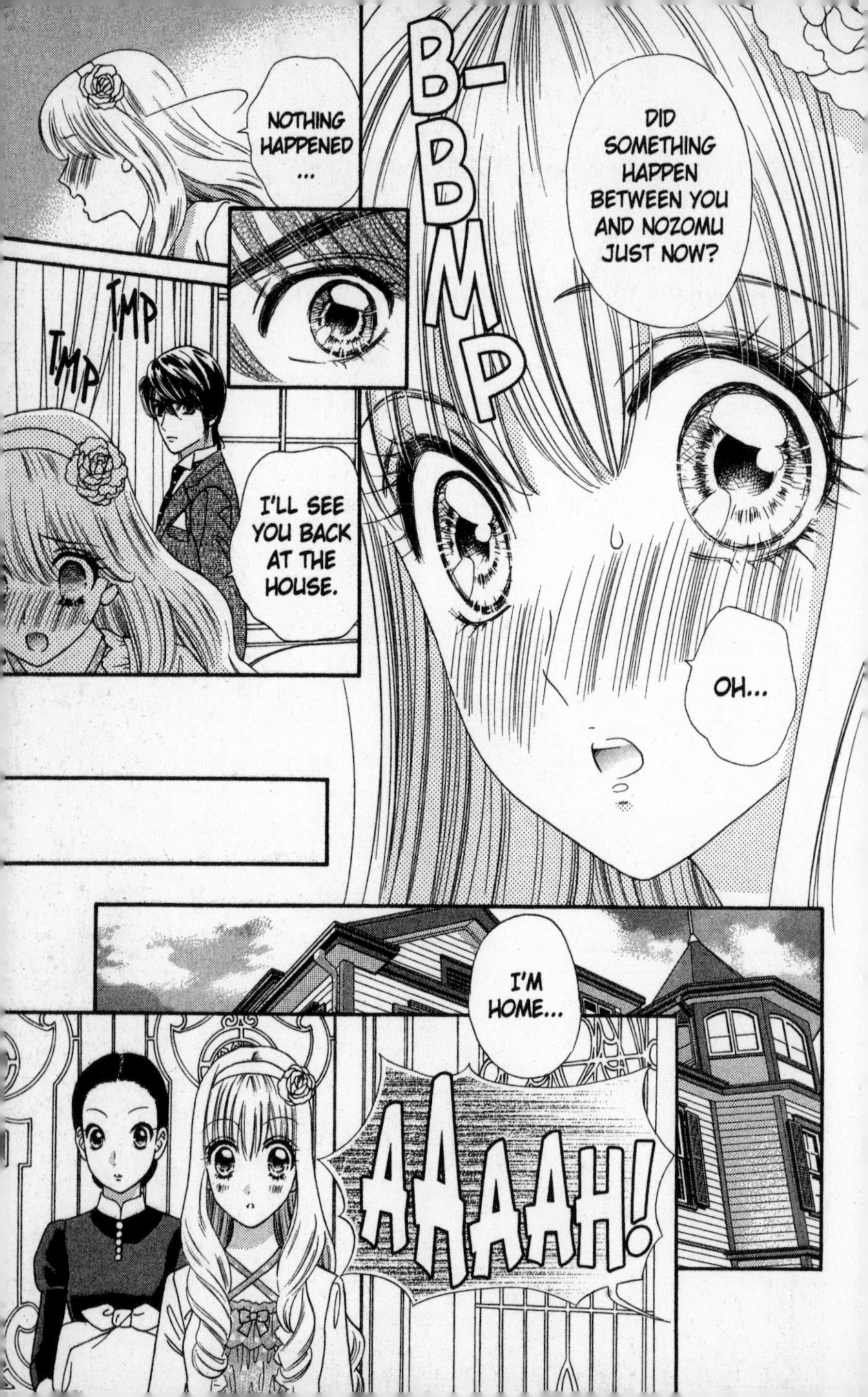
B-BMP
DID SOMETHING HAPPEN BETWEEN YOU AND NOZOMU JUST NOW?
OH...
NOTHING HAPPENED ...
TMP
TMP
I'LL SEE YOU BACK AT THE HOUSE.
I'M HOME...
AAAAH!

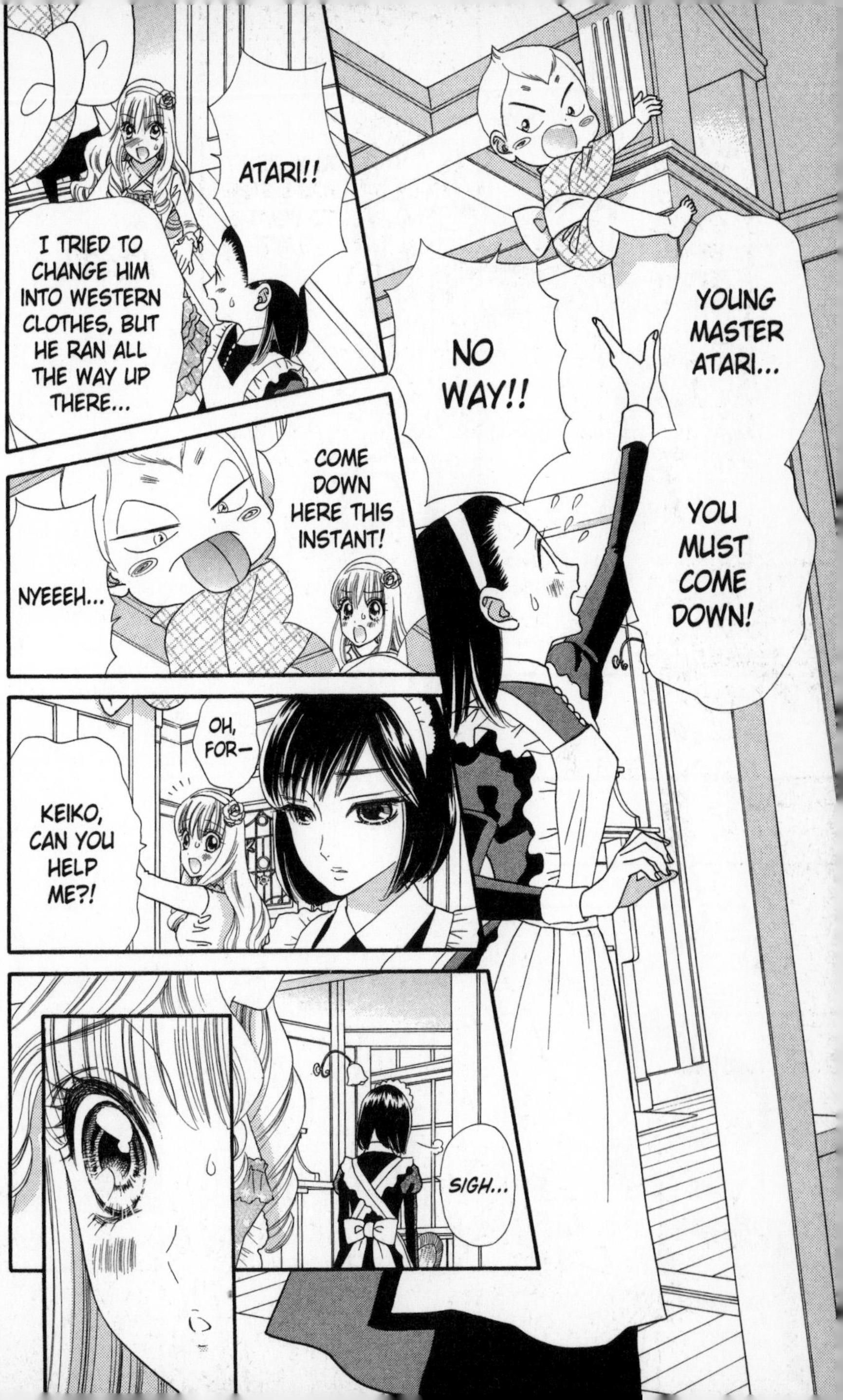
YOUNG MASTER ATARI...
NO WAY!!
YOU MUST COME DOWN!
COME DOWN HERE THIS INSTANT!
ATARI!!
I TRIED TO CHANGE HIM INTO WESTERN CLOTHES, BUT HE RAN ALL THE WAY UP THERE...
NYEEEH...
OH, FOR—
KEIKO, CAN YOU HELP ME?!
SIGH...

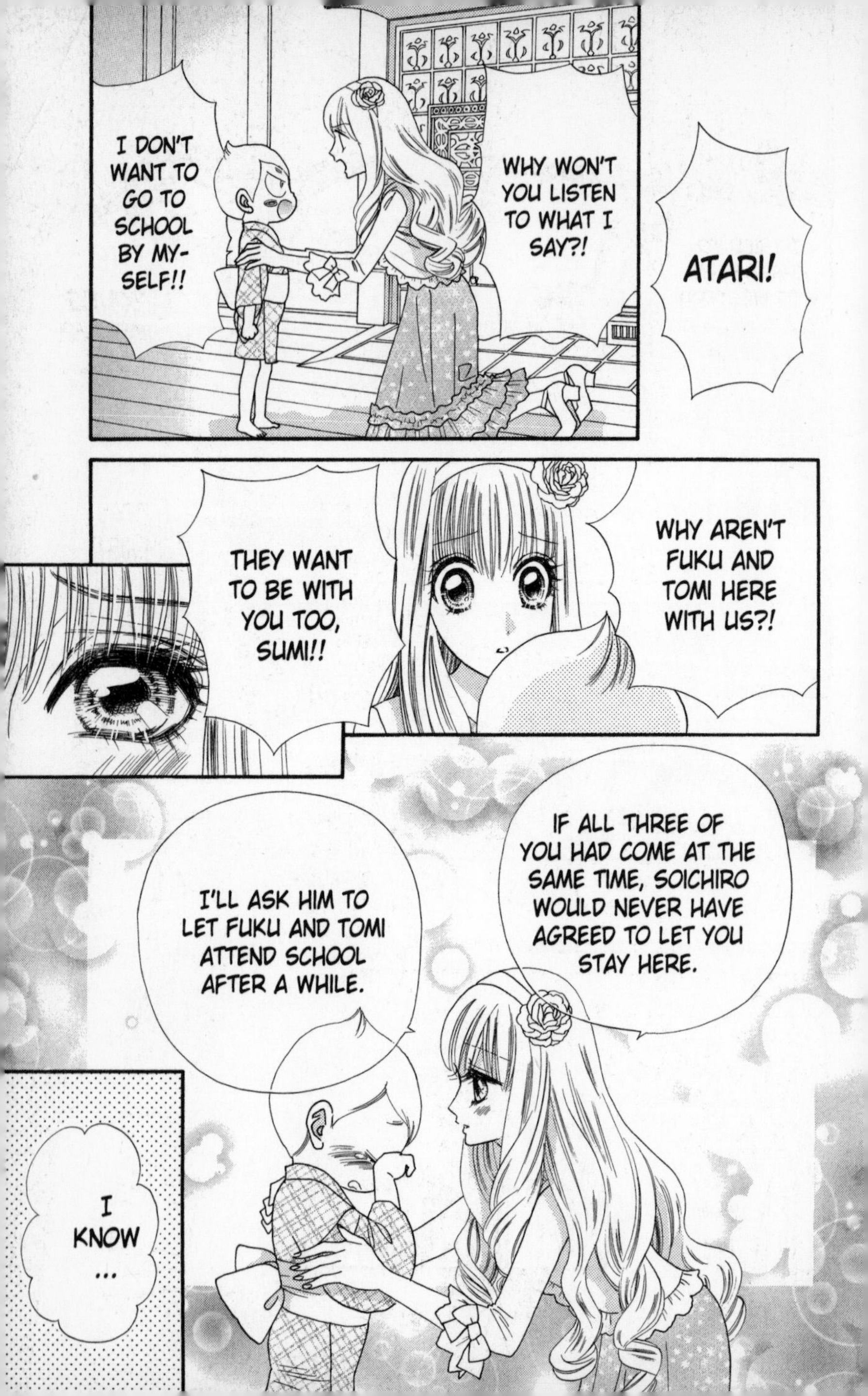
ATARI!
WHY WON'T YOU LISTEN TO WHAT I SAY?!
I DON'T WANT TO GO TO SCHOOL BY MY-SELF!!
WHY AREN'T FUKU AND TOMI HERE WITH US?!
THEY WANT TO BE WITH YOU TOO, SUMI!!
IF ALL THREE OF YOU HAD COME AT THE SAME TIME, SOICHIRO WOULD NEVER HAVE AGREED TO LET YOU STAY HERE.
I'LL ASK HIM TO LET FUKU AND TOMI ATTEND SCHOOL AFTER A WHILE.
I KNOW ...

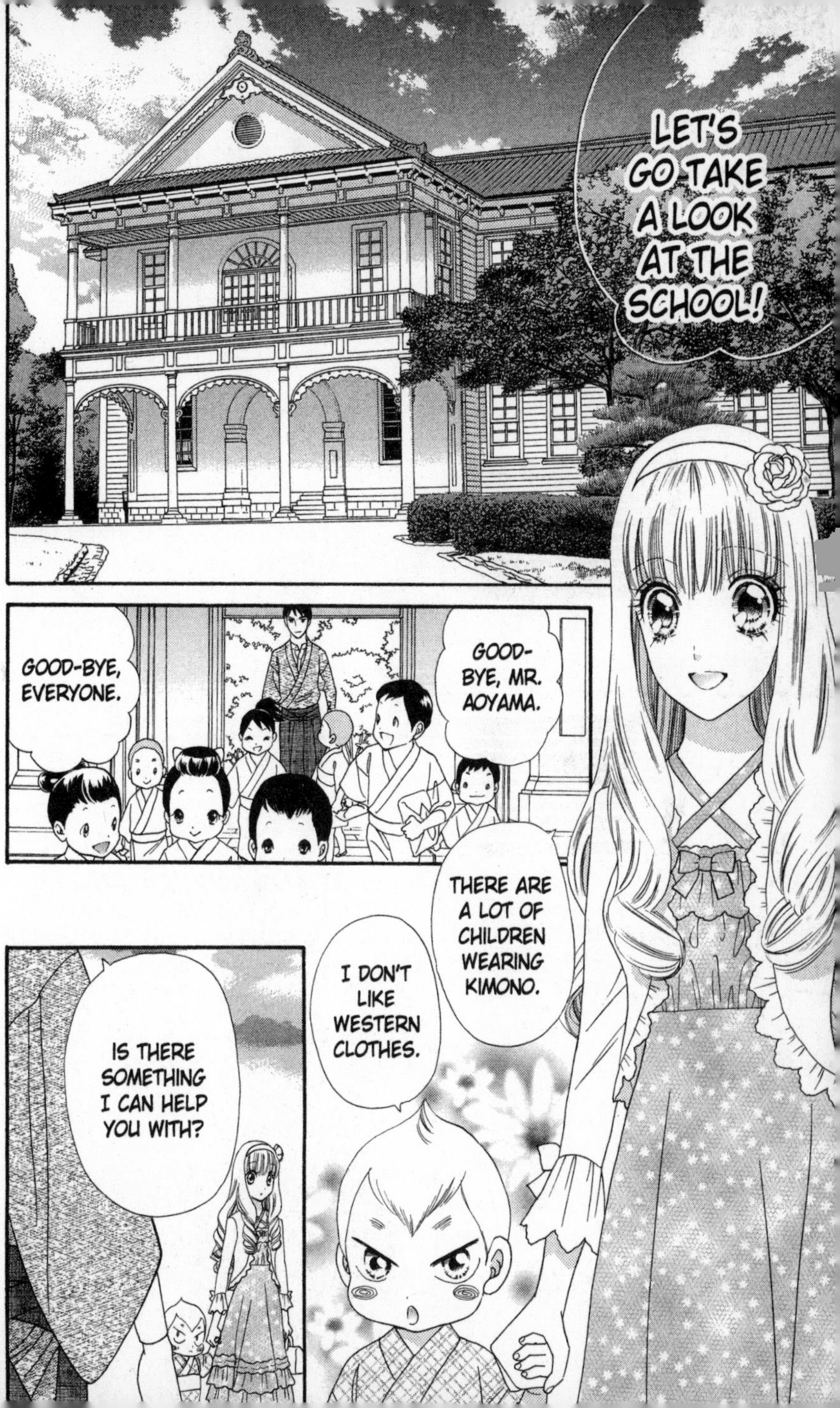
LET'S GO TAKE A LOOK AT THE SCHOOL!
THERE ARE A LOT OF CHILDREN WEARING KIMONO.
I DON'T LIKE WESTERN CLOTHES.
GOOD-BYE, MR. AOYAMA.
GOOD-BYE, EVERYONE.
IS THERE SOMETHING I CAN HELP YOU WITH?

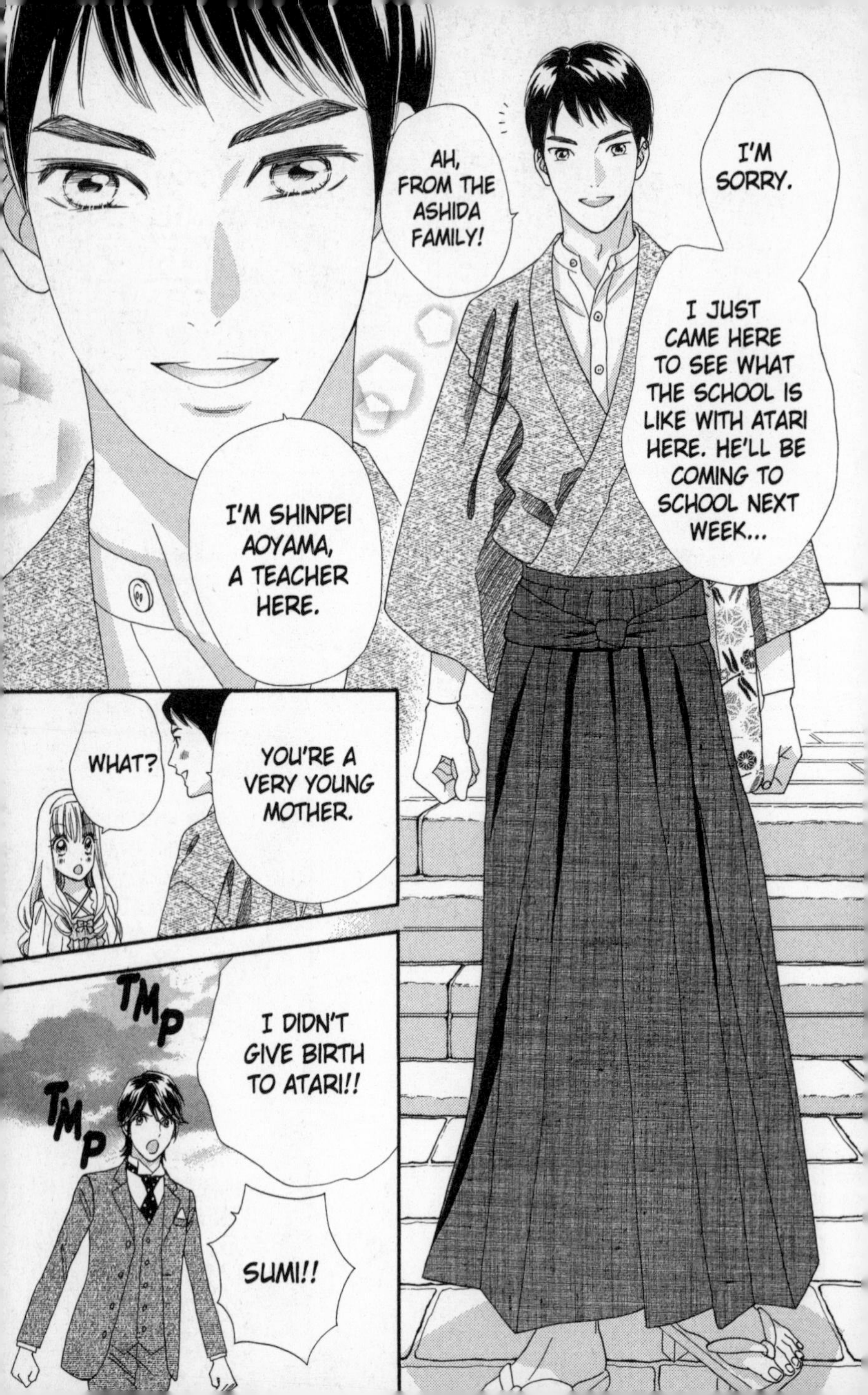
I'M SORRY.
AH, FROM THE ASHIDA FAMILY!
I JUST CAME HERE TO SEE WHAT THE SCHOOL IS LIKE WITH ATARI HERE. HE'LL BE COMING TO SCHOOL NEXT WEEK...
I'M SHINPEI AOYAMA, A TEACHER HERE.
YOU'RE A VERY YOUNG MOTHER.
WHAT?
I DIDN'T GIVE BIRTH TO ATARI!!
TMP
TMP
SUMI!!

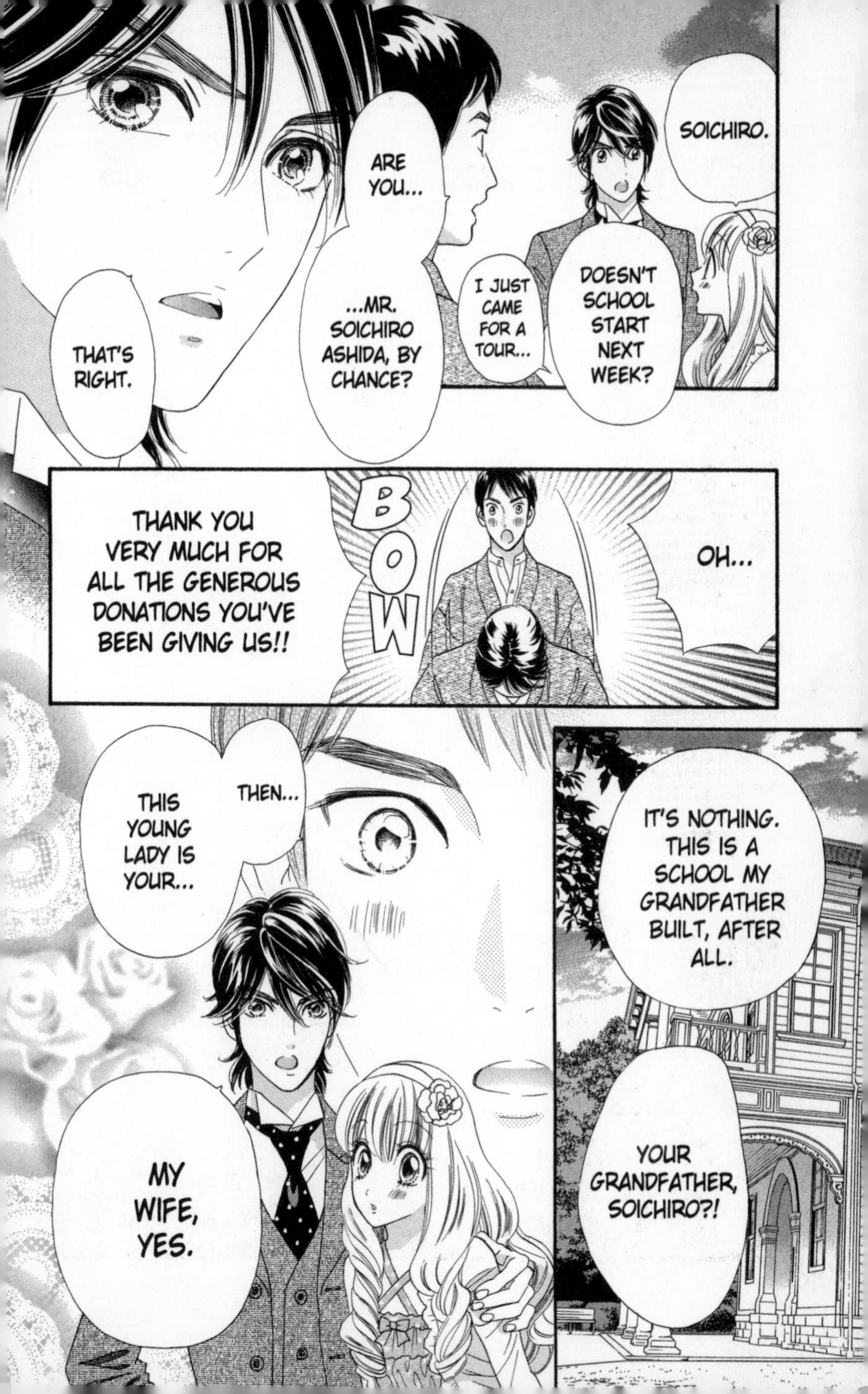
SOICHIRO.
DOESN'T SCHOOL START NEXT WEEK?
I JUST CAME FOR A TOUR...
ARE YOU...
...MR. SOICHIRO ASHIDA, BY CHANCE?
THAT'S RIGHT.
OH...
BOW
THANK YOU VERY MUCH FOR ALL THE GENEROUS DONATIONS YOU'VE BEEN GIVING US!!
IT'S NOTHING. THIS IS A SCHOOL MY GRANDFATHER BUILT, AFTER ALL.
YOUR GRANDFATHER, SOICHIRO?!
THEN...
THIS YOUNG LADY IS YOUR...
MY WIFE, YES.

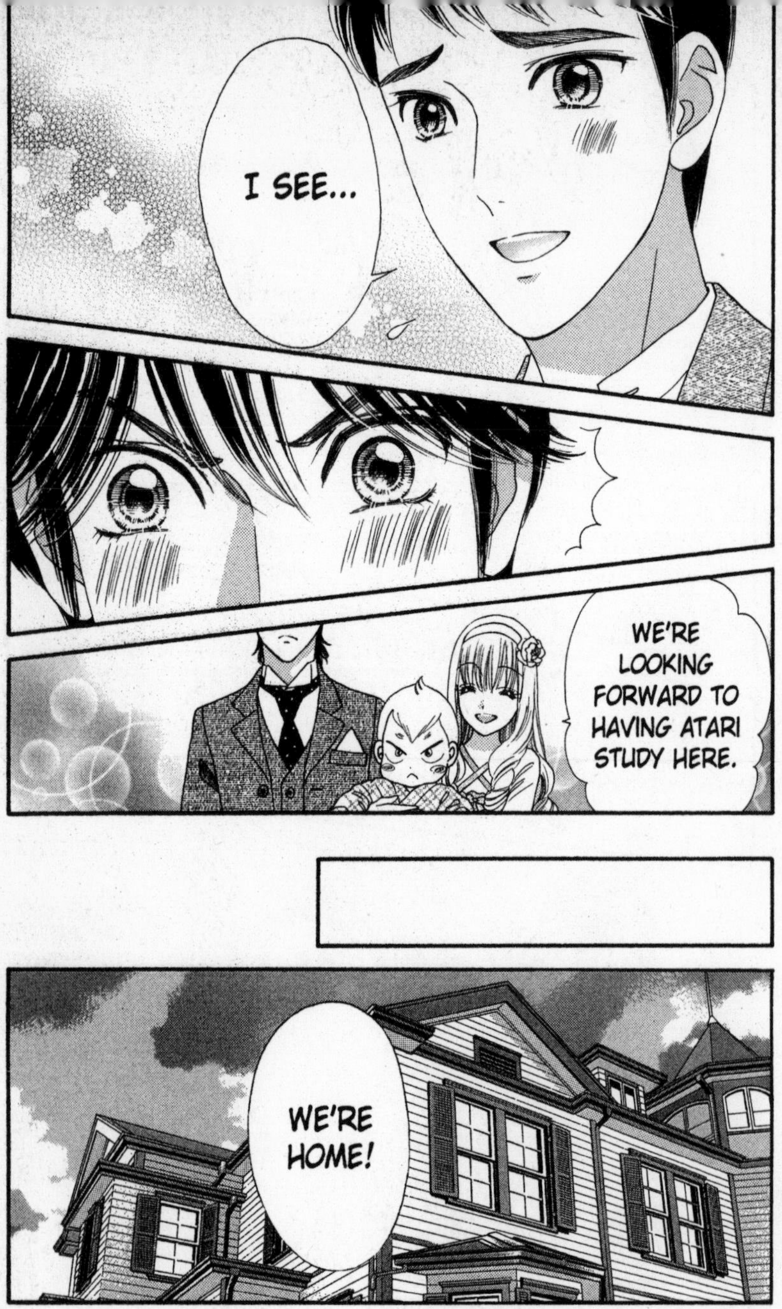
I SEE...
WE'RE LOOKING FORWARD TO HAVING ATARI STUDY HERE.
WE'RE HOME!

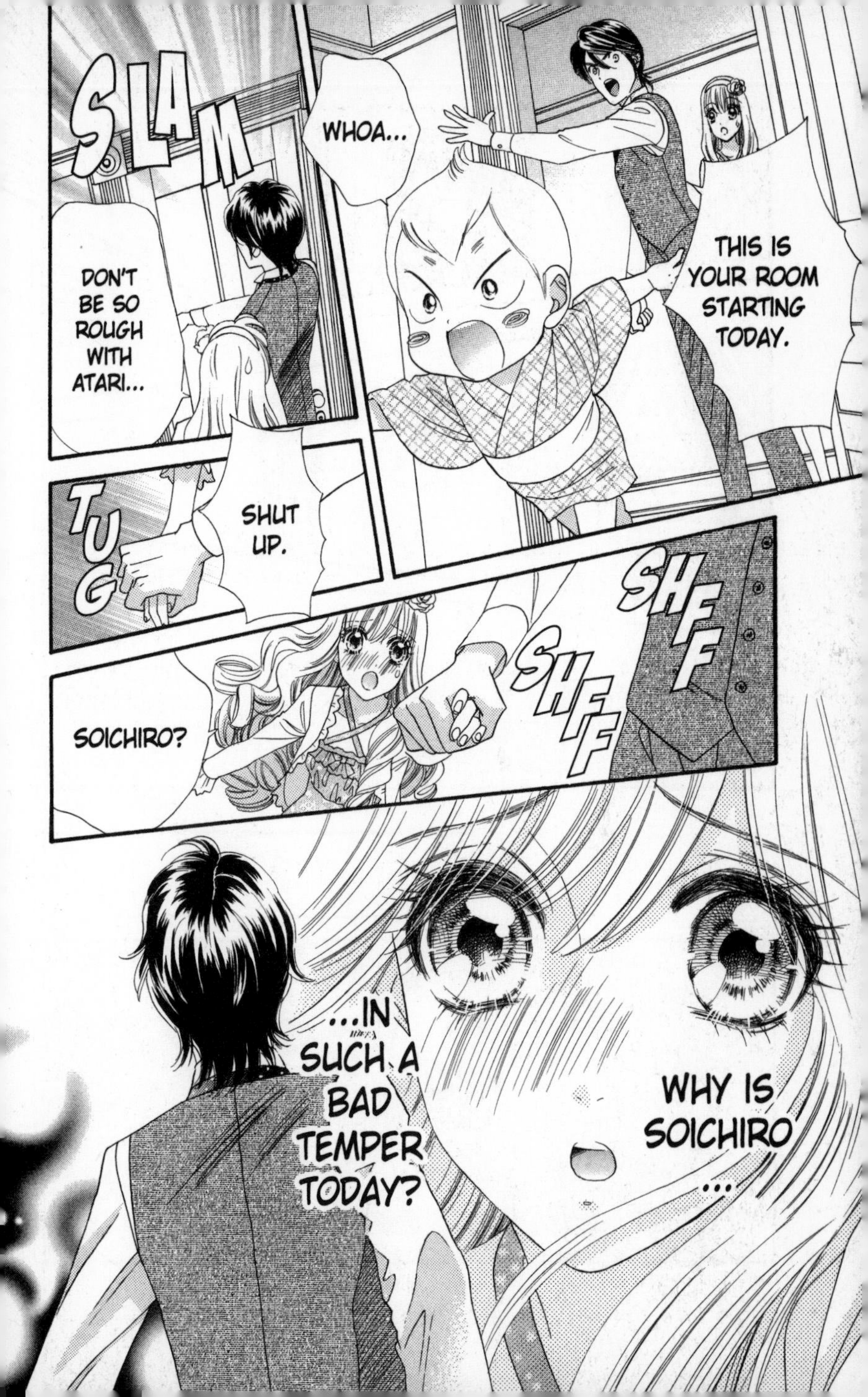
THIS IS YOUR ROOM STARTING TODAY.
WHOA...
SLAM
DON'T BE SO ROUGH WITH ATARI...
TUG
SHUT UP.
SHFF
SHFF
SOICHIRO?
WHY IS SOICHIRO ...
...IN SUCH A BAD TEMPER TODAY?

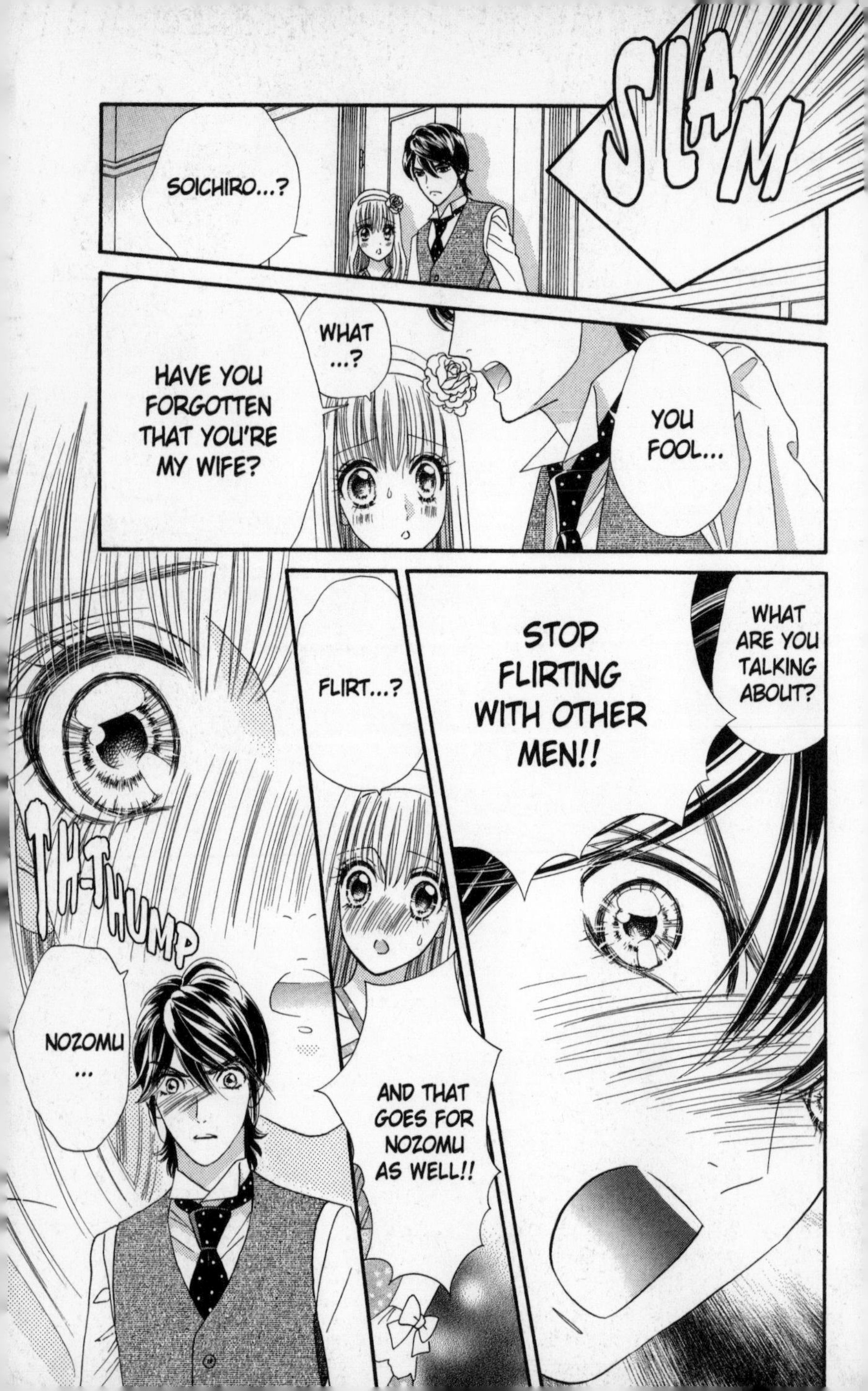
SLAM
SOICHIRO...?
YOU FOOL...
WHAT ...?
HAVE YOU FORGOTTEN THAT YOU'RE MY WIFE?
WHAT ARE YOU TALKING ABOUT?
STOP FLIRTING WITH OTHER MEN!!
FLIRT...?
AND THAT GOES FOR NOZOMU AS WELL!!
TH-THUMP
NOZOMU ...

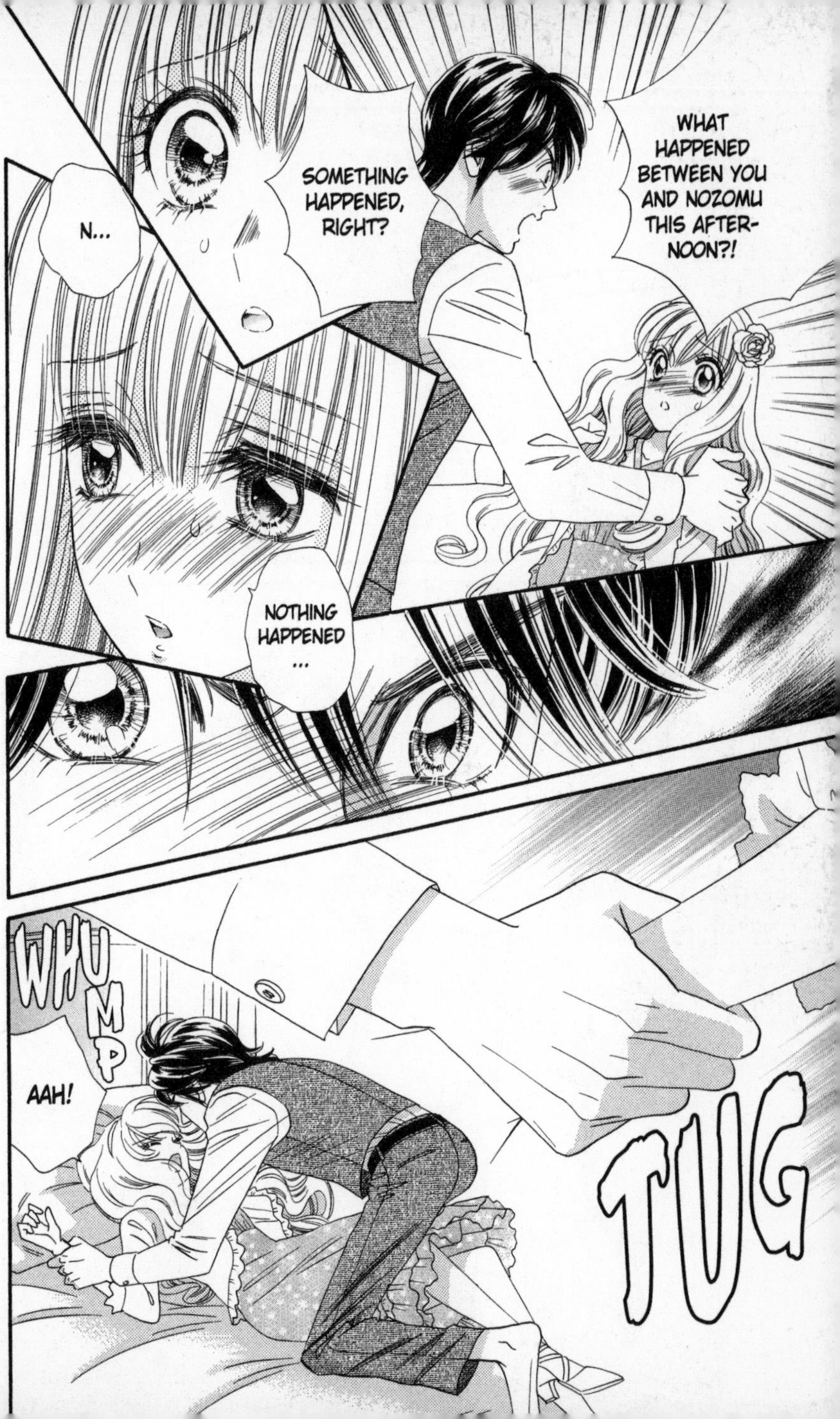
WHAT HAPPENED BETWEEN YOU AND NOZOMU THIS AFTER-NOON?!
SOMETHING HAPPENED, RIGHT?
N...
NOTHING HAPPENED ...
TUG
WHUMP
AAH!

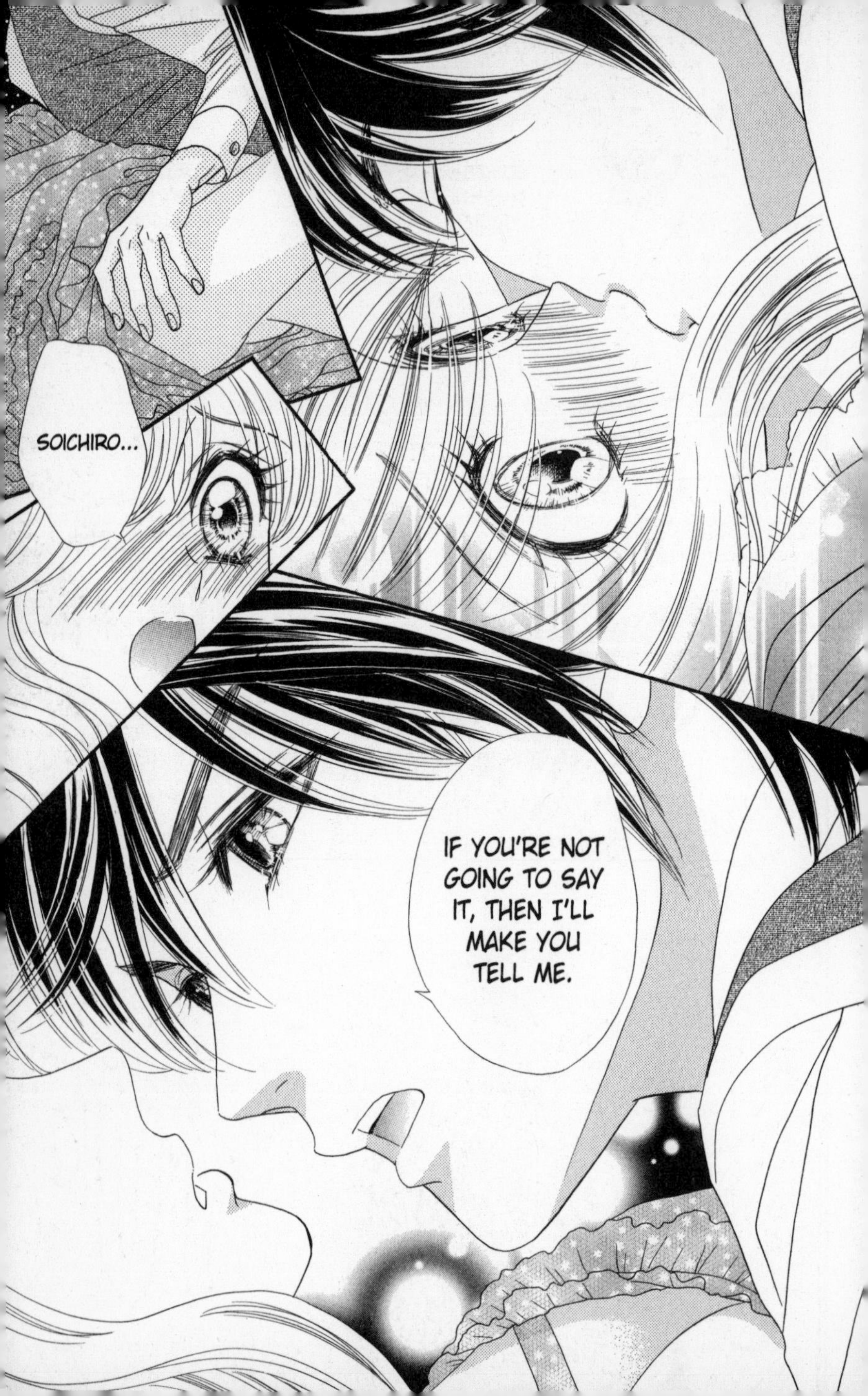
SOICHIRO...
IF YOU'RE NOT GOING TO SAY IT, THEN I'LL MAKE YOU TELL ME.

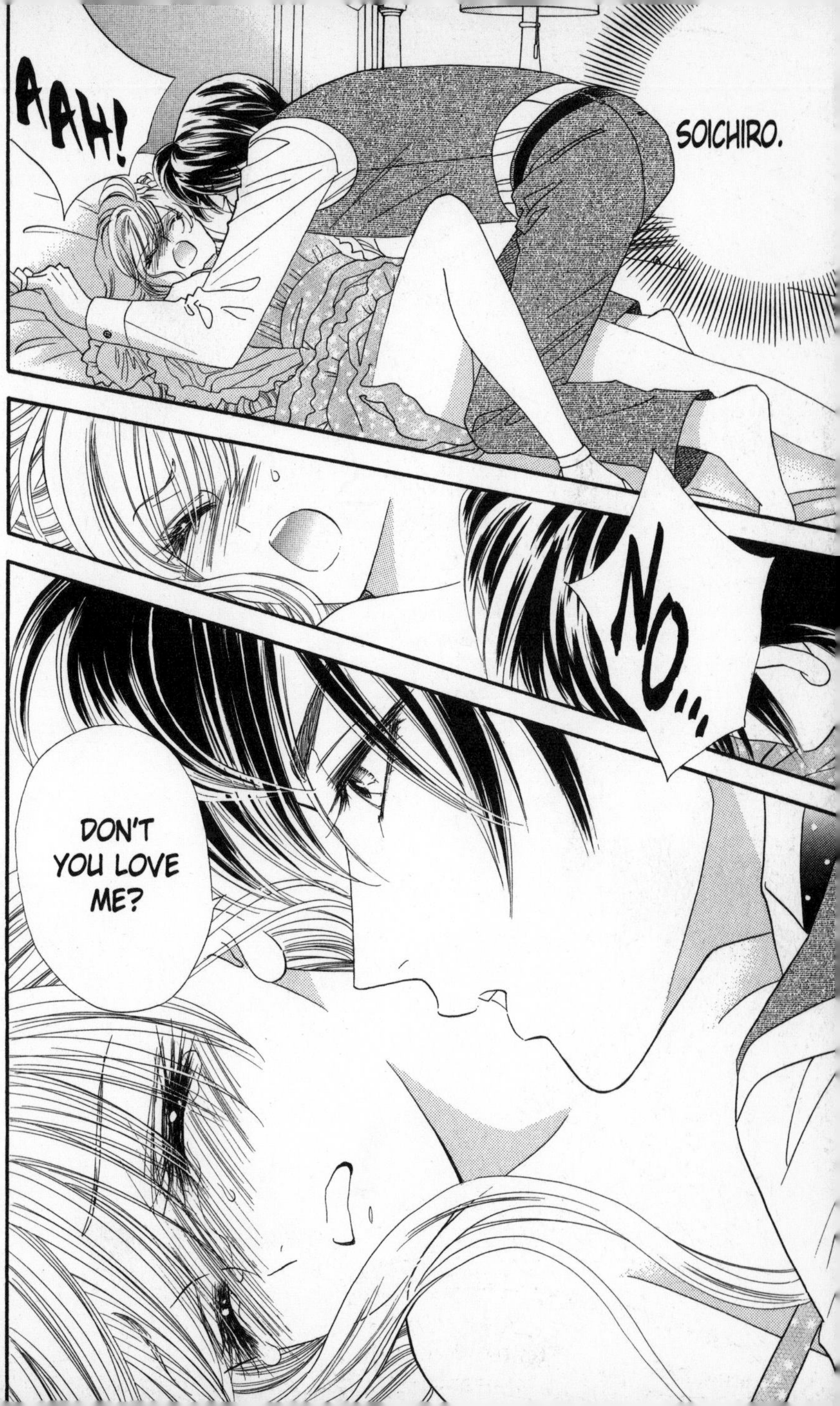
SOICHIRO.
AAH!
NO...
DON'T YOU LOVE ME?

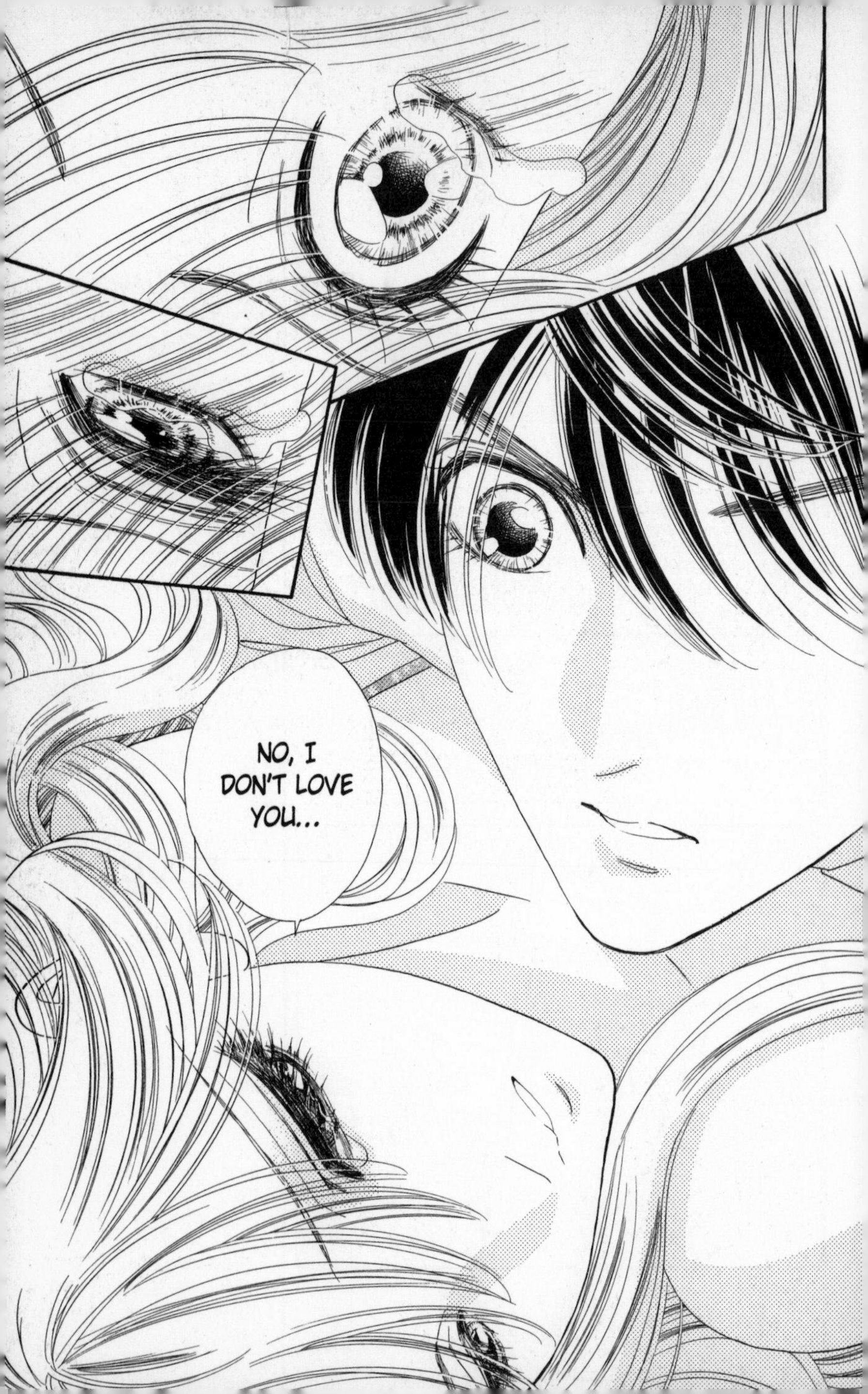
NO, I DON'T LOVE YOU...

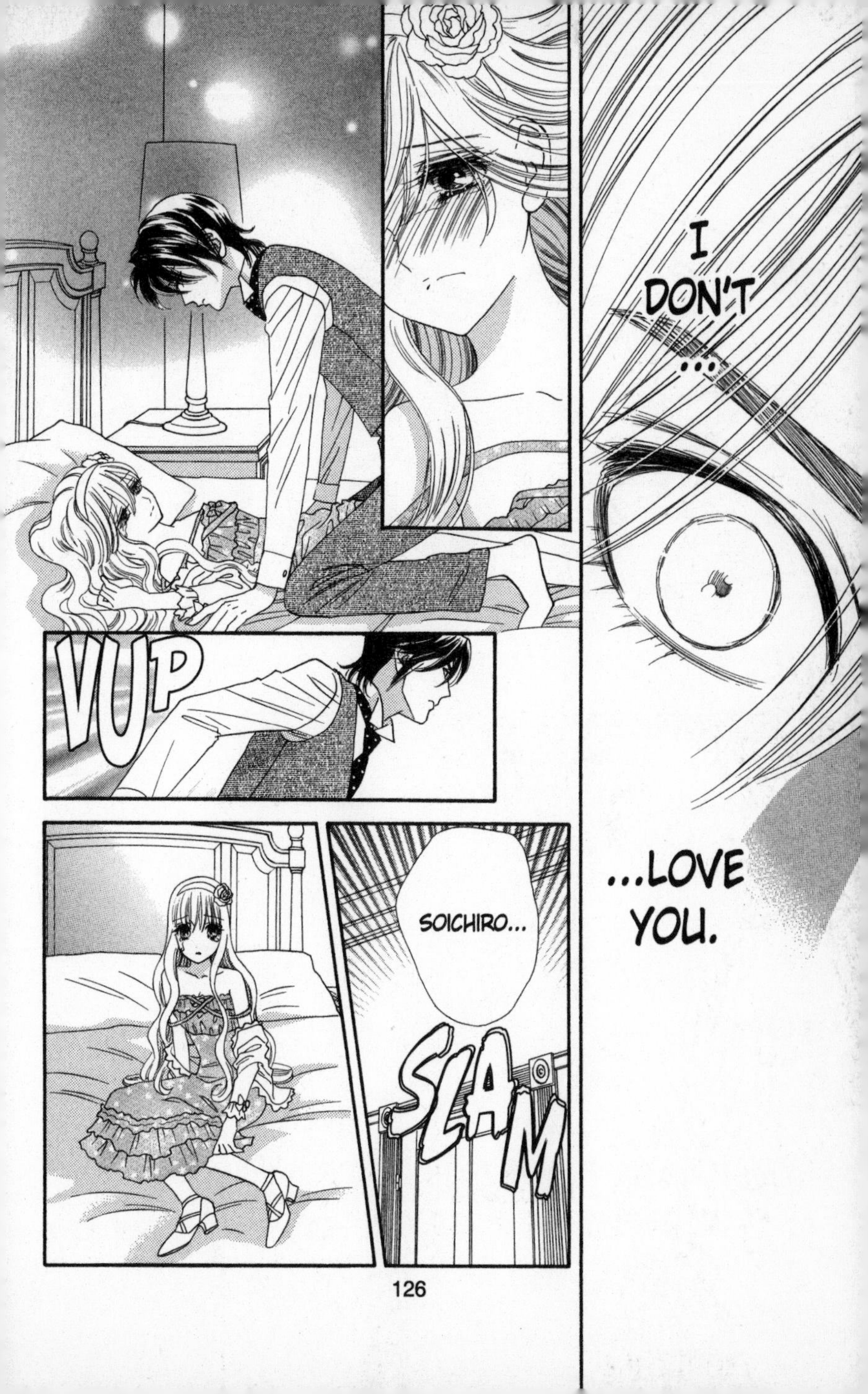
I DON'T ...
...LOVE YOU.
VUP
SOICHIRO...
SLAM

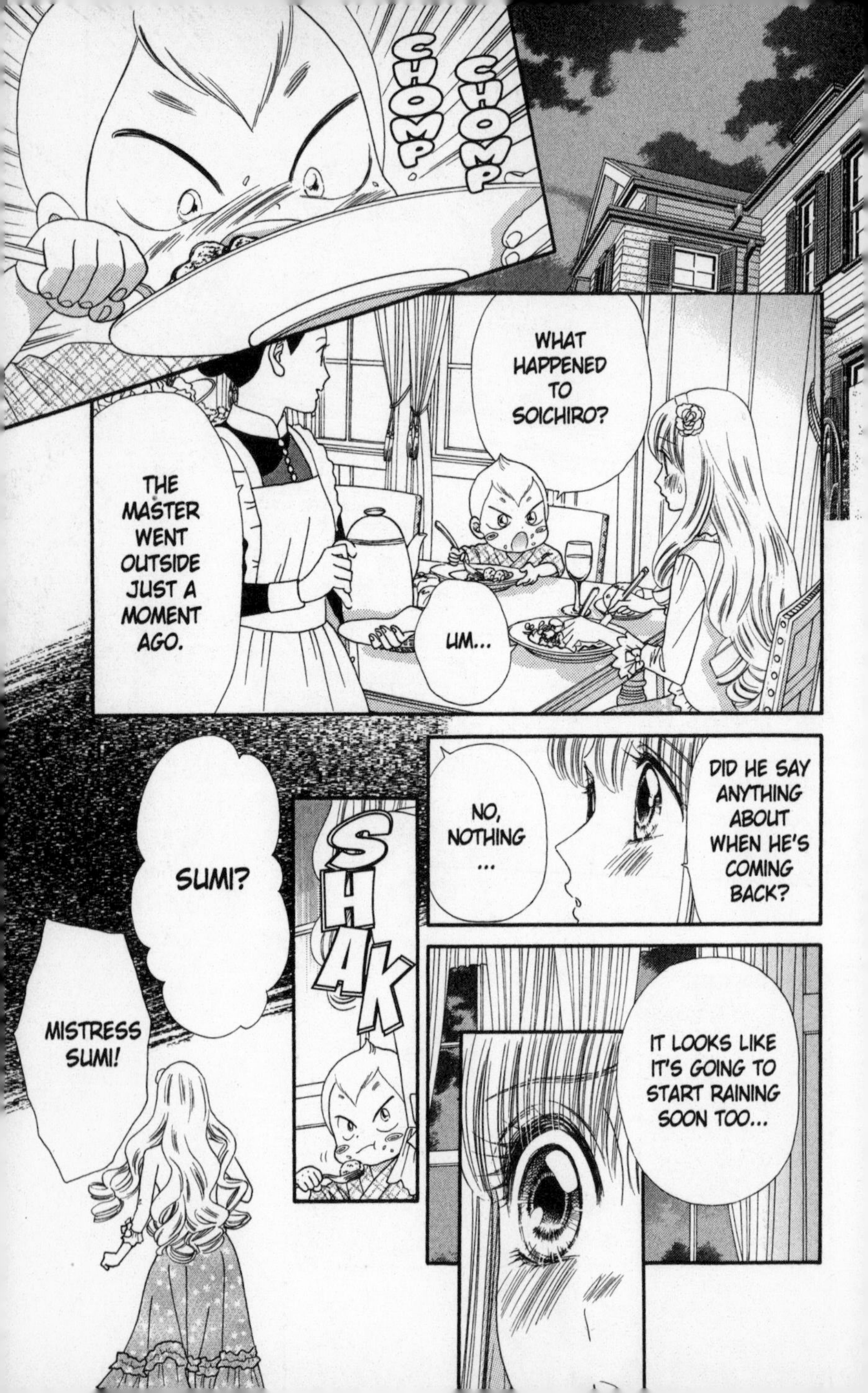
CHOMP CHOMP
WHAT HAPPENED TO SOICHIRO?
THE MASTER WENT OUTSIDE JUST A MOMENT AGO.
UM...
DID HE SAY ANYTHING ABOUT WHEN HE'S COMING BACK?
NO, NOTHING ...
IT LOOKS LIKE IT'S GOING TO START RAINING SOON TOO...
SHAK
SUMI?
MISTRESS SUMI!

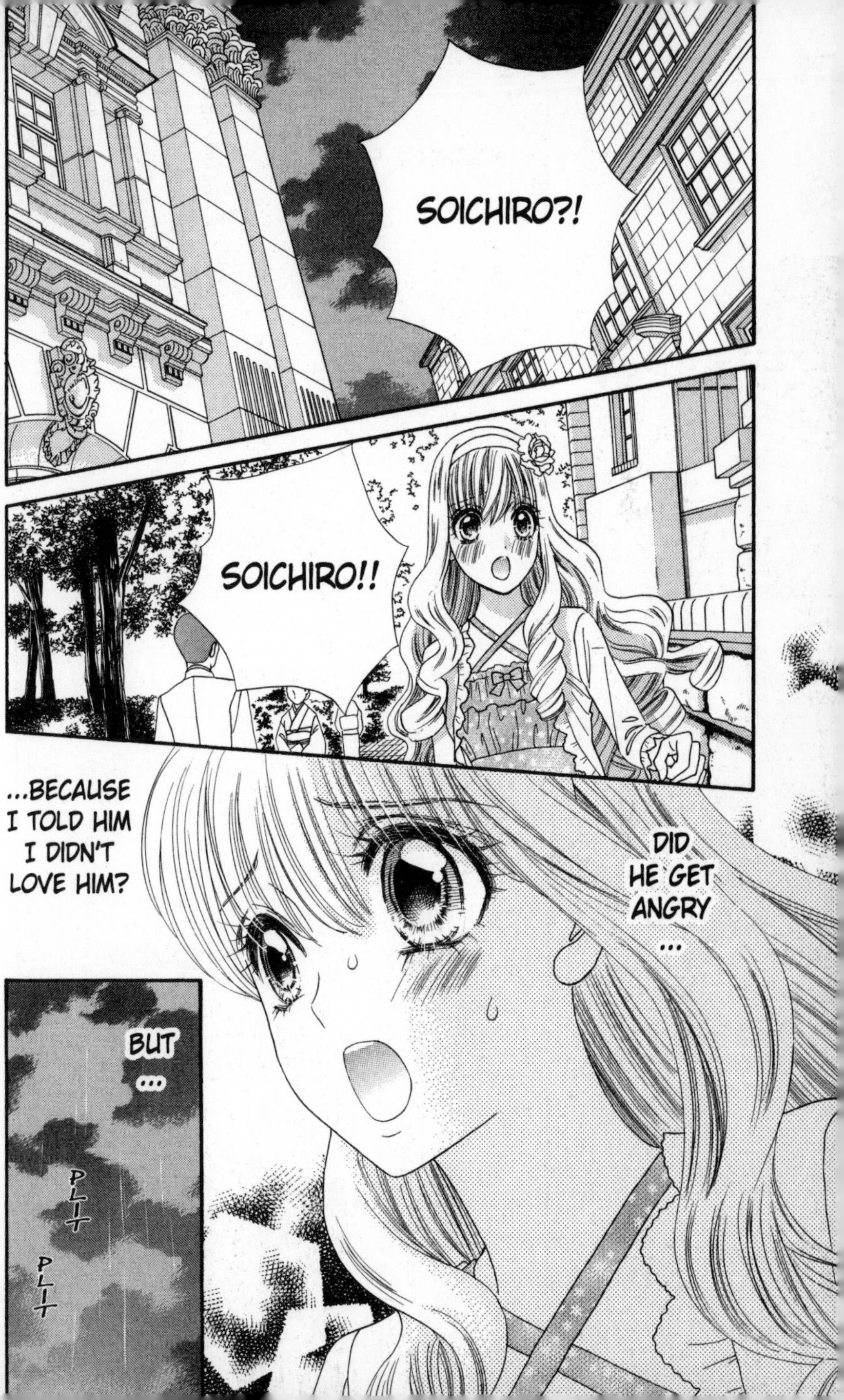
SOICHIRO?!
SOICHIRO!!
DID HE GET ANGRY ...
...BECAUSE I TOLD HIM I DIDN'T LOVE HIM?
BUT ...
PLIT
PLIT

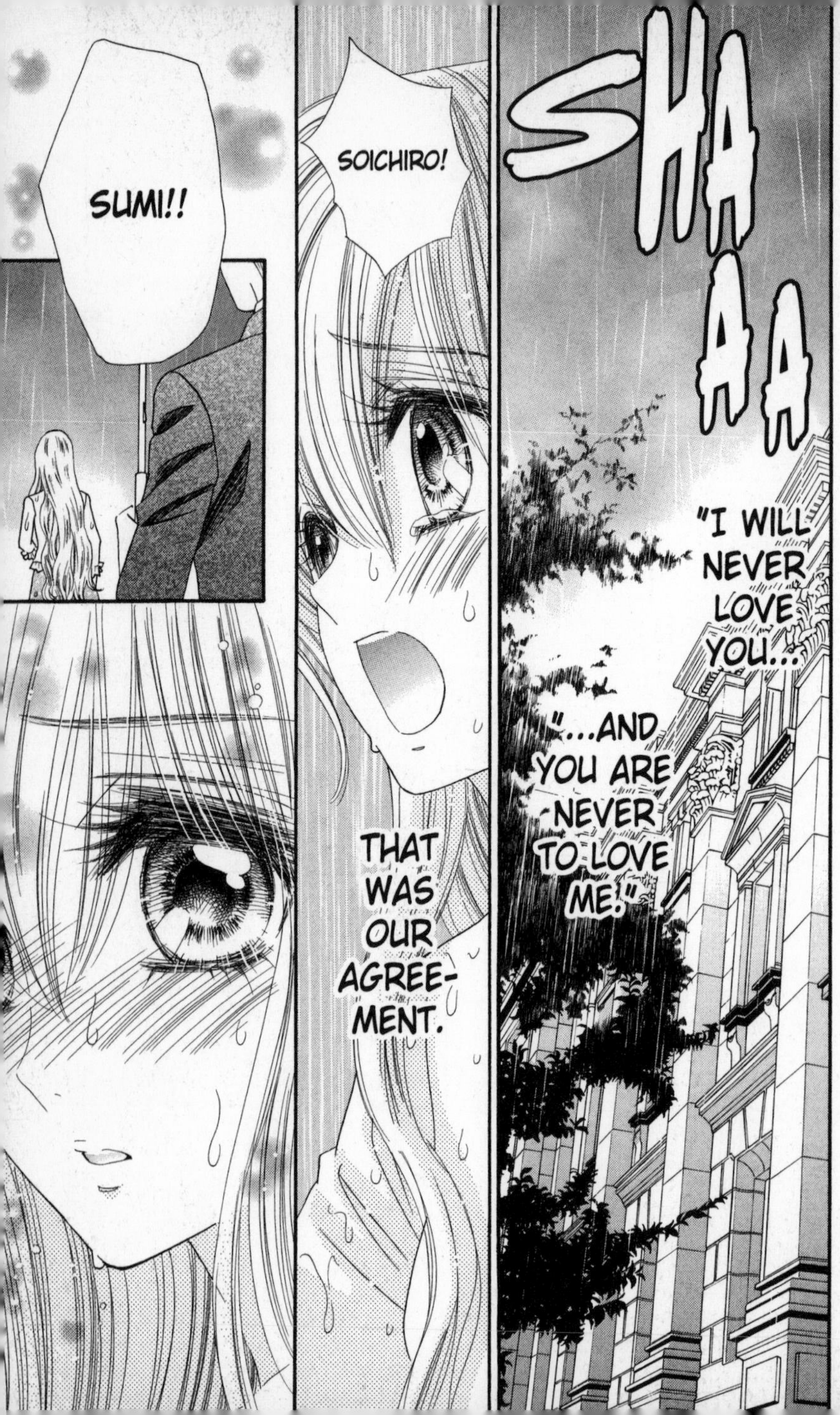
SHAAA
"I WILL NEVER LOVE YOU...
"...AND YOU ARE NEVER TO LOVE ME."
SOICHIRO!
THAT WAS OUR AGREE-MENT.
SUMI!!

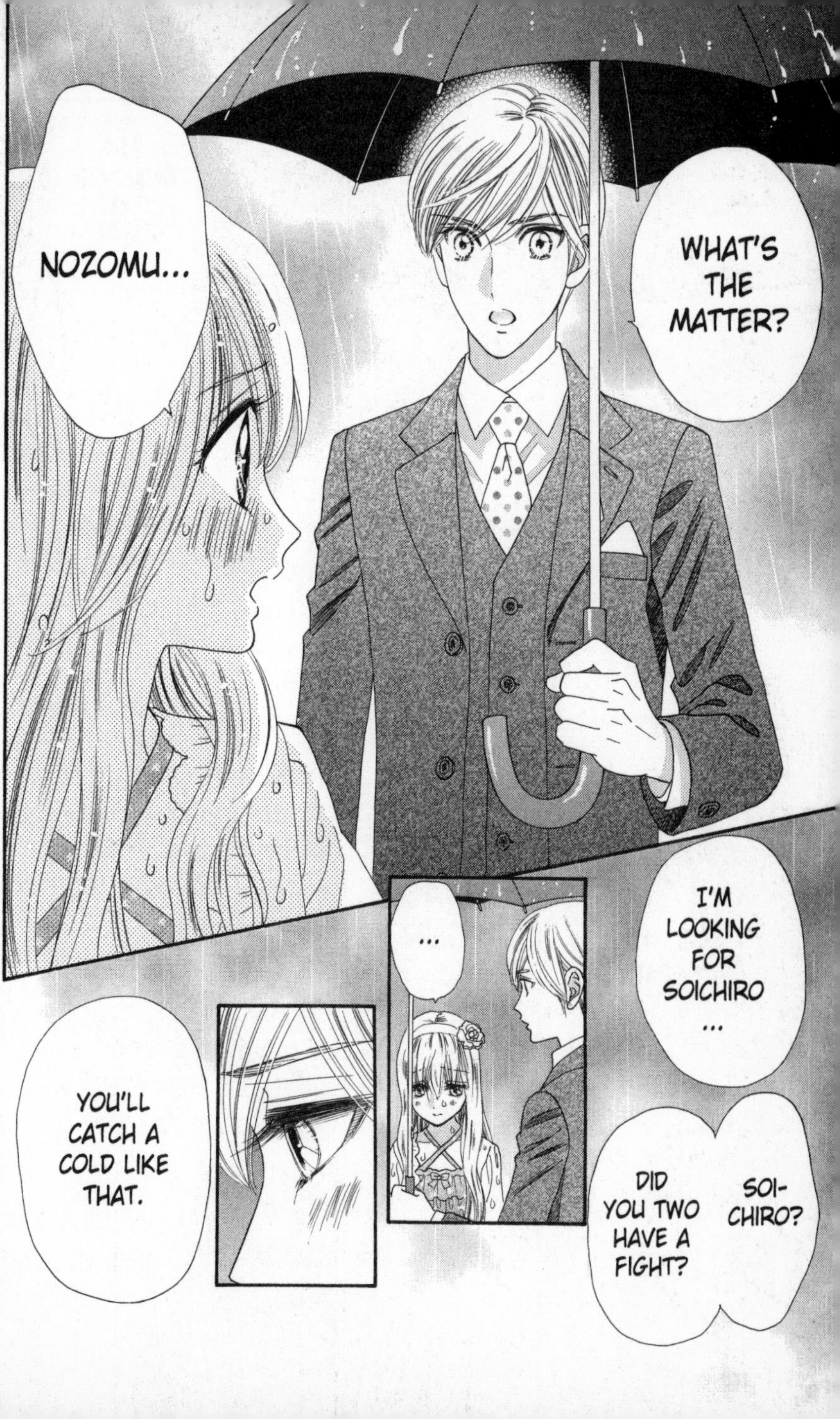
WHAT'S THE MATTER?
NOZOMU...
I'M LOOKING FOR SOICHIRO ...
SOI-CHIRO?
DID YOU TWO HAVE A FIGHT?
...
YOU'LL CATCH A COLD LIKE THAT.

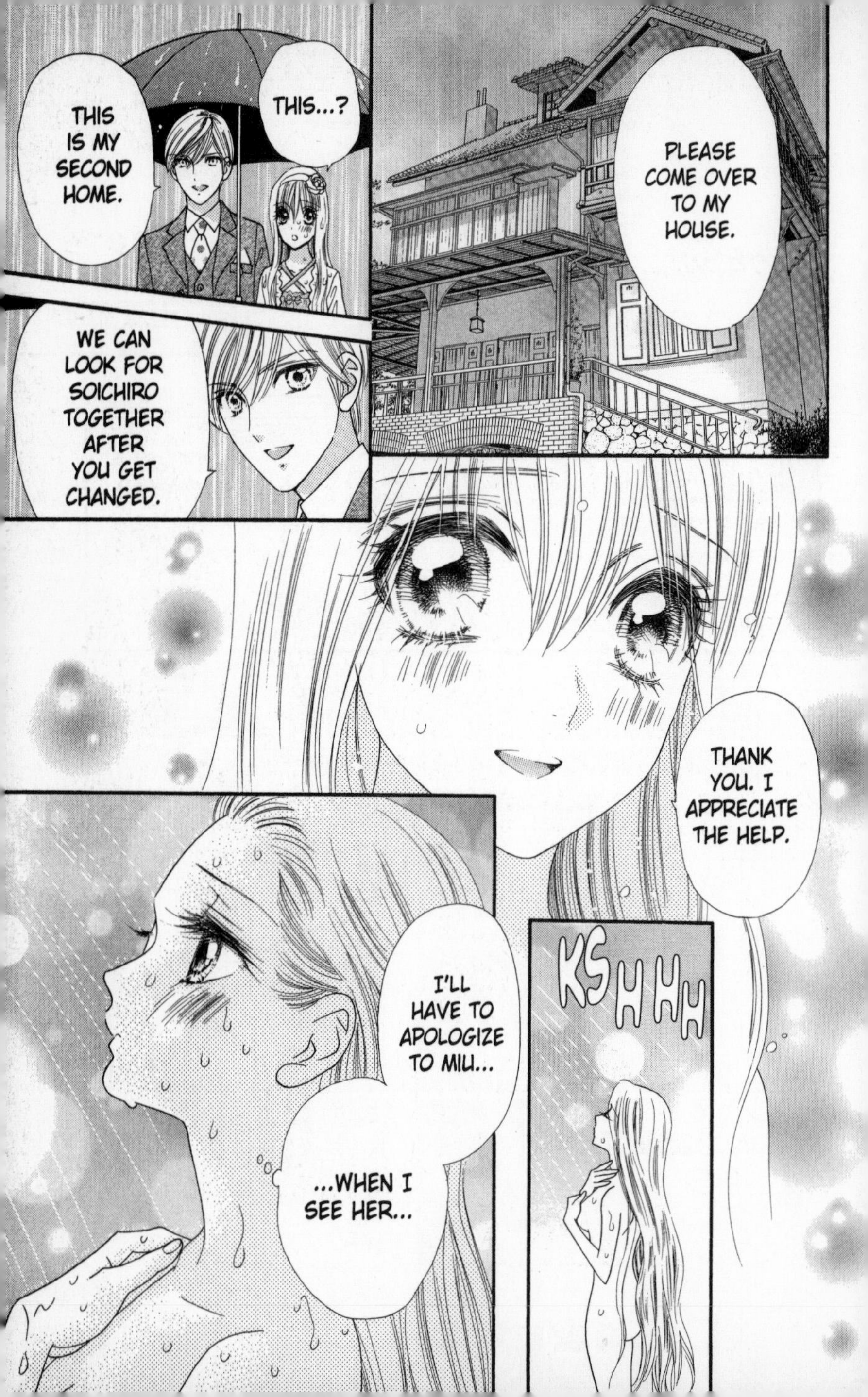
PLEASE COME OVER TO MY HOUSE.
THIS...?
THIS IS MY SECOND HOME.
WE CAN LOOK FOR SOICHIRO TOGETHER AFTER YOU GET CHANGED.
THANK YOU. I APPRECIATE THE HELP.
KSHHHH
I'LL HAVE TO APOLOGIZE TO MIU...
...WHEN I SEE HER...

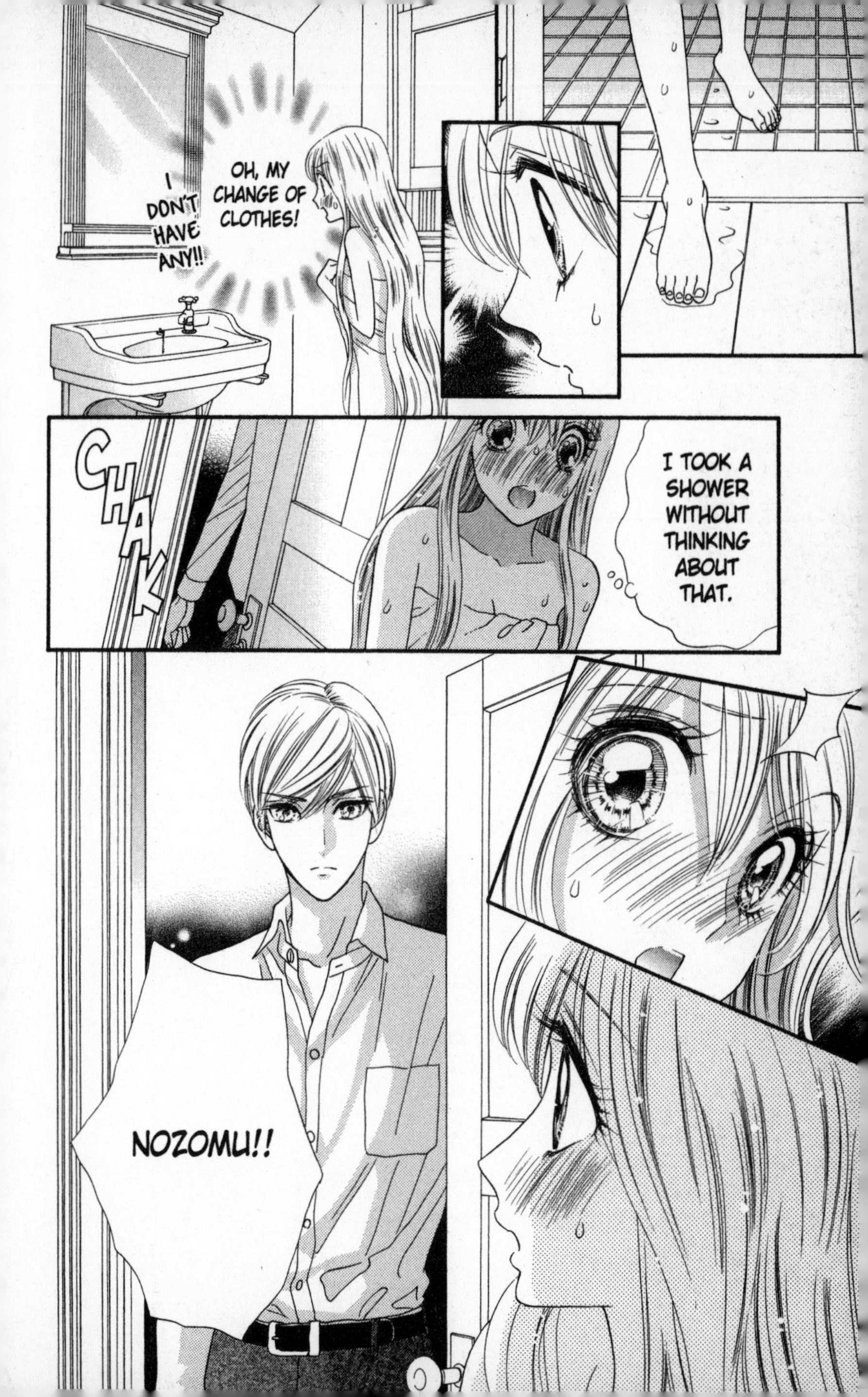
OH, MY CHANGE OF CLOTHES!
I DON'T HAVE ANY!!
I TOOK A SHOWER WITHOUT THINKING ABOUT THAT.
CHAK
NOZOMU!!

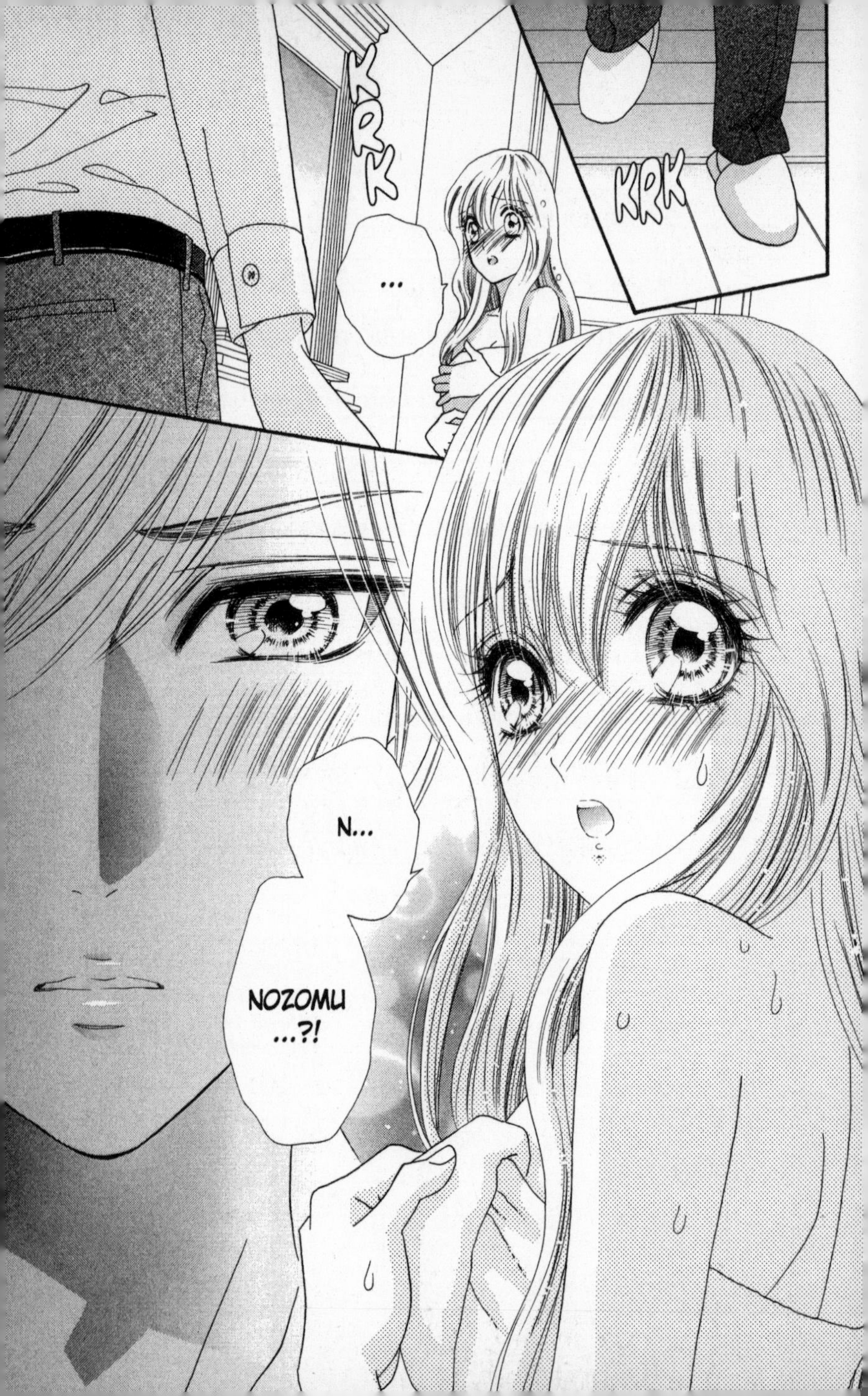
KRK
KRK
...
N...
NOZOMU ...?!

No. 5

Date

RANDOM CHITCHAT

✿ MY BLOOD TYPE IS B. THAT'S WHAT I WAS TOLD BY MY MOTHER AS A CHILD. THE TEST RESULTS OF MY BLOOD TYPE (WHICH THEY DID WHEN I WAS A BABY) SAID THIS TOO. I AM A MOODY, TEMPERAMENTAL PERSON WHO SAYS THINGS OUTRIGHT, TYPICAL OF A BLOOD-TYPE B PERSON.

AT LEAST, THAT'S WHAT I THOUGHT UNTIL A WHILE AGO...

✿ THE DOCTOR CHECKED MY BLOOD TYPE AS A PART OF MY HEALTH EXAM AFTER I GOT PREGNANT, AND I COULDN'T BELIEVE IT WHEN THEY TOLD ME MY BLOOD TYPE IS A! ALL MY THIRTY-SOMETHING YEARS OF JOY AND SORROW FROM BLOOD-TYPE FORTUNE-TELLING AND WHATNOT FOR BLOOD-TYPE B PEOPLE WAS ALL MEANINGLESS...

FROM TYPE B TO TYPE A... THAT'S A VERY BIG CHANGE!!

I DON'T KNOW WHAT I'M SUPPOSED TO BELIEVE ANYMORE.

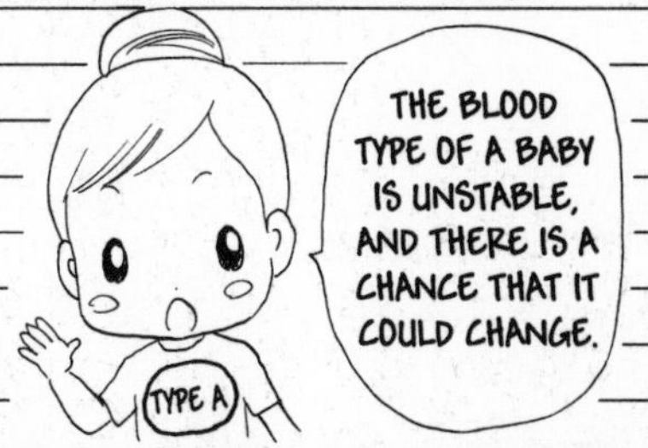
THE BLOOD TYPE OF A BABY IS UNSTABLE, AND THERE IS A CHANCE THAT IT COULD CHANGE.
TYPE A

✿ MY PROFILE ON THE *MARGARET* HOMEPAGE HAS ALREADY BEEN CORRECTED.

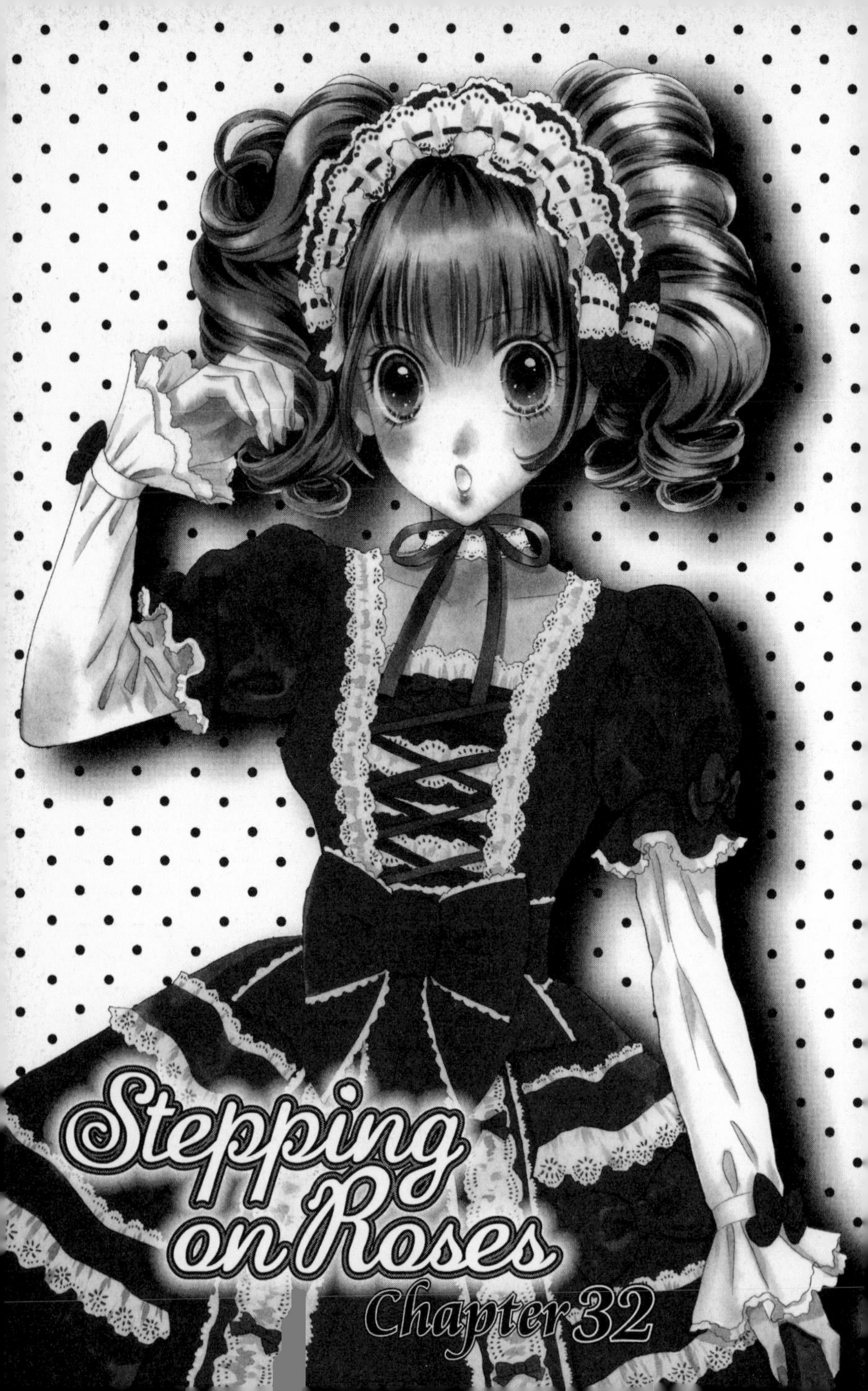
Stepping on Roses
Chapter 32

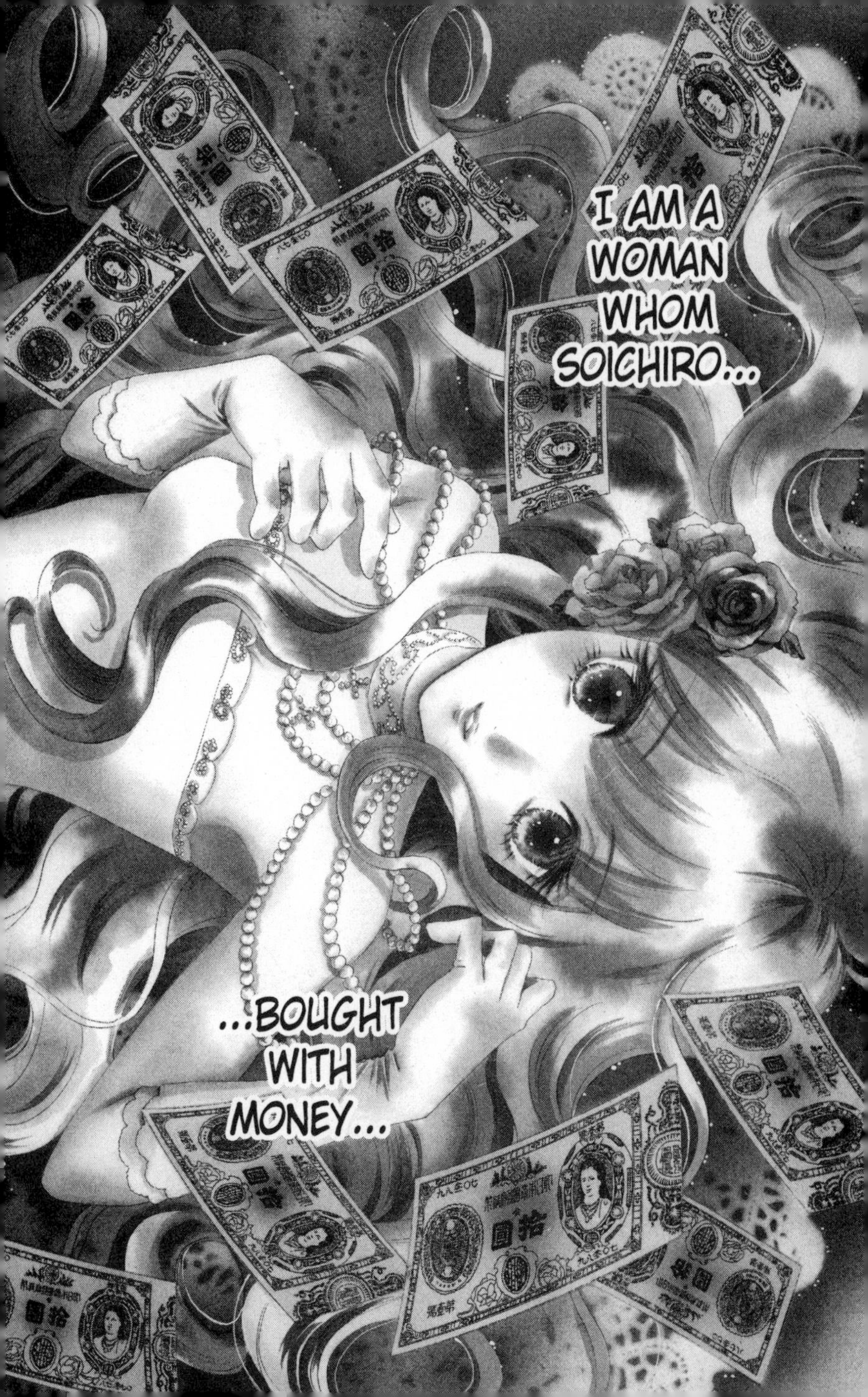
I AM A WOMAN WHOM SOICHIRO...
...BOUGHT WITH MONEY...

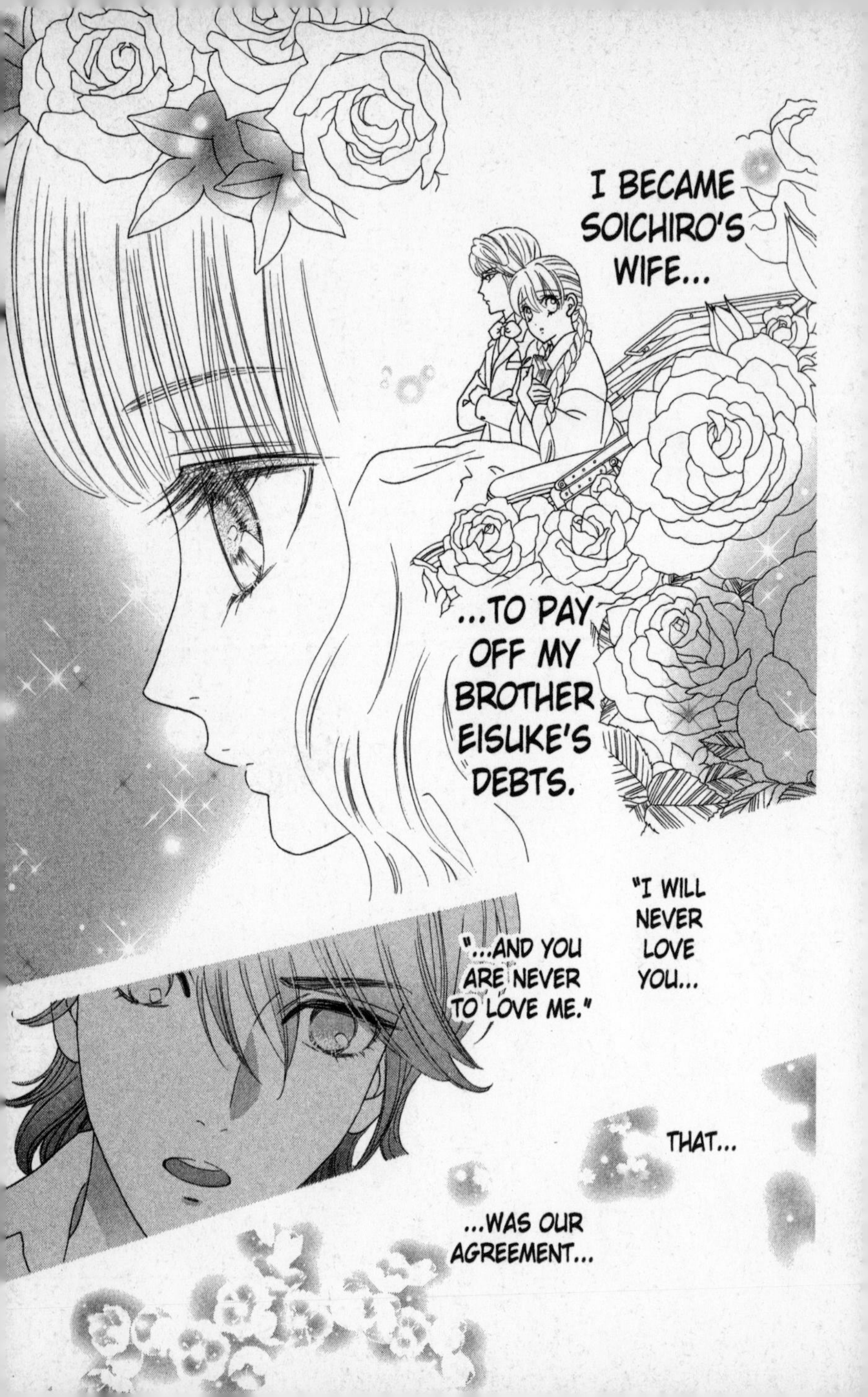
I BECAME SOICHIRO'S WIFE...
...TO PAY OFF MY BROTHER EISUKE'S DEBTS.
"I WILL NEVER LOVE YOU...
"...AND YOU ARE NEVER TO LOVE ME."
THAT...
...WAS OUR AGREEMENT...

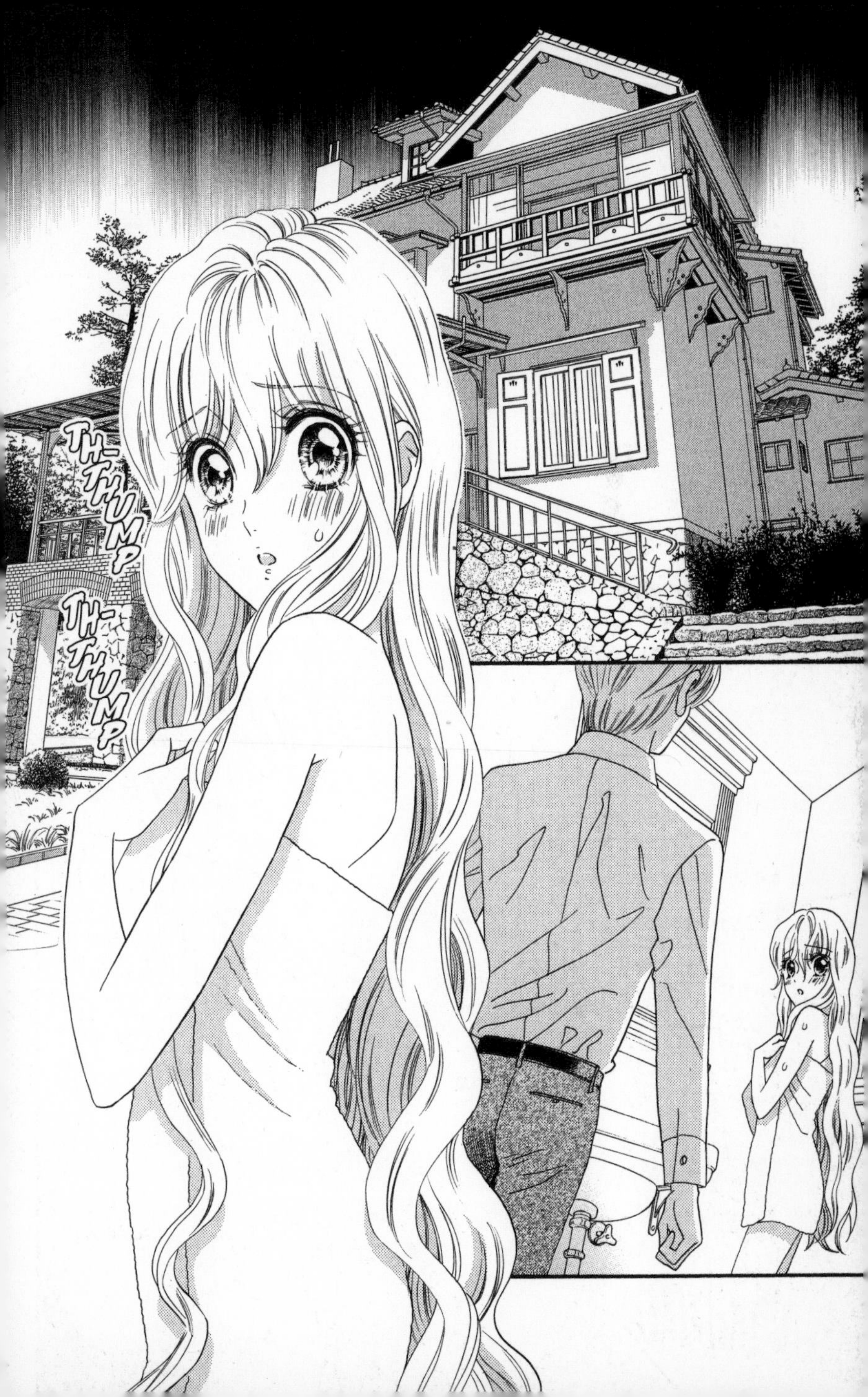
TH-THUMP
TH-THUMP

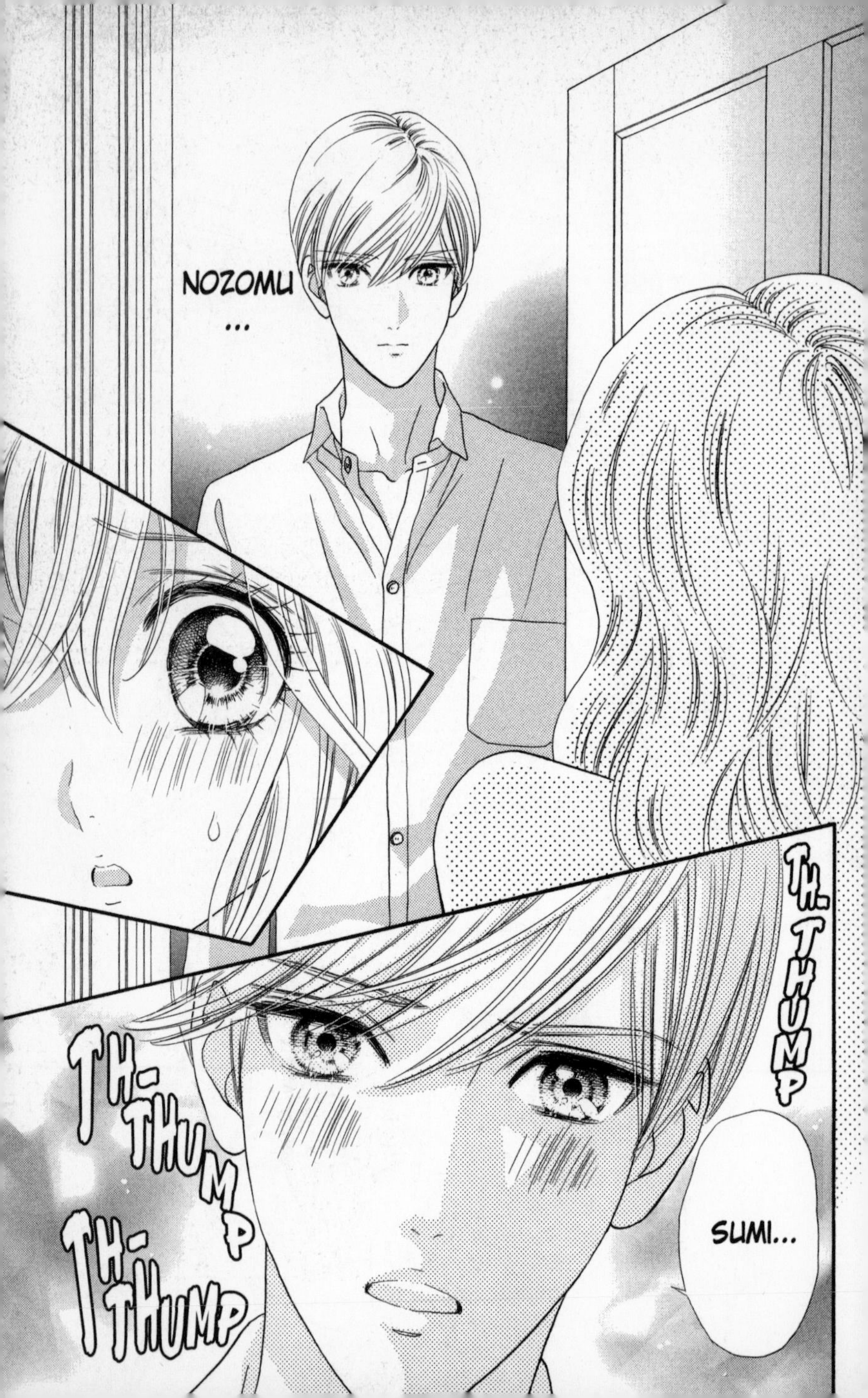
NOZOMU ...
TH-THUMP
SUMI...
TH-THUMP
TH-THUMP

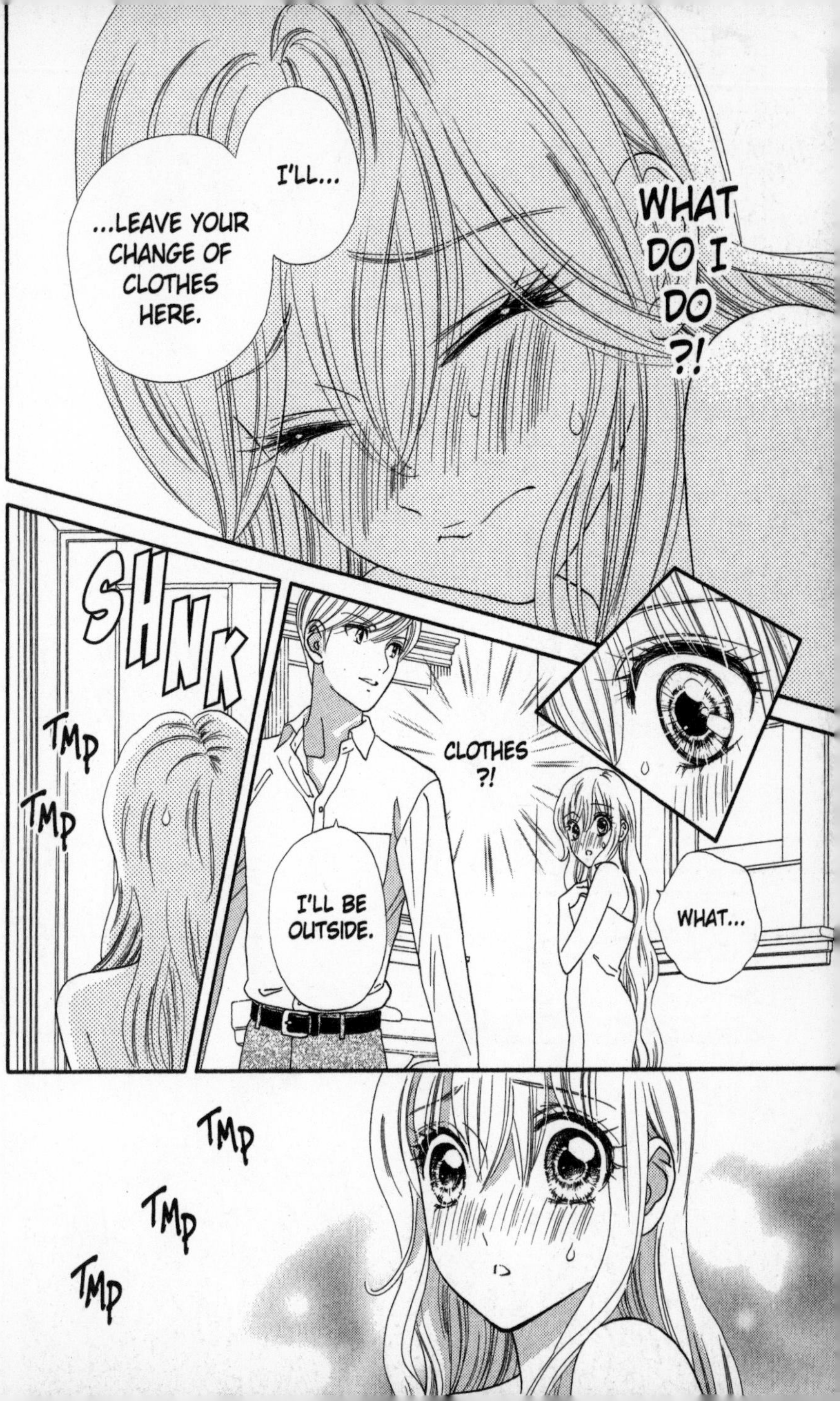
WHAT DO I DO ?!
I'LL...
...LEAVE YOUR CHANGE OF CLOTHES HERE.
WHAT...
CLOTHES ?!
I'LL BE OUTSIDE.
SHNK
TMP
TMP
TMP
TMP
TMP

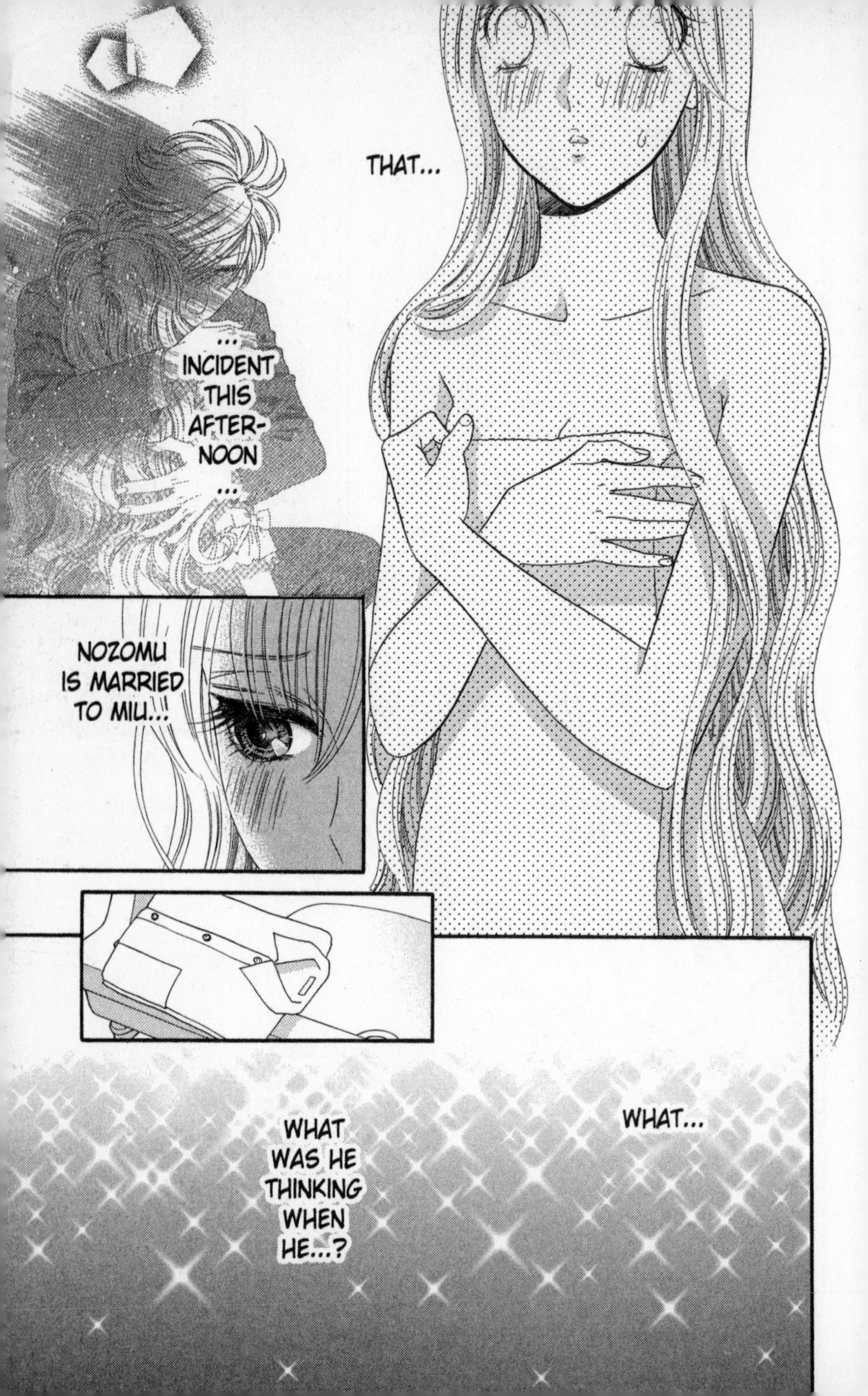
THAT...
...INCIDENT THIS AFTER-NOON...
NOZOMU IS MARRIED TO MIU...!
WHAT...
WHAT WAS HE THINKING WHEN HE...?

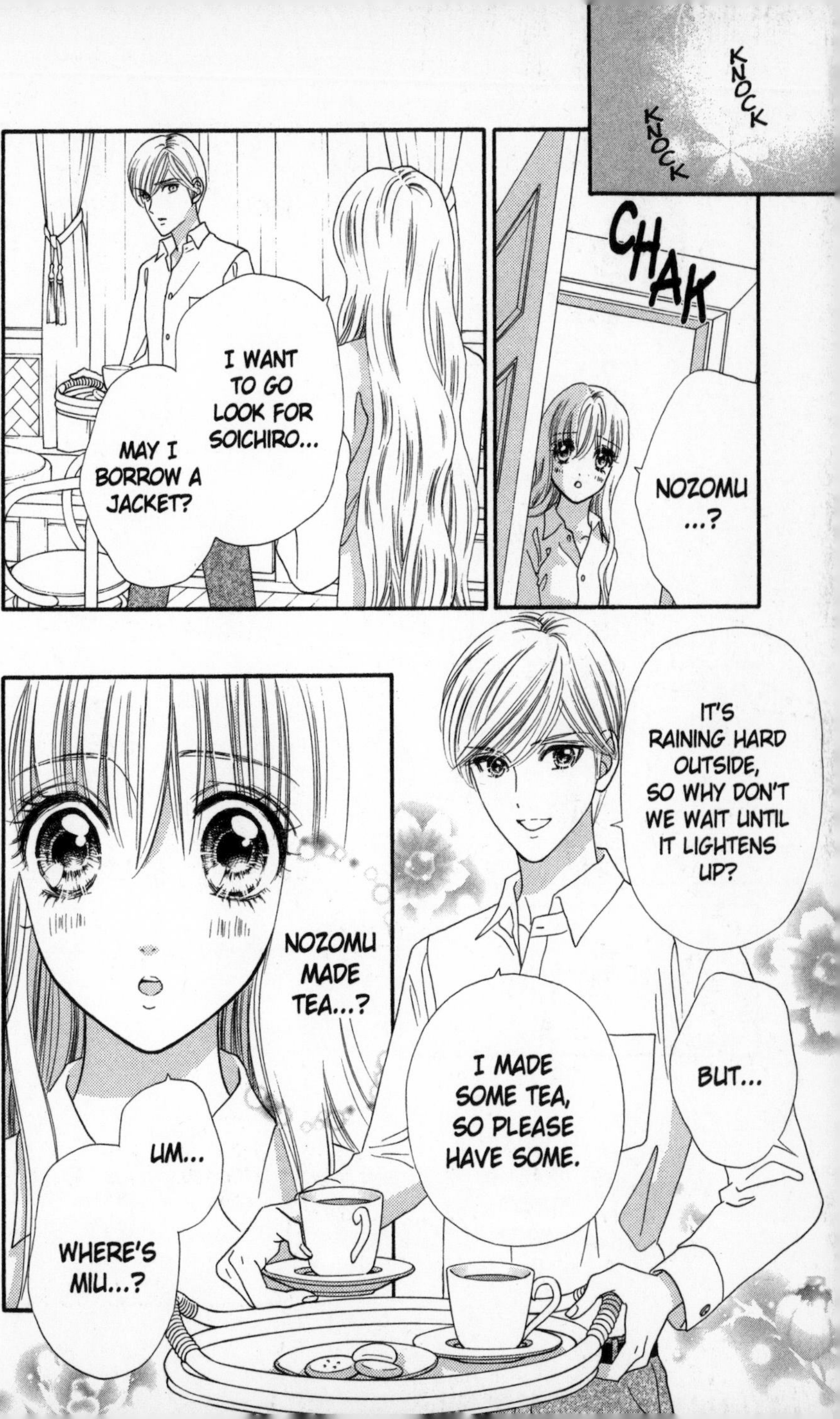
KNOCK
KNOCK
CHAK
NOZOMU ...?
I WANT TO GO LOOK FOR SOICHIRO...
MAY I BORROW A JACKET?
IT'S RAINING HARD OUTSIDE, SO WHY DON'T WE WAIT UNTIL IT LIGHTENS UP?
BUT...
I MADE SOME TEA, SO PLEASE HAVE SOME.
NOZOMU MADE TEA...?
UM...
WHERE'S MIU...?

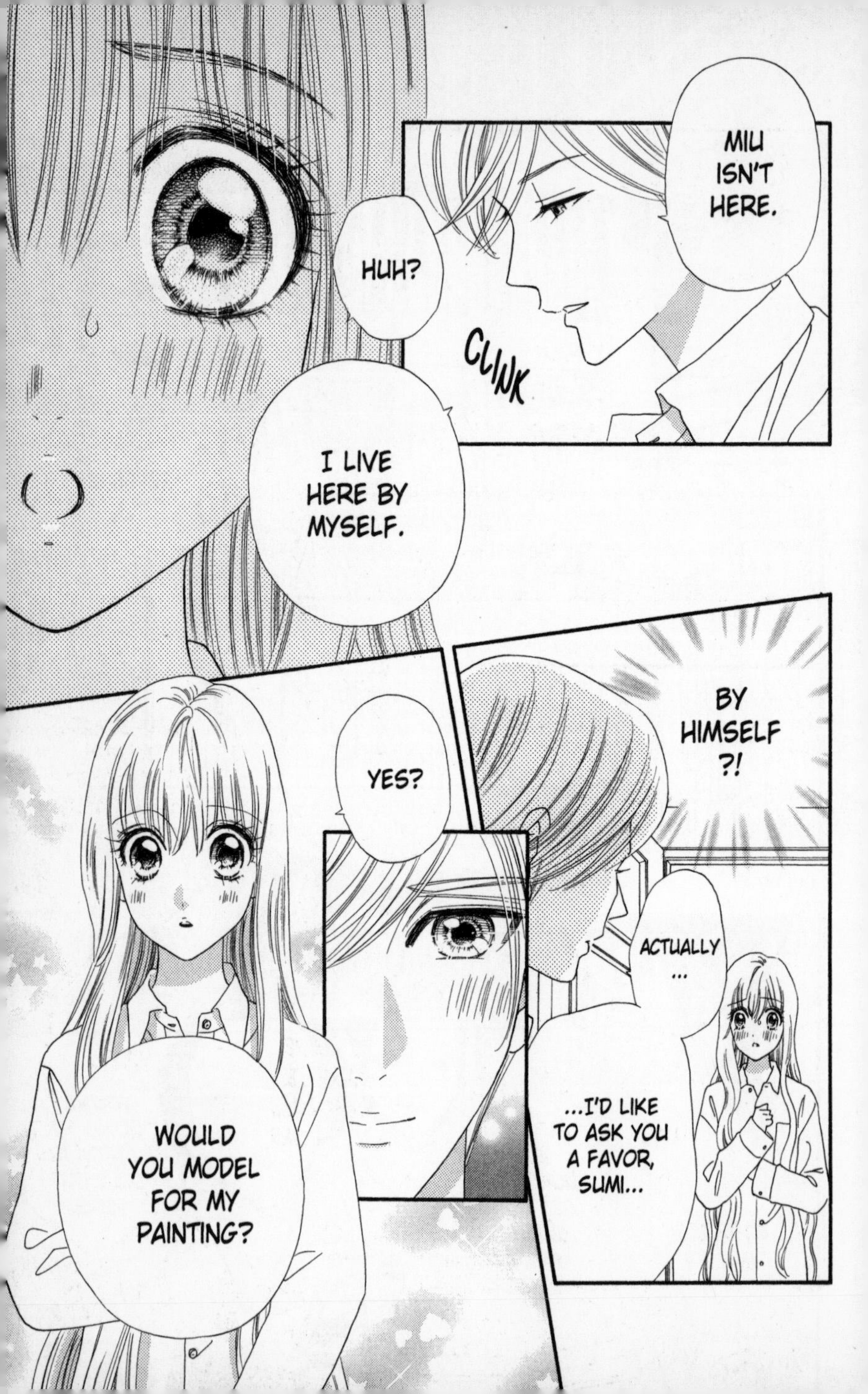
MIU ISN'T HERE.
HUH?
CLINK
I LIVE HERE BY MYSELF.
BY HIMSELF ?!
ACTUALLY ...
...I'D LIKE TO ASK YOU A FAVOR, SUMI...
YES?
WOULD YOU MODEL FOR MY PAINTING?

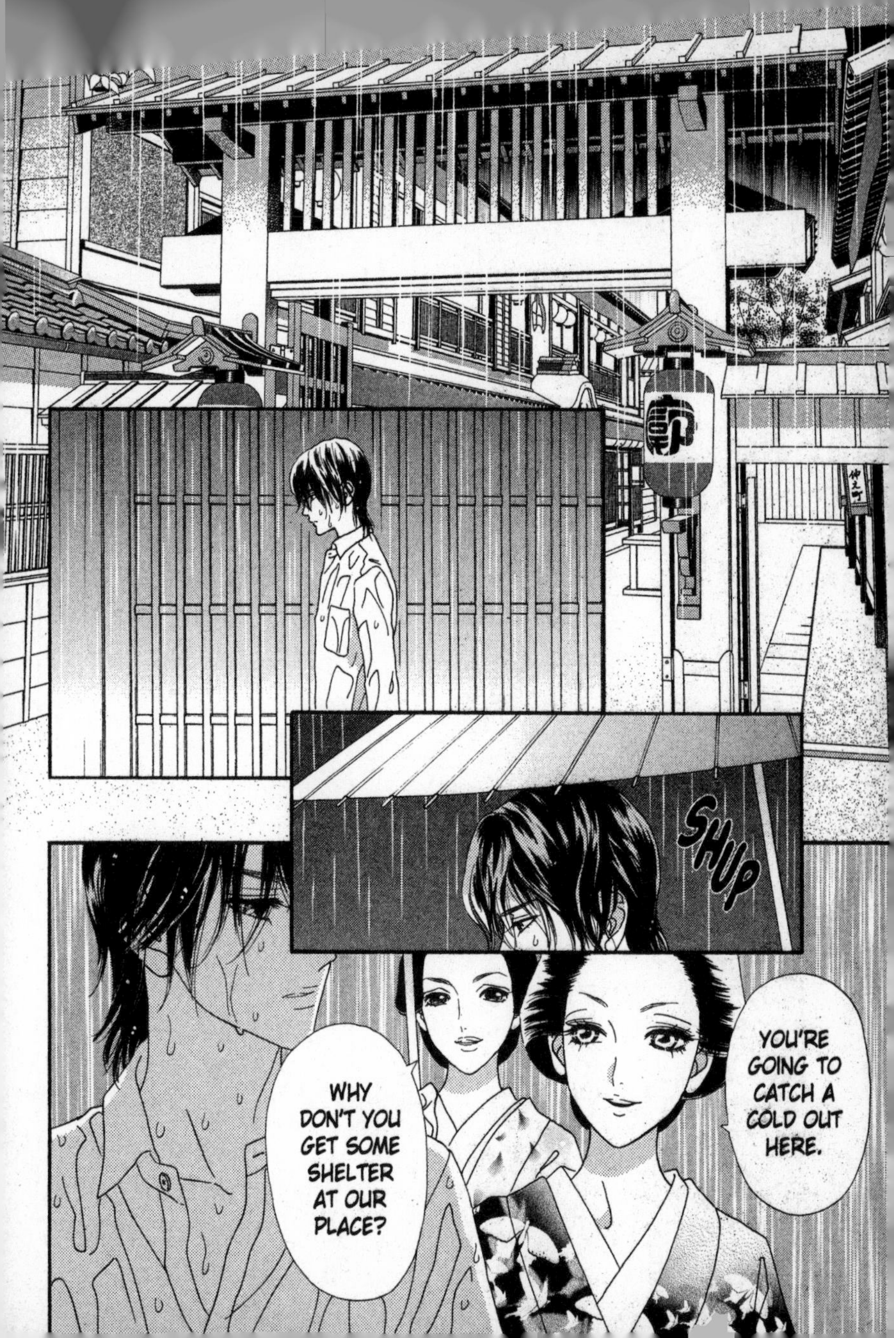
SHUP
YOU'RE GOING TO CATCH A COLD OUT HERE.
WHY DON'T YOU GET SOME SHELTER AT OUR PLACE?

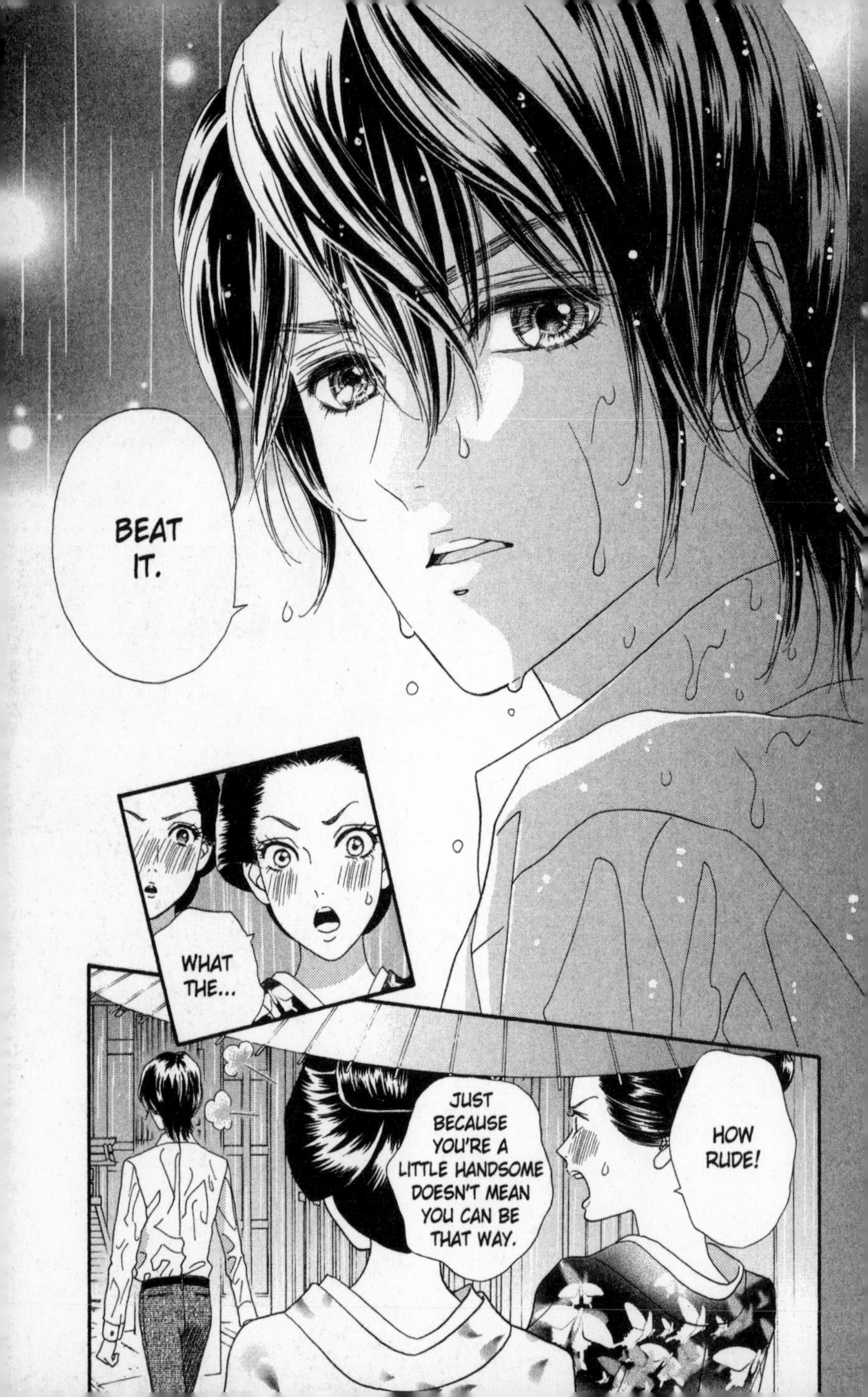
BEAT IT.
WHAT THE...
HOW RUDE!
JUST BECAUSE YOU'RE A LITTLE HANDSOME DOESN'T MEAN YOU CAN BE THAT WAY.

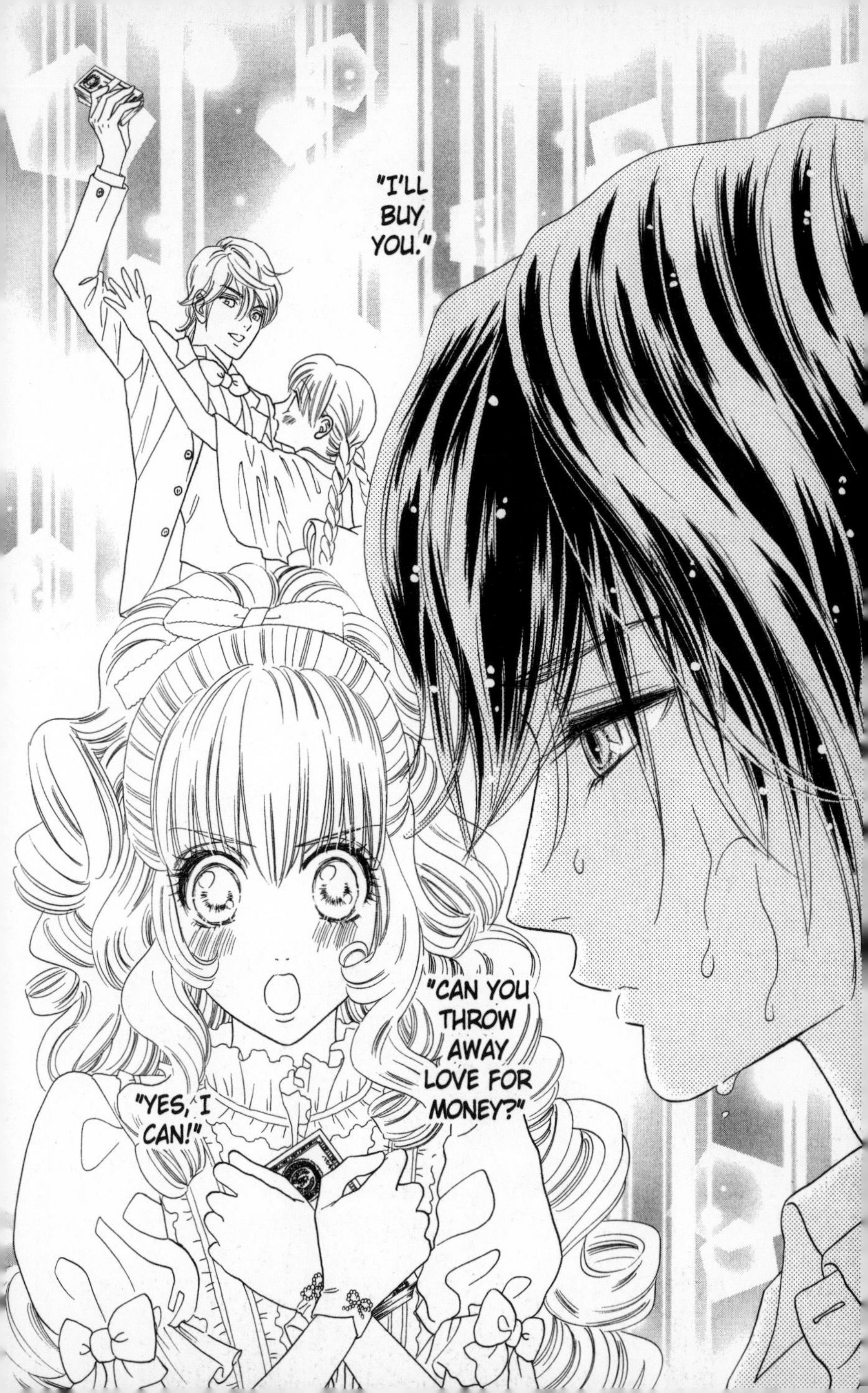
"I'LL BUY YOU."
"CAN YOU THROW AWAY LOVE FOR MONEY?"
"YES, I CAN!"

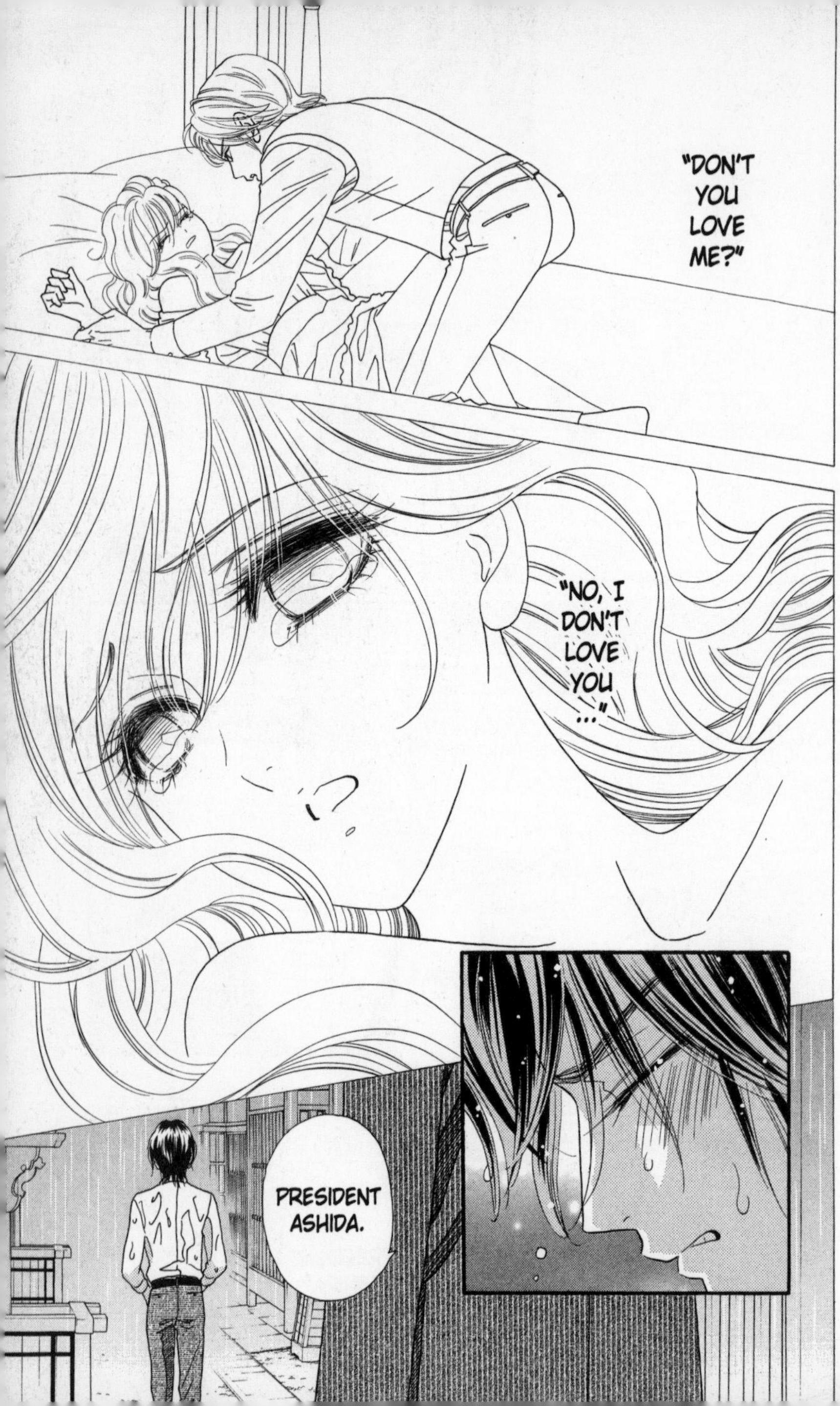
"DON'T YOU LOVE ME?"
"NO, I DON'T LOVE YOU ..."
PRESIDENT ASHIDA.

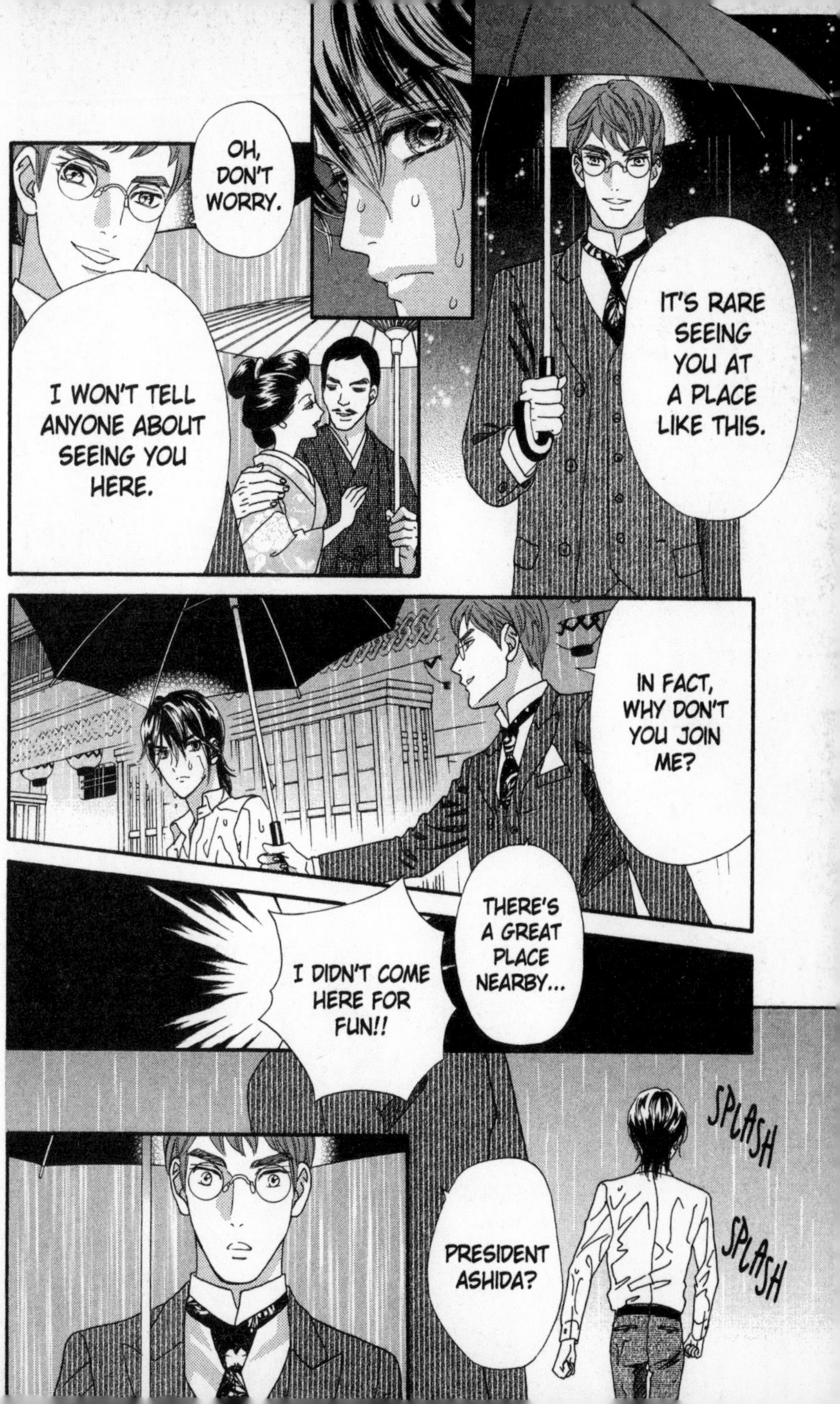
IT'S RARE SEEING YOU AT A PLACE LIKE THIS.
OH, DON'T WORRY.
I WON'T TELL ANYONE ABOUT SEEING YOU HERE.
IN FACT, WHY DON'T YOU JOIN ME?
THERE'S A GREAT PLACE NEARBY...
I DIDN'T COME HERE FOR FUN!!
SPLASH
SPLASH
PRESIDENT ASHIDA?

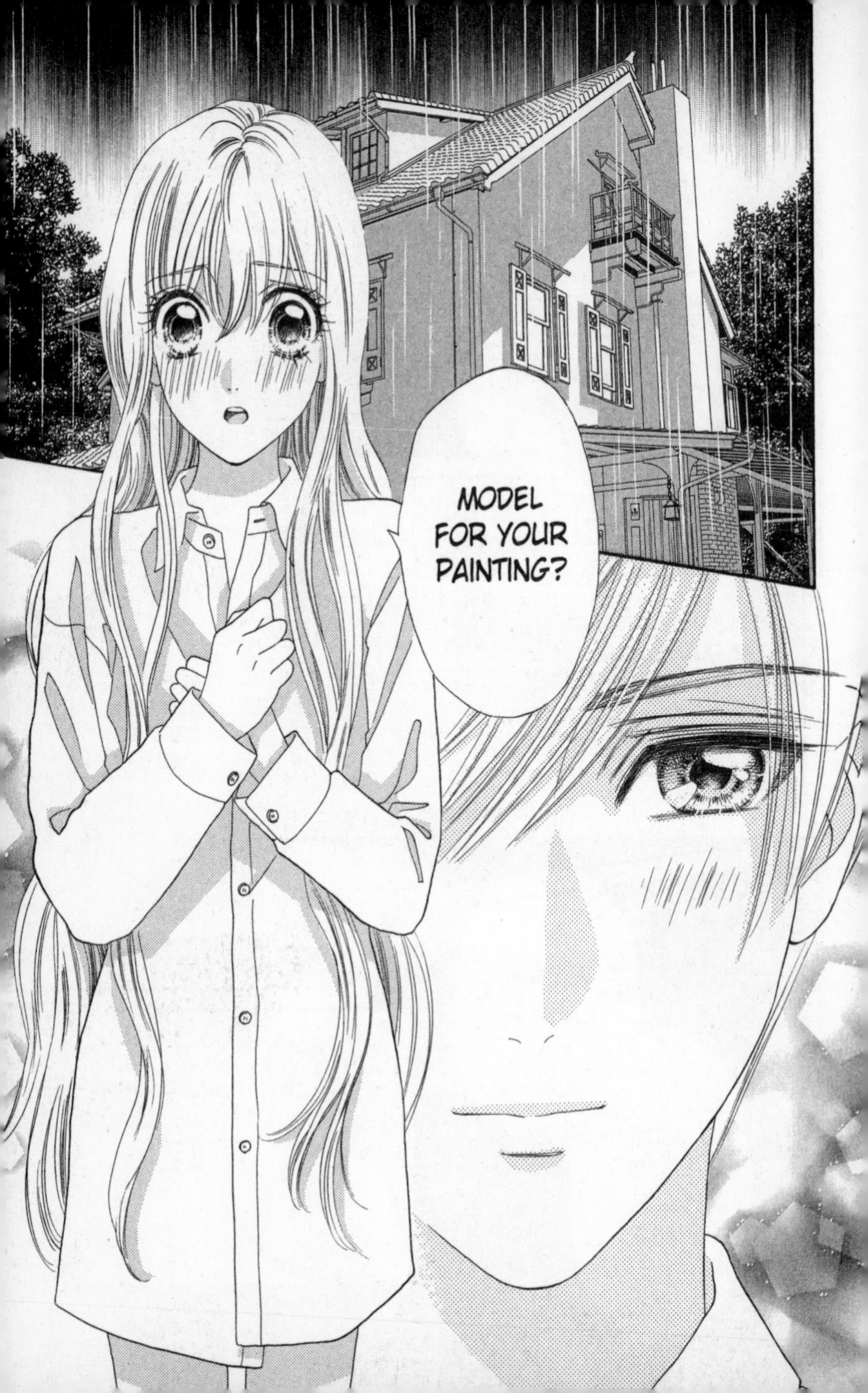
MODEL FOR YOUR PAINTING?

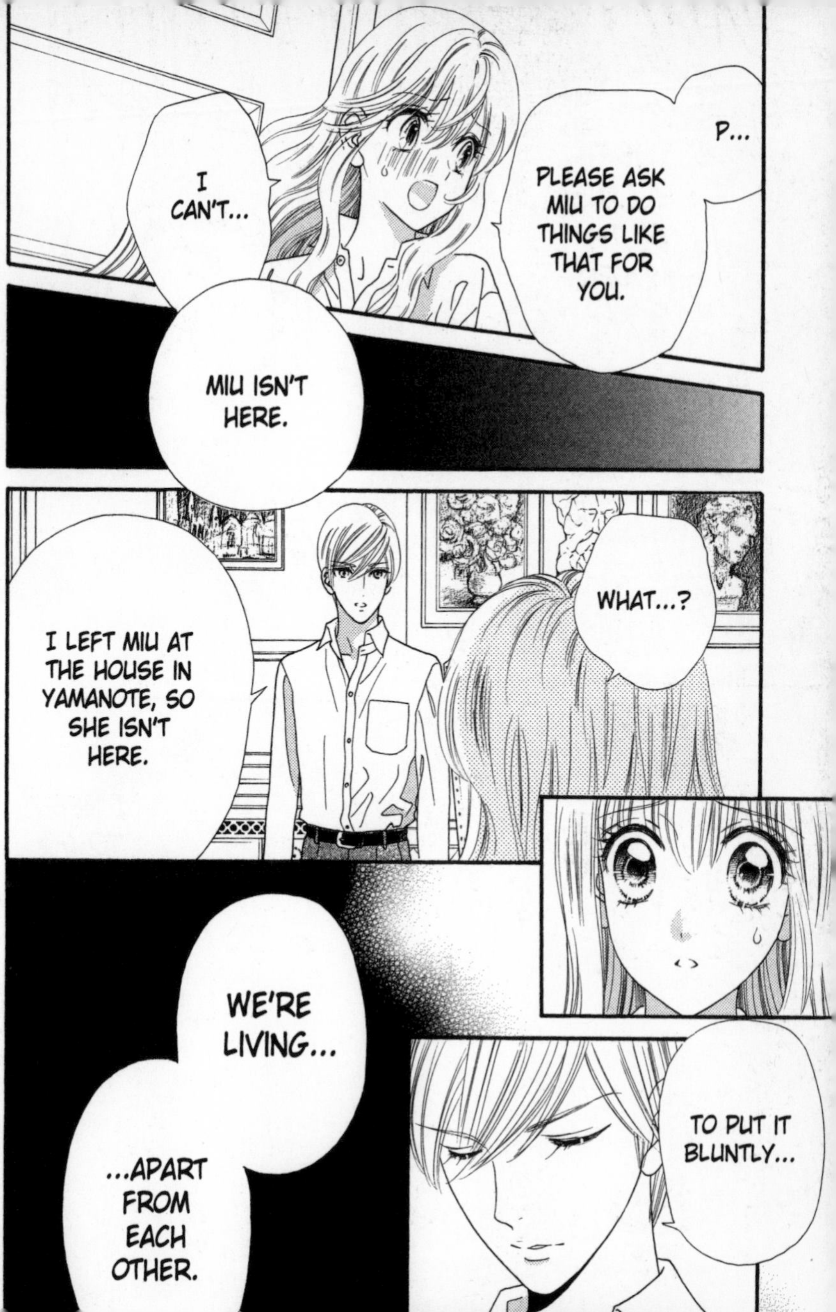
P...
PLEASE ASK MIU TO DO THINGS LIKE THAT FOR YOU.
I CAN'T...
MIU ISN'T HERE.
WHAT...?
I LEFT MIU AT THE HOUSE IN YAMANOTE, SO SHE ISN'T HERE.
TO PUT IT BLUNTLY...
WE'RE LIVING...
...APART FROM EACH OTHER.

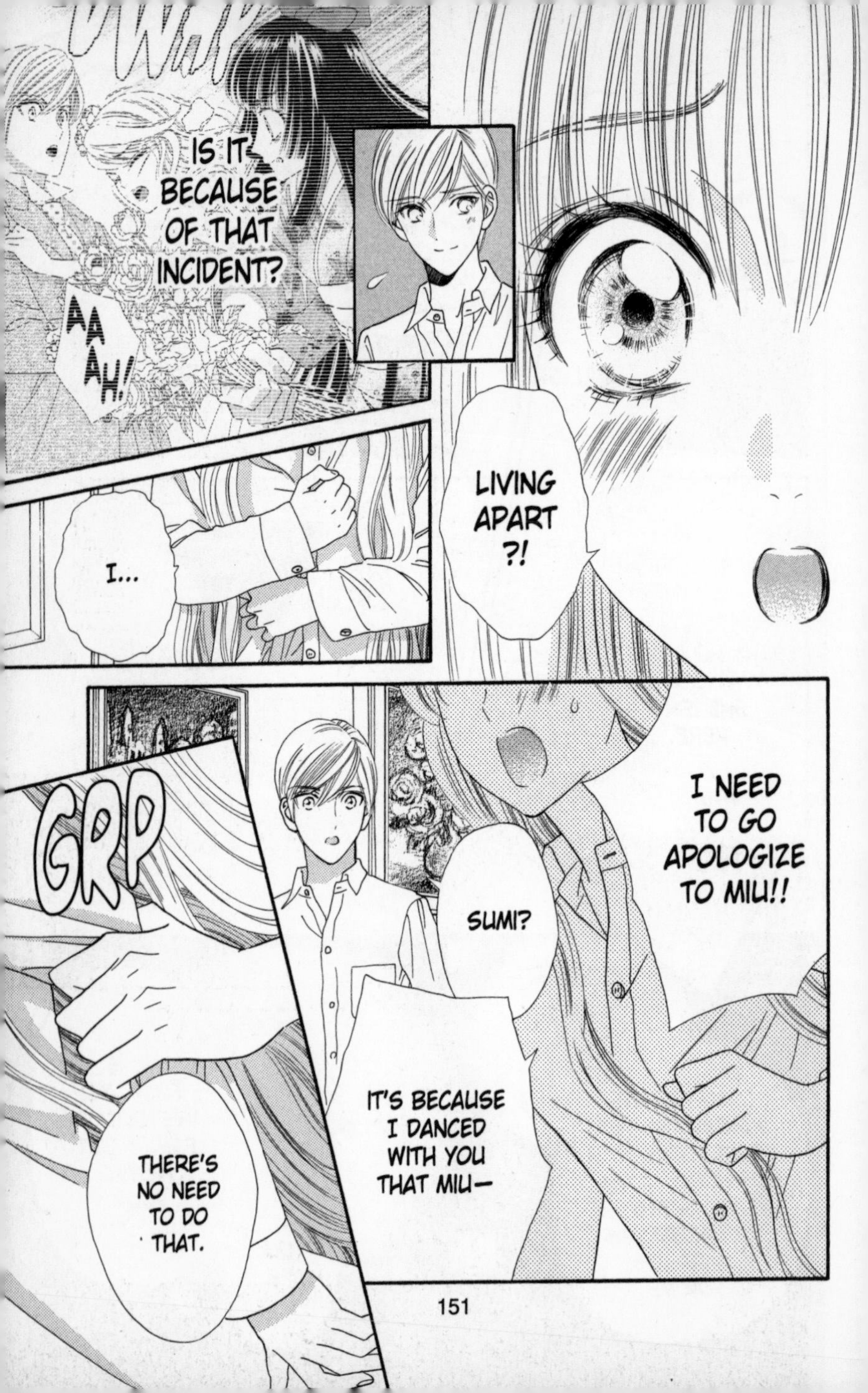
LIVING APART ?!
IS IT BECAUSE OF THAT INCIDENT?
AAAH!
I...
I NEED TO GO APOLOGIZE TO MIU!!
SUMI?
IT'S BECAUSE I DANCED WITH YOU THAT MIU—
GRP
THERE'S NO NEED TO DO THAT.

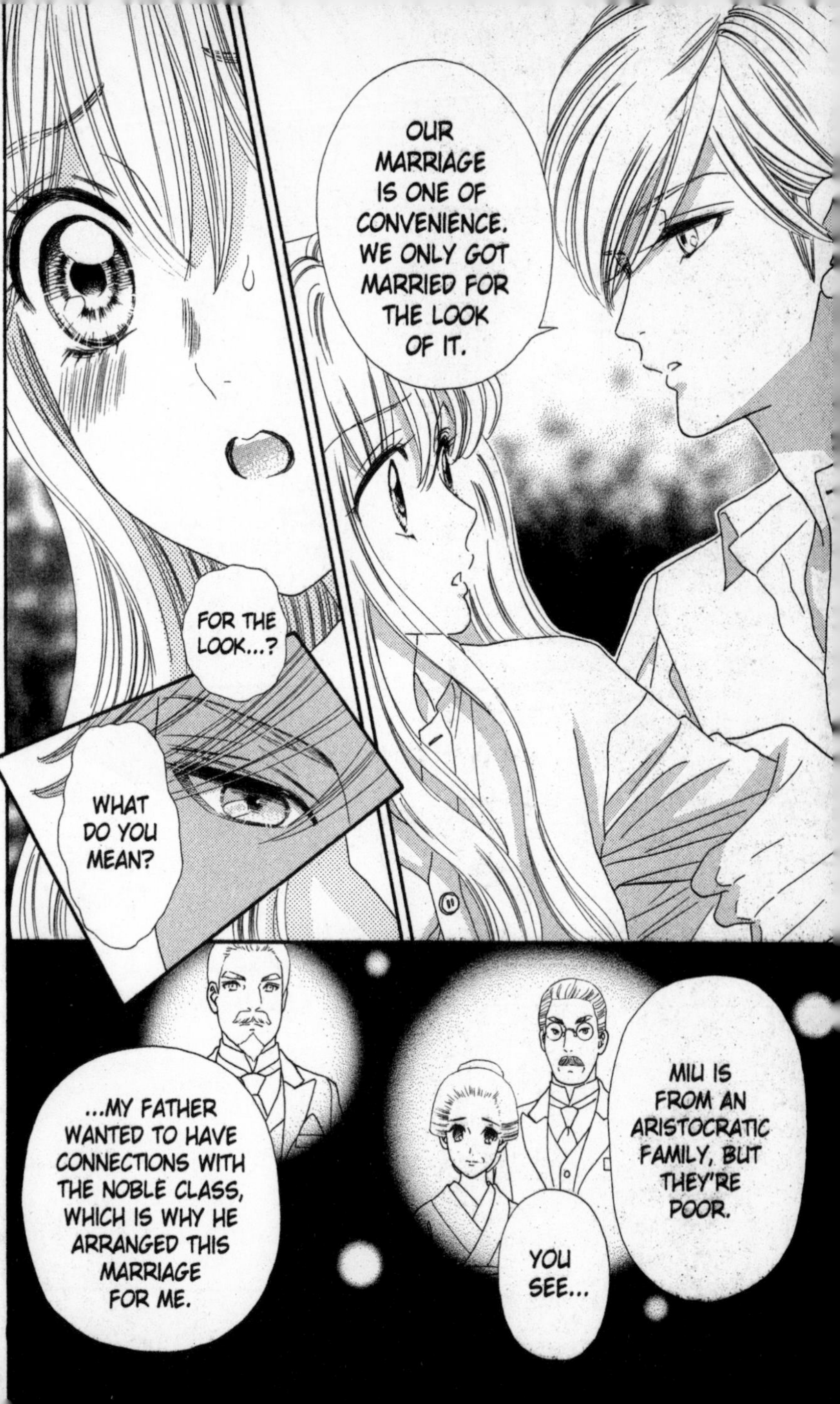
OUR MARRIAGE IS ONE OF CONVENIENCE. WE ONLY GOT MARRIED FOR THE LOOK OF IT.
FOR THE LOOK...?
WHAT DO YOU MEAN?
MIU IS FROM AN ARISTOCRATIC FAMILY, BUT THEY'RE POOR.
YOU SEE...
...MY FATHER WANTED TO HAVE CONNECTIONS WITH THE NOBLE CLASS, WHICH IS WHY HE ARRANGED THIS MARRIAGE FOR ME.

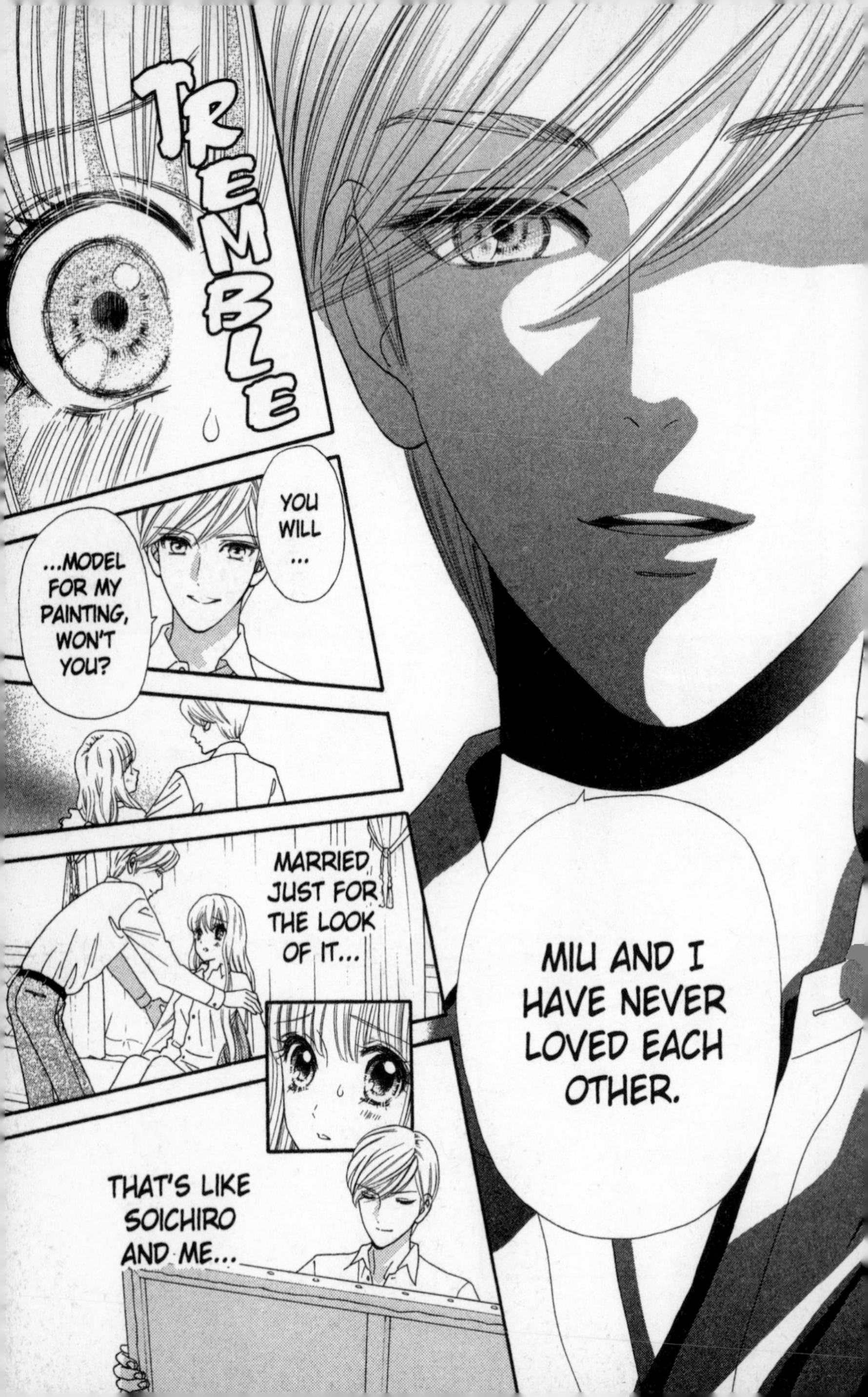
MIU AND I HAVE NEVER LOVED EACH OTHER.
TREMBLE
YOU WILL...
...MODEL FOR MY PAINTING, WON'T YOU?
MARRIED JUST FOR THE LOOK OF IT...
THAT'S LIKE SOICHIRO AND ME...

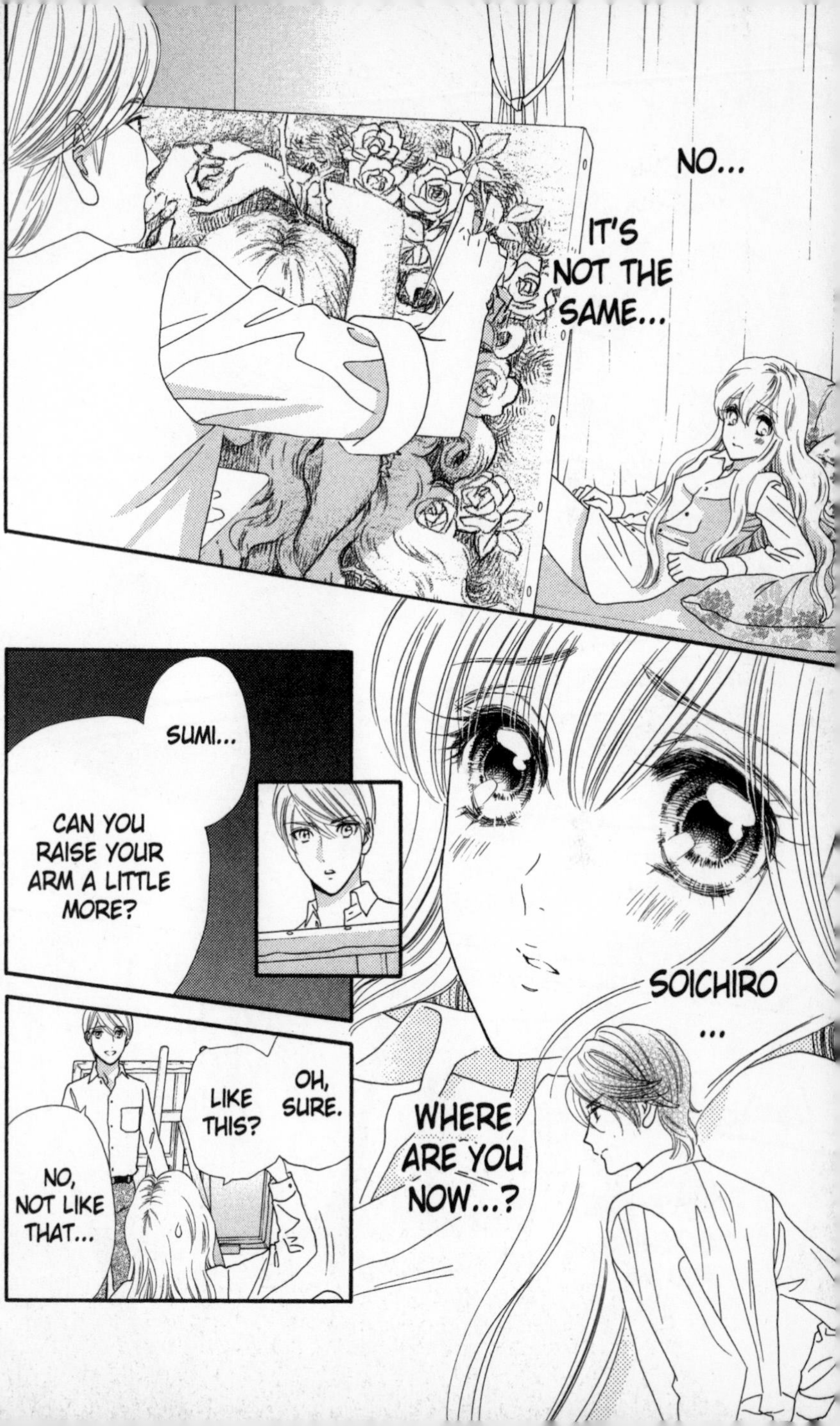
NO...
IT'S NOT THE SAME...
SOICHIRO ...
WHERE ARE YOU NOW...?
SUMI...
CAN YOU RAISE YOUR ARM A LITTLE MORE?
OH, SURE.
LIKE THIS?
NO, NOT LIKE THAT...

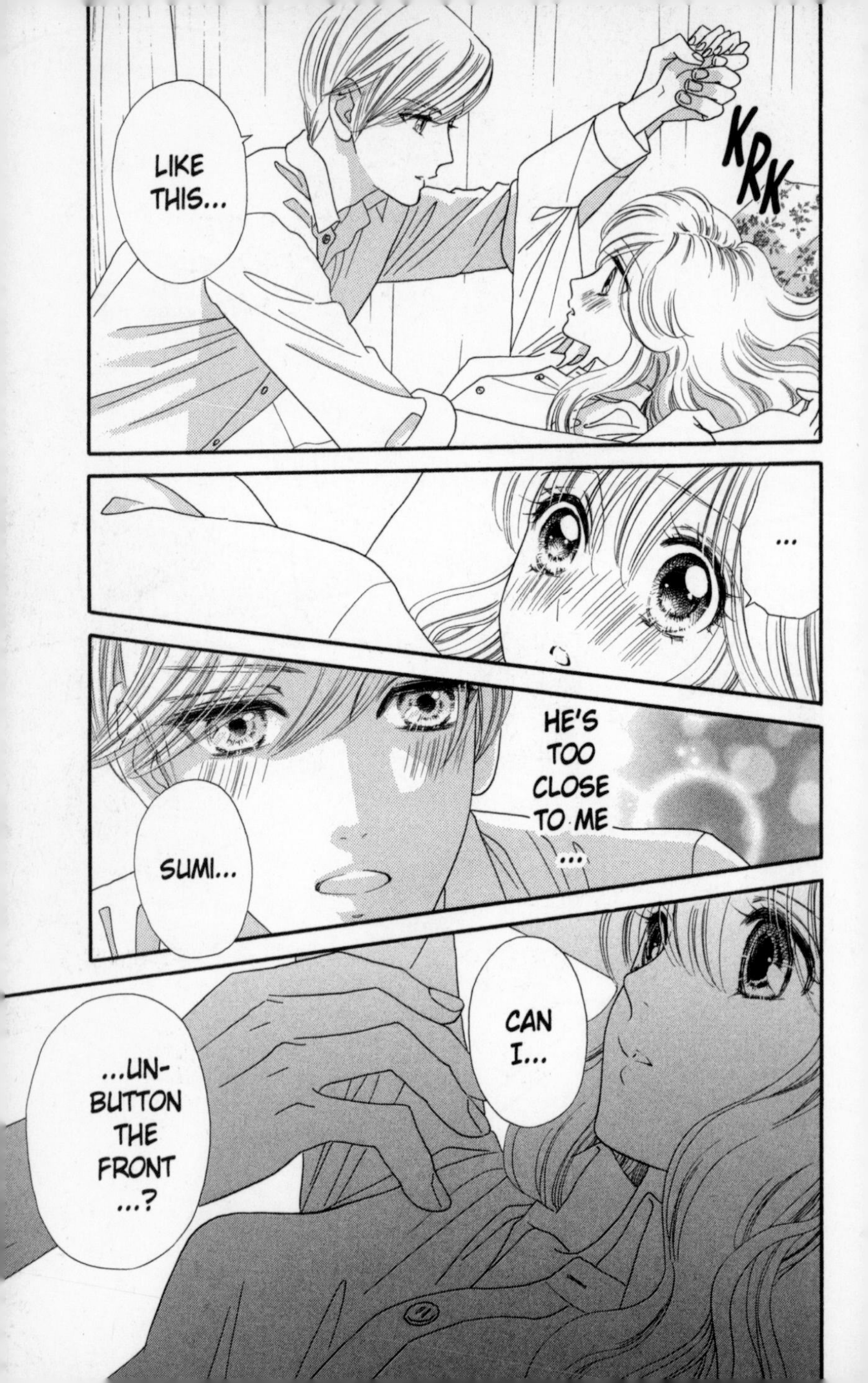
KRK
LIKE THIS...
...
HE'S TOO CLOSE TO ME ...
SUMI...
CAN I...
...UN-BUTTON THE FRONT ...?

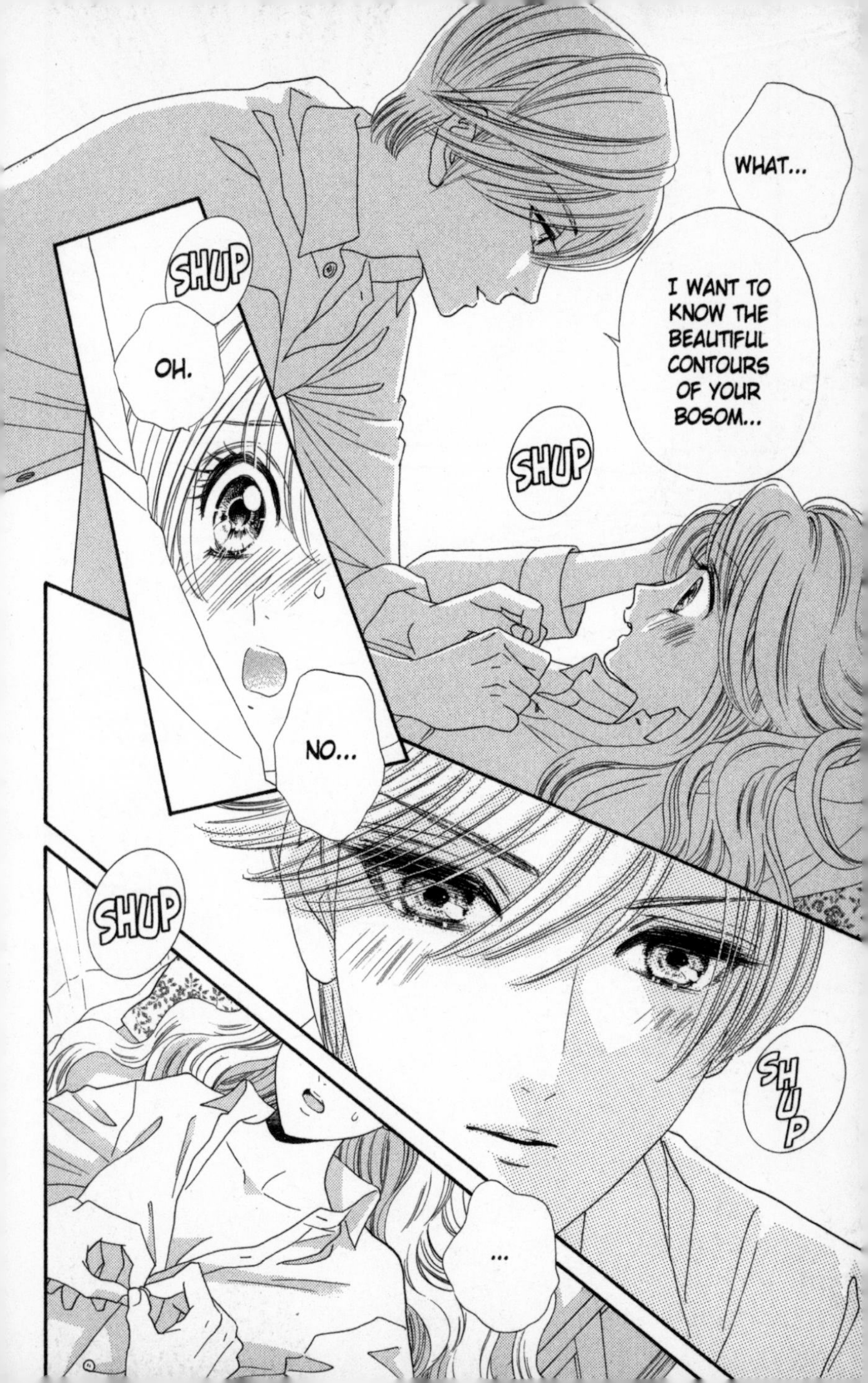
WHAT...
I WANT TO KNOW THE BEAUTIFUL CONTOURS OF YOUR BOSOM...
SHUP
SHUP
OH.
NO...
SHUP
...
SHUP

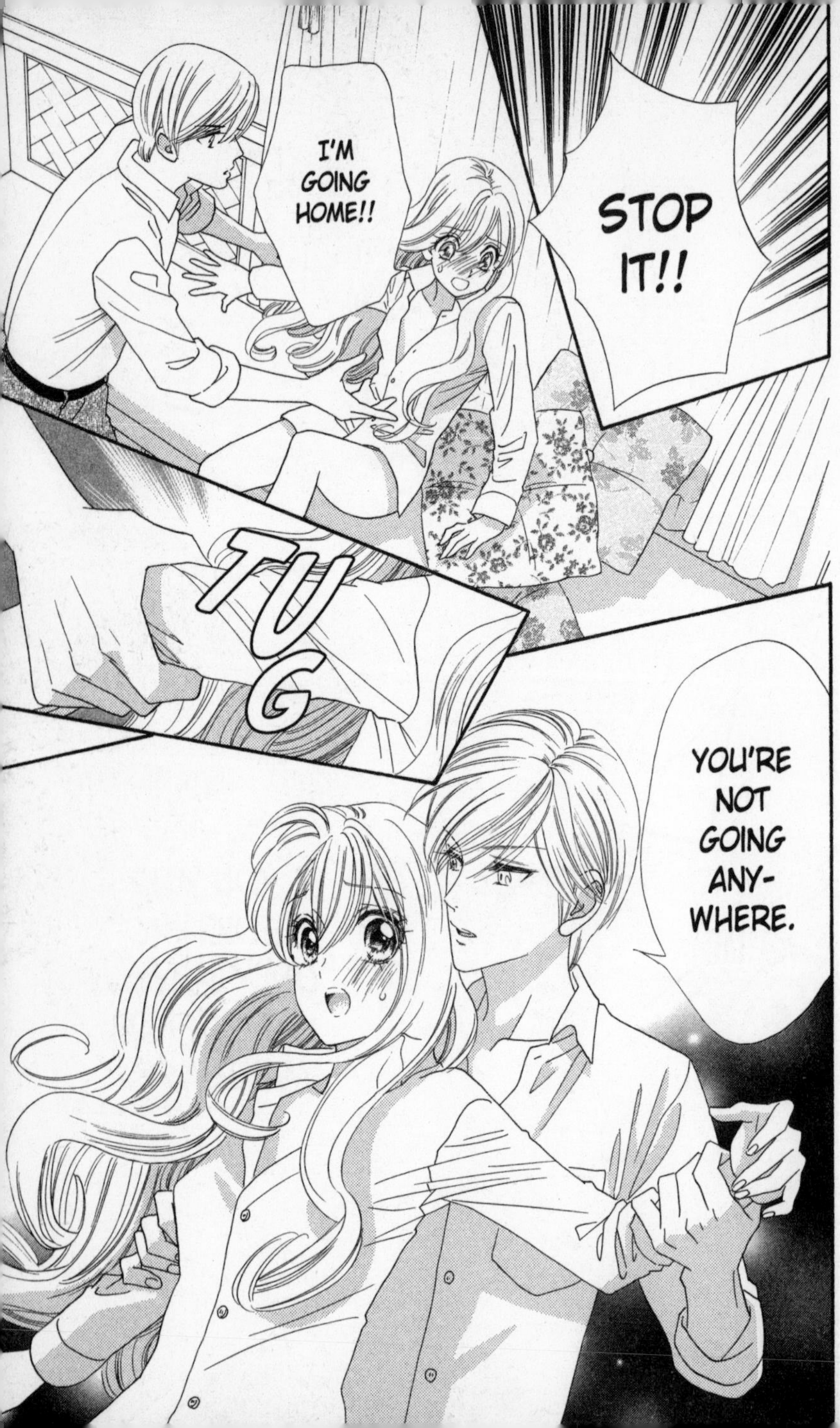
STOP IT!!
I'M GOING HOME!!
TUG
YOU'RE NOT GOING ANY-WHERE.

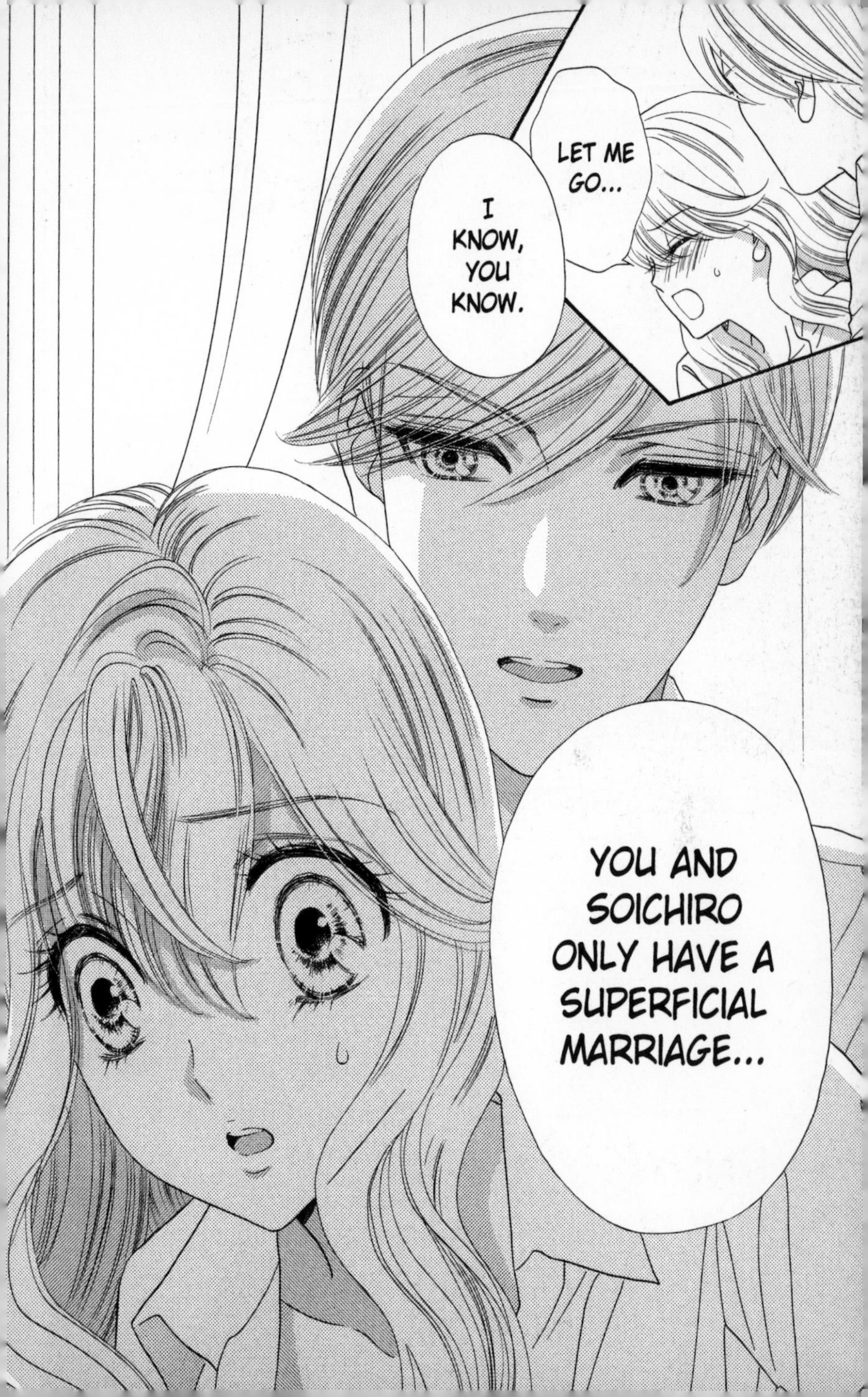
LET ME GO...
I KNOW, YOU KNOW.
YOU AND SOICHIRO ONLY HAVE A SUPERFICIAL MARRIAGE...

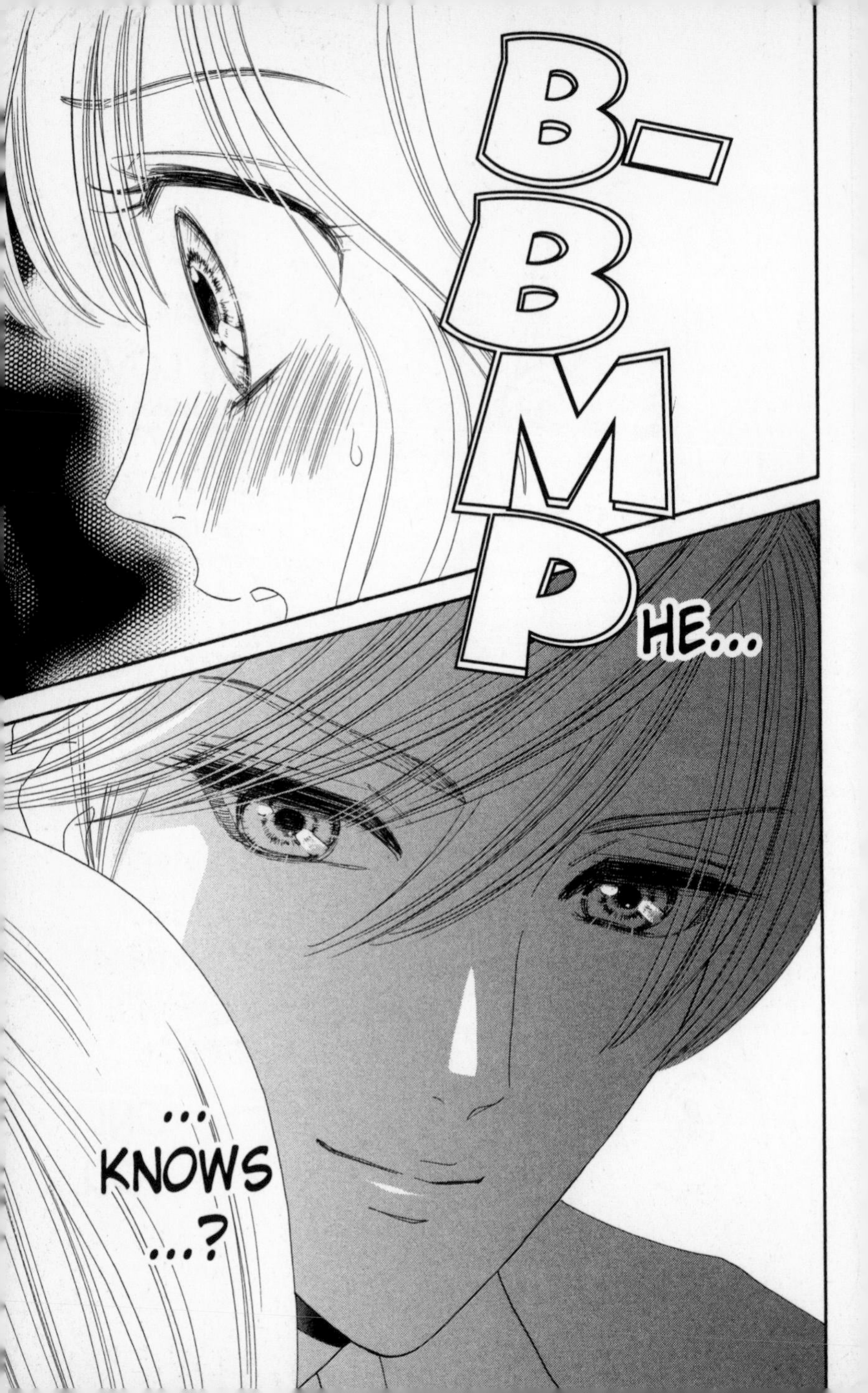
B-BMP
HE...
...KNOWS ...?

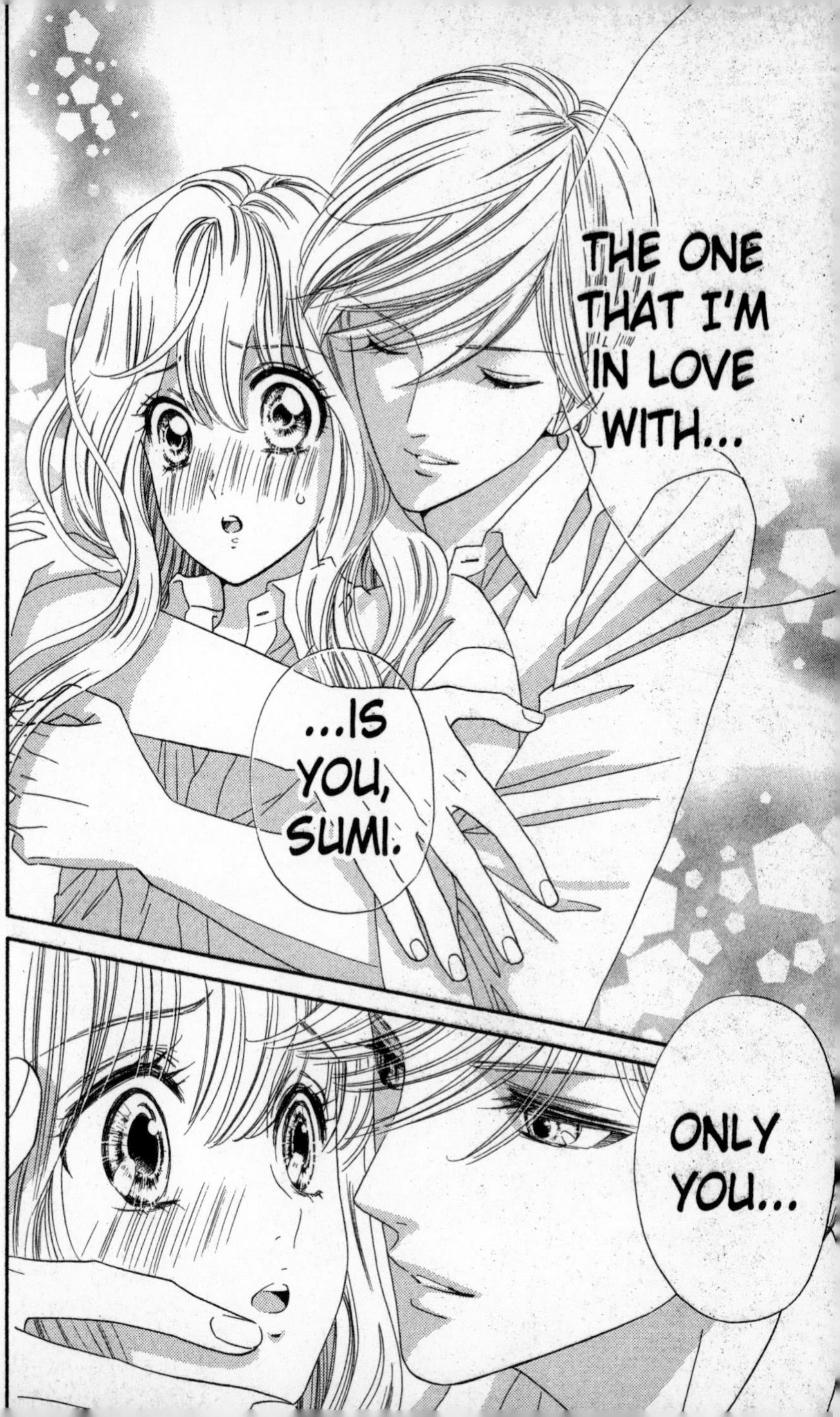
THE ONE THAT I'M IN LOVE WITH...
...IS YOU, SUMI.
ONLY YOU...

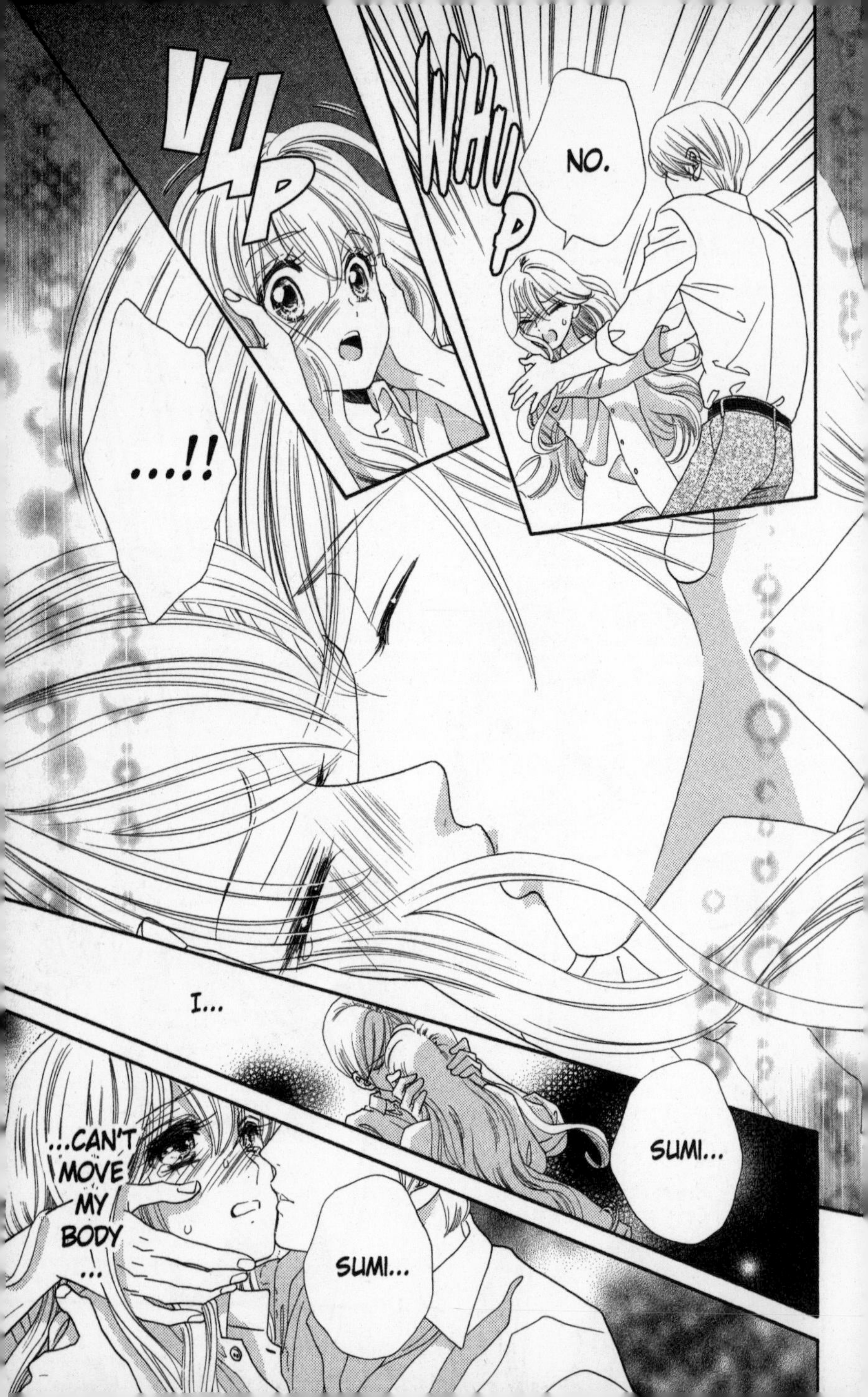
WHUP
NO.
VUP
...!!
I...
SUMI...
SUMI...
...CAN'T MOVE MY BODY...

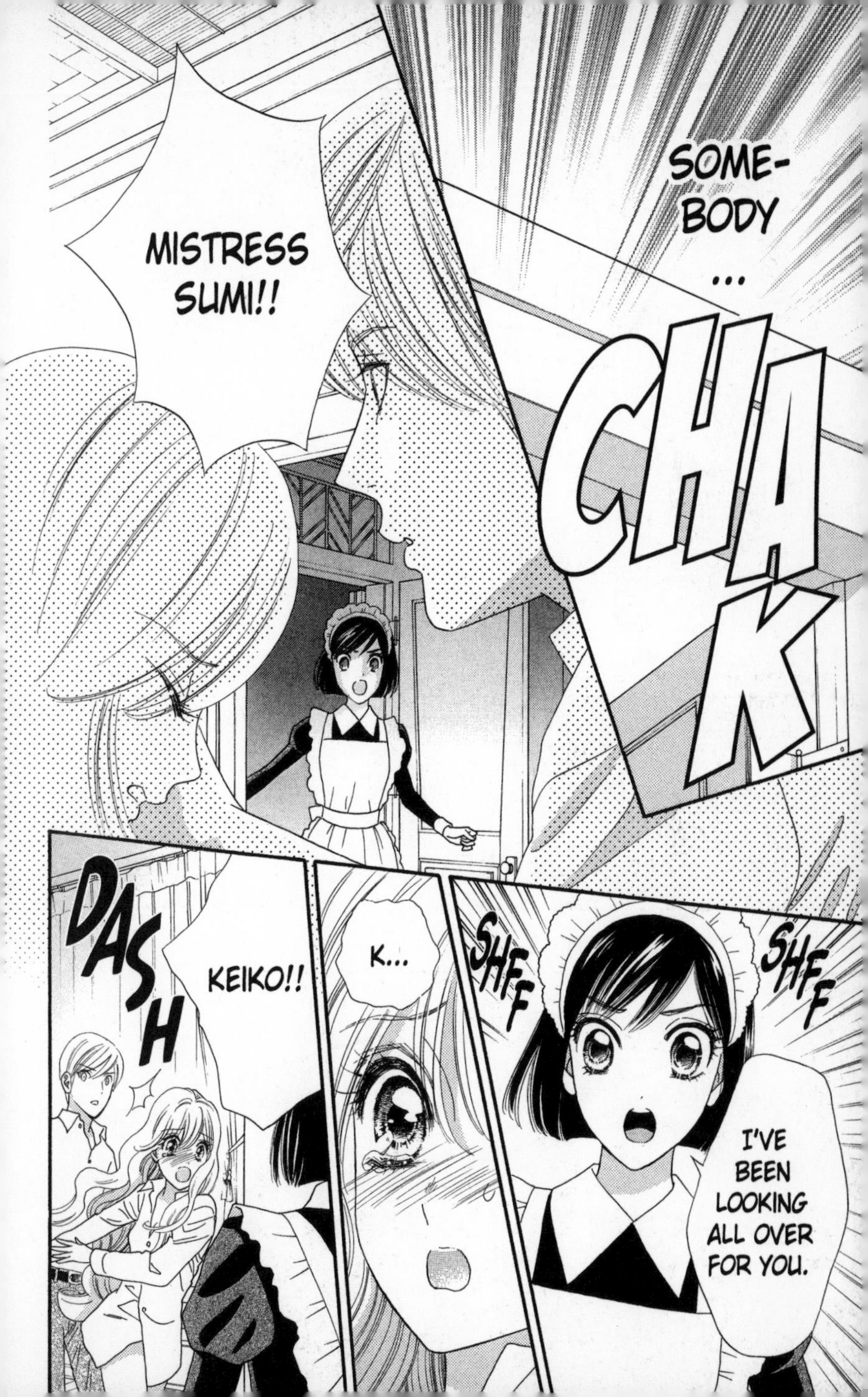
SOME-
BODY
...
CHAK
MISTRESS SUMI!!
SHFF
SHFF
I'VE BEEN LOOKING ALL OVER FOR YOU.
K...
DASH
KEIKO!!

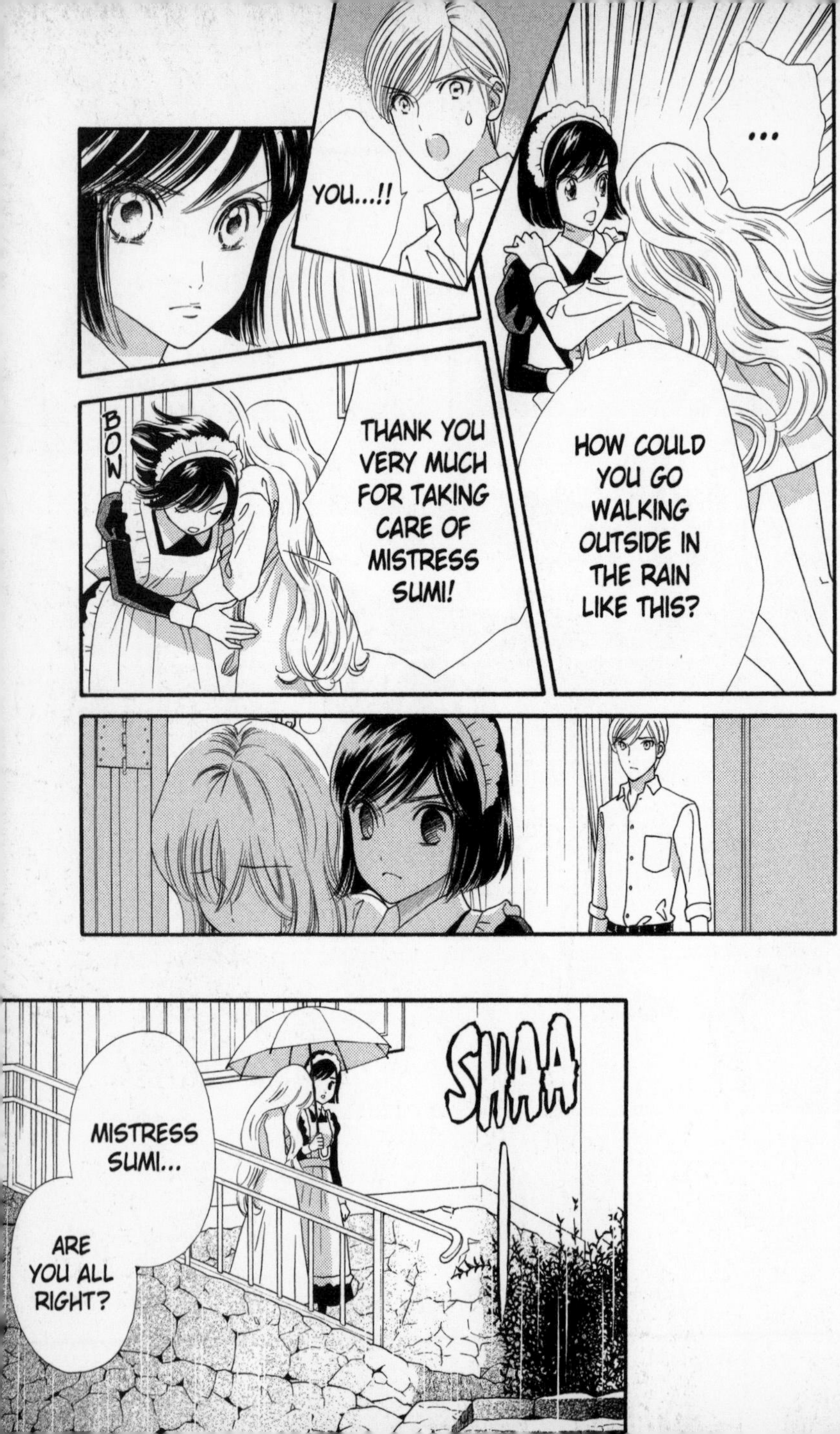
...
HOW COULD YOU GO WALKING OUTSIDE IN THE RAIN LIKE THIS?
YOU...!!
THANK YOU VERY MUCH FOR TAKING CARE OF MISTRESS SUMI!
BOW
SHAA
MISTRESS SUMI...
ARE YOU ALL RIGHT?

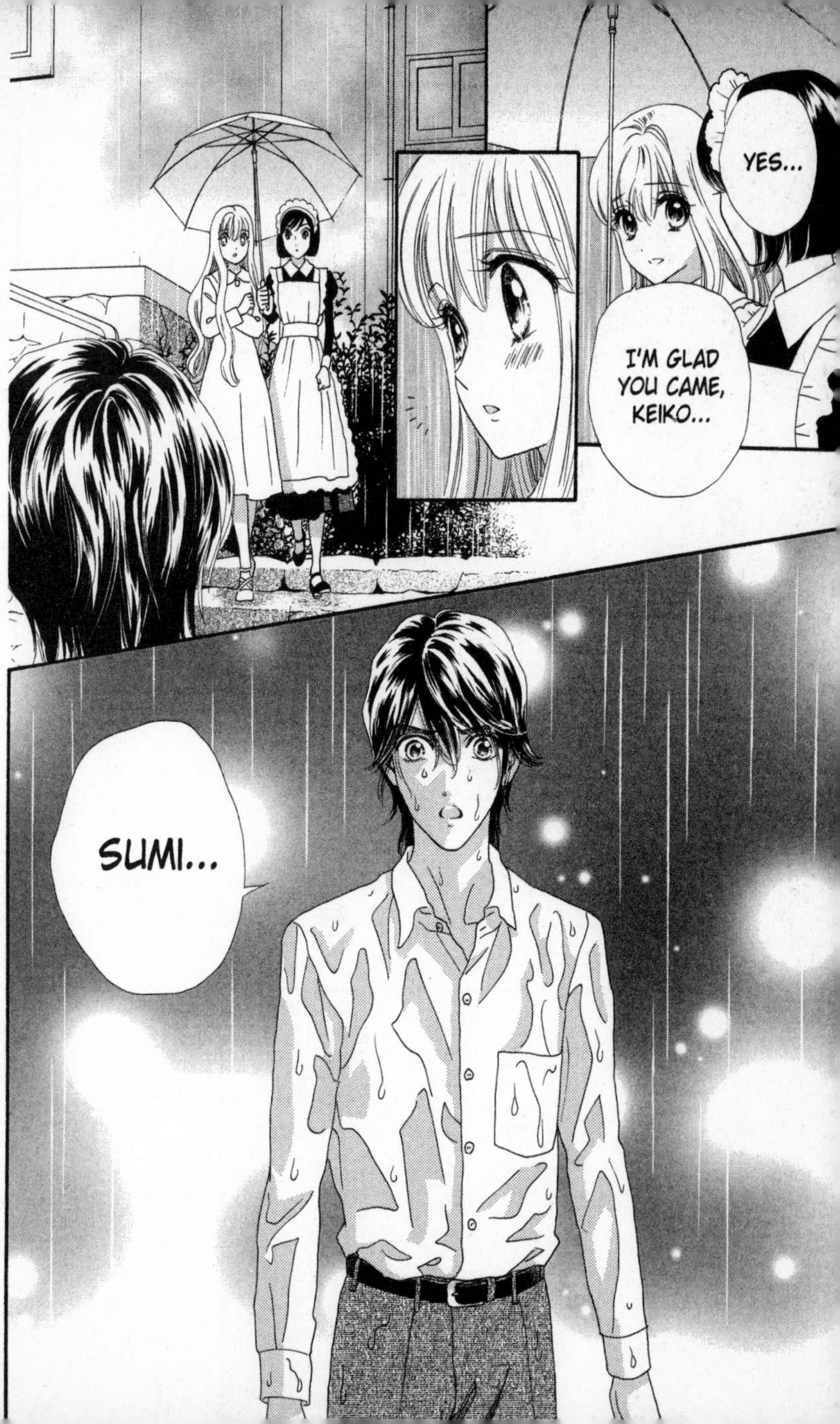
YES...
I'M GLAD YOU CAME, KEIKO...
SUMI...

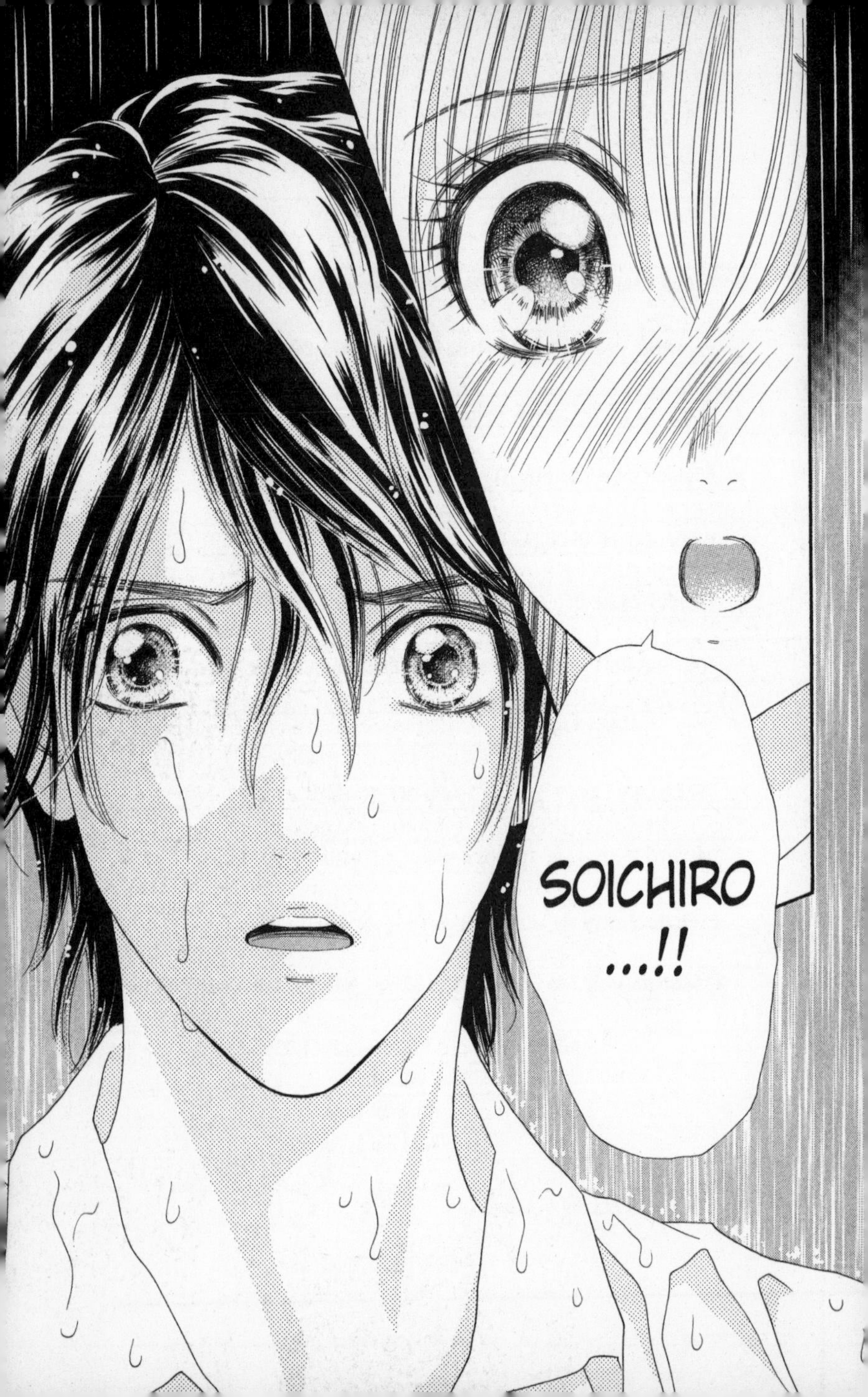
SOICHIRO
...!!

RANDOM CHITCHAT

Date · ·

✿ I TOOK HALF A YEAR OFF WORKING ON *MARGARET*, BUT I ACTUALLY STARTED

DRAWING MANGA TWO MONTHS AFTER I GAVE BIRTH. RAISING A CHILD AND

WORKING AT THE SAME TIME IS EXTREMELY TOUGH. IT'S SO TOUGH THAT I

FEEL LIKE I'M CONSTANTLY FAINTING SINCE I GAVE BIRTH.

MY DAUGHTER IS DOING FINE, AND I GET A LOT OF SUPPORT FROM MY FAMILY,

THE EDITORIAL OFFICE, AND MY ASSISTANTS. I SHOULD FEEL GRATEFUL

FOR THE HELP, BUT THE HARDSHIP I FEEL IS OVERWHELMING, AND I CAN'T

STOP WHINING ABOUT IT.

I FEEL LIKE I KEEP SAYING "HANG ON" TO BOTH MY WORK AND MY

DAUGHTER... I'D LIKE TO WORK HARDER SO THAT I CAN BE MUCH MORE

EFFICIENT WITH MY WORK AND WITH RAISING MY CHILD.

✿ SEND YOUR LETTERS OF SUPPORT TO UE-RIN, WHO IS FEELING A LITTLE DISCOURAGED!!

RINKO UEDA C/O STEPPING ON ROSES EDITOR

VIZ MEDIA

P.O. BOX 77010

SAN FRANCISCO, CA 94107

✿   ~ ♡   Rinko ☺ Ueda ☺

SEE YOU ALL IN VOLUME 6!

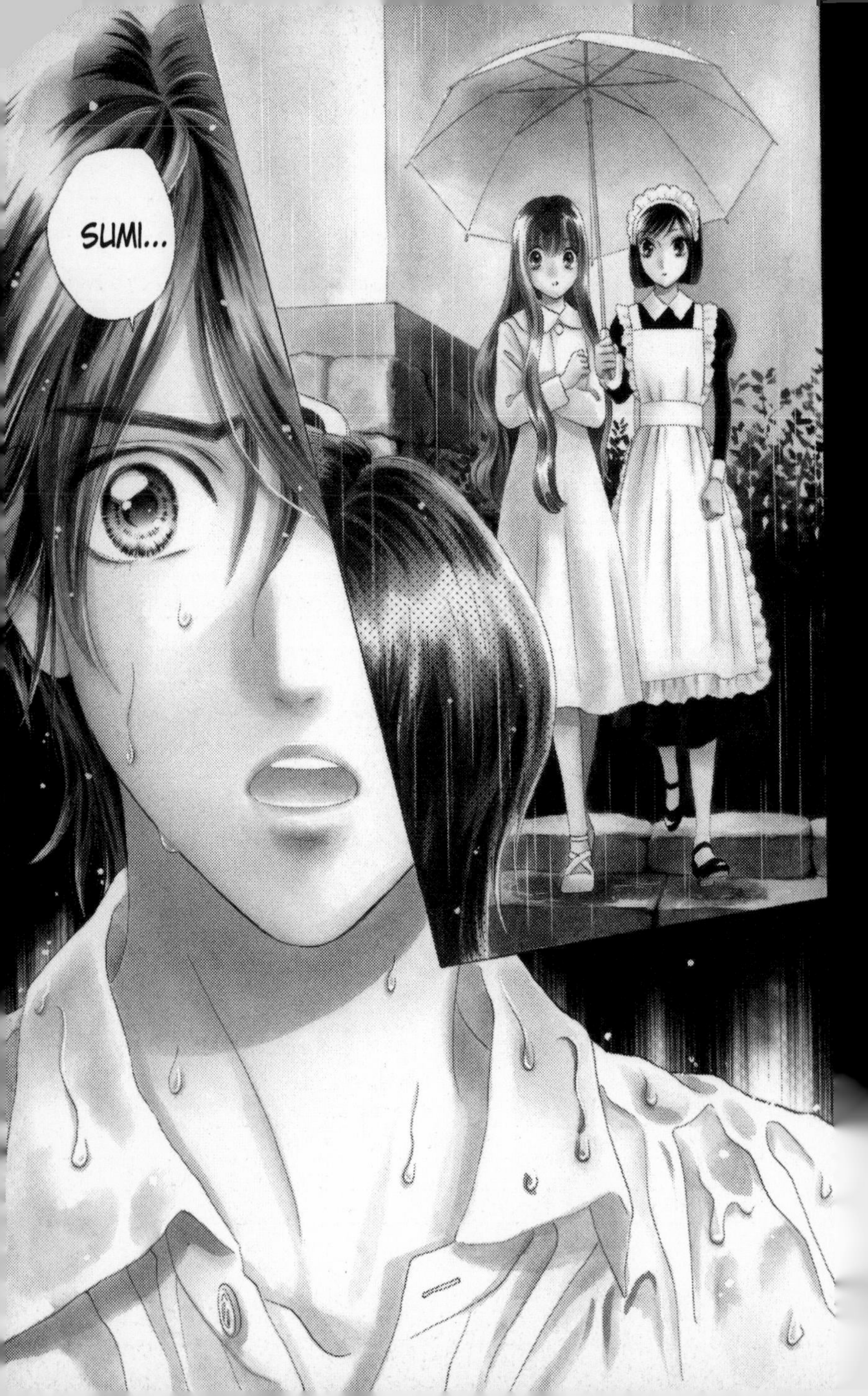
SUMI...

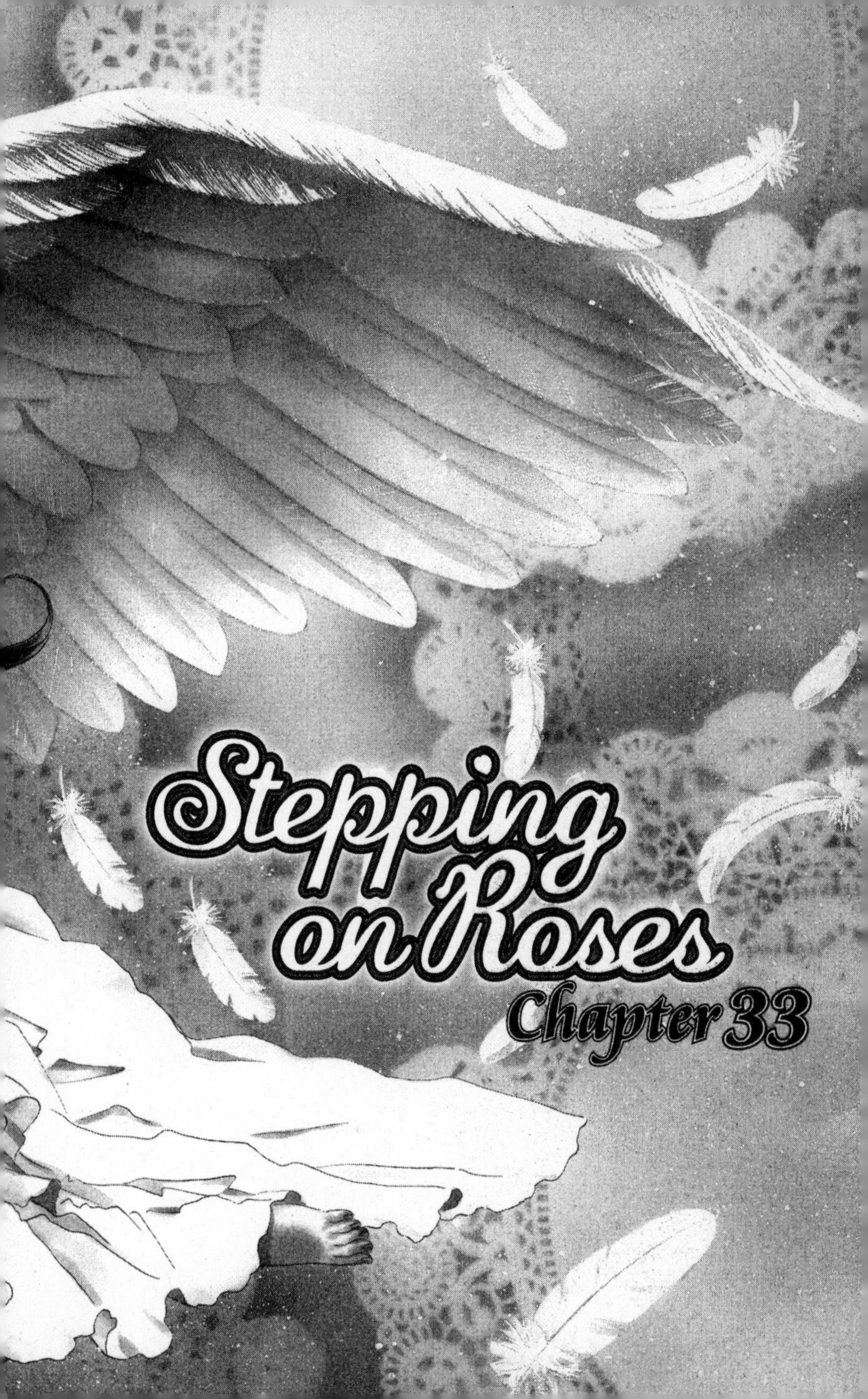
Stepping on Roses
Chapter 33

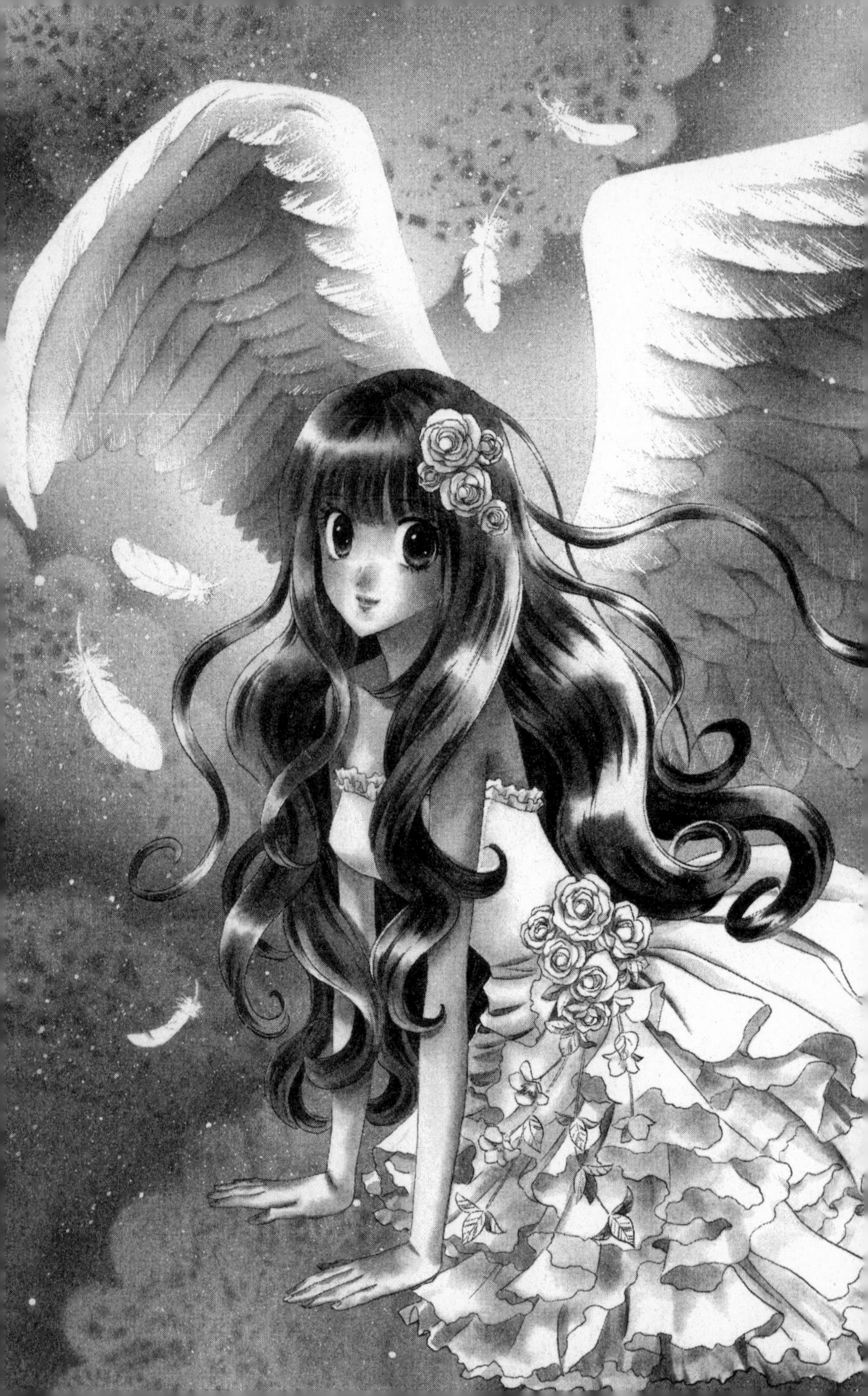

Stepping on Roses

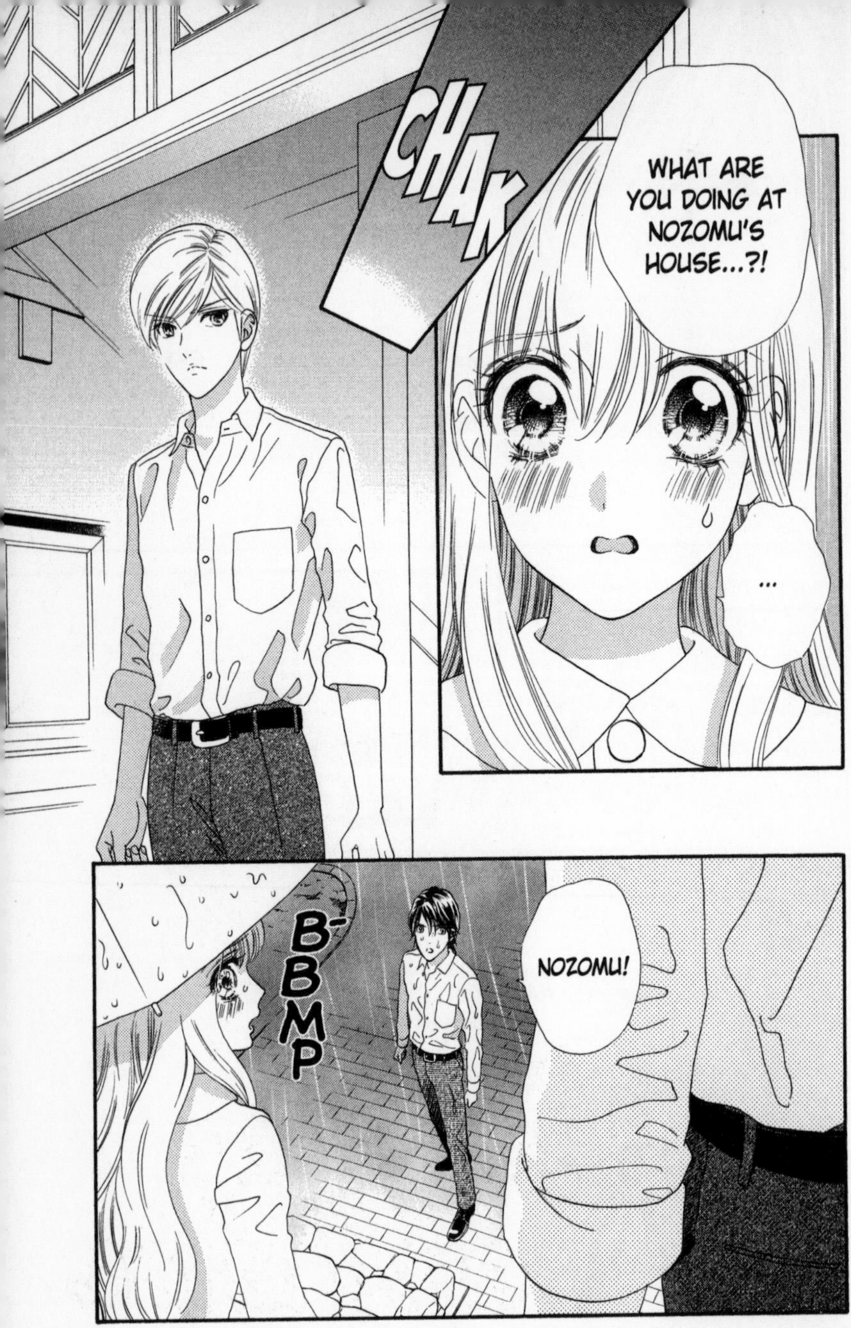
WHAT ARE YOU DOING AT NOZOMU'S HOUSE...?!
...
CHAK
NOZOMU!
B-BBMP

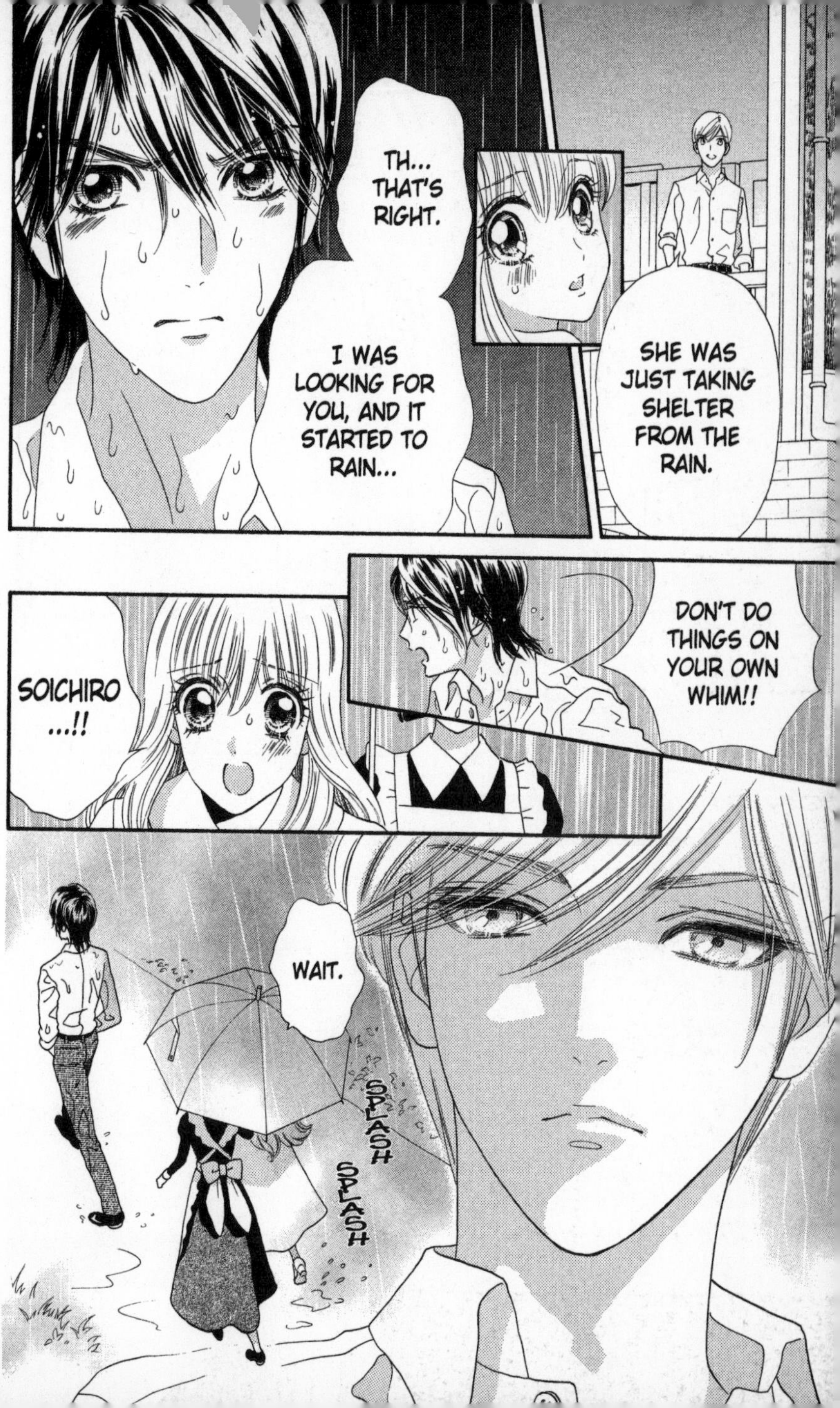
SHE WAS JUST TAKING SHELTER FROM THE RAIN.
TH... THAT'S RIGHT.
I WAS LOOKING FOR YOU, AND IT STARTED TO RAIN...
DON'T DO THINGS ON YOUR OWN WHIM!!
SOICHIRO ...!!
WAIT.
SPLASH
SPLASH

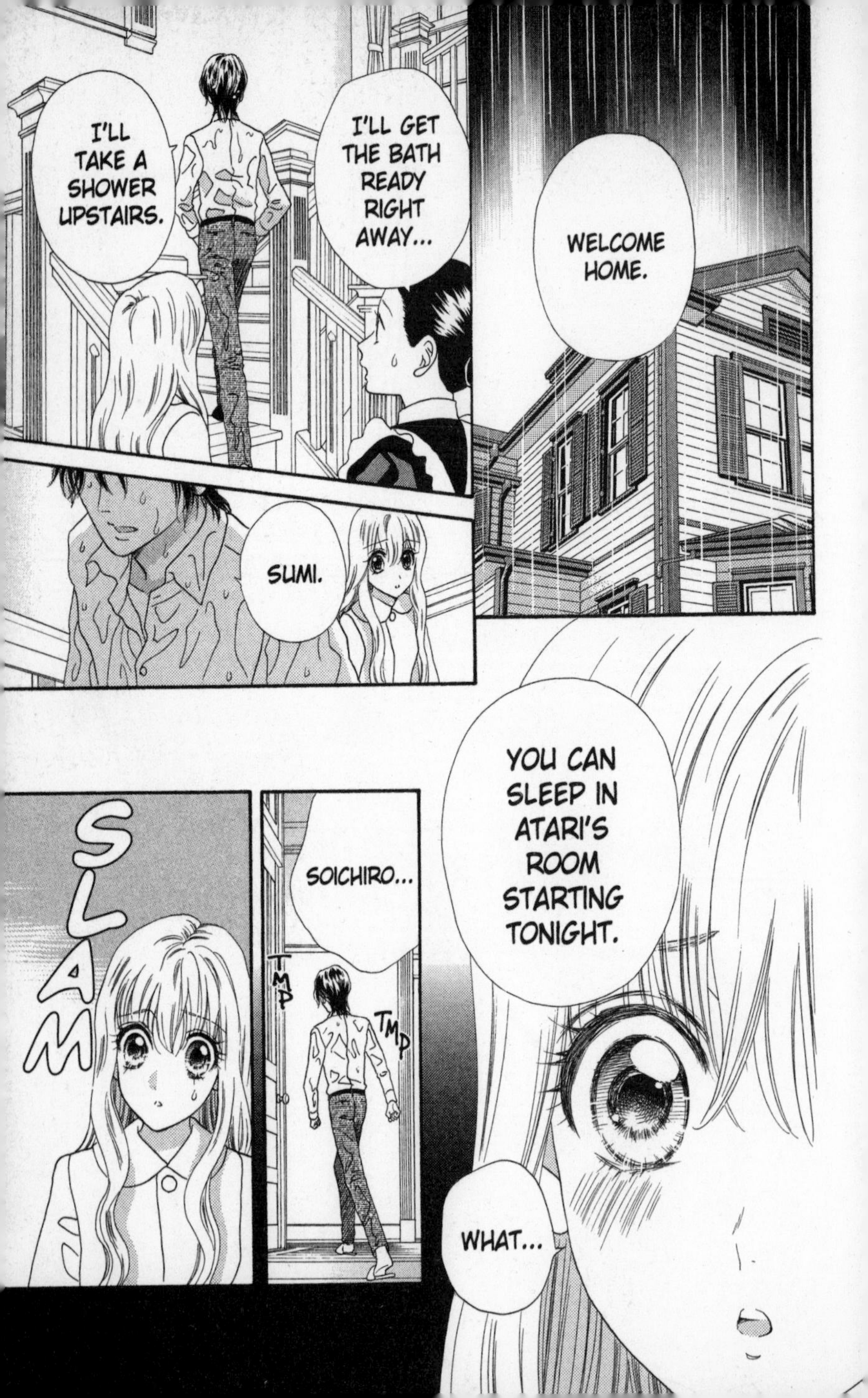
WELCOME HOME.
I'LL GET THE BATH READY RIGHT AWAY...
I'LL TAKE A SHOWER UPSTAIRS.
SUMI.
YOU CAN SLEEP IN ATARI'S ROOM STARTING TONIGHT.
WHAT...
SOICHIRO...
TMP
TMP
SLAM

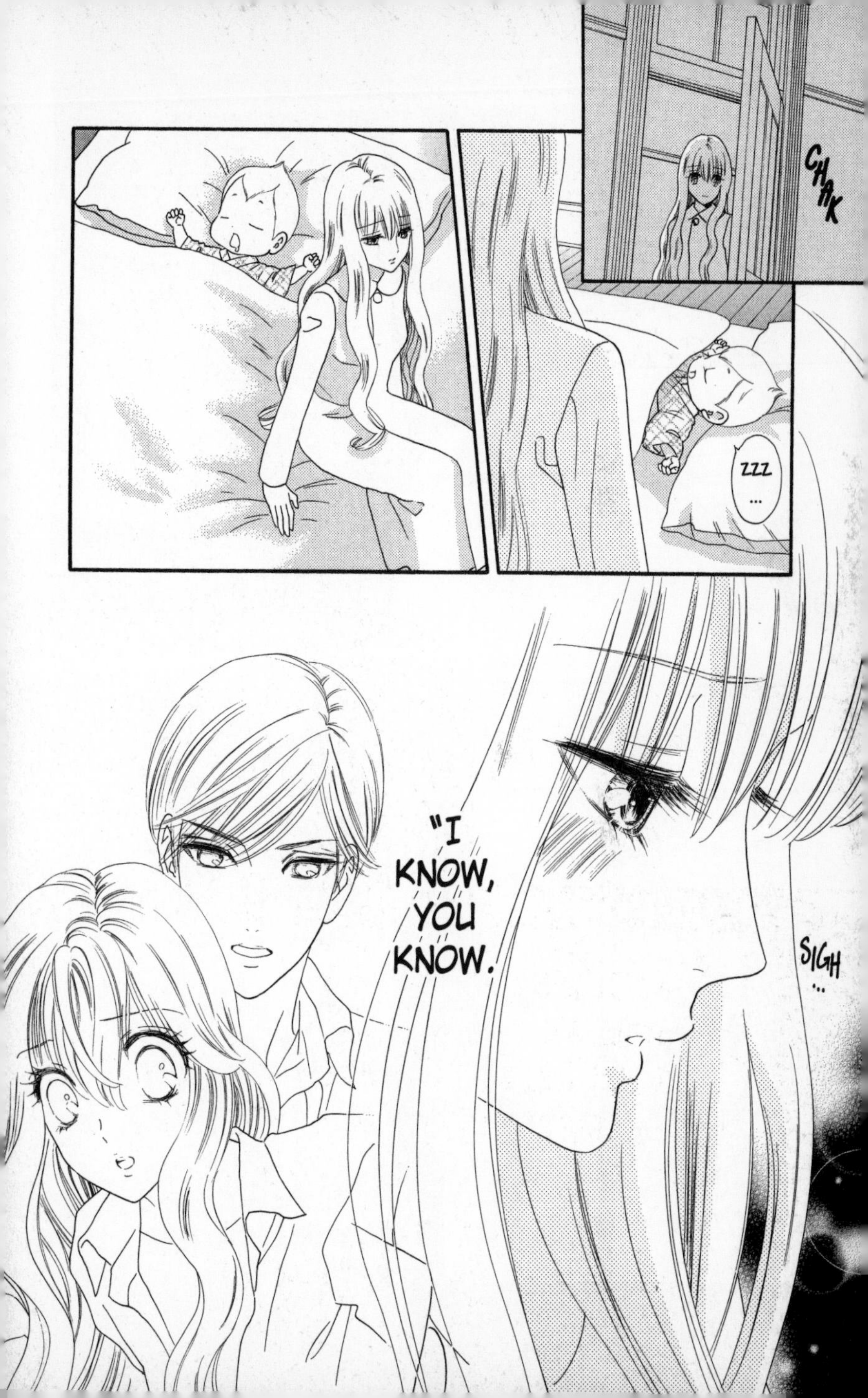
CHAK
ZZZ ...
"I KNOW, YOU KNOW.
SIGH ...

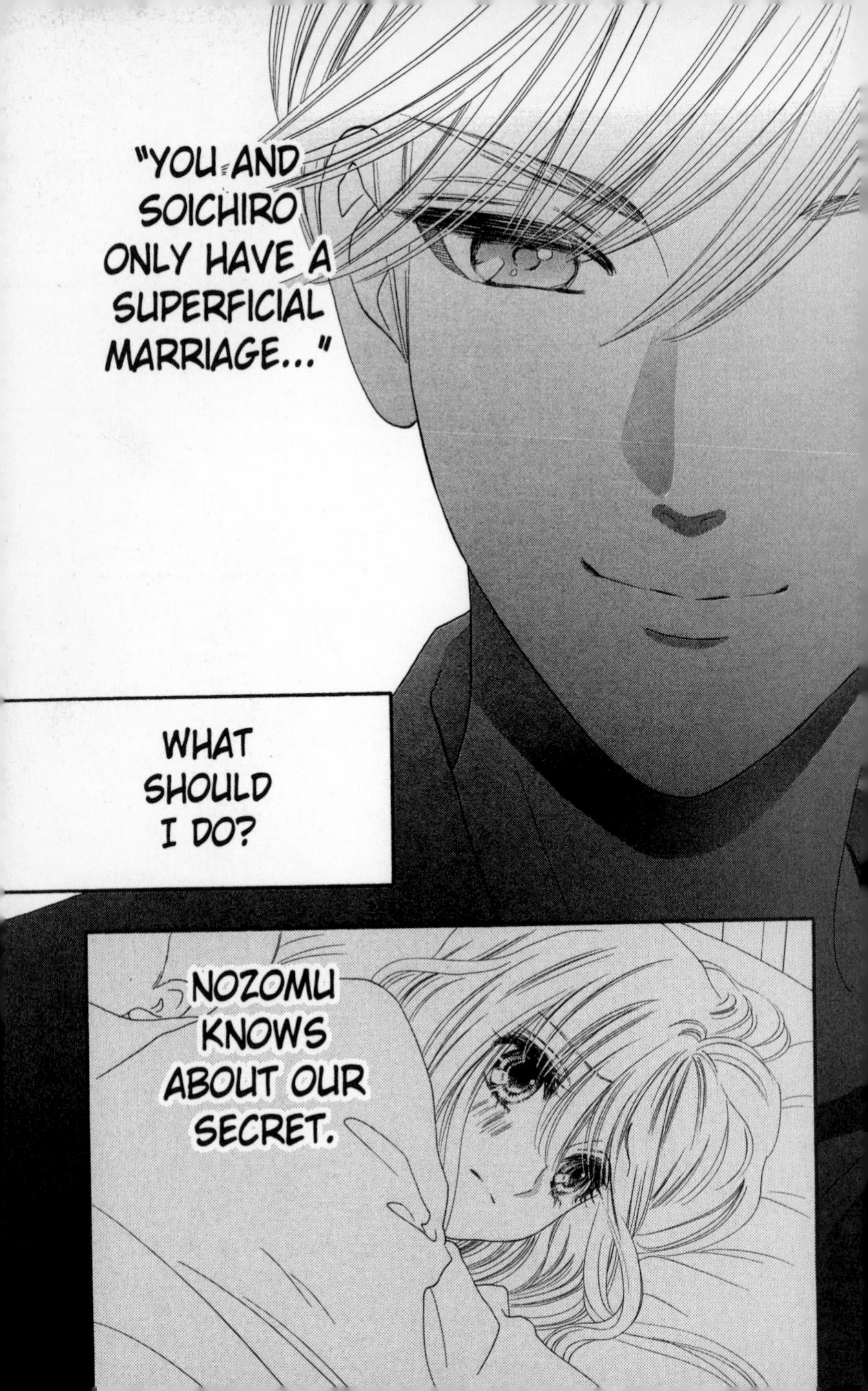
"YOU AND SOICHIRO ONLY HAVE A SUPERFICIAL MARRIAGE..."
WHAT SHOULD I DO?
NOZOMU KNOWS ABOUT OUR SECRET.

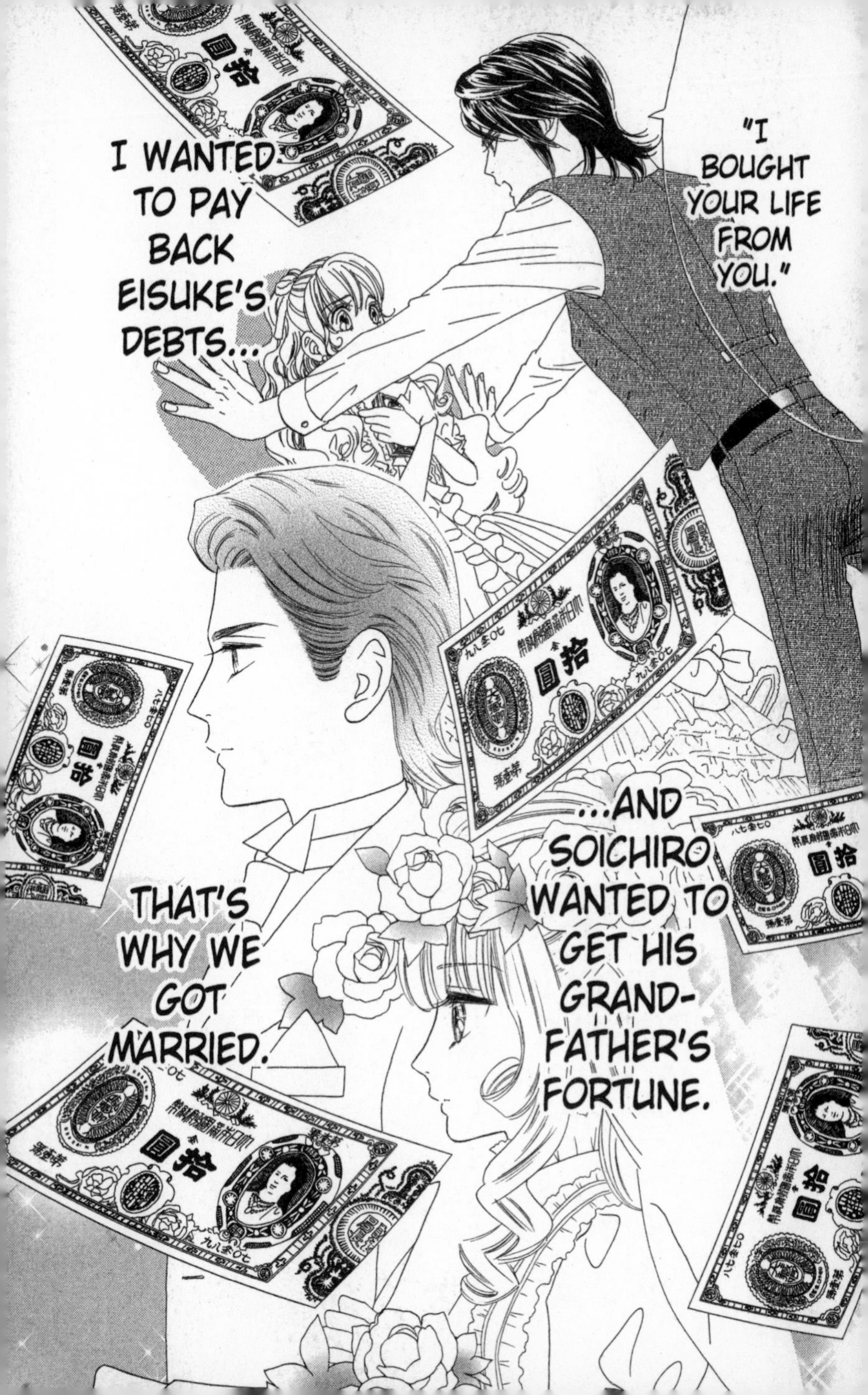
"I BOUGHT YOUR LIFE FROM YOU."
I WANTED TO PAY BACK EISUKE'S DEBTS...
...AND SOICHIRO WANTED TO GET HIS GRAND-FATHER'S FORTUNE.
THAT'S WHY WE GOT MARRIED.

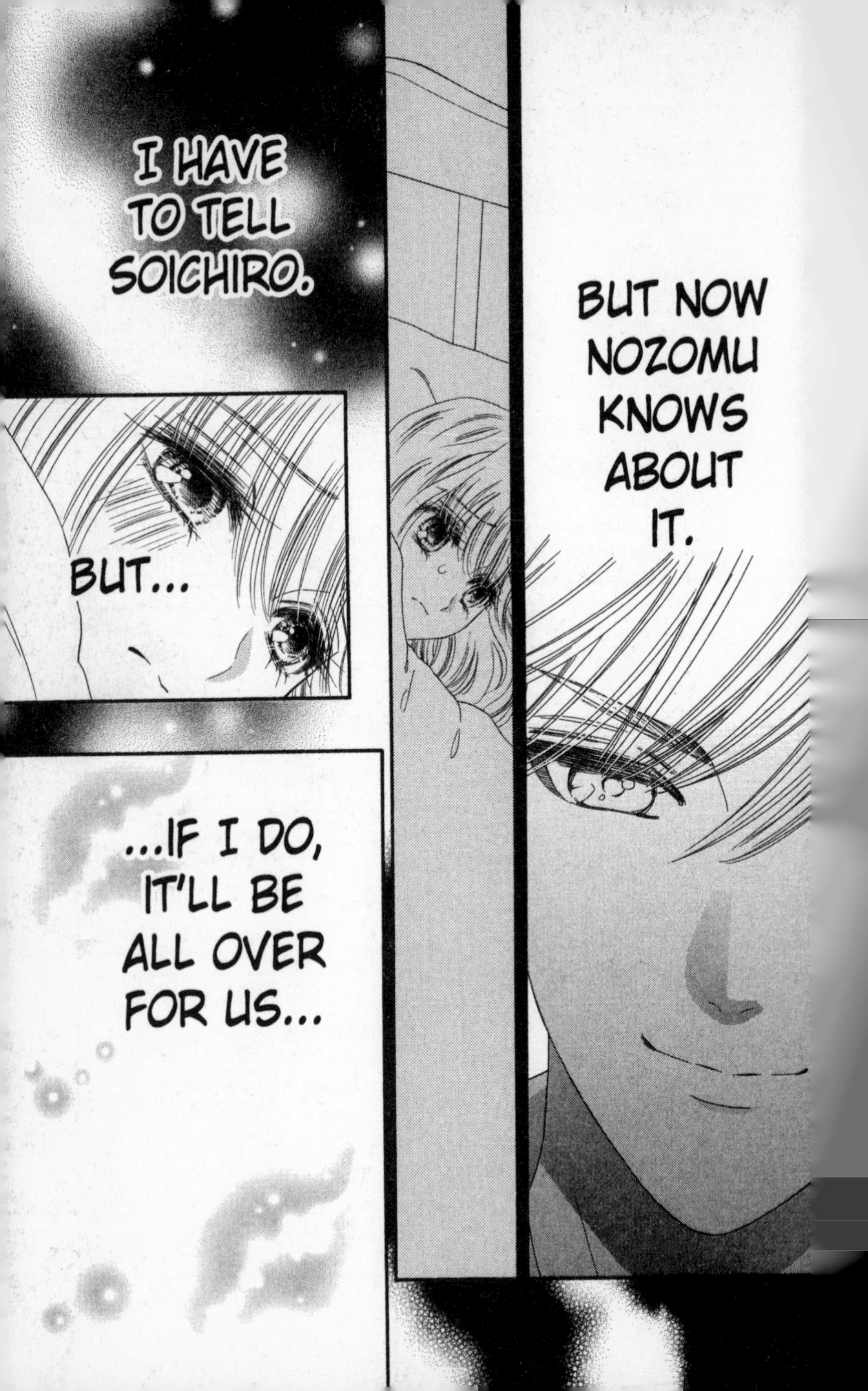
BUT NOW NOZOMU KNOWS ABOUT IT.
I HAVE TO TELL SOICHIRO.
BUT...
...IF I DO, IT'LL BE ALL OVER FOR US...

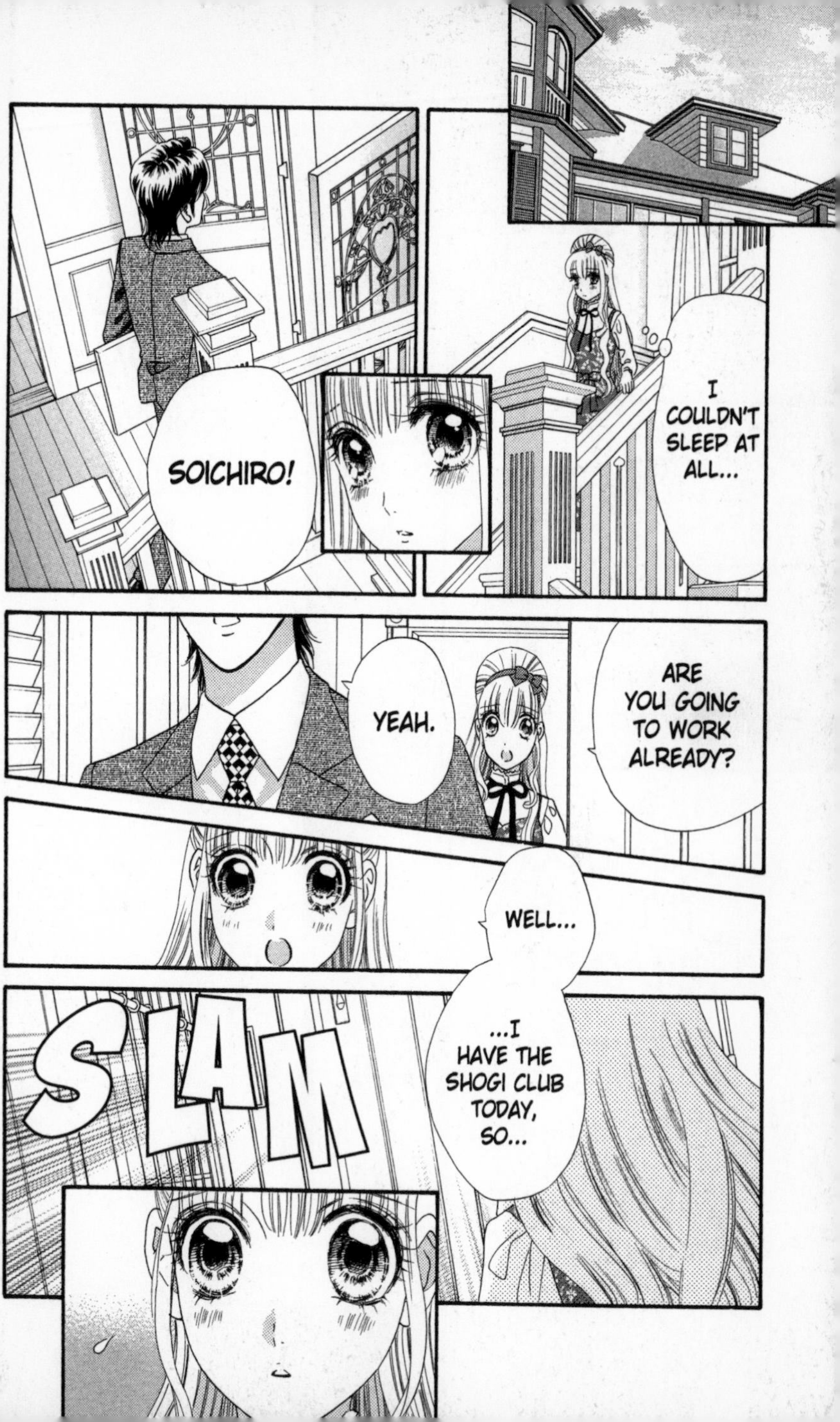
I COULDN'T SLEEP AT ALL...
SOICHIRO!
ARE YOU GOING TO WORK ALREADY?
YEAH.
WELL...
...I HAVE THE SHOGI CLUB TODAY, SO...
SLAM

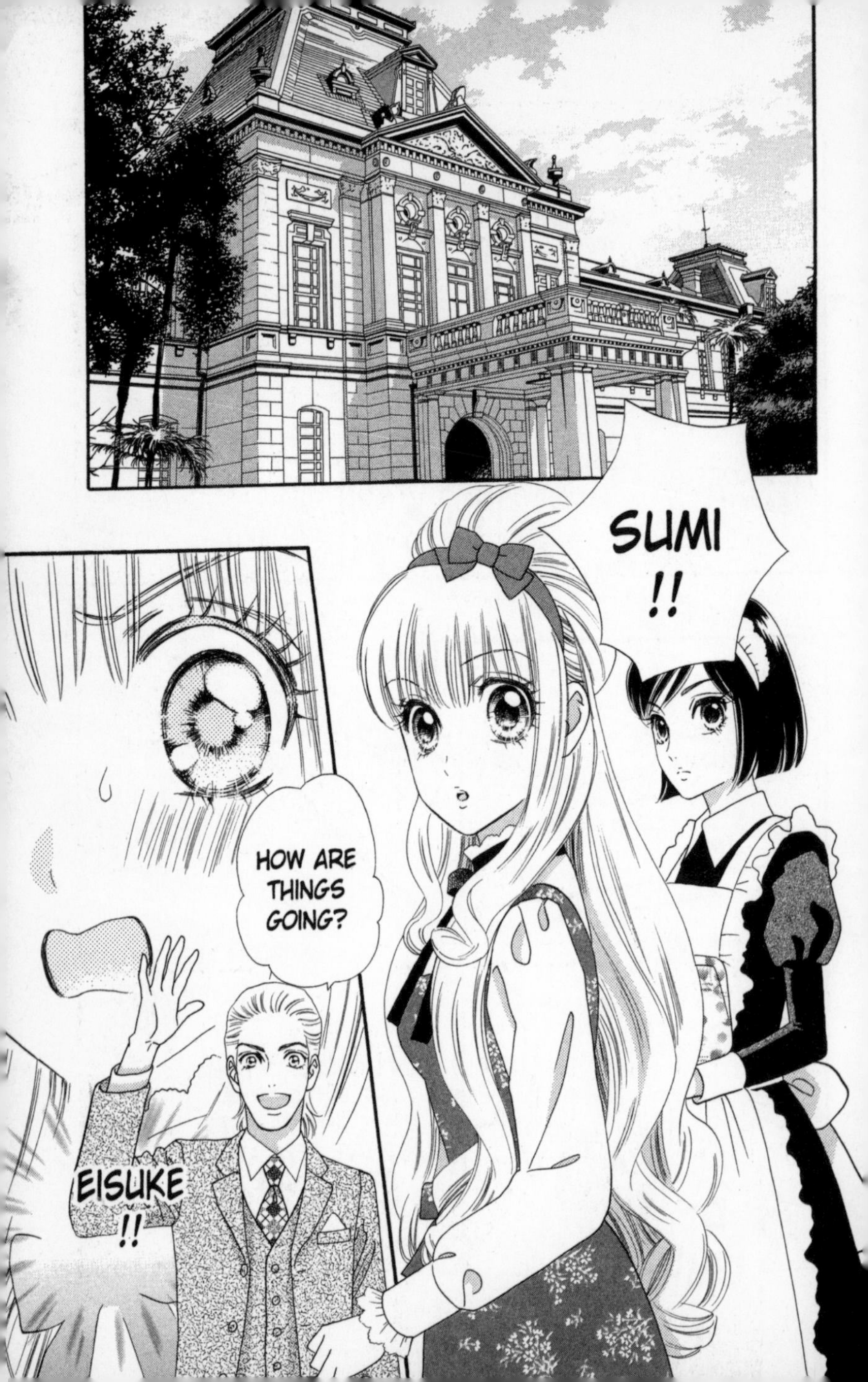
SUMI !!
HOW ARE THINGS GOING?
EISUKE !!

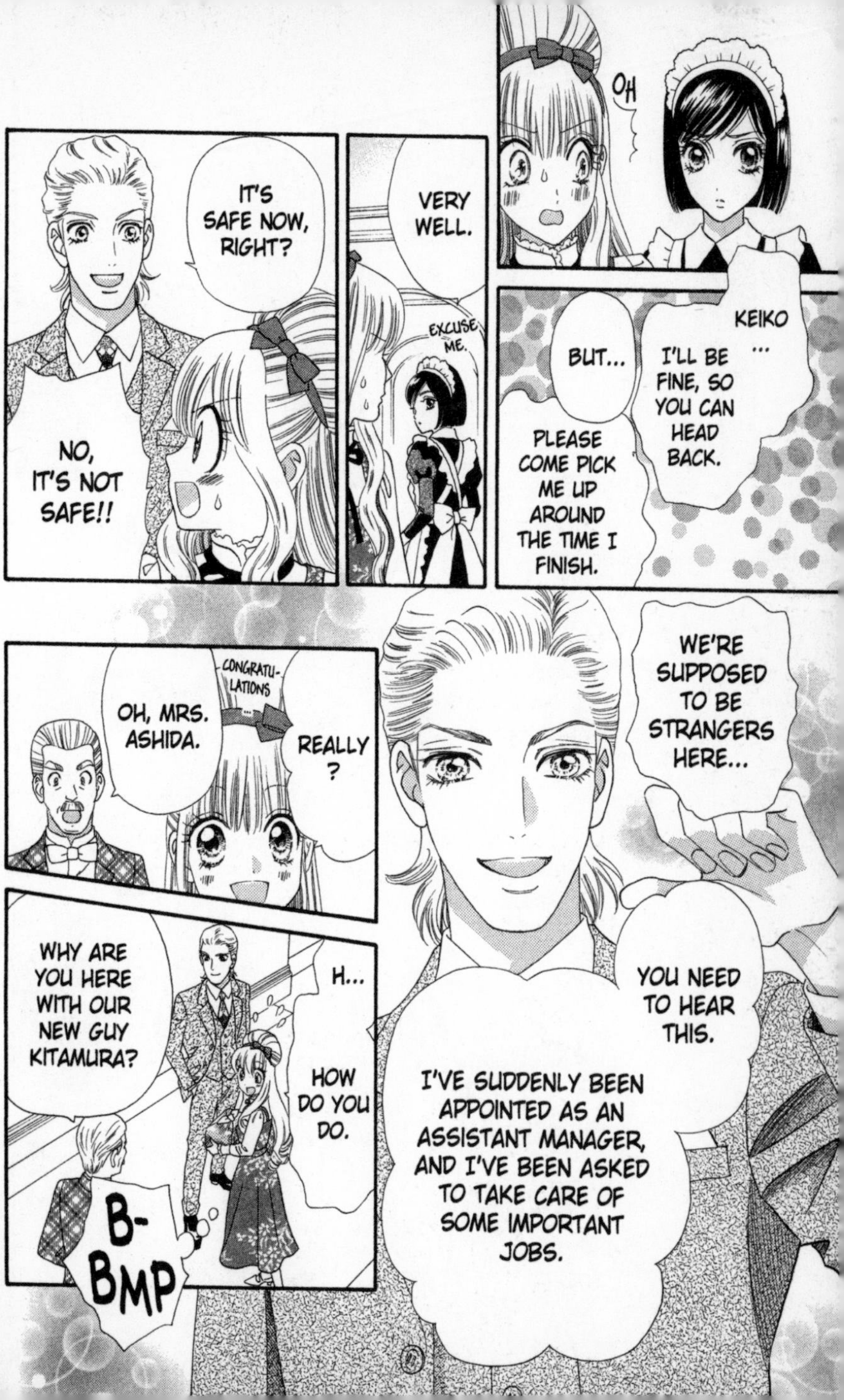
OH...
KEIKO...
I'LL BE FINE, SO YOU CAN HEAD BACK.
BUT...
PLEASE COME PICK ME UP AROUND THE TIME I FINISH.
VERY WELL.
EXCUSE ME.
IT'S SAFE NOW, RIGHT?
NO, IT'S NOT SAFE!!
WE'RE SUPPOSED TO BE STRANGERS HERE...
YOU NEED TO HEAR THIS.
I'VE SUDDENLY BEEN APPOINTED AS AN ASSISTANT MANAGER, AND I'VE BEEN ASKED TO TAKE CARE OF SOME IMPORTANT JOBS.
OH, MRS. ASHIDA.
CONGRATULATIONS...
REALLY?
WHY ARE YOU HERE WITH OUR NEW GUY KITAMURA?
H...
HOW DO YOU DO.
B-BMP

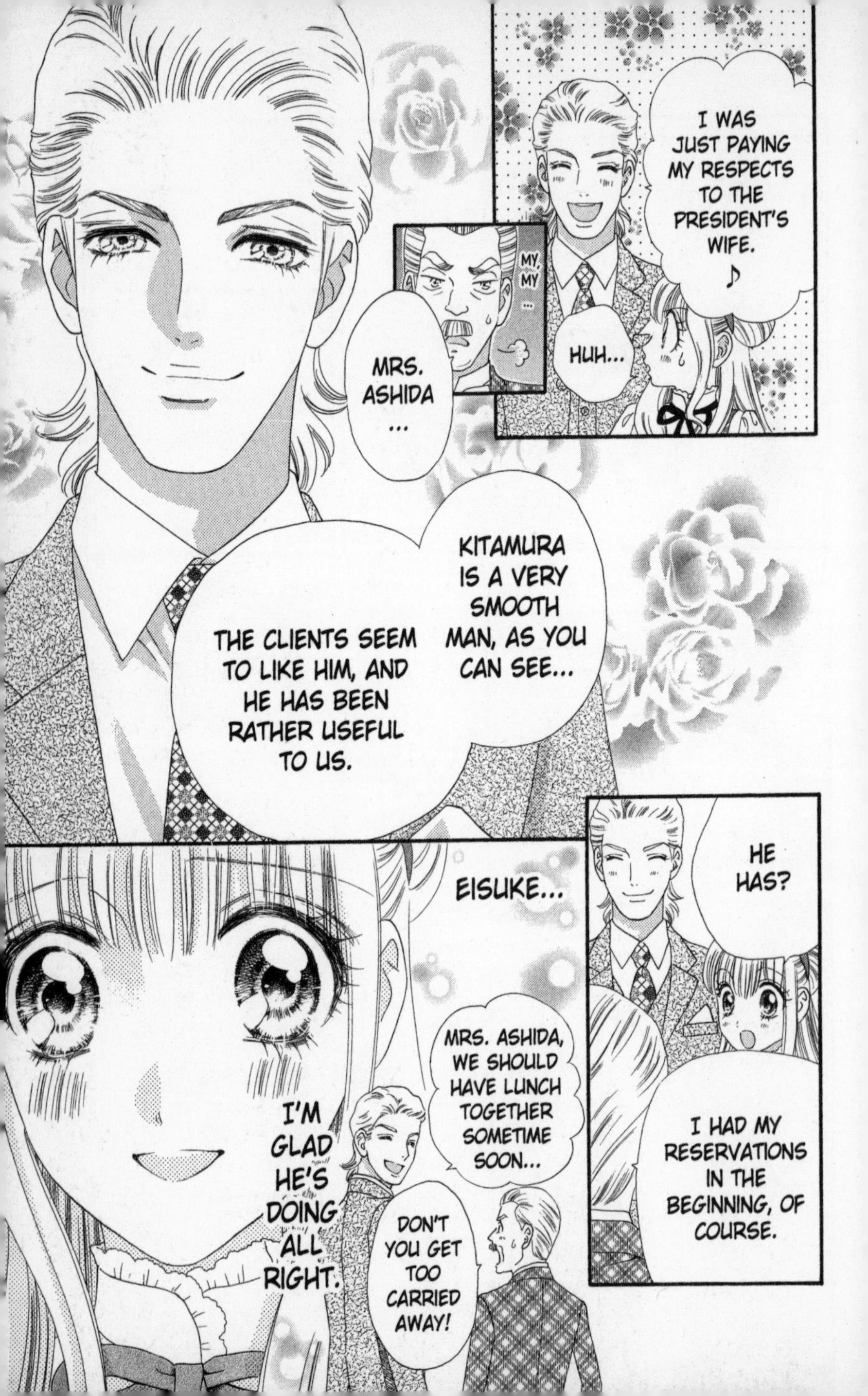
I WAS JUST PAYING MY RESPECTS TO THE PRESIDENT'S WIFE. ♪
HUH...
MY, MY...
MRS. ASHIDA...
KITAMURA IS A VERY SMOOTH MAN, AS YOU CAN SEE...
THE CLIENTS SEEM TO LIKE HIM, AND HE HAS BEEN RATHER USEFUL TO US.
HE HAS?
I HAD MY RESERVATIONS IN THE BEGINNING, OF COURSE.
EISUKE...
MRS. ASHIDA, WE SHOULD HAVE LUNCH TOGETHER SOMETIME SOON...
DON'T YOU GET TOO CARRIED AWAY!
I'M GLAD HE'S DOING ALL RIGHT.

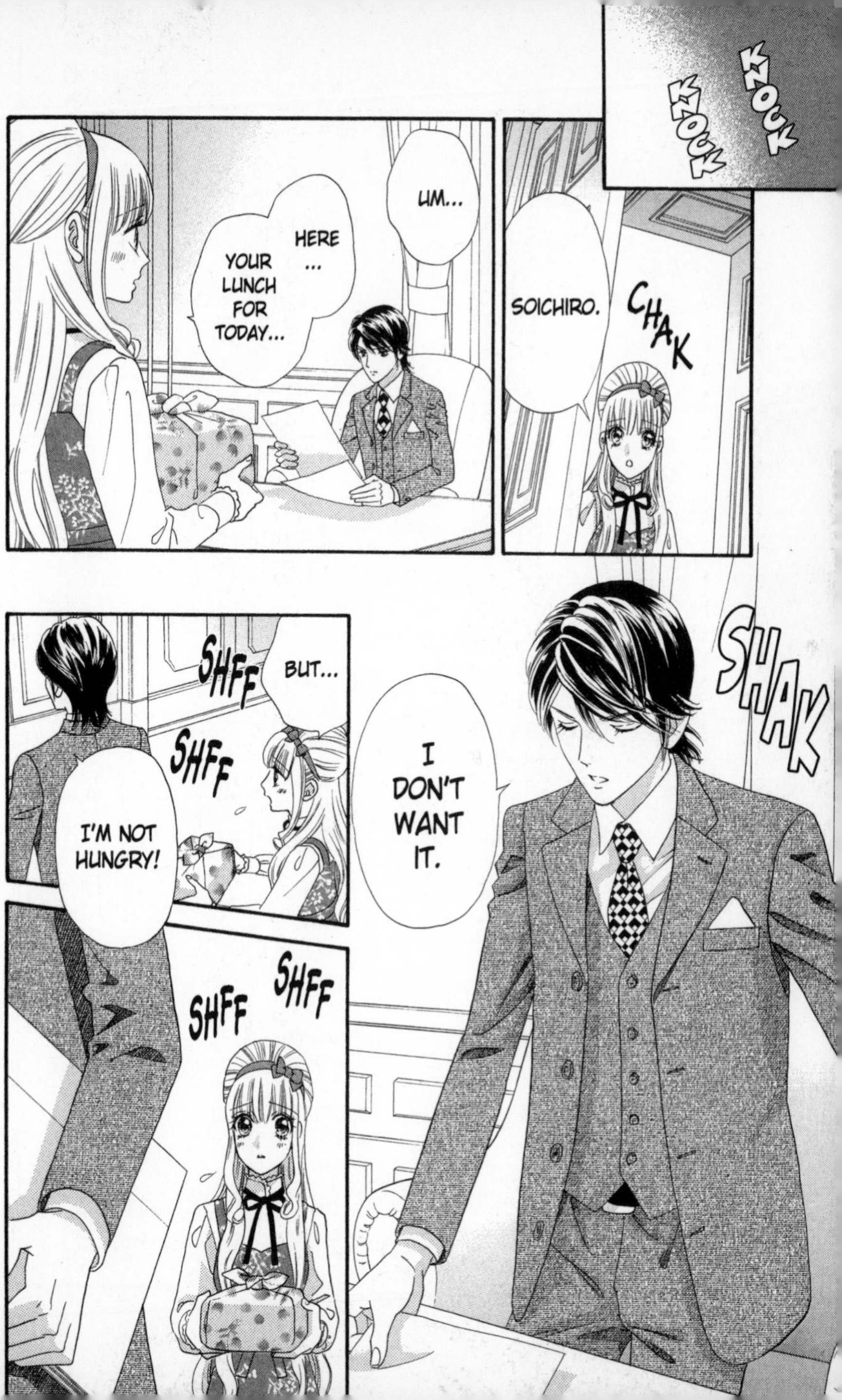
KNOCK
KNOCK
SOICHIRO.
CHAK
UM...
HERE... YOUR LUNCH FOR TODAY...
SHAK
I DON'T WANT IT.
SHFF
BUT...
SHFF
I'M NOT HUNGRY!
SHFF
SHFF

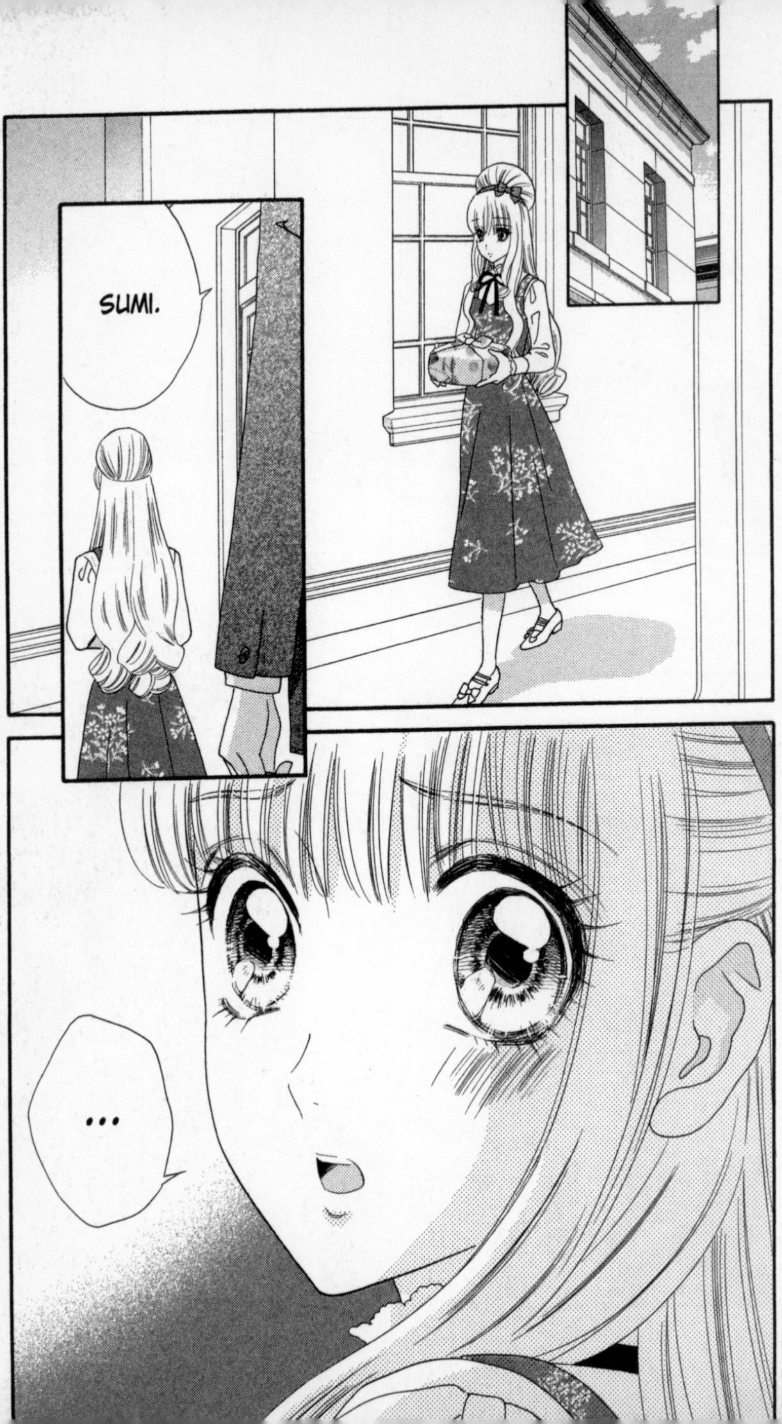
SUMI.
...

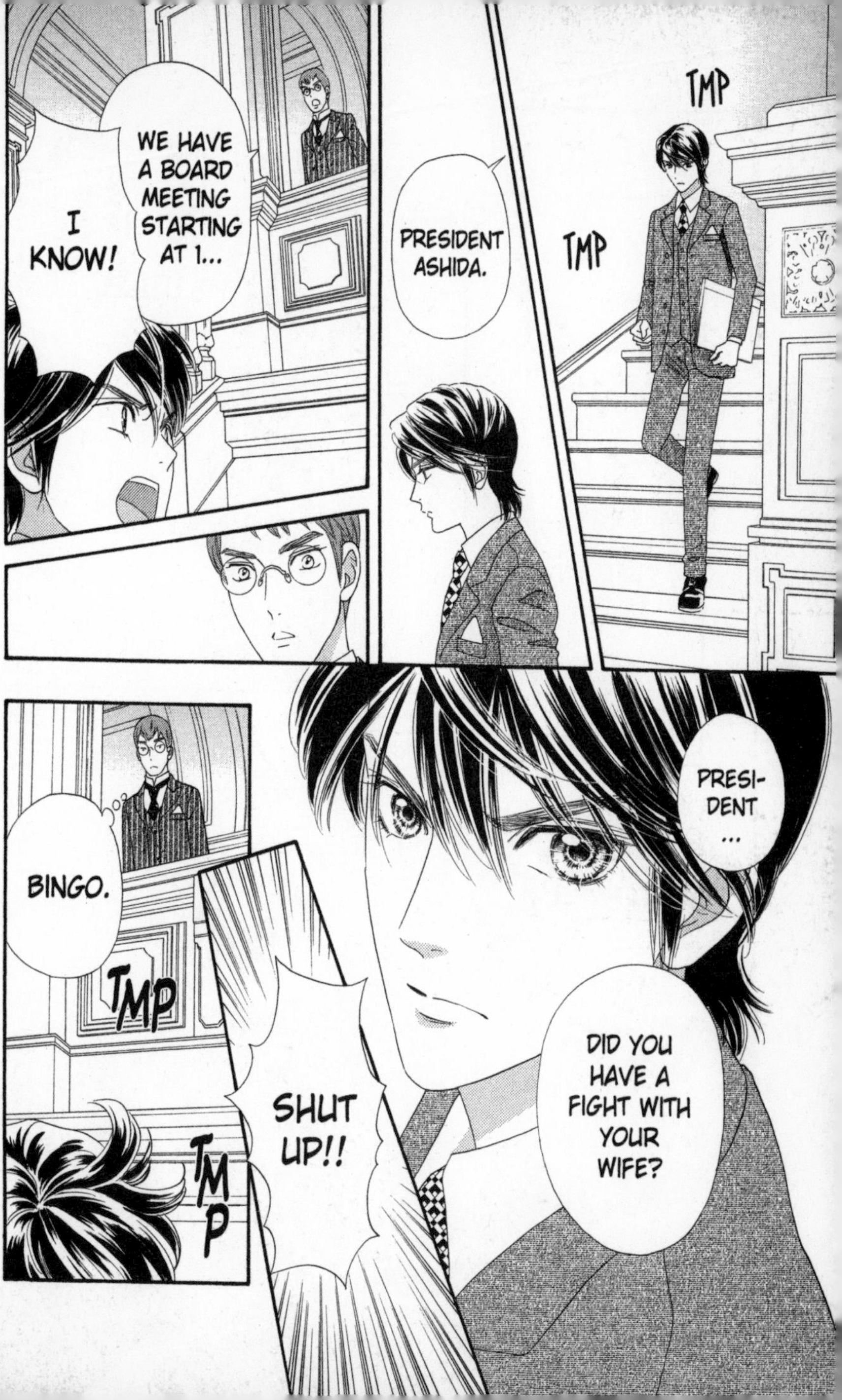
TMP
TMP
PRESIDENT ASHIDA.
WE HAVE A BOARD MEETING STARTING AT 1...
I KNOW!
PRESI-DENT ...
DID YOU HAVE A FIGHT WITH YOUR WIFE?
SHUT UP!!
BINGO.
TMP
TMP

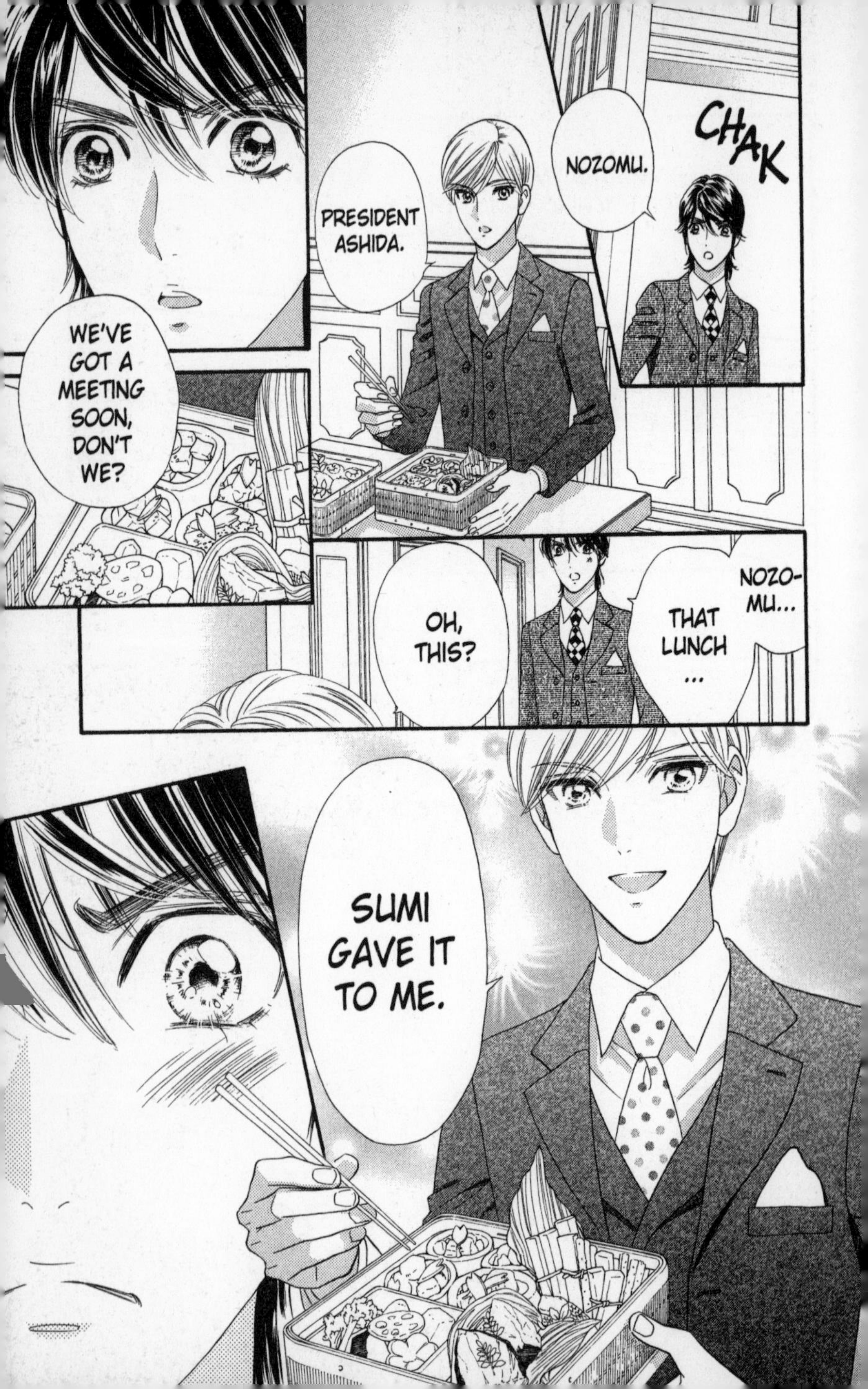
CHAK
NOZOMU.
PRESIDENT ASHIDA.
WE'VE GOT A MEETING SOON, DON'T WE?
NOZOMU...
THAT LUNCH...
OH, THIS?
SUMI GAVE IT TO ME.

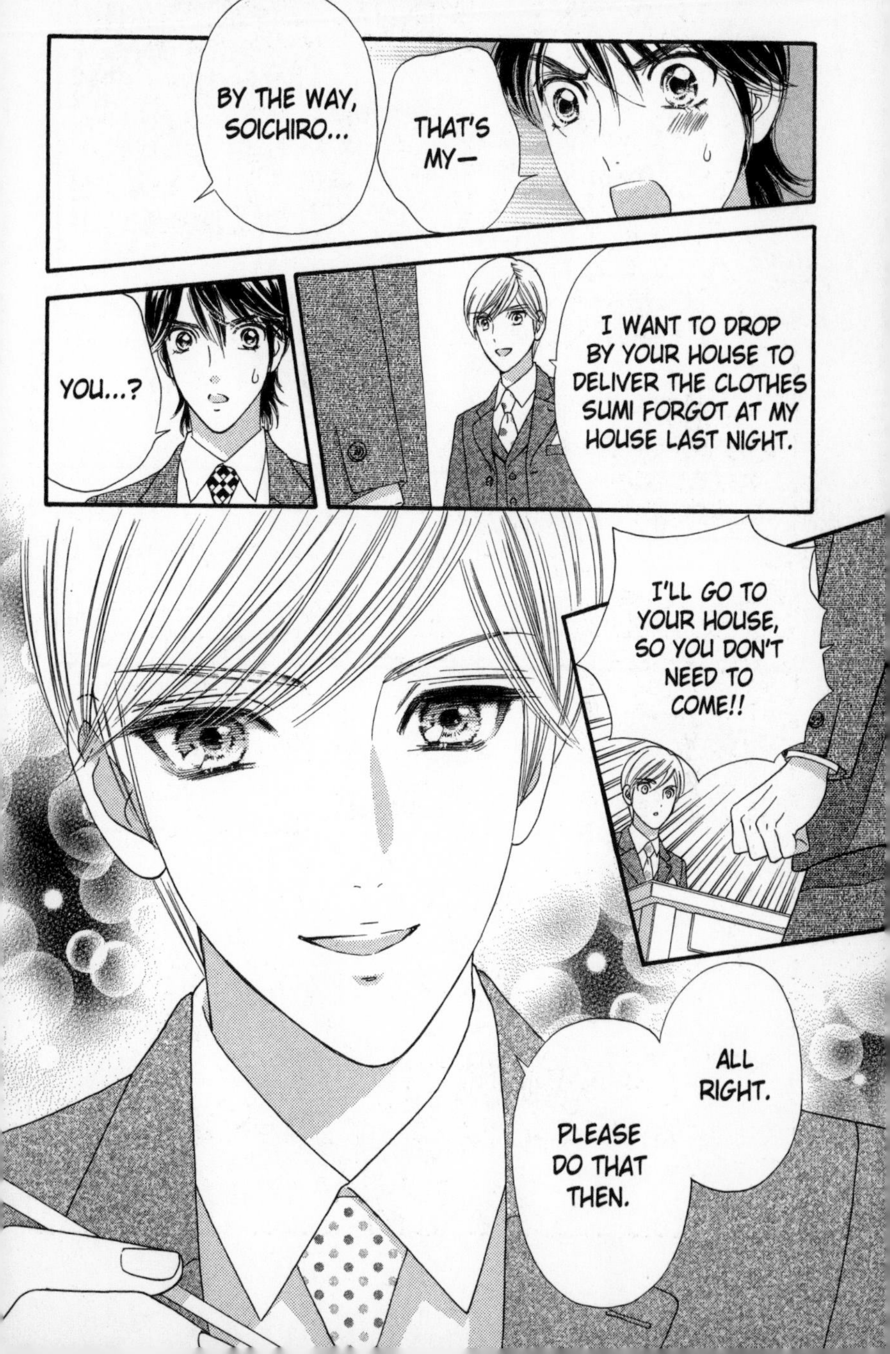
THAT'S MY—
BY THE WAY, SOICHIRO...
I WANT TO DROP BY YOUR HOUSE TO DELIVER THE CLOTHES SUMI FORGOT AT MY HOUSE LAST NIGHT.
YOU...?
I'LL GO TO YOUR HOUSE, SO YOU DON'T NEED TO COME!!
ALL RIGHT.
PLEASE DO THAT THEN.

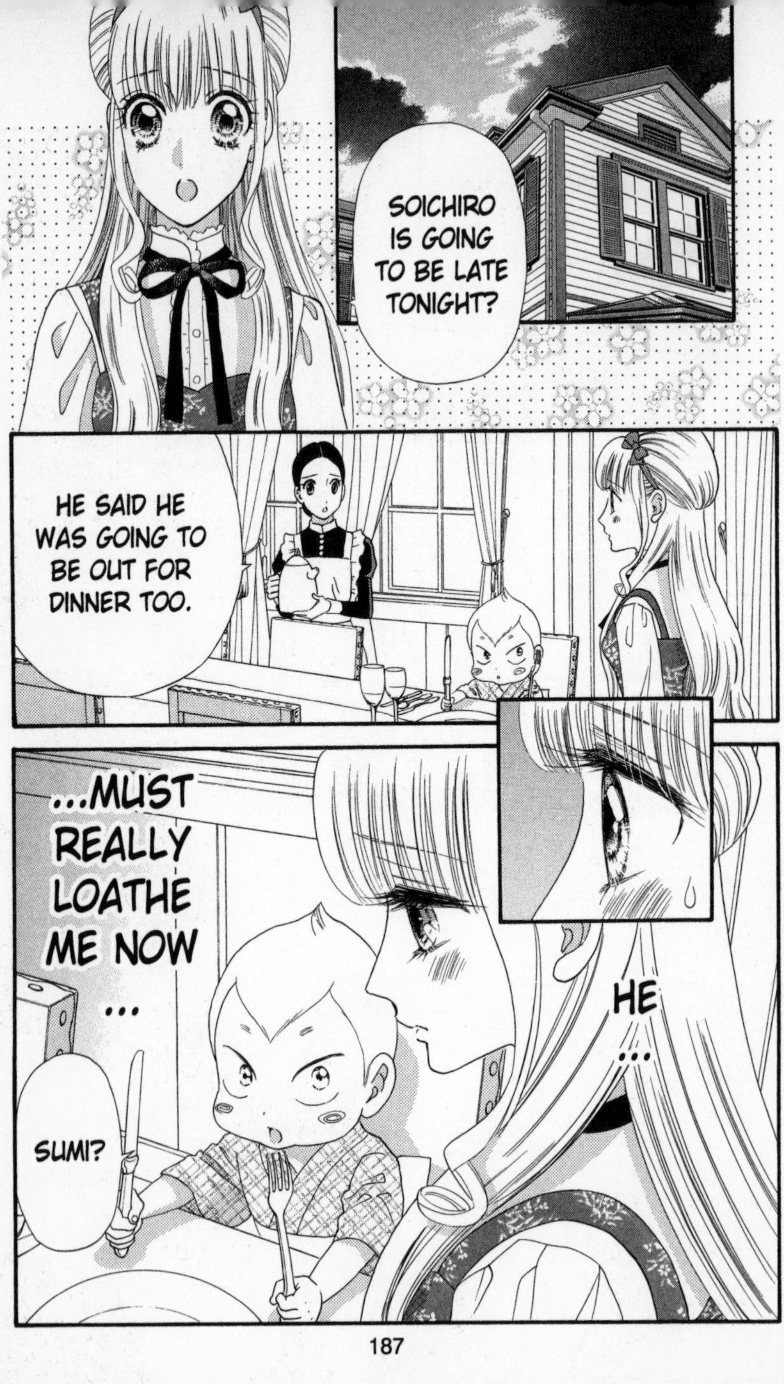
SOICHIRO IS GOING TO BE LATE TONIGHT?
HE SAID HE WAS GOING TO BE OUT FOR DINNER TOO.
HE ...
...MUST REALLY LOATHE ME NOW ...
SUMI?

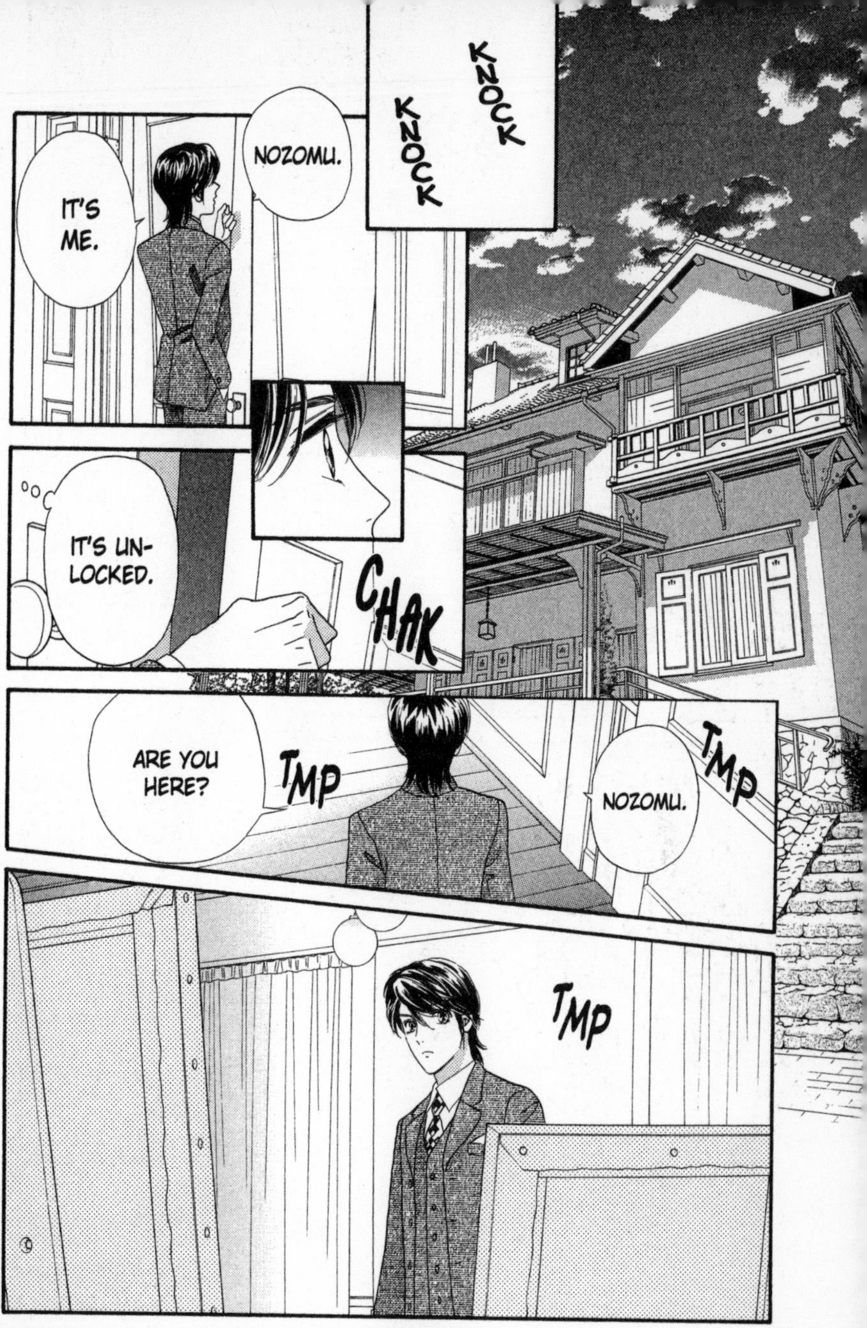
KNOCK
KNOCK
NOZOMU.
IT'S ME.
IT'S UN-LOCKED.
CHAK
TMP
NOZOMU.
TMP
ARE YOU HERE?
TMP

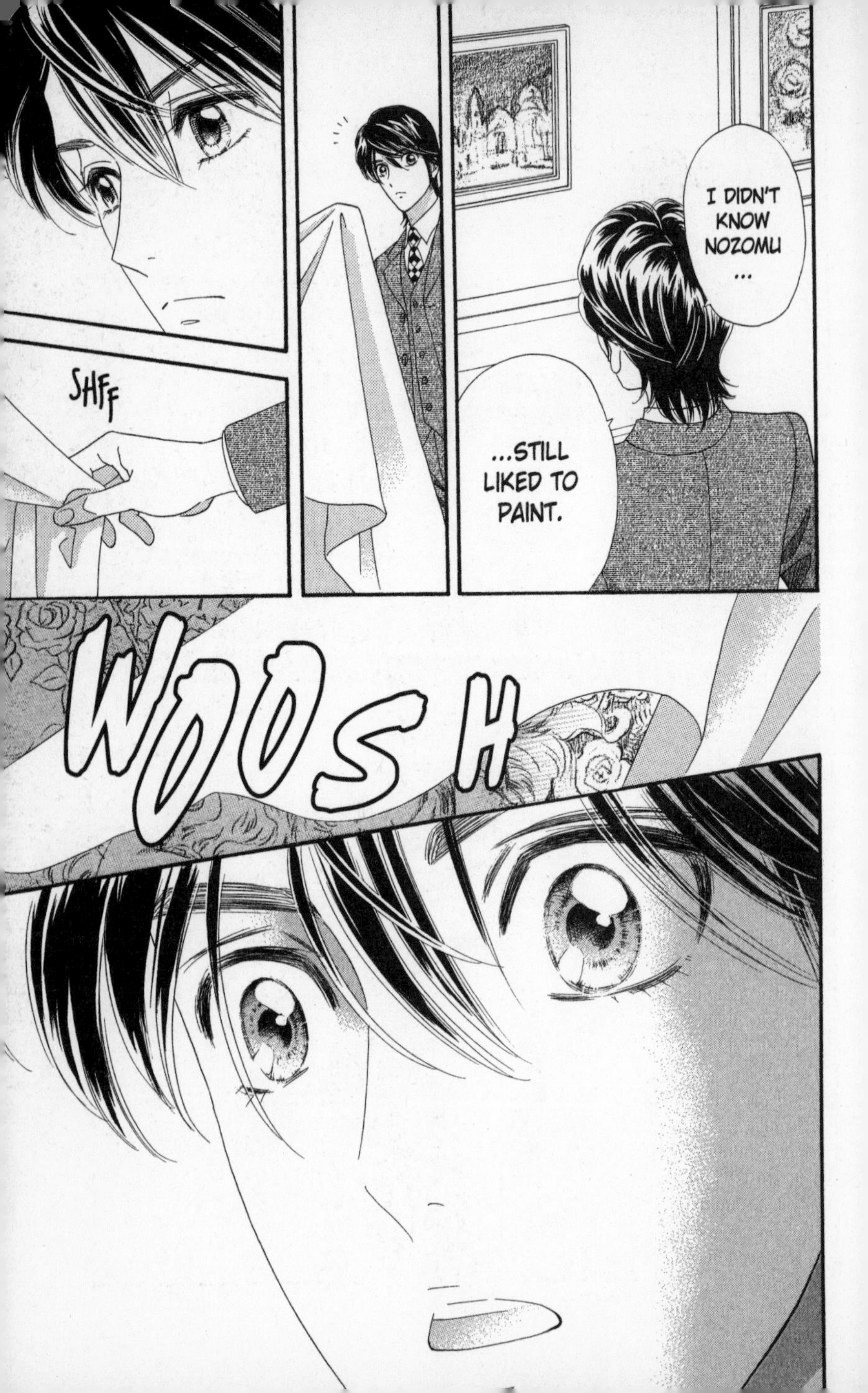
I DIDN'T KNOW NOZOMU ...
...STILL LIKED TO PAINT.
SHFF
WOOSH

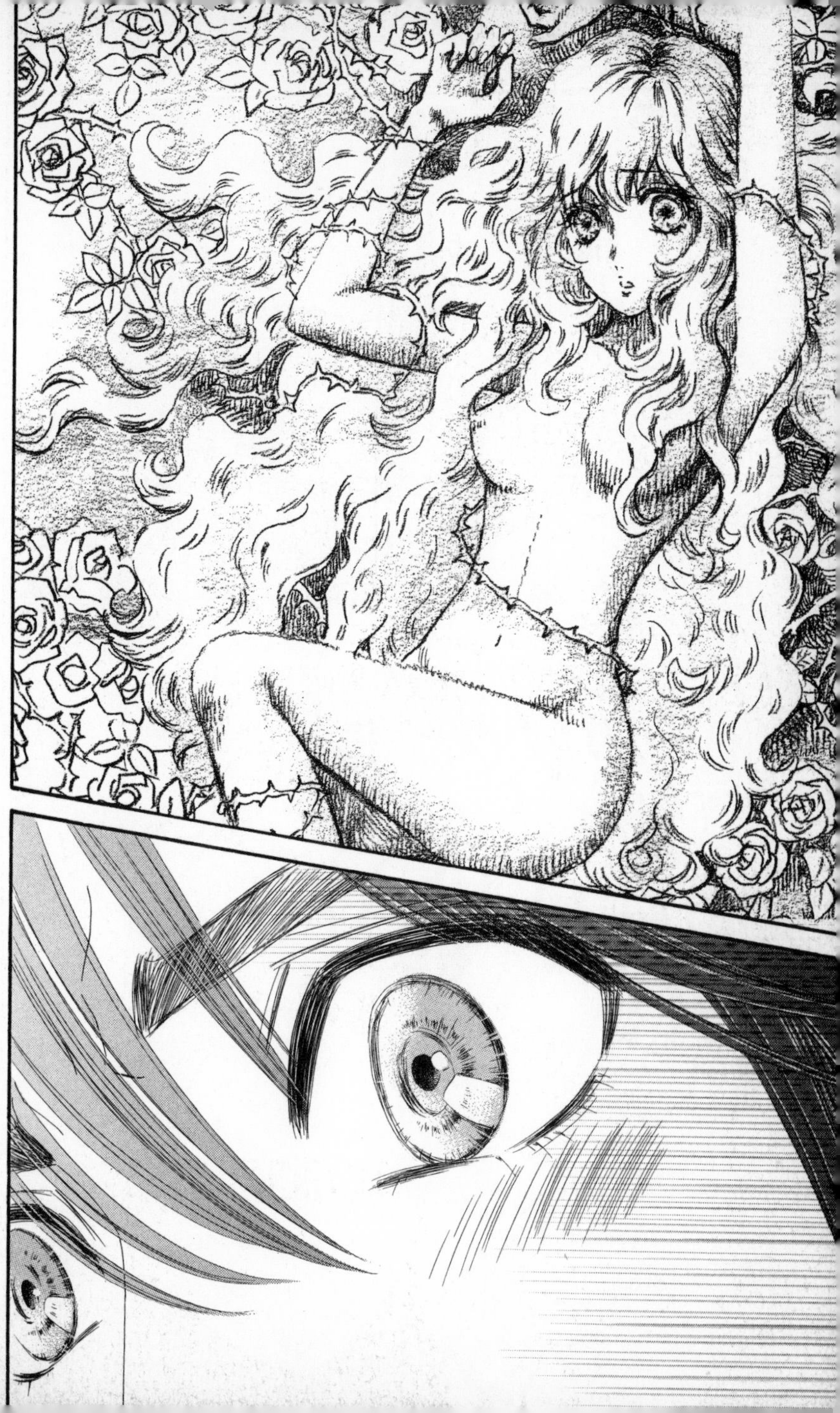

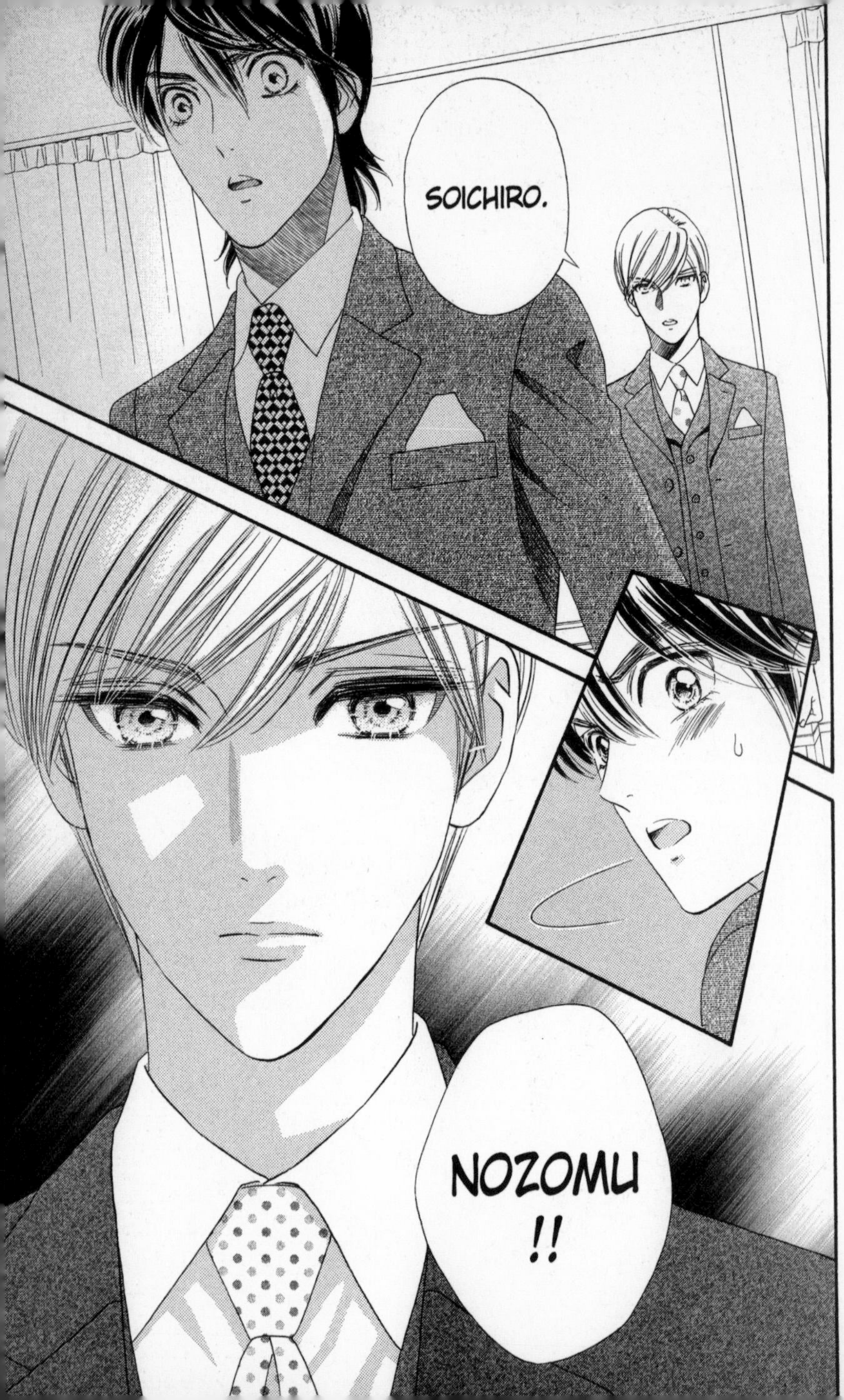
SOICHIRO.
NOZOMU !!

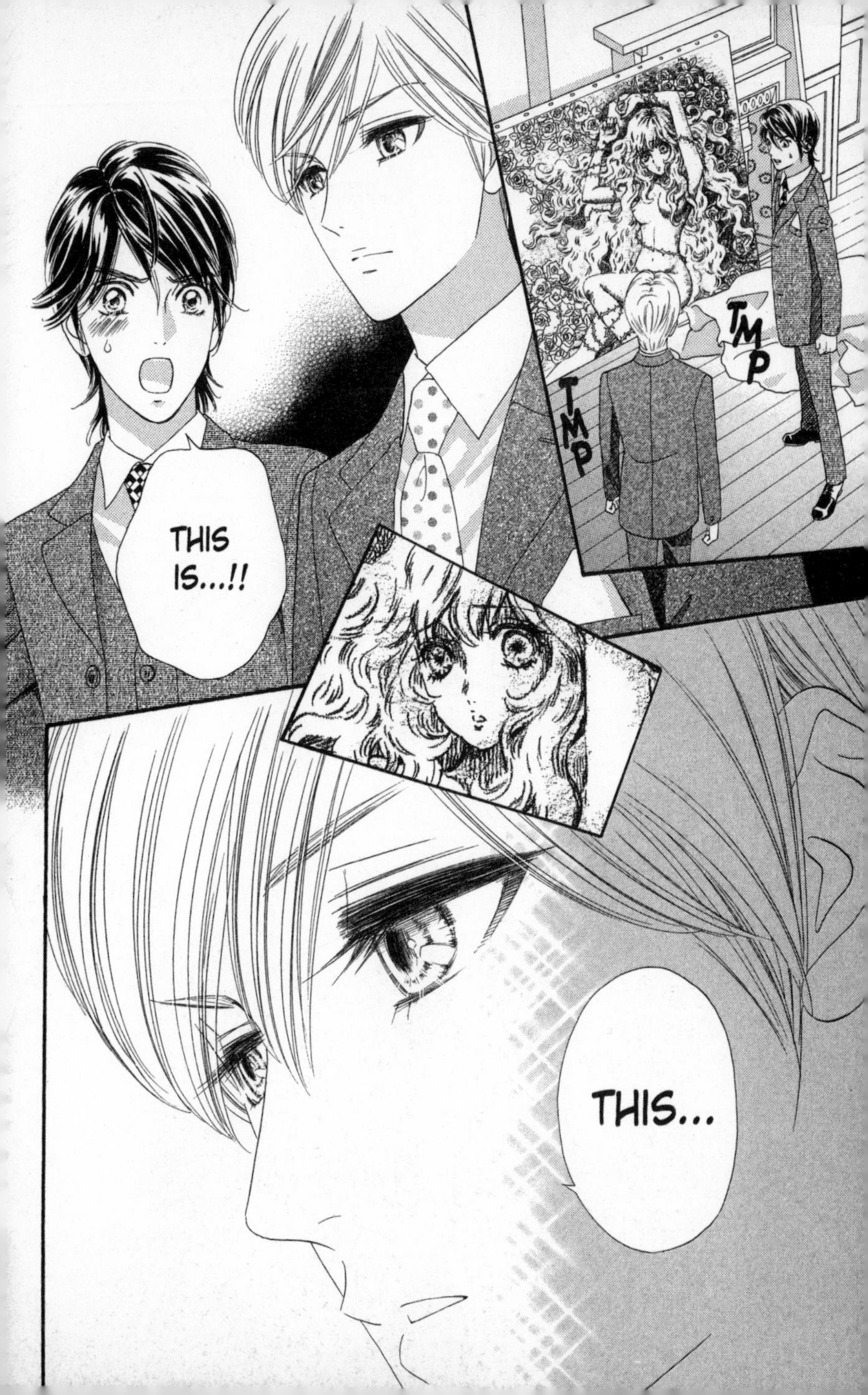
TMP
TMP
THIS IS...!!
THIS...

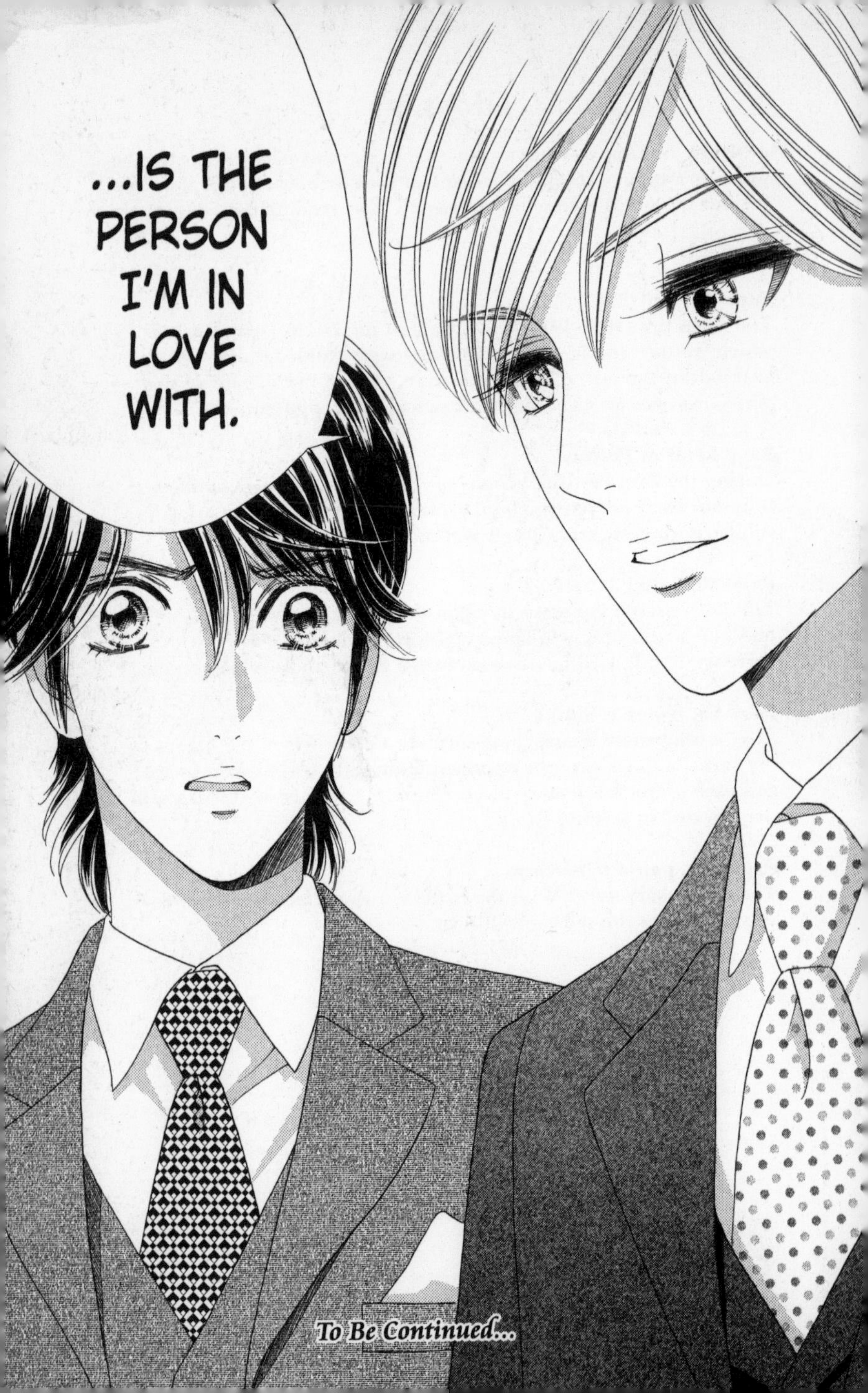
...IS THE PERSON I'M IN LOVE WITH.
To Be Continued...

Glossary

The setting of *Stepping on Roses* plays an important part in the story, as it showcases a unique time of change and transformation in Japan. Check out the notes below to help enrich your reading experience.

Page 2: Meiji Era
The Meiji Era (1868–1912) was a time of reform in Japan during which Western models and technology were studied, borrowed and adapted for the sake of modernization. One of the slogans of this period was *bunmei kaika*, or "civilization and enlightenment."

Page 54: Bon Festival
During the Bon Festival, people get together with their families to honor their ancestors. Here, Rinko Ueda is remarking on its similarity to New Year's in respect to family and celebration.

Page 60, panel 3: Sen
The *sen* is an old currency in Japan that is the equivalent of one-hundredth of a yen. These coins are no longer used, but the currency is still used in stock exchange prices and exchange rates.

Page 78, panel 2: Shogi
Shogi is a Japanese board game similar to chess where the object of the game is to capture the opponent's king. It's played on a board and each player has twenty pieces. Sumi is a master at shogi, a skill she revealed in volume 3.

Page 144, panel 1: Kuruwa
The kanji character (廓) on the lantern means "an enclosed area," and it signifies the red-light district.

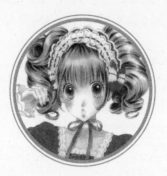

If I check the time on my cell
phone or on a digital clock, I
immediately forget what they say.
But for some reason, I can clearly
remember the time when I look
at the hands of an analog clock.
Also, I can immediately figure
out which buttons are for open
and close in an elevator if they're
written in kanji characters, but
if they use the open and close
symbols instead, I go completely
blank...

-Rinko Ueda

Rinko Ueda is from Nara
Prefecture. She enjoys listening
to the radio, drama CDs and
Rakugo comedy performances.
Her works include *Ryo*, a series
based on the legend of Gojo
Bridge; *Home*, a story about love
crossing national boundaries; and
Tail of the Moon (*Tsuki no Shippo*),
a romantic ninja comedy.

STEPPING ON ROSES
Vol. 5
Shojo Beat Edition

STORY AND ART BY
RINKO UEDA

Translation & Adaptation/Tetsuichiro Miyaki
Touch-up Art & Lettering/Mark McMurray
Design/Yukiko Whitley
Editor/Amy Yu

HADASHI DE BARA WO FUME © 2007 by Rinko Ueda
All rights reserved. First published in Japan in 2007 by SHUEISHA Inc., Tokyo.
English translation rights arranged by SHUEISHA Inc.

The rights of the author(s) of the work(s) in this publication to be so identified
have been asserted in accordance with the Copyright, Designs and Patents Act
1988. A CIP catalogue record for this book is available from the British Library.

Printed in the U.S.A.

Published by VIZ Media, LLC
P.O. Box 77010
San Francisco, CA 94107

10 9 8 7 6 5 4 3 2 1
First printing, April 2011

www.viz.com   www.shojobeat.com

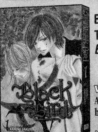

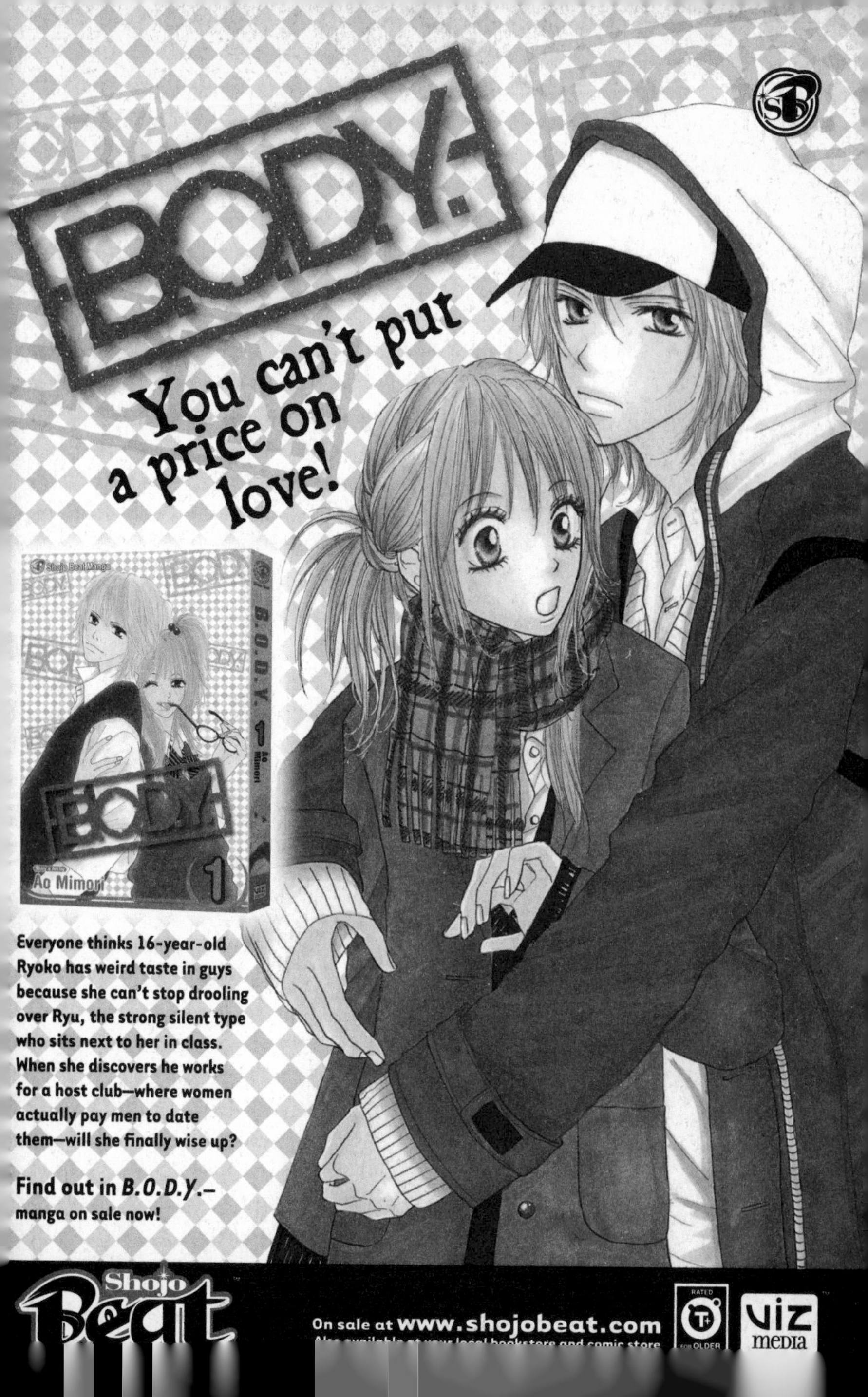
B.O.D.Y.
You can't put a price on love!
Shojo Beat Manga
B.O.D.Y.
1
Ao Mimori
Everyone thinks 16-year-old Ryoko has weird taste in guys because she can't stop drooling over Ryu, the strong silent type who sits next to her in class. When she discovers he works for a host club—where women actually pay men to date them—will she finally wise up?
Find out in B.O.D.Y.—manga on sale now!
Shojo Beat
On sale at www.shojobeat.com
Also available at your local bookstore and comic store
RATED T+ FOR OLDER TEEN
VIZ media

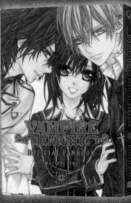
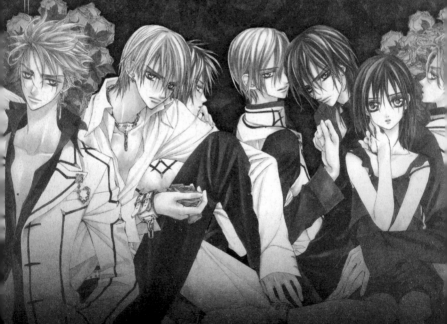

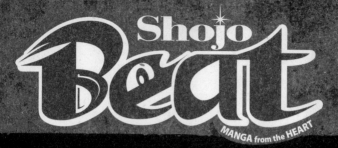
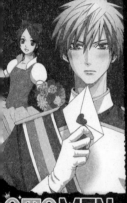
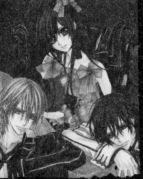
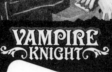

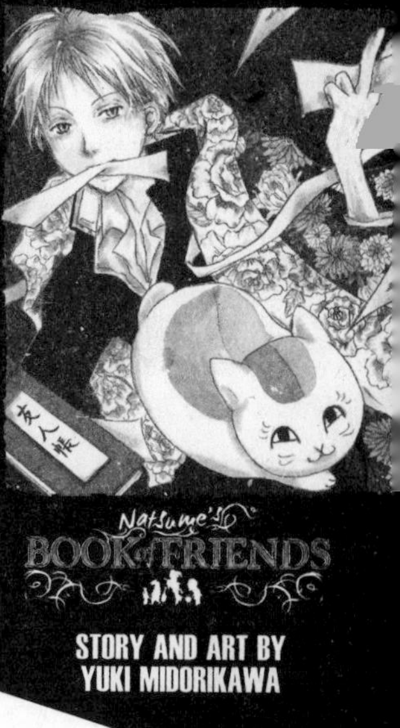